W9-ARG-093

HISTORY
OF RUSSIA

Sergei Mikhailovich Soloviev

The
Academic International Press
Edition
of
Sergei M. Soloviev

History of Russia From Earliest Times

G. EDWARD ORCHARD
General Editor

Contributing Editors

HUGH F. GRAHAM

JOHN D. WINDHAUSEN

ALEXANDER V. MULLER

K.A. PAPMEHL

RICHARD HANTULA

WALTER J. GLEASON, JR.

WILLIAM H. HILL

G. EDWARD ORCHARD

LINDSEY A.J. HUGHES

NICKOLAS LUPININ

GEORGE E. MUNRO

DANIEL L. SCHLAFLY, JR.

ANTHONY L.H. RHINELANDER

PATRICK J. O'MEARA

T. ALLAN SMITH

SERGEI M. SOLOVIEV

History of Russia

Volume 12
Russian Society Under Ivan the Terrible

Edited and Translated
By

T. Allan Smith

Academic International Press
1996

The Academic International Press Edition of S.M. Soloviev's
History of Russia From Earliest Times in fifty volumes.

Volume 12. *Russian Society Under Ivan the Terrible.*
Unabridged translation of the text of Chapter I of Volume 7 of
S.M. Soloviev's *Istoriia Rossii s drevneishikh vremen* as found in
Volume IV of this work published in Moscow, 1959–1966, with
added annotation by T. Allan Smith.

ISBN: 0-87569-180-3

Composition by Sharon Lackey

Printed in the United States of America

A list of Academic International Press publications is found at
the end of this volume.

ACADEMIC INTERNATIONAL PRESS
Box 1111 • Gulf Breeze FL 32562-1111 • USA

CONTENTS

WEIGHTS AND MEASURES

Linear and Surface Measure

Arshin: 16 vershoks, 28 in (diuims) 72.12 cm
Chetvert (quarter): 1/4 arshin, 1/2 desiatine, 1.35 acre (sometimes 1.5 desiatinas or ca 4.1 acres)
Desiatina: 2,400 square sazhens, 2.7 acres, 1.025 hectares
Diuim: 1 inch, 2.54 cm
Fut: 12 diuims, 1 foot, 30.48 cm

Obza (areal): c. 10 chetverts, 13–15 acres
Osmina: 1/4 desiatina, 600 sq. sazhens, .256 hectare
Sazhen: 3 arshins, 7 feet, 2.133 m
Vershok: 1.75 in, 4.445 cm, 1/16 arshin
Verst: 500 sazhens, 1,166 yards and 2 feet, .663 miles, 1.0668 km
Voloka (plowland): 19 desiatinas, 20 hectares, 49 acres

Liquid Measure

Bochka (barrel): 40 vedros, 121 gallons, 492 liters
Chetvert (quarter): 1.4 bochkas, 32.5 gallons

Kufa: 30 stofy
Stof: Kruzhka (cup), 1/10 vedro, c. 1.3 quarts, 1.23 liters
Vedro (pail): 3.25 gallons, 12.3 liters, 10 stofy

Weights

Berkovets: 361 lbs, 10 puds
Bezmen: c. 1 kg., 2.2 lbs
Chetverik (grain measure dating from 16th century): 1/8 chetvert, 15.8 lbs
Chetvert (grain measure): 1/4 rad, 3.5 puds, 126.39 lbs, c. 8 bushels
Funt: 96 zolotniks, .903 lbs, 14.4 ozs, 408.24 kg
Grivenka: 205 grams
Kad: 4 chetverts, 14 puds, 505.56 lbs

Kamen (stone): 32 funt
Korob (basket): 7 puds, 252 lbs
Osmina (eighth): 2 osmina to a chetvert (dry measure)
Polbezmen: c. 500 g, 1 lb
Polosmina (sixteenth): 1/2 osmina
Pud: 40 funts, 36.113 lbs (US), 40 lbs (Russian), 16.38 kg
Rad: 14 puds, 505.58 lb
Zolotnik: 1/96 lbs, 4.26 grams

Money

Altyn: 6 Muscovite dengas, 3 copecks
Chervonets (chervonny): gold coin of first half of 18th century worth c. 3 rubles
Chetvertak: silver coin equal to 25 copecks or 1/4 ruble (18–19th centuries)
Copeck: two Muscovite dengas
Denga: 1/2 copeck
Grivna: 20 Muscovite dengas, 100 grivnas equals 1 ruble, 10 copecks
Grosh: 10 peniaz
Grosh litovsky (Lithuanian grosh): 5 silver copecks
Kopa grosh: 60 groshas, one Muscovite poltina, 1/2 ruble
Moskovka: 1/2 copeck
Muscovite Denga: 200 equals 1 ruble
Novgorod Denga: 100 equals 1 ruble

Novgorodka: 1 copeck
Peniaz: 10 equals one grosh (Lithuania)
Poltina (poltinnik): 50 copecks, 100 dengas, 1 ruble
Poltora: 1 1/2 rubles
Polupoltina (-nik): 25 copecks, 50 dengas
Ruble: 100 copecks, 200 dengas
Shiroky grosh (large silver coin): 20 Muscovite copecks.

Foreign Denominations
Chervonnyi: c. 3 rubles
Ducat: c. 3 rubles
Efimok: c. 1 ruble, 1 chervonets or chervonnyi
Levok: Dutch silver lion dollar
Thaler (Joachimsthaler): c. 1 ruble, 1 chervonets or chervonnyi

Note: Weights and measures often changed values over time and sometimes held more than one value at the same time. For details consult Sergei G. Pushkarev, *Dictionary of Russian Historical Terms from the Eleventh Century to 1917* (Yale, 1970).

PREFACE

This book is an unabridged translation of Volume VII, Chapter I, which comprises pages 7-189 in Book IV of Soloviev's *Istoriia Rossii s drevneishikh vremen* (History of Russia from Earliest Times), published from 1959 through 1966 in Moscow. For the sake of convenience I have divided Soloviev's text into nine chapters. Chapter I of the translation corresponds to pages 7-14, Chapter II to pages 14-29, Chapter III to pages 29-34, Chapter IV to pages 34-47, Chapter V to pages 47-67, Chapter VI to pages 67-112, Chapter VII to pages 112-141, Chapter VIII to pages 141-155, and Chapter IX to pages 155-189 of the edition of 1959-1966. The uneven length of these chapters reflects the space devoted by Soloviev to a given theme.

The present translation endeavors to render the text and Soloviev's thought as accurately as possible. No attempt has been made to reproduce his style and text word for word for this would have yielded a bizarre Russianized text. The main consideration has been to make his history as readable as possible consistent with accuracy while retaining at least something of the flavor of the language of the era. An effort has been made to find English-language equivalents for all technical terms Soloviev employs (ranks, offices, titles, legal, administrative and so forth) in the belief that English is no less rich in such terms than other languages. This is intended to smooth the flow of the narrative for the reader and to avoid marring the pages with annoying untranslated words. The exception involves Russian words which have become common in English—boyar, tsar, cossack. In all of this the translator remains painfully aware of the inevitable shortcomings that may remain.

Soloviev's pages are featureless and interminable, one long and complex sentence marching after the last. To make the text easier to follow for today's readers, long paragraphs and sentences have been broken into shorter ones. Most of the subtitles are based on the descriptive topic headings clustered at the beginning of the Russian original. These headings have been moved into the body of the text as subtitles to mark and ease for the reader the transition from one subject to another. In some cases the topic headings have been used as chapter headings in the translation. New subtitles have been created to show topics not listed by Soloviev. Soloviev's arrangement of the material has been followed strictly.

Brief explanatory or interpretive materials have been inserted into the text enclosed in brackets, or added as footnotes to each chapter at the end of the book. All material enclosed in brackets was added by the present editor and all material in parentheses is the author's. Emphasized words or phrases in italics are the author's.

The general policy followed in annotating has been to identify prominent personalities at first mention, and to give explanations and elucidations of less common or obscure terms and passages, assuming the typical reader to have relatively little familiarity with Russian history. These appear as numbered footnotes at the back of the book by chapters. Explanations for the numerous ranks, financial and legal terms appearing in this volume have been taken from *Real- und Sachwörterbuch zum Altrussischen* (Lexikon for Old Russian Terminology) ed. H.W. Schaller et al. (Neuried, 1985). With a few exceptions, Soloviev's own notes are not included because of their highly specialized archival, documentary and bibliographic nature. Similarly, most of the notes added by the editors of the edition published in the Soviet Union which are also technical in nature— fuller bibliographic citations than those in Soloviev's notes—have not been included. When the author's notes and those of the Soviet editors are included, they are so designated. All other notes are those of the present editor.

Russian personal names are preserved in their Russian form with a few exceptions: Alexander, Alexis, Nicholas, Jonas, Joseph, Peter, Sergius. The names of many important ecclesiastical figures have been recast into their Latin or Greek equivalents. This applies to prominent individuals; Russian forms usually are used for the less prominent. Certain other names and terms have been anglicized for the sake of clarity and because they are used widely—Casimir, Sophia, boyar, versts, Dnieper river, and others.

The editors of the edition published in the USSR frequently added patronymics and other names, and these have been retained without brackets; patronymics appearing in the original edition have been included. Plural forms for names and terms which might be confusing have been anglicized—Voguls and not Vogulichi, the Shuiskys and not the Shuiskie, and so forth. Most Slavic surnames show gender, and this has been preserved. Since an "-a" at the end of a name usually signifies a female,

Saburov would have a wife or daughter Saburova. The final "-iia" in feminine personal names has been shortened to "-ia"—"Maria" and "Evdokia" instead of "Mariia" and "Evdokiia."

Non-Russian names, locations, terms, ranks and so on are spelled according to the language native to the person or particular to the city, region or culture when this can be determined. Confusion arises at times because the text is not clear about nationalities. Individuals whose names were once non-Russian but had been in Russian service for generations are named by the original spelling of the family name. Turkish, Tatar, Persian and other names and terms are spelled in the original according to accepted forms in scholarly books. In some instances, if not otherwise ascertainable they are translated from the Russian as given by Soloviev. The names of geographical locations conform to commonly accepted English usage— Podolia, Moscow, Copenhagen, and so forth.

Finally, with respect to transliteration, this translation follows a modified Library of Congress system omitting diacritical marks and ligatures, and rendering initial "Ia-" and "Iu-" as "Ya-" and "Yu-" ("Yaroslav" and "Yury"), the suffixes "-yi," "-ii," have been simplified to "-y" ("Dmitry Poliansky," instead of "Dmitrii Polianskii"), and the form "-oi" has been replaced by "-oy" ("Kosoy" not "Kosoi"). Except for final "-ei" in "Andrei" and "Sergei," "-ei" has been rendered "-ey" ("Girey" not "Girei"). In some cases "i" has been inserted in place of hard and soft signs, or apostrophes indicating these signs. Hence "Soloviev," not "Solov'ev." The soft sign is not indicated by an apostrophe, as in some transliteration systems, but is dropped completely. In bibliographical citations the Library of Congress system has been adhered to more strictly.

All dates, as in the original, except where otherwise specified, are according to the Julian calendar ("Old Style"); that is, for the sixteenth and seventeenth centuries, ten days behind the Gregorian used in the West. The discrepancy arises beginning with the year 1582 when the Gregorian calendar was introduced in the West. A table of weights and measures is included at the front of this volume for the convenience of the reader.

This particular section of Soloviev's work contains a number of liturgical and theological terms peculiar to Eastern Christianity. In an attempt to alert the Western reader to the existence of other expressions of the Christian religion, I have opted for translations currently in use by Orthodox Christians who worship in the English language. Thus, the word *bogoroditsa* occasionally is rendered as "Theotokos" and the epithet for her, *prechistaia* is translated as "most pure" and not "immaculate." In the latter case, the word "immaculate" conveys theological and spiritual nuances which presuppose a Roman Catholic theological tradition not shared by Eastern Christianity. For the same reason the feast day commemorated on August 15 is called the Dormition (of the Holy Theotokos) and not the Assumption (of the Blessed Virgin Mary).

In preparing this volume I have drawn on the resources of the libraries of the University of Saskatchewan in Saskatoon, the Pontifical Institute of Medieval Studies in Toronto and the McLennan Library at McGill University in Montreal. I would like to express my sincere appreciation to the editor, G. Edward Orchard, for his numerous helpful suggestions. For their encouragement and patient listening to my thoughts about Soloviev's text I thank Joseph and Daniel Doane.

T. Allan Smith

INTRODUCTION

Sergei Mikhailovich Soloviev (1820-1879) was the son of an archpriest and religion teacher at the Moscow School of Commerce. Like many nineteenth-century Russian intellectuals from priestly families, he did not follow his father's path and seek ordination, choosing instead to dedicate his life to the study of Russia's past. The principal fruit of his scholarship is the monumental *History of Russia from Earliest Times*. After the publication of the first volume of his History in 1851, the remaining twenty-eight volumes appeared in annual succession down to the final one published posthumously in 1879, testimony to Soloviev's industriousness and devotion.

In the present volume Soloviev leaves the reader with a composite picture of the economic, political, religious, legal and cultural situation of Russia during the reign of Ivan IV. The richness of the material he presents to the reader conveys an age of tumultuous change, an era seemingly without direction, shaped by the spiritual and intellectual convulsions of its central symbolic figure, Ivan IV. Unfortunately Soloviev's desire to show the age of Ivan IV in all its many facets has produced a volume which is difficult to read. Discussing the literary debate between Ivan IV and Prince Andrei Kurbsky, Soloviev cites a passage from the latter's first letter to Ivan IV which might well have been directed against Soloviev himself. "I have received your wide-ranging and obstreperous letter, comprehended and understood that it was belched out of indomitable anger with venomous words that would be unworthy not only of a tsar so great and universally renowned, but also of a simple, wretched soldier. In particular much in it is picked up from Sacred Scripture and these words are introduced with great fury and ferocity, not in lines or verses as is the custom of the skilled and the learned who enclose much reason in brief phrases, but rather beyond all measure and entangled, with whole books, liturgical readings and letters! In it is talk about beds and quilted jackets and odds and ends just like the fables of frantic old women, and everything is so barbaric that not only learned and skilled men but also the simple, yes even children, are surprised and laugh, especially in foreign countries where there are people who are skilled, not only in grammatical and rhetorical learning, but also in dialectics and philosophy."

While Soloviev cannot be accused of writing in anger, the principal charge of wandering from topic to topic with little or no connection stands. Many times in the volume Soloviev abruptly changes direction or interjects a topic which has little if any connection with that preceding it. Some subjects are introduced only immediately to be dismissed. This gives the work an uneven quality. Further complicating the use of this volume is the fact that its material pertains to Soloviev's narrative and discussion of events contained in Volume VI of the original work.[1] Thus the reader needs to have read that volume beforehand in order to appreciate fully what the present volume holds. Directly linked with the compilatory nature of the volume is its lack of analysis. Soloviev presents an abundance of source material but rarely if ever comments on it. When Volume VII appeared in 1857 these and other shortcomings were noted. This is not said to dissuade the modern student from turning to this particular volume; on the contrary, as is the case with the others in the series, the reader will gain much from being exposed to the primary documents used by Soloviev in his efforts to recreate a distant past; but the work must be read in its context.

Soloviev is justly renowned for his use of archival sources to give an objective character to his presentation of the flow of Russian history, but this does not mean that he avoided referring to contemporary scholarship. Prominent among those works cited by Soloviev are N.M. Karamzin, *Istoriia gosudarstva Rossiiskogo* (History of the Russian State) (St. Petersburg, 1842, originally published 1818-1819); an article by I. Beliaev,

"O storozhevoi, stanichnoi i polevoi sluzhbe" (On the Service of Guard Troops, Cossack Squadrons and Steppe Patrols)[2] and K.A. Nevolin,[3] *Istoriia rossiiskikh grazhdanskikh zakonov* (History of Russian Civil Laws) (St. Petersburg, 1851). As a young boy Soloviev read Karamzin's work assiduously; he would understand his own work, however, as a counterbalance to Karamzin's subjectivist presentation of Russian history. By inserting chapters dealing with social developments Soloviev hoped to demonstrate that Russian history was not merely a chronicle of the fortunes of a dynasty and its attendant nobles, but more profoundly the interplay of a growing state and a developing society made up of various groups of people. On the level of methodology he shares Nevolin's aim of furnishing a discriminating and rich selection of sources.

In addition to chronicles, collections of letters and official documents, Soloviev incorporated material from such works as Mikhalon Litvin, "O nravakh tatar, litovtsev i moskvitian (On the Morals of Tatars, Lithuanians and Muscovites)," *Arkhiv istoriko-iuridicheskikh svedenii, otnosiashchikhsia k Rossii* (Archive of Historical Juridical Knowledge Pertaining to Russia), ed. N. Kalachov, Book 2, Part 2 (Moscow, 1854); *Zhizn' kniazia Andreia Mikhailovicha Kurbskogo v Litve i na Volyni* (The Life of Prince Andrei Mikhailovich Kurbsky in Lithuania and Volhynia) (Kiev, 1849), and Makarii (Bishop), *Istoriia russkogo raskola, izvestnogo pod imenem staroobriadstva* (History of the Russian Schism Known by the Name Old Ritualism) (St. Petersburg, 1855). He also included material from Giles Fletcher, *Of the Russe Commonwealth*, 1591, and *Hakluyt's Collection of the Early Voyages*, Vol. 1, in his section dealing with foreign trade and commerce. The reliability of these Russian and foreign works is often questionable, and in this volume of his *History* Soloviev only occasionally engages in an evaluation of their trustworthiness; the selections made from them do bring more color to the narrative flow of the volume and as such complement the other documents incorporated in the text.

The reader of this volume will discover what articles of clothing and table furnishings could be found in the tsar's apartments; how a typical Russian house and yard were constructed; what type of taxation the populace endured; how trials were conducted and sentences meted out; what types of manual labor and industry peasants were engaged in. The system of local government, military recruitment and service, as well as the state of the church and cultural achievements, all find a place in Soloviev's depiction of sixteenth-century Russia.

A brief sketch of Soloviev's approach to the study of history will shed some light on the loose collection of materials awaiting the reader of this volume. For Soloviev, history is the science of national self-awareness. Such self-awareness is not gained by means of narcissistic reflection, but rather through comparison with other nations. Knowledge of the history of other peoples, and especially of those who played some part in one's own national growth, is an essential tool for the historian. For this reason the reader will find parallel accounts of daily life and institutional reforms in Eastern and Western Russia, that is, Muscovy and Lithuania. While the incorporation of such knowledge about other nations into a history of one particular nation occasionally blurs the focus of historian and reader, it nevertheless satisfies another conception of the nature of history under which Soloviev operates, namely that history is an organic development. The science of history is immensely more complex than the simple retelling of the past and, as Soloviev recognized, it cannot be content with mere biography of important figures. A host of factors combine to produce a given nation, and it is out of desire to do justice to the complexity of the historical process that Soloviev wrote such a segment as the "Domestic Conditions in Russia During the Reign of Ivan the Terrible."

For example, the reader is alerted to the very different types of economic activity in Northern and Southern Russia respectively through Soloviev's use of the correct word for the basic taxation unit. In the North it was the "bow" and "saltpan," indicating that hunting and the manufacture of salt were the principal sources of income, whereas in the South the word was "plow," indicative of tilling the soil. Each of these human activities is in turn a product of the physical geography of the respective region. In other words, there is an organic link between the abstract terminology for taxation unit and the concrete reality of human labor, the former developing out of the latter. These terms become characteristic of Russian identity, and Soloviev's drawing attention to them seems to have been motivated by his desire to show that everything in a given society, even down to the idiosyncrasies of vocabulary, has been shaped by the historical process. It must be admitted that digressions into such minute details tend to disturb the reader's attention. Soloviev also does not always make explicit why a given bit of information is important, leaving it to the reader to make the appropriate inferences.[4]

Soloviev attributes great significance to four factors which he considers to be determinants of a given nation's history and hence identity. These are geography, intellectual achievements, government and the people. That the present volume deals almost entirely with government and intellectual achievements is no doubt partly responsible for the harsh criticism to which it was subjected by his contemporaries. In particular the absence of any discussion of the village commune, pointed out by the Slavophile K.S. Aksakov among others, gave the volume an old-fashioned spirit out of step with the well-known interest in popular movements and "the people" in the middle of the nineteenth century.

Instead, Soloviev describes the introduction of a new Code of Law in 1550, some significant changes in urban and rural government legislated by Ivan IV, and the system of taxation imposed on various types of activities and regions. It is true that these changes altered the way people lived in Muscovy, and the reader will discover many examples of the slow adjustment made by the people to these changes, illustrated in petitions to the tsar or local officials. Yet the people, which for Soloviev included all classes from noble to slave, remain by and large passive, reacting to government initiatives from on high.

With one notable exception mentioned below, the people appear as mere caricatures of themselves, as for instance in the vignette taken from Soloviev's depiction of daily life in Western Russia. "We run across information which shows as well the activity of a life-giving source that used to awaken an individual and point out the higher goals of life. On the road along which a drunken lord with his likewise intoxicated wife would travel returning from a feast, and whether drunk or sober having no respect for the life, honor and property of their lesser brethren; on the road along which a lord with his armed detail of servants and peasants went to attack the estate of his opponent; on the road along which manservants and maidservants walked in order to bear false witness at court or shamelessly to declare false what was correct—on this same road it was possible to meet a young man who, having experienced hardship, recognized it as divine punishment and would take upon himself some ascetic feat to purify himself of an infamous sin. He would go on foot to collect money for an ecclesiastical institution."[5] While such scenes may have edified Soloviev, they ill serve his purpose of depicting sixteenth-century Russia and express rather more clearly a sentimental yearning for a religious atmosphere slowly being eroded by enlightened secularism.

If history is organic development, its essence is progress, a belief Soloviev shared with nineteenth-century liberal intellectuals inside and outside of Russia. He did not believe in endless progress, for his study of history showed him the fate of many peoples who appeared on the historical stage, flourished and then vanished from sight. For Soloviev sixteenth-century Russia was still in the process of maturation. The inability of society to deal effectively with the arbitrary violence of criminals and nobles alike, and the blood-soaked outbursts of Ivan IV against former allies are for Soloviev but two examples of social immaturity. He decried the low level of education which debilitated potential intellectual greatness among clergy and laity, and found lamentably obscurantist those voices which sought to stifle new learning or the introduction of technological advances. In his view, education would have cured many of society's ills, and Soloviev greeted with a paean worthy of any liberal thinker the advent of the printing press in Moscow in 1563.

Part of the progress which Soloviev documents in his complete *History* is the development of the authority of the state, and although in this volume he refrains from explicit discussion of the point, two parts of the collage which comprises this volume point towards such development, namely the *oprichnina* or crown estates, and the new Code of Law of 1550. It must be stated immediately that direct references to the crown estates are few and far between, which is indeed surprising to anyone familiar with the plethora of studies devoted to it by later scholars. Neither does Soloviev venture any possible reasons for its institution nor does he elaborate on the terror into which it plunged Russia. This he did in Volume VI (Volume 10 of this series). He notes that with the introduction of the crown estates service ranks were affected, taxation increased considerably, and the influence of certain boyar families at court was curtailed effectively and ruthlessly. There are some brief glimpses of the human suffering caused by the crown estates henchmen and Ivan himself, but they get lost among the other documentary depictions of sixteenth-century Muscovy. The result is that although Soloviev refrains from an explicit evaluation of the crown estates the reader having only this volume would be justified in concluding that for Soloviev the crown estates were a necessary and positive measure, designed to promote further concentration of authority in the hands of the tsar.

Soloviev devotes more space to the new Code of Law (Sudebnik) of 1550 and the corresponding Statute of 1556 for Lithuania. His belief in the benevolence of the central government responding to the requests of its subjects comes out strongly when he maintains that "since throughout the sixteenth century there was a strong demand for measures against abuse by government figures and judges, this demand could not help but be expressed in the Code of Law of Ivan IV." Here is one of the few times where Soloviev assigns the people an active role in altering the shape of their nation. It is true that since 1497, when Ivan III issued a Code of Law for

Muscovy, complaints about corrupt judges and venal officials steadily multiplied. The scope of the changes included in the new Code of 1550 suggests a lengthy preparation which indeed could have been motivated by popular dissatisfaction with the justice system. Yet similar discontent, not to mention outright abhorrence, over the crown estates brought no such response from the state. On the contrary, as Soloviev himself documents in the fate of Metropolitan Philip, complaints incurred swift and cruel reprisals. How such apparent attentiveness to the needs of society in 1550 on the part of the government can be reconciled with utter disregard for law and civility during the period of the crown estates is a question which Soloviev does not address in this volume. Curiously enough, he singles out the aristocracy of Poland-Lithuania for its exemplary disregard for basic human rights, remarking that "nowhere did disdain for authority and law by the powerful reach such a level as in Poland and Lithuania."

In keeping with his belief in progress as the motive force in history, Soloviev presented the Code of Law of 1550 as an improvement over the previous state of affairs, which in many cases it was. The Code attempted to rectify judicial abuse and corruption by intensifying and extending the types of punishment for legal transgressions; it dealt with compensation for injured honor, and spelled out in no uncertain terms the limits of competency for governors and rural district officials. But within a decade of its promulgation the Code lost much of its clout, especially those sections pertaining to the governors and rural district officials. Without himself making the connection, Soloviev draws attention to one of the factors now thought to have contributed to the early demise of the Code of Law of 1550—the replacement of governors and rural district chiefs by locally elected magistrates. He points out that this change in local govern-ment had a lengthy history, beginning during Ivan's minority, and seems to have reached a peak around 1556. Districts purchased freedom from maintaining the governors and rural district chiefs, yet the fees for this liberty went directly to the treasury in Moscow. Replenishment of the crown treasury, strained by the conquest of Kazan and Astrakhan, would have been a powerful motive for staying the recently enacted regulations concerning governors and rural district officials.[6] The institution of the crown estates further undermined the authority of the 1550 Code of Law.

Soloviev's theory of the organic development of a nation's history allowed him to explain extraordinary moments in that history as out-growths of one or another feature of the national physiognomy. The great personages of a nation are thus not so much inexplicable phenomena as they are the embodiments of good or bad principles inherent in a given nation. For Soloviev the great personages of this age were Ivan IV and Prince Andrei Kurbsky. The primitive, rude nature of sixteenth-century Russia found its perfect representation in the terrifying tsar who both shaped and was shaped by his environment. As Soloviev put it, "The phenomenon of Ivan the Terrible, agreeing as it did with the state of contemporary morality, had in its turn a harmful influence on morality, inculcating cruelty, violence and disdain for the life and welfare of one's neighbor." Soloviev attempted to shed light on the characters of Ivan IV and Kurbsky by presenting selections from their famous correspondence. He drew attention to the different styles typical of each man's writing and argued that personality played an important part in shaping their written words.

Following Kurbsky's lead, Soloviev holds that Ivan was inept as a writer, never fully in control of his pen; Ivan's irascibility prevented him from attaining that disciplined and harmonious style favored by Kurbsky and, apparently, Soloviev. He doubts that Ivan understood the art of rhetoric, choosing sonorous phrases with little thought for their content. "In keeping with his own day's means of intellectual formation," he writes, "Ivan was an autodidact who read Scripture by rote, and the same happened to him as can be seen nowadays in those similarly educated by rote. The forms of the language in which he read, the forms which for him held an important, sacred meaning, these very forms crowded densely in his memory and when he wished to use them, then without studying the peculiarities of the forms and guided only by his memory, he was often unable to control them or the structure of a phrase. He threw together words and clauses without conjunctions, jumped from one subject to another and without having completed one thought he began another."[7] Ivan is, in other words, a victim of the same empty formalism which so annoyed Soloviev in the *Domostroi*, or "Household Manager." Modern scholars do not share Soloviev's views and delight in the throbbing, passionate stream of words issuing from Ivan's pen.[8]

Kurbsky, on the other hand, benefited from a more formal education. His claiming Maxim the Greek as a teacher opened to Kurbsky an entirely different manner of expression, according to Soloviev. Kurbsky's ability to maintain composure under stress and his sense of being persecuted combined to give his writings the quality of controlled passion as opposed to the violent eruptions of venom characteristic of Ivan's pen. Soloviev sees in Kurbsky the representative of the other side of sixteenth-century culture, liberal, humanitarian, open to change. If the low level of education and the immature state of society prevented this side from gaining the upper hand the seeds were there which eventually grew into the enlightened culture of the nineteenth century.

The present volume gives only a few brief glimpses into Soloviev's evaluation of Ivan as a ruler. He points out Ivan's fits of anger, drawing attention to his diseased moral nature and predilection for coarse entertainments. Although Ivan is presented as a product of his age, the fact that Kurbsky or Metropolitan Philip, to name two figures, did not emulate their sovereign compels Soloviev to search for another factor to account for the phenomenon of Ivan IV. This factor might be called the moral obligation to do the good, which in Soloviev's view Ivan ignored.[9]

Soloviev devotes nearly one third of this volume to ecclesiastical matters, including the establishment of the diocese of Kazan in 1555, the precarious situation of the Orthodox in Poland-Lithuania, and the treatment of certain heretics at trials in the middle of the century. The conquest of Kazan and Astrakhan brought the church new opportunities for evangelization. As Soloviev notes, "once the towns became Russian, they also had to become Christian." For Byzantine ecclesiology, Christian state and church are coterminous realities, and the establishment of the church goes hand in hand with the establishment of the civil authority of a Christian state in formerly non-Christian territories. This is certainly true of the expansion of Russian Orthodoxy into the Volga region, and the documents which Soloviev cites leave no doubt that Ivan IV shared this church-political outlook. Echoing sixteenth-century sentiments, Soloviev interprets the military victory over the Kazan khanate as a religious victory of Christianity over Islam. The lengthy description of the consecration of Archbishop Gury and his stately procession from Moscow to Kazan to take possession of his newly created diocese were indeed a first in Russian church history, as Soloviev remarks.

When reading this section it is essential to bear in mind the intertwining of state and church interests. Gury was given explicit instructions on how to conduct missionary work among the Tatars, not from the church, but from Ivan IV. The mission was subsidized heavily from the tsar's treasury, Gury receiving a large salary and the right to a tenth of all taxes levied in the Kazan region. Further financial support was to come from the metropolitan and other Russian dioceses. Such massive crown support for the Christian mission resulted initially in the conversion of large numbers of Tatars to Christianity. The fact that the church was linked so closely with the conquering Russian state eventually led the Tatars to transfer their hatred for their new civil authorities onto the church. As Josef Glazik ably shows, the supposed triumph of Christianity over Islam quickly evaporated.[10]

It is intriguing that Soloviev chose to highlight precisely the missionary tactics employed by Gury in Kazan. When for example he broaches the topic of monasteries, the Council of 1551 or the situation of Orthodox Christians in Poland-Lithuania, Soloviev restricts his view primarily to administrative, jurisdictional and financial matters; but immediately after the section on Kazan, Soloviev moves to Northern Russia and briefly presents the missionary work among the Lapps conducted by Feodorit of Kola and Trifon of Pechenga. His foray into missionary practices is in fact the only time that Soloviev looks at spiritual matters in his treatment of the church.

Events occurring in his own day may account for this momentary shift away from non-religious themes. When the volume first appeared in 1857, Russia just had waged an inconclusive war against the Ottoman empire in the Crimea (1853-1856). In the same period Russia solidified its presence in Central Asia with erection of the fortresses of Perovsk on the Syr-Daria and Verny, modern-day Alma Ata. More to the point was the reopening of the Theological Academy of Kazan in 1842, and the founding of a Missions Institute at the Academy in 1854 by the layman Nikolay Ivanovich Ilminsky. A Translation Commission was inaugurated in 1847 with the approval of Archbishop Grigory Postnikov, and in 1850 Ilminsky's Tataric translation of the Liturgy of St. John Chrysostom appeared, followed in 1852 by a Book of Hours.[11]

Ilminsky's missiology was ahead of its time. He advocated the acquisition of a thorough knowledge of Islamic and Tatar culture by all clergy serving in Tatar areas. Active attempts at conversion were to be avoided; rather, the missionaries should concentrate on already baptized Tatars, strengthening their knowledge and practice of Christianity. They should facilitate encounters between Christian and non-Christian Tatars, and in that way advance the cause of Christianity.[12] This approach differs from the methods ordered by Ivan IV in the sixteenth century, although on one important point there was agreement, namely that no coercion of any sort was to be employed in winning converts, which for its time was progressive. Soloviev thus paid tribute to these renewed efforts at evangelization, at the same time demonstrating the validity of his understanding of history as an organic process. The contemporary missions in the Volga region and

Siberia rose on the shaky foundations laid by Ivan IV and Gury, whose memory Soloviev conveniently brought back into public consciousness.

Comments on daily life in sixteenth-century Russia are found in Soloviev's presentation of the *Household Manager*. He was interested primarily in this document for the light it might shed on the character of Sylvester, an archpriest at the Moscow cathedral of the Annunciation and confidant to Ivan IV. A lengthy quotation from Sylvester's letter to his son provides Soloviev with the key to unlock Sylvester's influence over Ivan IV. Soloviev compares the letter to the *Instruction* of Vladimir Monomakh, which then allows him to claim that the relationship between Sylvester and Ivan IV was that of teacher and parent to pupil and child. Using this same insight, he also can account for Sylvester's later fall from favor. Sylvester continued to treat Ivan as a pupil and son, and "forgot the tsar in Ivan and saw only a young man." Soloviev suggests that it was this attitude which caused Sylvester to side with the boyars against Ivan in the matter of the Livonian war. Sylvester expected Ivan to obey the older and wiser boyars; when he went his own way, Sylvester had to yield.

Soloviev was particularly disgusted with the obsequiousness which Sylvester's letter inculcated, and refers many times to Sylvester's injunction to avoid conflict and animosity at all costs. In fact, Sylvester's advice to "beat one's servant for an offense he did not commit so that a quarrel with his master can be avoided" causes Soloviev to digress a second time into the theological sphere. This time he is concerned with the essence of Christianity. From Soloviev's perspective, Sylvester perverted the Christian message and erected a pseudo-Christian existence on empty formalism. "In spite of the fact," he writes, "that Sylvester's exhortation to his son has to all appearances a religious, Christian character, we cannot help noticing that its purpose is to impart worldly wisdom. Meekness, patience and the other Christian virtues are portrayed as means of acquiring worldly advantages and people's benevolence. Good deeds are prescribed, but immediately the material advantage to be gained from them is brought to the fore. By prescribing tractability and the avoidance of animosity, all the while basing this on a seemingly Christian commandment, Sylvester ended up by prescribing something quite contrary to Christianity, servility to other human beings." Though these words are directed against Sylvester they could apply also to certain conservative religious groups in Soloviev's own day, and in particular to the hierarchy, which in many respects was more concerned with formality and externals than with the spiritual force of Christian belief.

The *Household Manager* further gives Soloviev the opportunity to comment on the lot of women in the sixteenth century. The reader must bear in mind that the teachings of the *Household Manager* were directed at what might be called the middle class, for noble women and peasant and slave women lived in a very different world than that envisaged by Sylvester. Soloviev highlighted those passages outlining the daily routine of the housewife, and as the reader will discover, it was a demanding regimen. Numerous restrictions were placed on a married woman, beginning with subordination to her husband, and extending into her choice of diversions and acquaintances. Her entire day was occupied with managing the household, a task which demanded expertise in culinary arts, all types of handicrafts, bartering, and management of servants. There was little time for relaxation, and even then the housewife was to be thinking about her household. Soloviev laments the absence of intellectual and spiritual stimulation but concedes that, given the times in which the *Household Manager* was composed, there was very little worthwhile entertainment available. He suggests that the repeated warnings in the *Household Manager* about alcohol may point to widespread use of this intoxicant as an escape from the harsh and tedious routine endured by women.

This is not the only place where Soloviev deals with women. When presenting the legal documents pertaining to inheritance laws he quotes those passages which stipulate the right of women to own, inherit and dispose of property, though not with the same liberty enjoyed by men. Again, developments in Soloviev's own day may account for this interest in the status of women. According to Richard Stites, the reign of Nicholas I saw the first literary and philosophical discussion of woman's place in society. He points out that in its desire to rid Russia of French influences, the intelligentsia promoted traditional Russian models for female conduct in society, upholding the model of a pious, faithful, obedient housewife as the essence of womanhood. Conservative voices noted that Russian women could own and dispose of property with much greater freedom than their West European counterparts, making any demands for an enhanced female role out of place. Still, there were other voices calling for a rethinking of women's role, and particularly urging the equality of the sexes.[13] The selections Soloviev made from his sources perhaps may be interpreted as his own method of contributing indirectly to the discussion just emerging in intellectual circles, showing as they do that the seeds for the social and legal equality of men and women were not imported from abroad but had lain dormant in Russia's historical subconscious.

Throughout this introduction I have attempted to show Soloviev's method at work, and taken the liberty of drawing conclusions only hinted at by the author. Too often in this volume the reader is left wondering why Soloviev chose this bit of information and not something else, or why he let pass without comment numerous observations; for instance, that chronicles continued to be written, or that holy fools were a religious phenomenon characteristic of the time of Ivan IV. The sources brought to light by Soloviev open up a distant past, and as such serve their purpose within the larger context of Soloviev's multi-volumed history. The attentive reader also will discover indications of a commentary on Soloviev's own time, something which makes the reading of this volume, for all its problems, doubly rewarding.

The interested reader may wish to consult more recent literature dealing with the reign of Ivan IV. Of considerable use are Robert O. Crummey, *The Formation of Muscovy, 1304-1613* (London, 1987); Richard Hellie, *Slavery in Russia, 1450-1725* (Chicago, 1982); R.G. Skrynnikov, *Ivan the Terrible*, edited and translated by Hugh F. Graham (Academic International Press, 1981). Readers looking for more information on the religious history of the period are less well served in English and must rely on relevant entries in standard reference works. Readers may turn to John Fennell, *A History of the Russian Church to 1448* (London, 1995) for the earlier history of the church in Russia. Fennel's untimely death in 1992 brought a sudden end to a planned second volume. Illuminating maps are found in Robert J. Kerner, *The Urge to the Sea. The Role of Rivers, Portages, Ostrogs, Monasteries, and Furs* (Berkeley, 1942).

I

THE COURT OF IVAN IV

THE TITLE "TSAR"

According to Herberstein's[1] words Vasily Ivanovich as grand prince finished what was begun by his father and, with respect to power over his subjects, surpassed all monarchs of the entire world. Vasily's son, as a result of the circumstances set forth above, fully recognized his own significance and how he differed from those sovereigns chosen by the tumultuous popular will, or to whom their country merely was ascribed. Ivan expressed this self-awareness above all when he assumed the title "tsar and autocrat" and introduced it into constant usage both domestically and externally in his efforts to justify this action and consolidate it on historical foundations by means available at the time.

At the start of his reign, in order to confer greater solemnity upon the title, Ivan began to make use of so-called theology. "O Trinity superessential and all-divine, most gracious to those true Christians who correctly believe in you, giver of wisdom, incomprehensible and all-glorious absolute summit! Direct us to your truth and to obey your commands, so that we may speak of your people in accordance with your will. For by the mercy and desire of this our God, who is glorified in the Trinity, do we hold the scepter of the Russian tsardom, we who are great sovereign, Tsar and Grand Prince Ivan Vasilievich, autocrat of all Rus, Vladimir, Moscow and Novgorod, tsar of Kazan, tsar of Astrakhan, sovereign of Pskov and grand prince of Smolensk, Tver, Yugra, Perm, Viatka, Bulgaria and other lands, sovereign and grand prince of [Nizhny] Novgorod of the Lower Lands of the Volga, sovereign of Chernigov, Riazan, Polotsk, Rostov, Yaroslavl, Beloozero, Udorsk, Obdorsk, Kondinsk, and of the whole Siberian land and the Northern countries, and hereditary sovereign of the Livonian lands and sovereign of many other realms." The magnificent expressions in the charters sent to him by Eastern rulers pleased Ivan, and we find some of these expressions in his charters.

CUSTOMS OF THE TSAR'S NEW COURT

Wedding ceremonies for the ruling family during Ivan's reign did not differ in the slightest from the wedding ceremony of Ivan's father. It is noteworthy that at the third and at the last wedding of the tsar his younger son Tsarevich Fedor, and not the elder son Ivan the chiliarch,[2] stood next to Ivan in the grand position, that is, as a substitute father. The reason for this is in all likelihood to be found in the familial relationship of Tsarevich Ivan. At the time of his father's third wedding he was himself betrothed,[3] but at the last wedding he was no longer married to his first wife. The senior Lithuanian ambassador, because he was married a second time, could not take the place of the bridegroom at the betrothal of Grand Princess Elena. In Novgorod in 1573 the so-called king of Livonia, Magnus,[4] married the tsar's cousin Maria, daughter of Prince Vladimir Andreevich. The bridegroom was Protestant, and thus we read in the description of this wedding, "The king was married at St. Dmitry's in Priboinaia street, at Slavnov, and with the king came a Roman priest,[5] but the princess was betrothed and married by the priest of St. Dmitry's. Having come to the wedding ceremony, the princess entered the church, but the king remained in the narthex. The king was married according to his religion, but the princess was married in keeping with the Christian religion."

In the event of his death the tsar fixed the coming of age of his son and heir Ivan at twenty years. The godfathers at the baptism of the children of the ruling house were as usual ecclesiastical figures. Tsarevich Ivan's godfather was Metropolitan Makary.[6] The baptism took place in the Miracles monastery[7] by the shrine of St. Alexis. The baptism of Tsarevna Anna[8] took place in the New convent, and when the tsarevna was born Ivan went there and founded the temple of St. Joachim and St. Anna, attended the all-night vigil and orthros,[9] and in the morning he lighted the church and participated in his daughter's baptism. The godfathers were two elders, Adrian from the Androsov hermitage, and Gennady from the Saray hermitage; nothing is said about godmothers. When a daughter was born to Prince Vladimir Andreevich, to his delight he was visited the next day by the tsar, Tsarevich Ivan, Tsar Alexander[10] of Kazan and many boyars, and they dined on vegetables. On the occasion of the birth of Tsarevich Ivan legal fees were remitted. "Since our son Tsarevich Ivan has been born," the tsar wrote to the crown secretaries, "if the fees on cases which were judged and completed before his birth have not yet been collected, none shall be collected."

In a description of the reception of Polish ambassadors during the time of Ivan IV's minority we read that near the grand prince there stood on guard on his right Boyar Prince Vasily Vasilievich Shuisky and on his left Boyar and Master of the Horse Prince Ivan Fedorovich Obolensky-Ovchina,[11] and near Prince Vasily stood Ivan Ivanovich, son of Ivan Andreevich Cheliadnin[12] in place of the uncle. For an orphan, the father's place was occupied of course by an uncle, who supervised his upbringing and behavior, especially in those cases where the mother, being a woman, could not be present. Also attested at this time is the word "under-tutor,"[13] meaning a man who is appointed to look after a child.

The tsar undertook official journeys for three reasons. The first was the inspection of places or circuit tour. Thus in 1566 Ivan went on a circuit tour of Kozelsk, Belev, Bolkhov and other borderland localities, ordering the boyars, noblemen and junior boyars to come with him with the whole service order. The second aim of the journeys was pilgrimage, and the third was amusement, or as they said then, refreshment. Celebrations occurred after the tsar's meal, their character being evident from the fact that they occurred after eating. Apart from donning mourning clothes, members of the tsar's household mourned by letting their hair grow long, a practice called "being hirsute."

In the inventory of Tsar Ivan's household possessions we find an enumeration of fifty-five various types of costume. Then are listed the sovereign's chamber images, and the crosses and icons which the sovereign wore. Various types of clothing are mentioned.[14] Also listed are golden and silver vessels of various names such as jugs, casks, flagons, beakers, bottles, wash-basins, wine bowls, cups, scoops, tureens, spoons, goblets, types of ladles, wash tubs, buffalo horns, tankards, damask steel knives, cobblers' knives from Murom, copper clocks gilded like booklets.

COURT PERSONNEL

By establishing the crown estates Ivan defined his relationship with the boyar council, as exemplified by the manner the council was convoked over the war with Lithuania. As of old, titled princes still took precedence over boyars, and in Ivan's last will and testament there is still talk of service princes in Muscovite and Tver lands. Boyars, lords-in-waiting, treasurers, the keeper of the seal, the official attending the boyars in court, conciliar clerks, noblemen of the first class, and noblemen and junior boyars of the second class figured at the assembly of 1566.[15] Since we do not see the princes listed here separately and above the boyars, lords-in-waiting and noblemen, neither do we see junior boyars listed separately and above the noblemen.

This is a clear sign that as a result of the increased importance of the grand prince, who was by then tsar, the importance of personal service to him or service at his court also increased, while the significance of one's origins, that is, of the prince and the junior boyar, withered away. The latter title replaced that of nobleman and already stood for a lower rank of servitor.

It is nonetheless curious that if the attempt was made from above to elevate the importance of court service at the expense of origins, from below the earlier notions held their ground. Consequently the juxtaposition of old and new notions in documents is admitted easily, given the uncertainty of the times. Thus in the opening lines of the above-cited assembly record of 1566 we encounter only the titles of boyars, lords-in-waiting, treasurers, keepers of the seals, officials at the boyar law court, conciliar clerks, noblemen of the first and second class. At the end of the document, before the adding of signatures, we read "We, the boyars and lords-in-waiting of our sovereign and tsar, the crown officials and secretaries named in this charter have kissed the cross to our sovereign and affixed our signatures and we, the lesser princes and junior boyars and noblemen, in this charter and in our own hand have kissed the cross to our sovereign."

If for the aforesaid reasons the importance of the nobleman increased, all the more so did the importance of the servitor increase for the same reason, because this title was the most distinguished for the period at hand. In 1554 Prince Mikhail Ivanovich Vorotynsky[16] bore it.

The importance of the lord-in-waiting gradually becomes clearer. "Behind the grand prince," it says in the order for the coronation of a tsar, "come his brothers and children, and behind them, the boyars, other magnates and lesser princes, the junior boyars and all noble pages. No one then will dare to cross the path of the tsar, but everyone shall stand with fear, each in his own place. For this reason do the lords-in-waiting and other officials then walk along both sides of the grand prince with all attentiveness and decorum, each according to his rank.... Solemn prayers are sung.[17] Then the lords-in-waiting and other officials of the grand prince walk about the entire church and make certain that the people stand in complete silence and humility and chaste attentiveness." In addition to boyars, lords-in-waiting and majordomos, some junior boyars also were members of the council during Elena's regency.[18] During Ivan's independent reign we find noblemen who are referred to as "great nobles." Together with the boyars they attended important affairs when other noblemen could not do so. "The tsar ordered the noblemen to step forward from the pavilion," we read in the description of the reception for the Lithuanian envoy Bykovsky, "but he kept by his side the boyars and chancellery clerks and the great noblemen, and commanded the Lithuanian envoy to deliver his speech." Then there are encountered noblemen who "live with the boyars at the sovereign's court." Further on we encounter the titles "boyars of the privy council" and "noblemen of the privy council." Finally, the title of conciliar noblemen also appears. In the description of the reception for the Lithuanian ambassadors who came from Bathory[19] to confirm the Zapolsky truce we read, "At a distance from the sovereign the boyars, lords-in-waiting, conciliar noblemen, treasurers and noblemen of equal birth sat on the great bench; but the lord-in-waiting Stepan Vasilievich Godunov and the great noblemen, and Cherkas and Tiumen princes sat in the place of the lords-in-waiting."

We likewise see noblemen of the first and second class in the description of the assembly of 1566. We find the titles boyar and majordomo, boyar and armorer, court carver, department steward, keeper of the seals, court secretary, chancellery secretary, palace secretary. How the secretary grew in importance is witnessed in the fact that one of them, the famous Rzhevsky,[20] was named vicegerent of Chernigov. We also meet the term "eminent men." Thus, in his description of the devastation of Novgorod the chronicler writes, "Other junior boyars in the town seized the wealthy merchants and the sovereign's chancellery officials, eminent men and traders." We meet the term "man of note" instead of "nobleman."

THE MOST IMPORTANT FAMILIES

Information regarding the order of places occupied by the boyars in the council can be obtained from the dealings of various Lithuanian lords with boyars. This information must be used with extreme caution because when sending their ambassadors and documents the lords sometimes did not conform to the order of precedence but rather to the particular importance, the particular proximity of the boyars to the sovereign. In 1552 Lithuanian lords sent an ambassador to Prince Ivan Mikhailovich Shuisky[21] and to the boyar and majordomo Danilo Romanovich Yuriev,[22] and in 1555 to Prince Ivan Mikhailovich Shuisky. In correspondence between Hetman

Chodkiewicz[23] and Ivan Petrovich Fedorovich Cheliadnin[24] the Muscovite governor of Livonia concerning the peace, the following are named as comprising the supreme council of Moscow: the boyar and supreme commander, vicegerent of Vladimir, Prince Ivan Dmitrievich Belsky;[25] the boyar and vicegerent of Novgorod, Prince Ivan Fedorovich Mstislavsky;[26] the boyar and vicegerent of Kazan, Prince Vasily Mikhailovich Glinsky;[27] the boyar and vicegerent of Tver, Danilo Romanovich Yurievich-Zakharin.[28]

Among the boyars participating in the assembly deliberations of 1566 we no longer encounter the names of Prince Vasily Glinsky or Danilo Romanovich. Here after Belsky and Mstislavsky follow Ivan Petrovich Yakovlia Cheliadnin,[29] and then Prince Ivan Ivanovich Pronsky,[30] Ivan Bolshoy Vasilievich Sheremetev[31] and Ivan Menshoy Vasilievich Sheremetev,[32] Prince Vasily Semenovich Serebriany,[33] Nikita Romanovich Yuriev,[34] Prince Mikhailo Ivanovich Vorotynsky, Ivan Mikhailovich Vorontsov,[35] Mikhailo Yakovlevich Morozov,[36] Vasily Mikhailovich Yuriev,[37] Ivan Yakovlevich Chobotov,[38] Vasily Dmitrievich Danilov,[39] Vasily Yurievich Maly and Semen Vasilievich Yakovlev.[40] We find here representatives of ancient Muscovite boyar clans, including two members of the Akinfov clan, Ivan Petrovich Cheliadnin and Ivan Yakovlevich Chobotov; four members of the Koshkin clan, Nikita Romanovich and Vasily Mikhailovich Yuriev, Ivan Bolshoy and Ivan Menshoy Sheremetev (stemming from Fedor Koshka through Konstantin Alexandrovich Bezzubtsev); one Voronstov and one Morozov. The Danilovs traced their family from the prince of Smolensk who served under the Germans and then went over to Ivan Kalita.[41] As for the boyar Maly, he was the offspring of the famous Trachaniotes,[42] Greek immigrants.

We do not observe the Shuiskys among the boyars at this time. Prince Ivan Mikhailovich died, and Prince Peter Ivanovich perished in the battle against the Lithuanians in 1564. The other members of this family were still too young; hence we meet them among the noblemen of the first class, namely Prince Ivan Andreevich, the subsequently famous Ivan Petrovich, and Vasily Fedorovich.

Among these noblemen of the first class are sixty-one members of non-princely families and thirty-three members of princely families. Of the noblemen of second class there are eighty-nine members of non-princely and only eleven of princely families. We encounter Prince Ivan Vasilievich, the ancestor of the subsequently famous Princes Starodubsky-Pozharsky,[43] as vicegerent of Pereiaslavl in 1547.

PRINCELY PATRIMONIES

Three noble families enjoyed the special favor of the tsar, namely the princes Mstislavsky, Glinsky and Romanov-Zakharin-Yuriev, all three being related to the ruling house. In Ivan's last will and testament we read concerning them, "As our father Grand Prince Vasily favored Prince Fedor Mikhailovich, and because I too have given to his son, Prince Ivan, so shall my son Ivan not march into his patrimony nor into that of his children. Because I have favored Prince Mikhail Vasiliev Lvovich Glinsky with a patrimony, my son Ivan shall not for any reason march into his patrimony or that of his children. Because I have favored the wife of Romanov-Yuriev and her son Nikita with districts and villages, my son Ivan shall not march into that patrimony nor the patrimony of their children." Princes Mstislavsky and Glinsky were newcomers from Lithuania, and depended on the favor of the sovereign for their means of support.

We see another kind of instruction relating to the Russian Rurikid princes who, though acting as servitors of the grand prince, still preserved their rich patrimonies. Prince Vorotynsky had his ancient patrimony, the town of Odoev and two other towns, taken from him, in exchange for which he received a patrimony in the North, the town of Starodub Riapolovsky, the Murom rural district of Moshok, the Nizhny Novgorod village of Kniaginino and the hamlet Fokino on the Volga. In Ivan's testament we find instructions on the removal of patrimonies from the descendants of the Starodub princes, the Gundorov, Pozharsky, Tulupov, Romodanovsky, Kovrov, Krivoezersky, Nagaev, Starodubsky proper and Paletsky families. "Whatsoever patrimonies I have taken from the Yaroslav princes," we read later in the testament, "belong to my son Fedor."

For a more speedy escheat of princely patrimonies the following directions were included in the supplementary edicts of the Muscovite Law Code. "Whatever patrimonies given as compensation for the princes of Yaroslavl, Starodub, Rostov, Suzdal, Tver, Obolensk, Beloozero, Vorotynsk, Mosalsk, Trubetsk, Odoev and for other service princes are ancient patrimonies. Those princes are not to sell their patrimonies, nor are they to exchange them or give them as a dowry for their daughters or sisters; but if any prince dies childless, those patrimonies revert to the sovereign. If any prince in his testament signs over to his daughter or sister his patrimony, and with that patrimony sets up a memorial for his soul, those patrimonies may not be given as a dowry to his daughters or sisters. The dowry and the memorial for his soul are to be taken from movable possessions. If any prince does not have enough movable property to provide a dowry for his daughter or sister or to commemorate his soul, the sovereign, judging according to the patrimony, will order it paid out of his own treasury, but the sovereign will order the patrimony to be taken for himself.

"If any prince bequeaths his patrimony to his brother, cousin or nephew, or to any other close relative except those degrees within which marriage is licit, the sovereign, examining this according to the patrimony, and the testament and the service, will bequeath to him some patrimony and order that an edict be made. If any prince dies childless and leaves a wife behind, and if her husband relinquishes some part of his patrimony in the testament, she is to live on that patrimony until her death; but when she dies the patrimony reverts to the tsar, and the sovereign will order a memorial for her soul to be paid from his own treasury. If any prince bequeaths in his testament his entire patrimony to his wife, and the patrimony is large, the sovereign will issue an edict regarding that patrimony."

Following these directions we meet charters with curious expressions. Here is one example. "I, tsar and grand prince, granted Prince Boris Dmitrievich Paletsky the patrimony of his father and brothers, in accordance with the testament of his brother Prince Andrei. Prince Boris shall live in those villages and rule them until death, but when he dies or if he is tonsured, then in accordance with our code money is to be given on his behalf to the monastery for those villages, which I the tsar and grand prince shall take for myself." A curious validation charter[44] to the sovereign exists concerning the purchase of a patrimony by the boyar Sheremetev. In the charter the purchaser says that he purchased it "in accordance with the tsar's charter."

DIMINUTIVES

The names used by servicemen in their formal replies to the sovereign reflected the changes occurring in the relationship of retainers with the grand prince of Moscow. Under Ivan III nobles signed with their usual names, for example, Ivan and Vasily, whereas lesser nobles used diminutives, Ivanets and Vasiuk. Under Vasily we meet the diminutive form expressing humility used by insignificant people, for example, Ileika. Under Ivan IV even nobles began to use this form. Thus Prince Alexander Strigin signed his name "your slave Oleshka Strigin." Then we meet "Fedko Umny-Kolychev" etc., but even the most noble servitors such as the boyar Cheliadnin used the form ending in "-ets" or "-iuk."

II

SYSTEM OF SERVICE

PRECEDENCE

Bowing ever more deeply before the majesty of the sole lord and autocrat, the members of the retinue who by now adopted the term "serviceman" jealously guarded their ancestral honor in conflicts with each other over service. Witness the ever-increasing number of precedence suits. We cannot attribute the increase of such incidents solely to the fact that a large amount of rather complete information about them has come down to us from the period. We have every right to assume that there were causes which actually increased precedence suits in the period under consideration.

As the principality of Moscow grew stronger at the expense of other Northeast Russian principalities, the retinue of the Muscovite princes swelled with outsiders who obtained a position through appointment by the grand prince welcoming them. If the position did not seem sufficiently respectable, they departed for other principalities; if they remained, they began their new service independent of previous traditions. Their number was not great, and the number of campaigns in which many of them might confront each other was also not great. The service relationships of their ancestors were so recent, so much on the minds of everyone, that it was difficult to give them occasion for disagreement in the very act of being appointed, and if disputes did happen, they were settled easily.

Princes began to arrive, and took the first positions, but what kind of precedence conflicts could there be between them? Their service was too new. Be that as it may, as the service of princely and servitor clans grew more venerable and the number of generations performing this service increased, as the court of the Muscovite sovereigns grew more numerous and the court celebrations more splendid, incidents involving precedence must have arisen all the more frequently and become all the more intricate. It is understandable that in keeping with the measure by which these incidents increased, so harmful to the service, the crown had to take measures to limit them. It had to strive to reduce the number of conflicts in the service by declaring that such and such positions stood in no

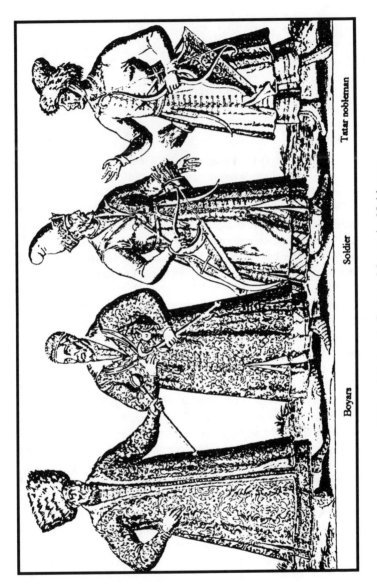

Boyars   Soldier   Tatar nobleman

Attire of Sixteenth-Century Muscovite Noblemen

relationship whatsoever to each other, neither as equivalents nor as subordinates. On the other hand, it had to try to define certain ancestral relations. This is why extreme caution is necessary when explaining ancient princely ancestral relations by means of the more recent definitions of seniority of ancestral degrees encountered in precedence cases, and clearly formed in accordance with the will of the government and its Code of Law.

In 1550 Tsar Ivan reached a decision with the metropolitan, his brother Prince Yury Vasilievich, his cousin Vladimir Andreevich and the boyars, commanding that the regimental service rankings of his boyars and commanders be written in the service warrant. The commander-in-chief was to head the great regiment.[1] This first commander of the great regiment was considered superior to the first commanders of the vanguard, right and left flanks, and rearguard. The commander-in-chief of the right flank was to take no account of the fact that someone was a deputy commander in the great regiment. With respect to subsequent appointments, the deputy commander was to be without rank. The first commanders of the vanguard and rearguard were not inferior to the commanders of the right flank; commanders of the left flank were not inferior to commanders of the vanguard; commanders of the left flank were inferior to the first commander of the right flank, and the deputy commander of the left flank was inferior to the second commander of the right flank.

Princes and grand nobles and junior boyars in the tsar's service with boyars and commanders, or with roving commanders for the tsar's affairs were without position. In the service warrant the tsar ordered it recorded that if junior boyars and grand nobles happened to be in his service with commanders not in keeping with their family heritage, their family heritage was not compromised. "If any grand nobles are now performing service for the tsar somewhere with inferior commanders not in keeping with their family heritage, and if henceforth any of these nobles happen to be commanders together with the same commanders, or happen to be somewhere on a mission, they shall make a report with the same commanders with whom they served and they are then to be commanders in keeping with their family heritage; but before this, although they served with certain inferior commanders, those nobles and the commanders in the report had no disparagement in their family heritage, in accordance with the sovereign's verdict."

In this way the number of cases in which commanders of different regiments could compete for seniority was restricted, and the right of young servicemen of noble origins to compete for seniority with commanders of less noble origins was obliterated. They received the right to compete for seniority only when they themselves became commanders, and then their former subordinate service had no influence at all.

The crown estates system did not exclude precedence although sometimes it upset well-known relationships, for afterwards we encounter the expression "This happened in the crown estates, and although such a rank existed, yet it was the sovereign's will in the crown estates." Commanders competed for seniority not only when being assigned regiments, but also when being assigned towns, for one town was more prestigious than another. Thus in the service warrant of 1570 we read "Any governors not in their proper position in any town shall be without position for the sovereign's business," that is, the present case held no influence on subsequent disputes.

From precedence cases during Ivan's era the way in which family relationships and calculations according to the genealogy tables determined the equality or inequality of those already in service is revealed clearly. "Your uncle Prince Ivan," we read in a document to Prince Fedor Troekurov[2] in 1573, "is equal to Prince Konstantin Kurliatev, and you therefore are equal to the third son of Prince Konstantin Kurliatev." We have observed, that in order to avoid diverse opinions and interpretations concerning genealogical calculations, opinions and interpretations drawn from different places and different principalities of ancient Rus, the Muscovite government needed to bring them into line with its own verdict and its own code, as exemplified in a document dealing with the case of Sheremetev and the princes Kurliatev and Khovansky. "According to our calculation," wrote the tsar, "Prince Alexander Kashin is an uncle in the seventh degree of Prince Konstantin Kurliatev; but according to our code the son of the blood brother is equal to an uncle in the fourth degree." This proves that, based on ancestral unity, an elder or equal in the clan of one rival was in a certain service case lower than his equals or juniors in the clan of another rival, a state of affairs known as "dragging down."

It is easy to understand how terrifying this was, and how clan members regarded someone who could drag them down, and consequently how important it was for each serviceman not to admit his junior position in front of a member of another clan. Such admission, this acceptance of an inferior position, entailed a lowering of all equal and younger members of his own clan before members of certain other clans. If it were discovered that two servitors appointed to the same service unit, one in a greater rank, the other in a lesser, were equal to each other with respect to ancestral relationships, genealogy and service, and according to the service warrant, this meant they were separated or discharged, such dismissal or separation serving also in the future as proof of their equality, of the impossibility of their being together.

Information from the service books for the year 1579 during the Livonian campaign provides an example of the harmful results of precedence and the measures which the crown had to take in the case of disobedience by commanders. The commanders wrote that they were not ranked properly. They were given the answer from Moscow that they must follow the official roster, but the commanders dug themselves in again and would not march to Kes [Wenden]. In anguish the tsar sent to them Andrei Shchelkalov, the crown secretary for foreign affairs, from Moscow, and the nobleman Danilo Saltykov from Alexandrov Village and commanded them to go to Kes and to look after his affairs, bypassing the commanders. The commanders he ordered to go with them.

The commanders competed for seniority in the regiments and in the towns, the artillery commanders competed for seniority in the artillery, and the courtiers did the same for positions at court ceremonies. "In 1577 the sovereign ordered Prince Ivan Sitsky to stand at the throne with the court carver Boris Godunov. Prince Ivan said that it was not in keeping with his station, and petitioned Boris's great brother, and Boris Godunov petitioned Ivan's father." Such cases were rare. The petitioner, because he considered his competitor for seniority to be unquestionably lower than himself by many ranks, petitioned directly to his opponent's senior relative whom he supposed followed him in rank, that is, was only one rank beneath him.

The reverse also happened. The respondent, considering it humiliating for himself to make petition and convinced that he was superior to his opponent, sometimes sent in his stead a junior relative to petition or to respond. One means of terminating such disputes, apart from redistribution or dismissal, was to declare a service to be without position, or not related to precedence; that is, having no influence on future cases. Punishment for unjustified petitions included extradition to the offended party, beating with a cudgel in front of the Chancellery of Crown Service and Appointments, imprisonment for a certain term and making monetary amends for the dishonor.

MAINTENANCE AND SERVICE

In the chronicle there is this information about Ivan's instructions concerning military service. "The tsar and grand prince with his brother, his cousin and the boyars reached a decision concerning the maintenance and service duties for all servitors in the future. At this time the boyars, princes and junior boyars sat in keeping with their maintenance in the towns and rural districts for the sake of administering justice for the people and putting the lands in order. For they themselves were there for peace and maintenance. In those villages and rural districts which had vicegerents and district chiefs they dispensed justice and established order. They turned them from various evil acts to goodness, and were satisfied with their quitrents and the lawful fees that the tsar imposed for them.

"A rumor reached the pious sovereign tsar that the vicegerents and district chiefs were making many towns and districts desolate, holding the fear of God and the sovereign's statutes in contempt. They were committing many insidious acts, being neither pastors nor teachers, but rather oppressors and ravagers. The peasants of those same towns and rural districts were committing much perfidy, and were murdering their men. When the vicegerents and district chiefs abandoned their maintenance the peasants sought compensation by means of many lawsuits, all of which resulted in much bloodshed and the ruin of souls. Many vicegerents and district chiefs lost their ancestral property. The sovereign commanded that elders, hundredmen,[3] fiftymen and tenmen be appointed in the towns and rural districts, and that his will be imposed through the ancient and horrible prohibition. These officials were to judge robbery, theft and all types of cases without showing enmity, nor should they have recourse to venality or false testimony, but should criminals be found in their midst they were to be handed over for punishment.

"The sovereign commanded the officials to impose quitrents on the towns and rural districts based on their industries and lands, and his own crown secretaries were to bring these quitrents to the tsar's treasuries. He furnished the boyars, magnates and all the soldiers with a maintenance and just payments, each according to his worth. He provided the provincial military servitors with a salary in the fourth year, and the others in the third year. Then the sovereign observed that some magnates and all soldiers owned many lands, but had grown impoverished by their service obligations, their service not being in accord with the sovereign's grant and patrimonies. The sovereign equalized them by means of land allotment. Each was given what he deserved, and what remained was divided among the impoverished.

"The service to be performed for patrimonies and service estates was laid down. For one hundred chetverts of good productive land the owner must provide a man and a horse fully outfitted, and two horses for distant campaigns. Anyone who rendered the service due from his land would be rewarded by the sovereign with a grant and maintenance, and a monetary salary would be awarded to those who served accordingly. If someone held land without performing service, the sovereign collected money from him to pay for servitors. If someone provided more men than required from the land, the sovereign would give him a large grant, and the servitors would be paid a third above the normal rate. The sovereign arranged everything so that service for him would be completely free of dishonesty or offense, and the original service records would be kept by the sovereign's head administrators and with the chancellery officials."

In 1550 the sovereign and his boyars decided "to distribute to the junior boyars, his best servants numbering one thousand men, service estates in the district of Moscow, and in half of Dmitrov, in Ruza, Zvenigorod, in Chisliaky, Ordynets, in fowlers' villages and Teterevichy, and in the qui-trent villages[4] sixty and seventy versts from Moscow. They would give any boyars and lords-in-waiting who were prepared for a mission, and who had neither service estates nor patrimonies in the Moscow district, service estates in the Moscow district of two hundred chetverts each. Junior boyars in the first class would receive service estates of two hundred chetverts each, junior boyars of the second class estates of one hundred fifty chetverts each, and those of the third class service estates of one hundred chetverts each. They would be given as many stooks of hay as are given to anyone from a quarter field, except for the peasants' hay, and the peasants would receive thirty stooks of hay per plowland. If one of those thousand servitors dies and his son proves unsuitable for service, another shall be chosen to replace him. But those boyars and junior boyars whose patrimonies are in the Moscow district or in another town some fifty or sixty versts from Moscow are not to be given service estates." Among those appointed for the allotment are mentioned provincial military service landholders and crown service landholders from Pskov, crown service landholders from Toropets, nobles from Volhynia and provincial military service landholders from Lutsk.

Sons or grandsons were appointed to replace men who retired because of old age or illness. If these sons or grandsons were still minors, they were granted a deferment for the appropriate number of years. The wounded were released from service until they recovered. A letter of discharge was given to those released from service. When a servitor's sons reached the time for service, that is, when they attained the age of fifteen, either they were coupled with the father on his service estate or granted an allotment from the father as their separate estate. When as a result of the increase in his family a servitor petitioned that he no longer could serve on the basis of his former estate, in keeping with the tsar's decree the depositions of the petition were verified against the declarations, cadastral surveys, registers of transfers and dowry registries and against all courier charters. The title "register of transfers" is explained by the words of the tsar's edict concerning the addition of two areals[5] to the former service estate of the landholder Saburov. "Let two areals be transferred to Nikita's old estate of ten areals, and see to it that these two areals and his old estate are recorded in the register of transfers." The edicts concerning the augmentation or partition of a service estate normally concluded with the words that this arrangement remain in force until the entry into service of the landholder's son.

After the death of the serviceman his estate either was partitioned equally among all his sons, or a new estate was given to some of them; the widow and daughters likewise were apportioned a part of the estate for sustenance. As soon as the daughters married, reached the age of fifteen or died, their plots escheated to the sovereign, who might direct them to be returned to the brothers. Widows had use of their plots until they died, took the veil or remarried. Landholders might exchange amicably their parcels of land on condition that this exchange was even, that the lands were of equal value as well as its revenue-bringing pastures and incomes, that the exchanged land was not deserted, and that by this exchange there be no losses in service or taxes to the sovereign. In the Novgorod region the distinction between petty landowners and servitors brought in from regions downstream still was preserved. Thus two servitors petitioned that the sovereign's crown secretaries at first transferred to them from the local landowners' service estates ten additional areals, but then these estates were taken from them and returned to the small landowners.

If the landholder petitioned that his estate had become desolate, and he had nothing with which to fulfill his service, the neighboring residents on all sides of the estate for three, four, five, six and more versts, including the abbots, priests and deacons among the clergy, and the junior boyars and peasants, were interrogated under oath concerning the reasons for the desolation of the estate. Was it desolate owing to famine, bad weather, taxes or because of the landholder himself, or others? If in the inquiry it was established that the estate was ruined by the landholder and his negligence the petitioner was left with his old estate. If they said it was not the landowner's fault that the estate was desolate it escheated to the tsar and was given back in quitrent or with a tax exemption for a certain number of years, and the petitioner was granted another estate.

Sometimes a landholder requested not an exchange of estates but an exemption from tax assessment because the peasants had died of the pestilence, and the survivors had fled because of famine. In 1548 Durov, an administrative steward, requested an exemption not only for his service estate but also for his patrimonial lands because one hamlet had burned and his other villages were ruined owing to the tsar's assessment and the obligation to provide for travelers and soldiers. The tsar gave an exemption for four years, during which the servitors and peasants on Durov's patrimonial lands and service estates were to pay neither tribute nor post station taxes or fodder fees. They were exempted from plowland taxes and public works. They were excused maintenance for the vicegerent, the rural district chief or their agent, nor were they liable for the salary of the exactor and bailiff, or to pay the hearth tax. They were not to feed the tsar's horses, mow the hay, dam up the ponds or bring stones, lime and stakes to town. They did not have to stand at the post-station with carts or repair the post-station yard.

When service estates were granted care was taken that the areals were allotted contiguously, not in separate parcels or spread out across the land. Service estates were expropriated on failure to appear for service, those who did not appear were called defaulters, and the lists in which their names were recorded were called defaulter lists. If the disgrace was remedied the defaulters received either their old service estates or new ones on the occasion of certain religious or crown celebrations such as the presentation of a miraculous icon or the birth of a tsarevich.

The mustering of junior boyars for service was carried out in this manner. Officials appointed from Moscow rode to a certain region. Here at the crown secretaries' office they took the district criminal judges, the town managers and as many dispatchers as were needed and they set about their business, armed with a list of all the junior boyars. If they met any junior boyars on the road, they released them on solid written bonds. After enrolling the junior boyars according to the list, all of them for surety bonds, they went with them to the sovereign's service. When they found remaining junior boyars who hid they beat them with the knout and then sent them off into service. They took children and servants from those who continued to hide. They went after them in places they were reported to be, hunted them down, beat them with the knout, put them on bail and sent them off to the sovereign's service. Once underway extreme caution was exercised lest the junior boyars desert in transit, commit acts of violence and theft against anyone on the road or seize provisions for men and horses by force. Apart from service estates, servicemen received tax-free service property in the towns where their families fled in the event of danger from enemies.

MUSKETEERS, ARTILLERYMEN AND FOREIGNERS

Apart from the noblemen and junior boyars we also observe in this period musketeers under the authority of their own commanders, after whom their companies were named. Beneath the commanders were the fiftymen and tenmen. In precisely the same way the town cossacks were differentiated by the company or group of their own commanders, and together with the musketeers they fell under the authority of the Chancellery of Musketeers.

Among the servitors in the artillery are mentioned the cannoneers who likewise were under the authority of their own commanders. "When the cannoneers come to you," the tsar wrote in 1555 to the Novgorod crown secretaries, "without delay command the Novgorod blacksmiths to make six hundred iron cannon balls, using the molds sent with the artillerymen, and order the blacksmiths to make the balls round and smooth, just as the cannoneers indicate. Give them ten canvasses, three hundred sheets of good, large, thick paper, twenty-two sheaves of soft, fine flax, eight flax cords, each cord twenty sazhens long, eight boxes for balls and for sacks, eight bast reins, twenty grivenkas of lead and eight sheepskins. Watch the artillerymen carefully lest they take any graft and gifts[6] from the blacksmiths."

When the artillery set out on a campaign, carpenters and blacksmiths with carpentry and smithing riggings went with them. In the towns, near the munitions, cannons and arquebuses were stationed arquebusiers, town gatekeepers, watchmen, blacksmiths and carpenters without interruption, day and night. All of them swore allegiance and were put on bond so that they would not leave the town. We know that in case of need towns sometimes drew their artillerymen and arquebusiers from among old and retired servitors. Finally, part of the Russian army were foreign detachments, principally Lithuanians.

ARMY RATIONS

Supplies of grain were sent to captured Livonian towns. It was the obligation of the taxpaying peasants to furnish these supplies. Sometimes the grain supplies were provided to the towns on a contractual arrangement. Thus in 1582 a certain Terekha Sitnikov was hired to provide from Nizhny Novgorod for Astrakhan grain supplies amounting to two thousand five hundred chetverts of meal and oat flour. The purveyor received a document which guaranteed him free and unimpeded passage everywhere. If anyone summoned a bailiff against the supplier or his men, or if his cossacks, not desiring to go to court, sought damages from him or his men or slandered him, the boyars, governors and crown secretaries need not send the bailiff or try him or his men in court. If anyone had some suit involving him or his men, the boyars would try them in Moscow. Similarly, the boyars, military governors and crown secretaries could not conscript Terekha's cossacks for the musketeer or cossack companies.

We learn that service Tatars and cossacks were given two dengas a day to buy fodder for each horse. When the Tatar tsarevich Kaibula departed on campaign to the Swedish borders orders were given to prepare maintenance for men and horses all along the way. At every encampment every eighty men were given a dry cow, a sixteenth measure of cereal and a pound of salt. Every ten men were provided with a ram, and a denga's worth of cereal and salt each. The hides from the dry cows and the sheepskin from the rams were left behind for those from whom the animals were taken. For every ten horses a quarter measure of oats was given, and each man received an armful of hay as fodder for his horse. In the edict it stated that "this must be laid in store so that the soldiers will not be without provisions, lest the peasantry on the road be attacked and provisions stolen."

The tsar did not forgive commanders who permitted their soldiers to behave violently in the Russian land. In the description of the campaign of Tsar Shah Ali and Prince Mikhail Glinsky against the Lithuanians we read, "This Prince Mikhail and his men, riding along the road, pillaged violently his own lands and on the boundary his men looted the villages of Pskov territory, slaughtered livestock and burned Christian homesteads. The tsar was incensed at him, and commanded that a search be conducted for those who were robbed on the road. They collected compensation from him for the thefts." Town cossacks and musketeers received annual salaries of fifty copecks each in addition to the grain dole. Arquebusiers, gatekeepers, watchmen, blacksmiths and carpenters each received one ruble a year, two puds of salt, twelve baskets of rye and the same amount of oats. The town cossacks even received lands. In 1571 the boyars decided that the cossacks of Putivl and Rylsk, if they wished, could recruit one thousand cossack cavalrymen or however many seemed suitable, depending upon how much land was available. They were to serve on steppe missions and guard the land without pay, and the sovereign ordered that whoever served would be granted lands.

MUSTERS

An order directed at Novgorod and its bytowns in 1545 exemplifies how military personnel were amassed. The sovereign commanded these towns to muster a total of 1,973 cavalrymen, taking one man from every three tax exempt properties and one man from every five taxpaying properties. From the Novgorod commercial districts and from the bytowns, commercial districts, trading rows and hamlets a total of two thousand arquebusiers were to be mustered, half of them mounted, the other half as foot soldiers. The arquebusiers on foot must have boats, which they were to provide at their own expense. The mounted men also must have boats to transport their food and supplies to Nizhny Novgorod. Each of these arquebusiers, whether mounted or on foot, must have a hand-held arquebus, twelve grivenka measures of gunpowder and the same amount of lead for bullets. All the men were to have a light or heavy dyed caftan.

The following month a rescript was sent to Novgorod which required the town to muster from the tax-exempt properties and from the merchants' properties one man per property, one man from every two cloth merchants' properties and one man from every five taxpaying properties as before. One pud of gunpowder was to be provided by every twenty properties without exception. A month later the prosperous people living on taxpaying properties had to provide from each property one man in addition to the previous levy of one man from every five properties. Freed from this recruitment were the properties of the archbishop's junior boyars, those of the priests from the cathedral of the Holy Wisdom and of all servitors of the archbishop.

Every six stipendiary priests were to provide one man and two grivenkas of gunpowder; every ten non-stipendiary priests must provide one man and two grivenkas of gunpowder. The deacons, clerks, sextons and altar bread bakers would help their own priests on the basis of church revenue. To those saying they were unable to procure gunpowder, saltpeter masters and arquebusiers were sent to show them how to prepare it. The Pskov chronicle reports for the year 1535 that its citizenry supplied five hundred arquebusiers, three thousand horse-and-wagons and men on horseback, three thousand chetverts of oatmeal porridge from oat flour, three thousand pig carcasses, three thousand chetverts of malt, three hundred sixty chetverts of peas and the same amount of hemp seed. They sent four hundred arquebusiers to Moscow and the people of Novgorod sent many auxiliary soldiers for the construction of the new town of Sebezh.

Sometimes the auxiliaries fled during a campaign, and the regions of their origin had to hire replacements. For the year 1561 the chronicle says that the tsar's governors lost many auxiliaries, and others fled because there was nothing to eat. Because of this Pskov, its bytowns and villagers incurred great expense in providing auxiliaries. To replace the runaway auxiliaries they hired others, twenty-two per plowland. They gave some men three rubles a month, and to others they gave three and a half rubles, each with horses and outfitted wagons. During the campaign against Polotsk there were 80,900 unmounted and mounted auxiliary recruits in Ivan's army. In Pskov, in the auxiliary division, each mounted soldier was paid five rubles, and each foot soldier was paid two rubles.

For 1570 the Pskov chronicle says that the tsar came to Great Novgorod, and many were slain. He then ordered that auxiliaries be raised in detachments to pave bridges in Livonia and to gather gunpowder ore. All the people of Novgorod and Pskov were impoverished by this levy and exaction. Because they had nothing to give, they went themselves as auxiliaries and died there a cruel death from hunger and cold, from bridge building and the military detail. In Pskov they hauled barges and large boats to Livonian towns as their auxiliary levy, but after hauling only a few they deserted into the woods. The boats rotted there and the peasants perished.

SERVICE IN THE MILITARY ENCAMPMENTS

Sixteenth-century Muscovy found itself in the same situation as ancient Rus at the time of St. Vladimir. Its southeastern boundary bordered on the steppe out of which nomadic marauders raced seeking plunder. For some time Muscovite sentinels, frontier guards or cossack patrols had fanned out in various directions into the steppe and took up their appointed posts, keeping a lookout for Tatars. During the reign of Ivan IV the Muscovite sentinels engaged in skirmishes with Lithuanians on the Dnieper. The tsar was attempting to show Sigismund Augustus[7] how advantageous it was for him to assist the Muscovite sentinels instead of quibbling about their being on Lithuanian soil.

In the second half of his reign Ivan, his attention entirely focused on the West, had to take all the more trouble that the southern border be defended lest the Crimean Tatars appear unannounced at the Oka river. With this goal in mind the sovereign in January 1571 put his boyar Prince Mikhailo Ivanovich Vorotynsky in charge of the cossack squadrons, the sentinels and the entire steppe military service. Speaking in the name of the sovereign, Vorotynsky told the crown secretaries in the registry that the sovereign commanded him to take charge of and organize the cossack squadrons and the sentinels, and he ordered them to try to find the earlier cossack squadron lists. He ordered them to send charters to the towns of Putivl, Tula, Riazan, Meshchera and other frontier towns and to Severia for the junior boyars, the military clerks and frontier captains, their troopers, the squadron commanders and the sentinels accustomed to ride from Putivl, Tula, Riazan, Meshchera and from Severian lands in the cossack squadrons to various perimeters in the steppe, and for any who rode some ten or fifteen years earlier, ordering them all to appear in Moscow.

When they arrived the sovereign commanded Prince Vorotynsky to spend time investigating the cossack squadrons, the sentinels and every steppe service unit, the captains, troopers and squadron commanders. This completed, he was to draw up a detailed schedule stating from which town, along which places and up to which places the cossacks best ride; where the sentinels should stand guard; up to what places, on which side, from which guard post, mounted patrols be undertaken; where in the steppe the captains should stand guard against the approach of enemy soldiers; from which towns and how many men each, with which commandant and what type of men must stand in the sovereign's service. This was done so that the sovereign would not be ignorant of the approach of enemy soldiers, and lest the enemy advance without warning against the sovereign's frontier territories.

After the inquiries Prince Vorotynsky, in conjunction with the junior boyars and the cossack squadron captains and members, reached a decision concerning the encampments in Putivl, Tula, Riazan and Meshchera, and concerning all monthly rotations of sentinels in the distant and near frontier guard posts. They determined from which town and to which perimeters the troopers best and most profitably should ride, as well as how many sentinels each of the towns must provide for the guard posts. The troopers must ride to their perimeters and the sentinels must stand guard in strategic locations from which they could observe enemy soldiers. The guards were to stand at their guard posts one after the other, not dismounting from their horses, and were to ride along the perimeters one after the other, to the right and to the left, two men each according to such orders as given by the commanders. They were not to pitch camp, and if they needed to cook their food they must not light a fire in the same spot, neither must they kindle a fire twice in the same place. No one might spend the night where he rested at noon. They were not to stop in the woods, but only in such places where they could keep watch.

If the troopers or sentinels observed enemy soldiers they were to send their comrades with this information to the nearest frontier towns. They themselves were to ride behind the enemy on the trails in order to estimate the number of soldiers along the trails and in the camps and having done this send their comrades with this information a second time to the same towns. The new messengers must ride to the right or the left, using whichever roads were closer, so that the news reached the frontier towns before the actual approach of the enemy. They themselves must pursue the enemy along the trail. If there were no trails then, having abandoned the trail on the right or the left as needed, they must proceed with caution and stealth, being especially vigilant. When they discovered against which frontiers the enemy soldiers were advancing, they were to hasten with accurate information to those same towns.

If the troopers caught sight of enemy soldiers on distant perimeters they were to send scouting patrols of three, four or as many men as were appropriate, to observe the soldiers and their actions from suitable sites, and not only from one place. Having reconnoitered accurately the enemy and their destination, they were to hasten as quickly as possible with their first-hand information to the towns upon which the enemy was advancing. If they were not on the trails and had not estimated the number of soldiers, nor learned in detail against which places the enemy soldiers were marching, the troopers and sentinels were not to ride with news, no matter how important, neither were the sentinels to leave the guard posts without awaiting replacements. If sentinels left their guard posts without being relieved, and war broke out during that time by enemy soldiers crossing the sovereign's frontiers, the sentinels were to be sentenced by the sovereign to death.

Any sentinels spending extra days in their guard posts beyond their assigned time without being relieved by their comrades collected twenty-five copecks per man per day from their replacements. If the commanders or captains sent men to supervise the squadrons and sentinels in the guard lines and posts, and those sent found them standing watch incautiously and imprudently, not riding as far as the perimeters even if they did not expect the approach of enemy soldiers, they were to beat those troopers and sentinels with the knout. The commanders and captains were to see to it that the sentinels had good horses and that they went on guard duty with two horses so that they might be able to leave if they spotted the enemy.

If any troopers or sentinels had poor horses and an urgent patrol arose, it was ordered that they obtain horses from their captains among the sentinels. If they must go quickly and there was no time for this, the commanders were to order them to take good horses from their captains. If the captains did not have so many horses, the commanders were to take good horses from their own troops according to their estimation and collect four altyns a day for each horse as rent from the captains, giving the money to those soldiers from whom the horses were taken.

The cossack squadrons were to ride from Putivl or Rylsk. The first squadron was to ride to the steppe in the spring on April 1, the second on April 15, the third on May 1, the fourth on May 15 and so on, and the eighth squadron was to leave on July 15. Then the first squadron began a second tour on August 1, and so on. The final expedition was to leave on November 15. If the squadrons needed to go on patrol and snow had not yet fallen, they must send troopers even later than November 15, according to the schedule. Two squadrons were to be despatched each month, allowing an interval of two weeks plus a day between squadrons.

In addition to junior boyars, townsmen and cossacks, hired inhabitants of Severian Ukraine, or Sevriuki, were used for the mounted patrols but later it was decided to dismiss them because they stood guard negligently. Enemy soldiers marched against the frontiers unannounced and they saw nothing; they never had reliable information but instead reported false information. Junior boyars from Putivl and Rylsk kept watch in the Donets guard posts. Those from Putivl or Rylsk had service estates or salaries.

In addition to the Donets guards, townsmen from the town quarters kept watch in the nearby guard posts of Putivl and Rylsk and in the joint and separate guard posts, as did the townsmen from Novgorod Seversk in the joint Putivl guard. Junior boyars of Mtsensk and Karachev with service estates and salaries kept watch in the joint and separate guard posts from Mtsensk and Karachev. Cossacks with service estates and salaries kept watch in the Orel, Novosil, Dedilov, Donkov, Epifan, Shatsk and Riazhsk guard posts. Tatars and Mordvinians from the surrounding lands served in the Kadom and Temnikov guard, and cossacks served in the Alatyr guard. Afterwards it also was decided to station six sentinels in each guard post instead of the former four so that they could patrol to the right and the left, changing continually two men at a time. To supervise the good working order of the guard posts, four border sentry officers were appointed to patrol the entire expanse of the steppe from the Volga to the Vorona, and from the Oskol to the Donets.

In October 1571, following the sovereign's edict, Prince Vorotynsky and his assistants decided to set fire to the steppe. They determined from which frontier towns and at what time, along what places, to which perimeters and how far, how many squadrons with how many men in each squadron should ride into the steppe and burn it. The burning of the steppe was set for autumn, in October or November before the first frosts, when the grass in the steppe was extremely dry. They did not wait for the snow but for fine and dry weather, so that the wind blew away from the sovereign's frontier towns, in the direction of the steppe, lest they set fire to the grass near the frontier towns, near forests or forest abatis or any fortifications built against the advance of enemy soldiers. To set fire to the steppe the squadrons rode from the towns of Meshchera, Donkov, Dedilov, Krapivna, Novosil, Mtsensk, Orel, Rylsk and Putivl. The conflagration was to spread from the upper reaches of the Vorona to the Dnieper and Desna.

In 1574 a new leader was appointed for the sentinels and squadrons, the boyar Nikita Romanovich Yuriev.[8] Under his leadership we observe a change with respect to the date of the squadrons' first expedition. Instead of falling on April 1, it was ordered to coincide with the beginning of spring. The service registrars and not the military governors from the towns were ordered to select the junior boyars for steppe service. In line with petitions from the monthly steppe sentinels the boyars decided that cossacks who served monthly guard duty in Shatsk, Riazhsk, Donkov, Epifan, Dedilov, Krapivna, Novosil and Orel were to receive service estates and salaries in compensation. They were given twenty to thirty chetverts per man to add to their old estates, and in the third year a salary of three rubles per man for guard duty. If they were horseless, they were to be given two good steeds each, or a good gelding in place of a steed.

The boyars ordered that scribes, junior boyars and scriveners be sent to those towns to examine all cossacks in person with their horses and with their whole service. Any cossacks who were ill-suited, horseless, or not in their guard service unit were to be dismissed from guard service. They were to serve in the cossack rank-and-file service unit, and did not receive the service estate supplement. Good mounted cossacks from the rank-and-file were chosen in their place. In Mtsensk and Karachev the junior boyars of minor rank with estates of fifty, seventy and one hundred chetverts were to stand watch in the guard posts from those towns because cossacks were

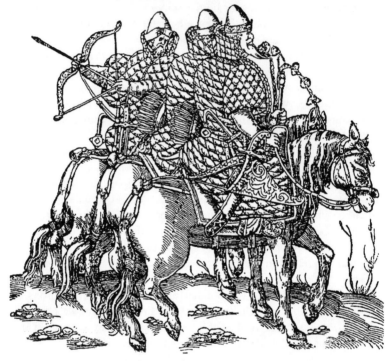

Russian Noblemen Armed for Battle
Based on a Sketch by Herberstein

not enrolled in those town rosters. Shatsk, Novosil and Orel were to send junior boyars in addition to the cossacks. At the time of Boyar Nikita Romanovich's tenure of office the Putivl squadrons rode as far as the upper reaches of the Tor, along the Miius, Samara and Arel toward the Dnieper as far as Pesi Kosti. The limits of the Tula squadrons' patrols extended towards Mozh and Kolomak to the Muravsky road, the Riazan squadrons patrolled as far as Severian Donets and Sviatye Gory and the Meshchera squadrons followed the Don river down to the Volga portage.

Such was the military organization in Northeast Russia in the Muscovite state. Here we see that the retinue paled more and more in significance before that of the sovereign. In Western Russia, on the other hand, the nobility jealously watched over the maintenance of their ancient rights.

GENTRY IN WESTERN RUSSIA

At the Wilno Sejm of 1547 the gentry demanded from their king protection against two estates, the clergy and the burghers. They requested that clerics not take part in land and secular courts and that they not summon people to ecclesiastical courts for temporal matters. With respect to the burghers the gentry complained that the Wilno artisans were collecting exorbitant fees for their labors and were increasing prices arbitrarily, thus impoverishing the gentry. The king promised to fulfill their request. At the Sejm of 1551 the gentry requested that simple slaves not be elevated above the gentry, that a simple slave or a noble of suspicious ancestry not hold ranks. The king challenged them to show him which slave or dubious noble was promoted by him. Then the gentry requested that the lords treat them respectfully at courts and other places. In 1576 the Braslav gentry presented King Stefan a petition that royal decrees be written to them in Russian and not in Polish.

COSSACKS OF WESTERN RUSSIA

We have noted the character of the Muscovite cossacks, those who lived on the steppes belonging to Muscovy and who nominally recognized its authority. The character of the Lithuanian or Little Russian cossacks, known at the time in Moscow by the name Cherkas, was precisely the same. Indeed their impunity was all the more assured by the weakness of the Polish-Lithuanian government. The behavior of the cossack captains such as Dashkovich[9] or Prince Dmitry Vishnevetsky,[10] whose adventures met a cruel end in Turkey, is well known. At the same time that the Polish government was making every effort to live in peace with the Crimea and Turkey, cossacks from Cherkasy, Kanev, Braslav and Vinnitsa repeatedly threatened caravans of Turkish and Crimean merchants travelling to and from Moscow along the steppe beyond Cherkasy, where over eight hundred congregated under the leadership of such senior cossacks as Karp, Andrusho, Lesun and Yatsko Belous. Moreover a Crimean messenger riding from the khan to the king was killed by cossacks in the steppe. Salt merchants travelling to Kochubeev for salt suffered constantly from their attacks.

In vain did the king write the khan that the marauders were the cossacks of their mutual enemy, Moscow, originating in Putivl, Chernigov and Novgorod Seversk, for Crimean and Turkish merchants knew very well how to distinguish Muscovite from Cherkas cossacks. Ataman Andrei Liakh and the cossacks of Prince Dmitry Vishnevetsky attacked the Muscovite messenger Zmeev in the steppes beyond Samara as he was going to the Crimea. Zmeev was accompanied by a Crimean messenger and, as usual, Turkish merchants and Armenians. The cossacks slew thirteen Turks and Armenians and lopped off the hands of three because they had purchased Lithuanian captives in Moscow.

Muscovite envoys living in the Crimea informed the sovereign about the frequent attacks by Ukrainian cossacks in the Crimea. Very intriguing is the information sent from Crimea to Moscow by the envoy Rzhevsky. "A cossack from the Dnieper," he wrote, "came to the Crimean tsar with news that the Muscovite sovereign sent a great grant to the commander Prince Bogdan Rozhinsky and to all the Dnieper cossacks, instructing them that if they needed additional cossacks he would send them as many as they needed and also would send saltpeter and all kinds of supplies. In the spring they must without delay attack the Crimean Tatar camps and advance on Kozlov."

The commander and the cossacks served the sovereign faithfully, and were exceedingly happy with the sovereign's generosity. Having heard this news, the khan called the princes and murzas[11] for advice. "If the cossacks come," he said, "first of all they will take Belgorod and Ochakov, and we will wait for them beyond the mountain ridge." "If many come in boats, the towns will not stop them. You know what a dog the cossack is. Even when Turkish musketeers advance against them in boats they kill them on the spot and take their boats!"

As in olden days when Rus princes needing an army for their domestic wars found ready-made retinues in the steppes where peoples of many names teemed, so too in the sixteenth century did the petty lords of the Danube principalities of Moldavia and Wallachia, who were fighting with each other, seek out and find assistance from the cossacks. Thus one of them, Ivon, being threatened by his rival Petrilla, whom the Turks supported, turned with a request for help to King Henry[12] of Poland, who refused to help on grounds that Poland was at peace with the Turks. Ivon then turned to the cossacks; that their king was at peace with the Turks meant absolutely nothing to them. They sent some men under the leadership of Svirgovsky to assist Ivon and initially had some success. In the end, they were crushed by the numerically superior Turkish regiments. Pod-kova,[13] the brother of the slain Ivon, who got his name because he could break a horseshoe, likewise found refuge among the cossacks and marched with them against Petrilla, defeating him.

Stefan Bathory did not want to break the peace with the Turks. He ordered his brother the prince of Transylvania to march out against Podkova, who was forced to withdraw and surrendered himself to the Poles, trusting in a safe conduct given to him in the name of the king, but the promise was broken. Podkova was put in fetters, and when prior to the war with Moscow[14] the Turkish ambassador insisted that he be executed, threatening war otherwise, Bathory carried out his demand and Podkova was executed in Lvov. Despite this, Podkova's brother Alexander and the cossacks routed Petrilla anew, but he fell into the hands of the Turks, who impaled him. Afterwards some cossacks set out against the Turks and burned down the fortresses of Yagorlik and Bendery. Bathory ordered his army stationed on the border to seize and put in chains the cossacks returning from that expedition.

III

FINANCES

The constantly increasing requirements of state in Muscovy demanded an increase in the financial resources to meet them. How did the government of Moscow act in this situation? Very simply, and of course according to the ideas of the time. Whenever a new requirement or new expenditure appeared, a new tax was imposed, hence that accumulation of various types of taxes which finally began seriously to hamper the financial performance of ancient Russia. Thus a musket impost was levied which amounted to 5,236 rubles from the Novgorod town quarter, bytowns, outlying district and hamlets. Those regions closest to the place of military action had to provide auxiliary soldiers for war. The auxiliaries' impost was two rubles per man. For the military provisions from privately owned lands , otherwise known as "white" lands, the so-called "white mainte-nance" was collected, forty-three altyns less two dengas for each Moscow plowland.

Intriguing are the receipts of payment pertaining to taxes and the expenses linked with their payment. For example, "I, Yushka, son of Mitrofan, a tenman, collected from Abbot Evfimy and the brethren of the Savior monastery taxes and ermine imposts and post taxes, except the donations for memorials to the clerk and for the Moscow region as well as the maintenance from Easter and the feast of St. Peter [June 29] completely, and I gave this receipt to him." Or, "So much post taxes and assessment levies were collected, such and such fees for clerical services, for public works and abatises, for clerks, for public clerks, for carpenters and blacksmiths, for assistance for the post-riders, for saltpeter works" and so on.

Apart from taxes, quitrents served the government as a source of income. In 1543 the Vologda scribes, in accordance with the grand prince's instruction, handed over to the abbot of the St. Cyril monastery for a quitrent two plots of taxable idle land belonging to the grand prince, because the idle land lay between the monastery's villages, but was separate from the grand prince's villages. For these idle lands, it was said in the document, the grand prince required no taxes, no auxiliary recruit service, no maintenance for the vicegerent, no fees for his agents, exactors or bailiffs, nor would litigation against the taxpaying peasants be brought. The monastery would pay the grand prince an annual quitrent of ten altyns for these idle lands.

Arable crown lands, hay fields, woods, rivers, mills and gardens were given out in exchange for quitrent. These properties came from the additional amount to whoever made an additional payment against the quitrent price paid by the previous landlord. The government hastened to make use of a vicegerent's income in the period between the old vicegerent's departure and the new vicegerent's appointment. In 1555 when the vicegerent of Novgorod, Prince Paletsky, left the town the tsar wrote to the crown secretaries, "Now select a good junior boyar from among the town administrators or the street wardens, one who fits the job and whom you can trust, and order him to bring to me from that half of Novgorod all revenues of the vicegerent and his tax collectors, and have him swear an oath and watch carefully over him so that our revenues not be lost."

How taxes were collected is evident from a royal charter to the Novgorod crown secretaries in 1556. "You wrote to us that it was commanded to send letters into all the quarters so that the princes, junior boyars and all servicemen, abbots, priests, deacons, elders, hundredmen, fiftymen, tenmen and all peasants chose from their quarters one good junior boyar each, and from the quarters one man for every three or four best men, and one man from each hamlet, one man from every two or three small hamlets. The elected elders were ordered to collect our post and assessment taxes, and all taxes for the plowland people and the saltpeter works, and every tax in keeping with the cadastral registers, and to bring it to you in Novgorod."

Ivan III gave a statute to the farmers of the excise and branding taxes in Beloozero. Under Ivan IV a commercial ordinance[1] was issued in Beloozero in 1551 which did not differ in the slightest from Ivan III's ordinance with respect to the collection of the excise, but a provision about collection of measuring and market fees was added. "The measuring fee is to be collected on wheat, rye, barley, malt, hemp, buckwheat, peas, oat flour, turnip, and all grain, hops and cured fish and on sparling and top-knots. From the vendors a denga is to be collected on four chetverts, but the excise shall not be collected on grain and dried fish. If anyone sells two or three cartloads of any type of grain without using a measure, or if anyone buys grain contrary to the authorized measure, a fine of two rubles is to be collected. One ruble is for the vicegerent and one ruble is for the measurement officials. Whoever sells four Muscovite chetverts of any grain, or whoever buys and sells grain other than in the authorized measure, must pay a fine of one ruble, a half of which goes to the vicegerent and half to the measurement officials.

"The fees in the market squares are the following. If someone arrives to purchase wares in the market squares the square manager collects from him as a market fee four dengas on every thousand Shuvay or Ustiug squirrel pelts and two dengas on every thousand Kliazma squirrel pelts. They collect the same amount on forty sable pelts as on the Shuvay squirrel pelts and one denga per forty marten pelts. They collect the same amount on ten beaver pelts as on a thousand Shuvay squirrel pelts. They collect three dengas on every bolt of Flemish or English cloth, and one denga on each bolt of cloth from Como and Troyes. The fee is one denga on honey in a vat of seven to ten puds, but if the vat is less than seven puds they collect a fee according to the schedule. If someone buys more or less than a ruble's worth of pepper they collect the fee according to the same rate. On a barrel of herring the fee is one denga; on a basket of caviar, one denga; on a barrel of plums, a half denga; on a cylinder of wax, four dengas and on a ream of paper a half denga. If someone arrives in Beloozero with meat or some other wares but does not set up a booth in the market square, stationing himself in someone's courtyard, and if the square managers accuse him before the vicegerent of having set up a booth other than in the market square without their leave, the vicegerent shall investigate the charge and collect a fine of twenty-five copecks for himself from him in whose yard the vendor set up shop, and the square managers shall collect twenty-five copecks from the vendor. The vicegerent's deputy will take four dengas as judicial escort fees.[2]

"The square managers collect nothing from anyone who brings goods worth less than two rubles, stations himself directly on the market and spends the night there. After examining the goods the square managers collect the market fee from anyone bringing in goods worth less[3] than two rubles and stationing himself in someone's yard and not in the market square. They collect four dengas a week for the warehouse. If someone comes without carts to set up a booth in the market square and has goods worth more than two rubles, the square managers shall give him a booth in the market square. If he does not obey the managers and does not approach them, they shall place him near their own booth across from the vicegerent's deputy, who will collect the escort fee of four dengas."

The commercial ordinance issued in 1563 to the village of Vesegonskoe belonging to the St. Simon monastery and located in the Gorodetsky township of Bezhetsky Verkh ordered that an excise tax of four dengas to the ruble be collected from merchants of other towns, including Moscow, Tver, Novgorod and Pskov. From local merchants the tax amounted to one and a half dengas. If traders arrived by boat on the Mologa river, the excise on their goods was collected from them in keeping with the commercial ordinance and one altyn was collected for each boat with or without a deck, or a boat with planks, posts and tow ropes, but three dengas were collected for a longboat.[4] When a merchant from Riazan or Kazan or some other foreigner entered the village of Ves, seven dengas per ruble's worth of goods were collected from them. The people of Bezhetsky Verkh, the townsmen of Gorodets and the village peasants farmed the excise and all commercial duties in the village of Ves, but in 1563 the St. Simon monastery, complaining that this was causing wrongs and great financial losses to their agents and peasants, obtained the right to farm the taxes in exchange for an annual payment of thirty-eight rubles for perpetual usufruct without increment.

In 1571 a Novgorod commercial ordinance was issued for the collection of taxes in the Merchants' Side,[5] in the crown estates. As in previous charters, beginning with the charter of Prince Vsevolod of Novgorod to the church of St. John-in-Opoki,[6] this charter gave preference to the people of Novgorod over those living in the bytowns and villages of the Novgorod land, as well as over inhabitants of other regions. Someone from Novgorod paid the excise duty on a Moscow ruble of one and a half moskovkas[7] while all others paid four moskovkas. If Novgorod merchants from the Sophia Side visited the crown estates on the Merchants' Side with goods, they would pay duties at par with the bytown and rural folk of Novgorod lands. Novgorod butchers did not dare purchase cattle from drovers on the road, who had to herd the cattle to Novgorod or to St. John-in-Opoki for sale. If anyone bought cattle outside town or on the road a fine was imposed, half on the buyer and half on the seller. When goods were exported from Novgorod by Gorodets peasants the customs agents gave small knots as their stamp upon collecting the excise. Novgorod Prince Vsevolod Mstislavich gave the church of St. John-in-Opoki wax weights.

In the period being described goods were weighed as before in St. John's but the duties obviously went directly into the tsar's coffers. We read in the charter of Ivan IV that wax, honey, tin, lead, alum, incense and thyme were weighed as of old, on the hook, at St. John's under the church in the Piatriatino courtyard, and the customs agents were not involved. The charter further states that honey, caviar and salt were not to be sold without being weighed; should anyone sell or buy any weighable goods worth at least a ruble without a pair of scales the fine was one Novgorod ruble, half from the buyer and half from the seller. If the purchase cost less than a ruble, the fine amounted to the price for which the goods were sold. If this was less than five altyns, the weighing agents would not collect the fine. No weighing agent should dare keep the weights at home; anyone convicted of doing so paid a fine of two rubles. The agents collected the excise, weighing fees and all duties on the goods of the tsar, metropolitan, bishop, vicegerent and boyar, on the villagers of the tsar, metropolitan, bishop, monasteries and boyars, on scholars and on everyone without exception.

When foreign merchants imported velvet, Chinese silk, precious objects and horses these wares could not be sold until after a selection on behalf of the sovereign was made. The customs agents were to take special care that no merchants or foreigners exported any money, silver or gold, any vessels, buttons, silver or golden objects in chests, baskets or cases from Novgorod to Lithuania or the Germans. The customs agents likewise were required to collect the lumber duties on the shores of the Volkhov river from boats and rafts and from the floating scales. The excise and all customs duties were to be collected by Muscovite and Novgorod whole-salers and merchants on their word, in whichever year they placed some-one in charge, and the Novgorod vicegerents and the crown secretary chose the sworn officials.

In 1577 a charter was granted to the sworn officials on the Merchants' Side detailing how they must collect duties from the merchants' courts and shops. They were to collect three dengas a week for one warehouse from each wholesaler if when numerous and, if there were few, two dengas and sometimes only one denga. There was a special rent for a shed.[8] Market fees in Novgorod were not collected by the square managers. The sworn officials must live in the market squares but they could not keep women with them. The excise and the weighing fees at St. John-in-Opoki were farmed out. In 1556 the tax farmers waived the weighing fees because wax and tallow stopped going to the Germans. Since they were unable to raise the required amount, they were placed in the stocks. Then the tsar ordered his crown secretaries to select unspecified men and entrust to them col-lection of the weighing tax in order to collect in a year the very same sum the tax farmers previously remitted, namely 233 rubles and 13 altyns. If they collected more, the tsar would favor them. What would happen if they collected less is not stated.

In the commercial ordinance for Oreshek the taxes enumerated are the excise, weighing fees, shop levies,[9] floor space tax,[10] the prow tax[11] on boats, the show tax, measuring fees, quitrent from forges, iron smelters and smithies. The Novgorod commercial ordinance ordered the collection of duties on all wares no matter who owned them. Similarly the tsar's charter given to the customs collectors of Dmitrov in 1549 strove to abolish any privileges with respect to levying trade duties. These collectors com-plained that peasants belonging to the metropolitan and bishops, to princes and boyars, to monasteries and others, Smolensk messengers, Moscow lords, tent makers and vegetable gardeners were coming to Dmitrov and Kimra and to the village of Rogachevo from the tsar's court villages, from Pereiaslavl and from the Mironositskaia suburb of Tsaritsyn, and traded in every kind of ware without paying any duties, saying they had charters of immunity from the tsar which freed them from the payment of customs duties. The tsar responded by abolishing all charters of immunity from customs and measuring duties except the immunity charters for the monasteries of Trinity-St. Sergius, Solovetsk, the New convent and St. Cyril, as well as the Vorobievsk suburb.

Finally, we must mention the "eighth," a new measure introduced in 1550. The way it was introduced is seen from the tsar's charter to the elders, hundredmen, sworn officials, and high, middle and lower rank villagers of Dvina. "I have sent to you in Dvina a new copper measure. When they bring this new copper measure to you, all you local officials shall fashion new wooden funnels from it in public, and you are to command publicly that a levy be put on all these wooden funnels in keeping with the stamp tax. Return them to the measuring officials so that they might give them to all the agents to measure every type of grain. The buyers and sellers and all officials shall measure levelly with the new measure without topping it off. Guard it securely. Order it cried out in the marketplace on a number of mornings that everybody must measure their grain with the new measures. If someone is discovered using the old measure, collect a fine of two rubles from him. If they expose him a second time, collect four rubles, and if they discover him a third time collect triple the amount. Then throw him in jail at our pleasure, but send the fines to Moscow."

In Lithuania the royal places paid a quitrent of fifty groshas on a field of the first order, forty groshas for a field of the second order and thirty for the lowest quality. On each pasture the quitrent was twelve groshas. A quitrent of seven peniaz was paid for each frontage for houses on the market place and five peniaz for each frontage for houses in the streets. On a vegetable garden two peniaz each was paid, on threshing barns in the suburbs for each frontage one peniaz, and for each morgen[12] three groshas. The excise was sixty groshas on mead, sixty groshas on beer and thirty groshas on spirits. Fifteen groshas were collected annually for the treasury from butchers for each stone[13] of tallow, but on market day a separate tax was paid in dengas to the tax office for each head of livestock. New arrivals in town paid two groshas into the treasury annually. Peasants on royal estates paid a quitrent of twenty-one groshas for a village plowland[14] of good soil, twelve groshas for one of average soil, eight groshas for poor soil and six groshas for the very worst soil, usually sand or marshland. They paid two barrels of oats each from a good and a moderate plowland, one barrel from a poor one, or five groshas for the barrel, and for the transport of each barrel, five groshas; then from every plowland one cartload of hay or three groshas, for the transport, two groshas. For a plowland of very poor soil neither hay nor oats were paid. In addition there was the requisition of geese, chickens and eggs. A plowland equalled nineteen Russian desiatinas; a Lithuanian grosha equalled five silver copecks.

IV

CIVIL ADMINISTRATION

REGIONAL GOVERNMENT

As early as the minority of Ivan the Terrible, at the time of the boyar government, something new and significant appeared in the life of the city and village population. After the vicegerent, rural district officials and their agents, a new authority of different provenance appeared. The inhabitants of town and village received permission from the government to hunt down, try and sentence thieves and brigands themselves, independently of the vicegerents and rural district officials. To this end they must elect junior boyars as their chiefs, three or four in a rural district, and team with them the elders, tenmen and best men. The men elected sometimes were called managers and sometimes elected officers or local magistrates. Sometimes the inhabitants of a town had to install tenmen, fiftymen and hundredmen in their midst to watch out for criminals. If these officers noticed someone suspicious they were to bring him to the town manager and together interrogate the suspect. The court administrator, sworn officials and best men must be present at the interrogation.

The relationships of the vicegerent, rural district officials and their agents to the local magistrate were determined in this way. "If they capture a thief in his first offense the plaintiff's fees are to be recovered from him, and he must pay the fine to the vicegerent, rural district official and their agents. As soon as the vicegerents, rural district officials and their agents collect their fees from the thief, then you, local magistrates, order him to be beaten with the knout and then banished."

The Pskov chronicler regards the criminal statutes as documents directed against the vicegerents as a result of their abuses. In criminal statutes coming down to us from Ivan IV's minority there are still no complaints against the vicegerents. "We have sent to you our investigators, but you complain that you incur heavy losses from our investigators and constables,[1] and you catch no brigands with our criminal investigators because you have great delays."

From the extant documents a complaint against the vicegerents and their agents first is encountered in 1552 in the petition of the people of the

Vaga basin. "Men of Vaga, Shenkursk and townsmen of the Velsk township, and the township and rural district peasants of the entire Vaga district petitioned and stated that in the trading quarters they have many households, but in the township and rural districts many villages have grown

Sixteenth-Century Southern Frontier Posts

desolate because of previous Vaga vicegerents, and their agents, bailiffs and investigation warrants, and because of villains, thieves, brigands and dice players. They stated they no longer could provide maintenance for the vicegerent of the Vaga district and the tax collectors, who caused many villages in their townships and rural districts to be deserted. Their peasants fled the trades and artisan quarters for other towns because of the violence, the fines and the robberies, and the peasants from the townships and rural districts fled to monasteries without heeding the legal departure dates[2] or formally being released. Other peasants dispersed to parts unknown. The vicegerents and their agents collect their maintenance from the remaining townsmen and peasants, whereas the exactors and bailiffs collect their stipends in full.

"Because of the vicegerents and their tax collectors and the fines they no longer could pay any taxes. Would the sovereign please dismiss the vicegerent and his agents and entrust the best men elected by the people of Vaga and Shenkursk, both townsmen and peasants, to execute the court sentences for all local cases according to the Law Code. The magistrates shall not collect fees for any judicial or criminal cases, and all fees previously payable to the vicegerent and his agent together with all stipends and incomes except the sovereign's quitrent shall be compounded by an annual quitrent of fifteen hundred rubles in cash."

The tsar fulfilled the request and commanded that they have elected magistrates. The townsmen of upper, middle and lower rank were to apportion the quitrent of one thousand five hundred rubles among themselves on the basis of their livestock and industries, and the peasants of upper, middle and lower rank were to divide it on the basis of their acreages, livelihoods and plowlands. Alternating between the two administrative districts[3] the magistrates and the best men would bring the quitrent to Moscow without waiting for the bailiff. Once arrived in Moscow with the quitrent, they were to give bribes and donations to no one. If they did not bring the quitrent on time the tsar would send his bailiffs for them and claim double the amount, together with the travel fees. Further, they were to select at their own discretion public clerks, who must record all the cases of the elected magistrates. This charter was called a redemption charter since the fifteen hundred rubles collected annually were known as the vicegerent's franchise.[4]

The statute charter of 1555 given earlier to the peasants of the Ustiug rural district speaks about the constant complaints of the town and village inhabitants against the vicegerents and rural district officials, just as it speaks about the complaints raised by the vicegerents and rural district officials against the townsmen and villagers. It also speaks about the replacement of vicegerents and rural district officials by elected magistrates as a general measure undertaken in consequence of these complaints. "Earlier," said the tsar, "we favored our boyars, princes and junior boyars. We gave them towns and rural districts for their sustenance, but from the peasants we receive lengthy petitions, and repeated and tiresome complaints that our vicegerents and rural district officials, our exactors and their tax collectors are charging them heavy fines and court costs above and beyond our ordinance. From the vicegerents, rural district officials, exactors and their tax collectors we have repeated and tiresome complaints and many petitions that the townsmen and country folk do not submit to their jurisdiction or post bond; they do not pay the maintenance and they assault them, which results in calumny and heavy lawsuits.

"As a result many peasant homesteads in the trading quarters and many villages and homesteads in the rural districts have fallen into neglect and our taxes and quitrents are not gathered in full. So we, taking pity upon the peasantry, dismissed the vicegerents, rural district officials and exactors from the towns and rural districts on account of these large fines and legal fees. In place of their incomes, taxes and court costs[5] we ordered the town and country peasants to pay the quitrent in cash, and that elected magistrates be installed in all towns, townships and rural districts to dispense justice among the peasants, collect the incomes of the vicegerent, rural district officials and exactors and bring them to us on time. The peasants themselves shall choose them from among their own, and elect them for the whole land. They shall not exact any fines, legal fees or damages, for those chosen know how to judge the peasants justly without bribery and lengthy delays. They can collect the quitrent for the vicegerent's income and bring it to our treasury on time without arrears."

The following year, in 1556, the people of Dvina received the right to choose magistrates, known there as elected judges, instead of vicegerents. These elected judges in the trading quarters, townships and rural districts of Kholmogory were to choose the hundredmen, fiftymen and tenmen who must be good, upright and acceptable to all the peasants, and order them to take special care that there be no brigands.

Although the replacement of vicegerents and rural district officials with authorities elected by the townsmen and villagers was presented as a general measure in one of the documents cited, this change did not occur in all rural districts. To explain this we must recall that the documents granting the rural districts the right to be governed by their own elected authorities were called redemptions. A rural district redeemed itself from the vicegerents and rural district officials for a certain sum of money which was deposited in the treasury. The crown extended it the right to be redeemed in consequence of its request. If the rural district did not submit a petition, if it considered the new order of things disadvantageous, it remained as before.

Why would a rural district decide against the change? There are various possible reasons. We know that when civic concepts are undeveloped, the meeting of social obligations seems difficult. People endeavor to avoid public appointments and public commissions, and it is difficult to find men to undertake to carry out and duly fulfill them. A rural district selected men who not only must devote their time to administration and justice, but who also were responsible for bringing the redemption money to Moscow, hastening from afar to arrive on time lest they incurred a penalty. It is not surprising that certain rural districts could not satisfy the new demands, preferring to stick to the old system.

In 1577 we run across the granting of a vicegerency as a maintenance. The charter was given to Prince Mortkin for the town of Karachev as a maintenance with everything remaining the same as under former vicegerents. "You, all the people of that town," it read, "must respect and obey him, and he will govern you and judge and visit you for all things according to the tax roll, as under previous vicegerents."

We detected a measure of suspiciousness displayed by the tsar towards a vicegerent of Perm in 1581. "The men of Perm and Usolie," he wrote, "collected the money among themselves, lest they suffer financial losses from you in the course of the levy." In addition, villages still were named for the maintenance of the vicegerent.

In strategically important border towns we see governors. In 1555 Prince Dmitry Paletsky[6] was named both governor and vicegerent of Novgorod. Evidently afterwards in Novgorod the governor attached to the vicegerent was considered higher in rank, but in an instruction to Archbishop Gury[7] of Kazan we see that the vicegerent took precedence over the governors. In 1581 the Sviiazhsk governor Saburov[8] was transferred to Kazan as governor and received this charter. "We have ordered the governor Prince Peter Buinosov-Rostovsky to be in our service in your place, and we have ordered you to be the governor in Kazan with Prince Grigory Bulgakov as your colleague, and with Crown Secretary Mikhailo Bitiagovsky,[9] all in concert together. When you hand over the town to Prince Rostovsky, first make a list of the artillery, the canons and arquebuses, the gunpowder, lead and other munitions in the treasury, our former instructions and commissions charters and all our affairs. When you arrive in Kazan you will be in our service in the fortress as before and the lists of junior boyars and the soldiers whom you had previously in your regiment you may take from Governor Prince Bulgakov. You shall be in our service in Kazan in the town and the fortress. Command your junior boyar soldiers, and concern yourself with our every affair, but with Governor Prince Bulgakov as your colleague, and with the clerk Bitiagovsky you shall be on an equal footing,[10] and there shall be no discord among you."

Remarkable in this instruction are the words that the governor Saburov had to serve alongside the governor Prince Bulgakov and the crown secretary Bitiagovsky, on an equal footing with both of them. The importance of the crown secretaries at the court and in the regional government strengthened greatly under Ivan the Terrible's father, and the reasons their position could not weaken during the reign of Ivan the Terrible himself are well known. Kurbsky[11] says that Ivan fully trusted his crown secretaries, whom he selected from among priests' sons or the common populace, because he hated his own magnates. Teterin, another émigré,[12] wrote to Morozov that "the grand prince has new proxies or plenipotentiaries, the crown secretaries, who provision him with less than half, taking for themselves the larger share; their fathers were not even fit to be slaves to your fathers, and now they not only control land, but they even trade with your heads."

The Pskov chronicler does not cease to point out the importance of the crown secretary in the administration of the town. Thus under the year 1534 he narrates how the grand prince removed the crown secretary Koltyria Rakov to Moscow, and the people of Pskov rejoiced because he imposed many taxes in Pskov. The tsar's document of 1555 to the Novgorod crown secretaries Yeremeev and Dubrovsky speaks about the relation of crown secretaries to governors. "We commanded our boyars and governors Prince Peter Mikhailovich Shcheniatev and Prince Dmitry Fedorovich Paletsky to take care of our affairs in Great Novgorod. You shall perform any of the tasks which our boyars have and listen to them when they speak of our affairs." When domestic policies were involved, evidently the tsar consulted directly with the crown secretaries, although for foreign policies, such as granting the Germans of Dorpat permission to trade in Novgorod and Pskov, the tsar turned to his vicegerent Prince Paletsky and to his crown secretaries Yeremeev and Dubrovsky.

Similarly he appealed to the vicegerent in judicial matters and when it concerned directives to the army. At the end of 1555 when the Novgorod vicegerent Prince Dmitry Paletsky set out on a campaign against the Swedes he relinquished the tsar's grant of Novgorod and took his men away, the tsar commanded the crown secretaries Yeremeev and Dubrovsky to select an agent and instruct him to judge all the vicegerent's affairs. They were also to choose constables. Then the tsar wrote to them, "Now we have sent to Great Novgorod Ivan Ivanovich Zhulebin, and we have ordered him, and you, our crown secretaries, to do our local business which the former vicegerents used to do. Whatever matters the agents cannot decide, you decide them with Ivan; and whichever even you are unable to decide, refer them to us." Zhulebin bore no particular title, and in all documents the tsar continued as before to address the crown secretaries alone. Only once did he address Zhulebin, when the matter concerned foreign relations, namely the forwarding of a document to the Swedish king. This document was forwarded in the name of the Novgorod vicegerent Prince Glinsky, though from the words of the document it may be concluded that Glinsky was yet to arrive in Novgorod.

We encounter numerous names for the commander of the town garrison.[13] In the criminal statute for the inhabitants of Galich it says that the elected hundredmen, fiftymen and tenmen brought criminals to the town garrison commanders and they interrogated them together. From other charters it is likewise evident that the commanders directed land, police and financial affairs. The commanders were elected by the whole land from the junior boyars, or as they used to say, "they were elected to the town office." Holdings of five plowlands each were distributed to them as service tenures.

Following the garrison commanders are mentioned the street wardens, also chosen from the junior boyars and receiving five areals each for an estate. During the reign of Grand Prince Vasily Ivanovich the crown secretaries in Novgorod ordered the positioning of gratings throughout the town with guards at the gratings to reduce robberies and murders. This piece of information explains to us the duty of the street wardens. In one of the charters of Tsar Ivan to the Novgorod crown secretaries we read, "You shall ask the commanders for street wardens, the best men available, and good scribes, ordering them to lay in store fodder for the horses and provisions for the soldiers in the encampments."

As of old we see in Novgorod elders for the city districts and the streets. When in 1548 the tsar showed his favor he relinquished control over the inns and taverns, and two kegs of beer, six pails of mead and half a pail of spirits for every thirty men were distributed among the elders of the city districts and streets. In 1555 the tsar wrote to the Novgorod crown secretaries, "Ivan Borzunov was made an elder in Great Novgorod; by our grant he received fifty rubles a year and he was given an estate for acting as an elder. Now I command this Ivan Borzunov to relinquish the eldership, and you shall forbid him to be in the law court alongside our vicegerents and majordomos; do not give him our favor, and transfer the estate to me until such a time as we choose another elder in his place." This Borzunov was a senior elder whose obligation it was, by the way, to go about the trading quarters, seize bootleg liquor and arrest drunkards. With him travelled the scribe, the street elder and townsmen. Disrespect towards the high elder carried a penalty of fifty rubles.

TOWNS

With respect to the urban population we encounter a distinction between those who possessed their own houses and others who did not, but lived with the householder and bore the title of boarder.[14] For example, a surety note given by certain people of Novgorod for the constable in 1568 states that "I, Potap, son of Foma, farm-yard worker from Varetsk street, live in my own house and I, Matvey Grigoriev son of a silk merchant live in my own house, and I, Ivan Ivanov son of Voronkov, damask merchant from Pavlova street live with Mitia, another damask merchant, as his boarder," and so on.

In Novgorod we meet the title "resettled merchant."[15] Town dwellers from Novgorod and Pskov continued to be resettled in Moscow and other towns downstream;[16] thus in 1555 ten disgraced families were transferred from Pskov to Kazan. In 1569 the tsar brought one hundred fifty families from Novgorod to Moscow, and five hundred families from Pskov. In 1572 forty families of resettled merchants from the Land domains[17] and sixty families from the crown estates moved from Novgorod to Moscow.

A description of Murom from the year 1574 has reached us which presents this town, that is, its trading quarter, in an unenviable position. The tsar's manor was located at that time in the Murom trading quarter, and in it the mansions, private apartments, summer bedrooms and entrance halls were rotting and collapsing; a single doorkeeper lived there. The tsar's other manor was the ice house where his stewards and cooks were housed during the tsar's fishing expeditions. In the trading quarter were the gunpowder yard and a variety of merchant shops including a row of butcher stalls, a row of fish stalls, salt stalls and fancy bread[18] stalls. The shops were divided into benches, shelves, partitions and booths. In the tsar's trading house[19] there were seventeen shops, all empty. In addition to the crown merchant courts there were two private ones. There were 111 taxpaying peasant properties with 149 residents, and 107 empty properties and 520 empty dwellings, whereas eight years before there were 587 inhabited properties, a loss of 476 taxpaying peasant properties. There were 202 occupied shops which paid a quitrent of 32 rubles and 15 altyns, and seventeen empty shops.

If for its own purposes the government established new towns on its western and southern borders, small towns appeared by themselves on the eastern borders, to which the population continued to move as before. The wealthy Stroganovs constructed some small towns using their own resources. Residents of the small town of Verkhneslobodskoy in Viatka region at first cleared woodland settlements[20] and hamlets situated in the woods. Then with these hamlets and settlements the inhabitants erected for themselves a small town at Shestakov on borrowed money. They obtained from the tsar a tax exemption charter according to which they could pay off the principal without interest over five years. The settlement vicegerent would have liked to ignore this charter, and the creditors were beginning to settle their accounts with the Shestakov people, who turned to the tsar with a complaint in which, among other things, they wrote, "Certain debtors came to Shestakov with nothing, and now they have fled from their creditors and abandoned their fields." From this we see first of all what type of men settled in the new remote towns and secondly, what they did. Debtors took to their heels and ran from their creditors, leaving their fields behind. How the tax exempt settlements got started is evident from the following information in a chronicle under the year 1572 which stated, "In Novgorod they shouted, 'Let any indentured men, be they monastic serfs or anyone else's, go to the sovereign's tax exempt settlement of Kholynia. The sovereign will give each five rubles and a tax exemption for five years.'"

Towns did not change their former appearance. As in earlier times we run across information about streets being paved with wood. Clusters of wooden buildings, of which the trading quarters were comprised, were still easy prey to flames. We mentioned the great Moscow fire; in 1541 the entire Slavensk quarter of Novgorod caught fire and 908 residences and twenty-two people were burned. In 1554 fifteen hundred residences burned down, set ablaze by arsonists. Strict measures prescribed by the government to prevent the frequent fires in the towns started under Ivan IV. In 1560 the crown secretaries ordered the people of Novgorod to put barrels and tubs of water by the chimneys about their residences and that in every log hut there be besoms on poles. In 1571 it was forbidden throughout Novgorod to heat log huts in the summer; the people of Novgorod built ovens in their gardens and around the yards, and there they baked their regular and fancy bread.

In the chronicles we find information about seals for towns, namely for Dorpat and Great Novgorod. The tsar ordered a seal made in his Livonian patrimony in the town of Yuriev,[21] and on the seal was the two-headed eagle device. In the eagle's right talon was a coat-of-arms, the seal of the bishop of Yuriev, and around the seal the legend "The seal of the boyar and vicegerent of his majesty the tsar in Livonia." He ordered the charters of the armistice with the Swedish king and charters destined for other realms to be affixed with this seal. The sovereign ordered a new seal made for Great Novgorod, and he ordered the vicegerents to affix it to charters of armistice with the Swedish king. The device of this seal was a pale with a staff in the middle. On one side of the pale was a bear and on the other side a lynx; under the pale was a fish. Around the seal the legend read "The seal of the boyar and vicegerent of his majesty the tsar." From these pieces of information it is evident that the seals were used for foreign relations, and in all likelihood were found only in Novgorod and Dorpat.

The Novgorod chronicler tells us about the following incidents in his town. In 1543 Ivan Dmitrievich Krivoy was sent from Moscow to Novgorod, where he constructed eight taverns, but after three years they were abandoned. In 1549 the tsar pulled down the rows of stalls in Novgorod and the trading licenses were gathered into the treasury.

VILLAGES

We have observed that under Ivan IV both village and town inhabitants began to receive licenses granting them the right to select from their own midst their rulers and judges. In 1555 the peasants of the Ustiug district obtained the right to choose their magistrates or judges who were to judge people and administer justice in keeping with the Code of Law[22] and statute charter, although in criminal cases involving rural district officials the district criminal judges judged and administered justice. The magistrates together with all upper, middle and lower rank peasants elected the sworn officials who were to sit in their court and make inspections, and the local clerks who were to record the court proceedings. They likewise elected officials to take the place of the bailiffs who were to place the accused on bond and bring them to trial. Rural district officials were elected to all of these public offices.

In the 1556 statute charter for Dvina the magistrates also were entrusted with criminal cases. "For trials and interrogations and all cases, the best men of the towns and rural districts are to assist the elected judges, so that they have no financial burdens or injuries or unseemly fines." In 1554 a statute charter was issued to two court villages, Afanasievsk and Vasilievsk, according to which the tsar's vicegerents, administrators[23] and agents did not judge the peasants of these villages at all except when caught in the act of murder or robbery. They were judged by the village managers, who held authority over these villages and hamlets. In 1556 the tsar showed his favor to the peasants of his court villages in Pereiaslavl when he removed them from the jurisdiction of the steward and village manager and ordered peasants whom they elected to be their judges in the same towns. The appanage prince Vladimir Andreevich[24] followed the tsar's example and gave the peasants of his district the right to choose from their midst their own magistrates. Concerning the wages of these elected officials, we know from the tsar's charter of 1565 to Vyshkovsk township that the elected assistant criminal judge received from the peasants who elected him a stipend of a half ruble per plowland.

In the tsar's charters the customary division of peasants into upper, middle and lower ranks is encountered. In the charters written by the peasants themselves we meet the division into farming, non-farming and woodland peasants. In one charter the miller, tailor and cobbler are named as non-farming peasants. Thus if tradesmen in the towns tilled the soil, on the other hand there were cobblers and tailors in the villages. In the new law code of Ivan IV the stipulation of the law code of Ivan III with respect to peasant departures is repeated, whereby peasants might move from one district to another and from one village to another only once a year, during the weeks before and after St. George's day in the autumn [November 26]. The departure fee[25] increased. According to the law code of Ivan III the peasant paid one ruble for his homestead in the fields and half a ruble for one in the woods; according to the law code of Ivan IV he paid one ruble and two altyns for a homestead in the fields and a half ruble and two altyns for a homestead in the woods, within ten versts of a stand of timber.

In addition to the definition of what is to be understood by the term "in the woods" we find the following additions in the law code of Ivan IV. The departure fee was to be collected at the gate, and for the delivery obligations two altyns per homestead were collected except from the peasant exempt from taxation. If a peasant still had grain in the field (that is, if he left after sowing grain), when he harvested this grain he paid two altyns on the harvested or standing grain. He paid the tsar's tax on rye for as long as it was in the ground, but did not have to perform labor services for the boyar under whom he had lived. If a peasant from arable land sold himself as a full slave, he might leave at any time, and no departure fee was collected from him. If any of his grain subject to the tsar's tax remained in the ground and he refused to pay the tax, he was to be deprived of his seed grain.

If a peasant caught stealing or doing some other criminal act in the field was handed over to the lord for whom he worked, or his master ransomed him, and if this peasant subsequently ran away, the owner must release him, but he must take out a written surety bond on the recruiter.[26]

If the peasant was prosecuted for any other matter, the landlord was to be present. Cases are encountered where peasants could be removed outside the legal departure dates. Thus, for example, the men of the Vaga complained that many villages in their townships and regions were deserted and the peasants went away to monastic estates outside the legal departure dates and without formal discharge, because of violence, fines and thefts. Incidentally, in granting them the right to elect their magistrates the sovereign said in his charter that they could call peasants to populate empty villages, waste plots and old settlements, remove their former taxpaying peasants from the monasteries outside the legal departure dates and without charge, and settle them in the villages where they lived before. Here departure outside the legal time and without formal notification was the condition for the return of the peasants to their former domiciles at any time and without duty having to be paid.

It is clear that in those times when the principality was still so young, when it was still making merely the first attempts at limiting the violence of the powerful, the soliciting of peasants, on account of which such important interests clashed, inevitably had violent consequences. Taking advantage of their helpless situation, landowners seduced peasants from their neighbors outside the legal departure date without formal notice of termination and without payment of fees.

The peasants of the taxpaying settlements of Pustorzhevsk submitted a petition because every day junior boyars of Rzhevsk, Pskov and Lutsk lured peasants for their own benefit from the taxable villages of Pustorzhevsk without regard for the departure date and without payment of fees, but when recruiters from the taxable villages came to them with a notice of termination within the lawful period for the purpose of removing peasants to the taxable villages, the junior boyars beat the recruiters and put them in irons. They would not release the peasants but, having caught them, tortured and robbed them and put them in irons. They collected the compensation from them, but not as prescribed in the law code, taking instead from five to ten rubles, on account of which it was absolutely impossible to bring a peasant from a junior boyar to the taxable villages.

This complaint about the detention of peasants, and about the collection of excessively high departure fees contrary to the law code, was not the sole complaint for the times. Sometimes the landowner, having taken all the taxes from the discharged peasant, robbed him. When the peasant went to complain the landowner declared him a fugitive slave and accused him of stealing. The junior boyars used their power against taxable villages and did not release peasants to them. The chancellery officials and peasants from the tsar's villages permitted themselves to perpetrate violence and flagrant robberies against monastic peasants. Thus the chancellery officials and all the peasants of the village of Khrepelevo which belonged to the convent of the Intercession complained that the sovereign's official in Dunilovsk sent his men and peasants who entered the village of Khrepelevo and plundered the monastery stables and great manor with abandon. They slew the village elder and the peasants, shooting with bows and guns, thrusting with boar-spears, hacking with sabers and axes, and they robbed monastic and peasant property worth one hundred sixty rubles. Sometimes a peasant who outlived his tax exempt years continued to pay no taxes and did not submit for judgment to the landowner. When the landowner sent him away, he would not go. The landowner appealed to a judge who, if he found his complaint justified, decided that the peasant must leave within a month without fail; otherwise he ordered him to be driven away without delay.

Peasant contracts with monastic landowners have come down to us from our period. They first of all state how much land the peasant holds, then how much quitrent the peasant is obliged to pay the landowner, whereby the quitrent in grain is distinguished from cash payments. In addition the peasant was obligated to pay the fees for the agents, stewards and managers, to give all apportionments of the tax assessment and to perform labor service for the monastery just like every other peasant. Sometimes if a peasant came to a new or deserted place he must plow up the village,[27] as they said then, fence in the fields, repair old barns and build new ones. Then he received from the landowner a subsidy in the form of money and a tax exemption for a number of years, and did not have to perform labor service. If the peasant did not live out the exempt years, but departed without fulfilling his obligations, he must return the subsidy to the landowner. In the event of quitrent default the government threatened the peasants who lived on taxable lands that "disobedient peasants are deported from the region and henceforth may not live there, but other residents are to be called to replace them." Setting up a farm in a new or deserted place was called "establishing the plow." Sometimes on one parcel of land were settled two peasants between whom there were evidently no ancestral ties.

SLAVES

In the new law code of Ivan IV we encounter changes from the law code of Ivan III regarding slaves. These changes tend to limit the number of cases in which a free man could become a slave. The old law code refers to a "slave according to service as an agent or village steward, with or without a confirmed slavery document."[28] The new code states that "no one can be a slave according to service as an agent without a full charter and without a confirmed slavery document; no one can be a slave according to service as village steward without a confirmed slavery document." Furthermore, the right to sell free sons, born before entry into slavery, was removed from the full and confirmed slaves. These free sons could sell themselves to whom they wished, either to the same lord whom their fathers served, or to some other lord. Monks and nuns likewise were deprived of the right to sell their sons and daughters.[29]

Certificates of manumission could be given only in Moscow, Great Novgorod and Pskov. If a free man borrowed money and for the interest indentured himself to serve his creditor, the money advanced could not exceed fifteen rubles. If two owners declared their claims on the same slave, or if two full charters or two confirmed slavery documents referred to the same slave, the slave was awarded to whoever's full or confirmed slavery document was older, in which case the money paid out was forfeited by the new lord, who in addition must reimburse the other lord for his losses if the slave left him by stealth. The second lord should consult with his broker (he who presented the slave to him as a freeman). If he sought compensation from the broker, he must bring legal action.

If a slave captured in battle escaped from captivity he was free and was no longer the slave of his former lord, unless he himself wished to return to him as a slave. If the slave fled with his lord or if he alone ran away into a foreign land and later came back to Moscow, he remained the slave of his former lord unless the sovereign granted him a charter of manumission. No one might accept as slaves junior boyar servitors or their children who had not yet served, except those whom the sovereign dismissed from service.

Whoever borrowed money at interest could not be in the service of his creditor. He must live by himself and pay the interest. If a creditor kept a debtor with him and the debtor ran away after robbing him, the creditor had no right to seek to recover his losses, and forfeited the money accruing from the indenture contract. Suppose someone entered another's service of his own accord without a sworn contract and then left him with or without notice of termination. The master then accused him of theft. In this case he might not lay charges since the accused served him voluntarily, and the lord was claiming damages against him because he did not wish to let him go. Anything missing from his possessions he has lost himself, because he trusted a voluntary man and kept him without a contract.

If anyone sued his peasants for stolen property, to enforce his claim he might allege that they were his slaves on the basis of a full slavery document or a confirmed slavery document, or that a woman became his slave through marriage to a male slave, or that a man became his slave through marriage with a female slave. Even if the slaves would have been freed by a judge, if anyone redeemed such slaves from the court and the slaves ran away under bond, the entire suit and all court fees were to be collected from the guarantors, from whom four rubles were collected for each slave. Although the lord still had not proven that they were his slaves, the slave was condemned as a fugitive; he was presumed guilty because he ran away. Wherever the lord found him, he could arrest him without a bailiff, but he did not have to return the money he took from the guarantors.

Concerning hirelings, it was stipulated that a hireling who departed without serving his full term for his master must forfeit his pay. If any lord was unwilling to give his hireling his wage and the hireling established his guilt, the lord must make good the wage twice over. Besides the term "hireling" which designates a laborer who voluntarily hires himself out, we continue to encounter in that sense the term "cossack" primarily in connection with non-agricultural industry. For example in a charter to the Trinity-St. Sergius monastery in 1543 it is stated, "if any of the cooks, chief bargemen and all cossacks go to live in Solia in the saltworks and the manors, our vicegerents and rural district chiefs and their agents shall not judge them. Any newly arrived hirelings who agree to live outside the monastery in the saltworks as cooks and chief bargemen, to cut timber, transport it and do every type of work, shall present themselves to our vicegerents for trial," and so on.

Confirmed slavery documents followed this procedure. The lord presented the vicegerent with the man enslaving himself to him and said, "Behold Sire! This is a free man of the tsar and grand prince. He takes such-and-such a sum of money from me and in exchange for this money he surrenders himself to me for the key in my village. On the basis of the key he surrenders himself to me in slavery."[30] The vicegerent inquired of him giving himself into slavery if it was really so. He confirmed the lord's deposition. Then the names of those who were in the revision decree are recorded. It was also recorded whether or not the parents of him entering slavery were still living, as well verifying that he was not someone else's slave.

If during the move of peasants there were cases where landowners permitted themselves breaches of the law by not recruiting the peasants during the legal time period, detaining them on their estates or taking more than was lawful for the departure fees, there were violations with respect to slaves enticed to another's household. Perhaps a fugitive slave sought by his lord declared to a judge that he was fleeing with stolen property from another lord, who promised to release him from a law suit. No instances have come down to us of enslavement of free men without their consent, for which the law code of Ivan IV specifies the death penalty.

NATIVES' FUR TRIBUTE

Certain natives paid the fur tribute directly to the government, while others paid it to their native rulers. In 1580 a charter was given to Ishey-Murza of Kadom for his father's fur tribute collected from the Mordvinians of Taldem on the Moksha river. The tribute amounted to seven rubles and fifty copecks annually, from which Ishey-Murza was obliged to perform the sovereign's service, maintain his sister and have her married.

V

COMMERCIAL SITUATION IN MUSCOVY
AND WESTERN RUSSIA

INDUSTRY

Whereas inhabitants of towns, that is, of their outlying districts, tilled the soil, villagers practiced various trades. As a result of the acquisition of new territories in the East and settlement of the still unoccupied wilderness, primary industry spread during the reign of Ivan IV. In particular the fishing industry expanded following the acquisition of the lower reaches of the Volga, where it was practised on a very large scale. The newly constructed Trinity monastery in Astrakhan asked for several sites at the mouth of the Volga suitable for fisheries, instead of being granted an emolument in grain or in cash.

From some old passages there is information about the condition of fishery districts in the Pereiaslavl town quarter. Here in 1562 there were ninety-nine fisheries with as many peasants, one of middle rank and ninety-eight of lower rank, twenty-one deserted homesteads and forty deserted sites. The fishers of Pereiaslavl paid into the Great Court[1] the transport taxes, money for plowland people and for fortifications and barricades. They gave the tsar a quitrent of four rubles and twenty altyns cash for pike and herring. In addition they gave the palace one hundred sazhen of fishing net and two sets of tackle. They caught herring for the tsar without a set limit. They went ice-fishing for the tsar two nights, one night for the tsaritsa, one night for the ice fishing supervisor, one night for the palace officer and one night for each of the two vicegerents. They fished the whole of Pereiaslavl lake and the Veksa river with seines, nets, dragnets, and wickerwork dikes in the spring when the water began to run. They were given some dry shore around Pereiaslavl lake, about ten sazhens from the water, as a place to hang their seines and nets.

We have received interesting information from our period about the palace falconers. They plied their trade in the distant North and were also settlers of the empty expanses. In 1548 three Vologda quitrent peasants of the Falconers' Office, the Blaznovs, requested that the tsar give them possession of some wilderness areas covered with forest, moss and swamps where their gerfalcon and falcon snares were located, three or four versts from inhabited places. The tsar gave them the requested lands, ordered them to build homesteads there, clear the forest for farming and flush the gerfalcons and falcons in the moss and swamps for the tsar's fowling. The unregistered and tax exempt people whom they attracted to their homestead were exempted from all taxes for ten years. After the expiration of the time limit the falconers were to give three falcons apiece into the tsar's falconry, but if the falcons had no feathers they were to pay a quitrent of one and a half rubles.

The salt industry expanded following the occupation of the wild territories adjoining the Kama by the Stroganovs and the acquisition of Astrakhan, thirty miles from which were found salt deposits. The producers quarried the salt and paid into the treasury one copeck per pud. In the old regions salt works are mentioned in 1543 as belonging to the Trinity-St. Sergius monastery in the district of Northern Starodub or Riapolovsk. The name Novaia Sol [New Salt] in Kholuy indicates that these saltworks were of recent origin.[2] For production of saltpeter a master powder maker was sent to erect a shed on the specified plot of land. The surrounding villagers were required to send to the shed earth, wood and ashes. During this period saltpeter was manufactured at Beloozero by the treasury, but in 1582 the monastery of St. Cyril of Beloozero received the right to erect sheds and prepare saltpeter for its entire patrimony at two puds per plowland, in all thirty-eight puds. The monastery was to send this quantity of well-filtered saltpeter, which was especially suited for gunpowder, to the Chancellery of Artillery in Moscow. Grigory Stroganov was commanded to prepare thirty puds of saltpeter in Solvychegodsk for the small town which he built, and not for sale. In the Dvina region near the Emets post-horse station the inhabitants manufactured a great deal of pitch and ash.

The Pskov masons lost none of their fame. When in 1555 the tsar proposed to fortify Kazan with stone walls, the Pskov crown secretary Bilibin, two elders, one from the church and one from the town, the master Posnik Yakovlev and the Pskov masons Ivashka Shiriay and associates received the order to select two hundred Pskov masons, bricklayers and stone cutters for dispatch to Kazan.

In general during this period trades evidently flourished among Russians in Novgorod and Pskov more than in Moscow. Thus the stone carvers from Novgorod wrote that in 1556 the tsar sent a missive to the Novgorod clerks saying, "We have sent to Novgorod a master of printed books, Marusha Nefediev, and ordered him to examine the stone prepared for the dais of the church of the Presentation of the Virgin. When Marusha examines this stone he will tell you if it is suitable for the church dais and if it is possible to put a face on it. You should examine this stone yourselves and assemble some stone masons who can put a face on it as at the church of the Holy Wisdom. If Marusha wants to become expert at facing stone himself, you should send him two or three stones for samples and tell him to try all three.[3] Marusha himself has told us that in Novgorod there is a certain Vasiuk Nikiforov who knows how to do all types of carving. You should send this Vasiuk to us in Moscow."

After the great Moscow fire, when the renovation of the churches commenced, iconographers were summoned from Novgorod and Pskov. At the time renowned among the Pskov iconographers were Ostan, Yakov, Mikhaila, Yakushka and Semen Vysoky Glagol, and in Novgorod the deacon Nikifor Grableny. The expert bell maker Ivan Afanasiev is mentioned, who cast the bell for Novgorod in Alexandrov Village. Under the year 1558 the Novgorod chronicler says that in the Savva hermitage the master builders Zakhar and Semen covered the church with a new roof. In 1535 masters from the Tver lands, the eldest among whom was called Yermolay, built the stone church of St. George in Khutyn "the likes of which were unknown in Novgorod lands." In 1536 the first heated church was built in Novgorod, the church of the Presentation on Dvorishche. Silversmiths from Novgorod were enlisted to make icon settings. Renowned in this trade were Artemy and Rodion Petrov with their brothers and children. In Novgorod stained glass window panes could be obtained, and were ordered for the tsar. Mention is made of a special skill for necklace-making in Moscow, and in Novgorod are mentioned caftan makers, wedding apparel makers and dyers.

According to the testimony of Mikhalon Litvin the towns of Muscovy abounded in experienced tradesmen who forwarded to Lithuania wooden cups, walking-sticks for the weak, the old and the drunk, saddles, spears, ornaments and various weapons. Even so, Russian master craftsmen were quite scarce. Ivan IV strove to secure harbors on the Baltic Sea so that foreign experts could reach his realm without obstacle. How great was the need for foreigners knowledgeable in all types of handicraft is evident from a document of the tsar to the Novgorod crown secretaries in 1556. "You should order proclaimed in Novgorod, the suburbs, the regions and the rows during market time on more than one morning that the junior boyars and all men must not sell their foreign captives to foreigners in Lithuania, but are to sell them in the towns of Muscovy. If the junior boyars learn that someone has sold foreign prisoners to foreigners, I will favor those junior boyars with my charter. If it is a taxable man who learns about someone doing this, settle with him for fifty rubles, but put the sellers into prison at our pleasure. Should one of the junior boyars or any other servitor have a captive foreigner who knows how to work silver ore, and who knows silver, gold, copper, tin and other types of metallurgy, you are to order the junior boyars to bring such captives to us in Moscow and we shall favor those junior boyars generously." In 1567 a doctor, a pharmacist, an engineer with assistants, a goldsmith, an assayer and other experts arrived in Moscow from England.

TRADE

The acquisition of Kazan and Astrakhan inevitably strengthened trade with the East, at least in comparison with the previous situation. Two contradictory pieces of information about trade through Astrakhan have come down to us from the East and the West for this period. According to the evidence of Muslim leaders who wanted to induce the sultan to take possession of Astrakhan, the Muscovite tsar's income from the Astrakhan customs duties was enormous. We cannot be content with this evidence, of course, knowing the passion of oriental peoples for exaggeration,

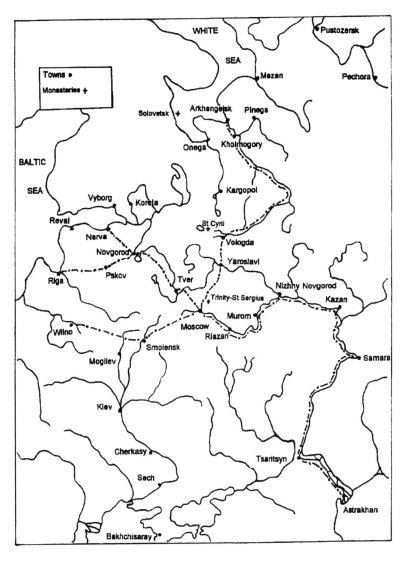

Major Muscovite Trade Routes

especially when it is a matter of wishful thinking. English travelers spoke otherwise about Astrakhan trade. According to their accounts, the Russians brought leather, wooden tableware, bridles, saddles, knives and various other trifles to Astrakhan as well as bread and other foodstuffs. The Tatars brought various types of woolen and silk goods and other items, but in such small quantities, and the merchants were so poor, that it was not worth talking about. Armenian and Turkish merchants travelled to Moscow as before. According to English information they paid ten percent on all wares except those sold by weight, for which they paid two dengas on the ruble. When horses were sold, they paid four dengas on a horse. Merchants from Bukhara also travelled to Moscow, bringing spices and furs bought up in Siberia. The Nogay Tatars continued to drive huge herds of horses to market. For example in 1555 they drove twenty thousand horses and more than twenty thousand sheep into Kazan.

In agreements with Sweden, Denmark and England attempts were by the Muscovite government to establish active trade relations with West European realms. It is possible to judge the significance of trade with Sweden from the fact that Gustav Vasa[4] ordered three hundred Russian merchants from Novgorod, Korela and Oreshek who were in his domains to be seized prior to the beginning of war with Moscow. Of course two questions can arise here. Is not this testimony exaggerated, given as it was in Moscow in answer to the Polish king who was petitioning for peace with Sweden? Would it not be interesting also to know where these Russian merchants were trading, in the border towns such as Vyborg, or in Sweden proper? We have noted that after the conclusion of peace with Sweden the tsar granted Swedish merchants the right to travel not only to Moscow, Kazan and Astrakhan, but also to cross Russia into India and China, on condition that Russian merchants be permitted to set out from Sweden for Lübeck, Antwerp and Spain.

In the agreement with the Danish king free trade was stipulated for Russian merchants in all towns of the Danish land, "but in neither country shall they have brokers or salesmen. They shall pay customs and tolls as was normal in each country. Should any of our merchants and wholesale merchants, Russian or foreign, go from Copenhagen to an overseas land with wares or if merchants from overseas lands pass through the Danish kingdom by the maritime gates, the Sound, the king must let them pass." Prince Romodanovsky,[5] travelling as ambassador to Denmark, was instructed to say that the king should order the tsar's wholesale merchants to settle their accounts for the merchant stalls just as for the merchant halls given in Novgorod and Ivangorod, where they were near the wharf, and that on either side of the Russian church there be no foreign churches. Should the king not give merchant halls in Copenhagen and Gotland, Romodanovsky was to tell him that the tsar would not allow halls to the Danish merchants in Novgorod or Ivangorod.

In the chronicles for the year 1567 it is stated "The sovereign sent off his wholesalers and merchants to coastal realms with his gift from the treasury. To the burgomasters and aldermen of Antwerp he sent the wholesale merchant Ivan Afanasiev and the merchant Timofey Smyvalov; to Hormuz he sent the merchants Dmitry Ivashev and Fedor Pershin; to Queen Elizabeth of England he sent the merchants Stepan Tverdikov and Fedot Pogorelov." Were these simply ambassadors dispatched as dependents of the tsar, or did they travel with wares from the tsar's treasury with the purpose of selling them in foreign countries and purchasing there other wares needed by the sovereign? Evidently both. According to English information the Russian ambassadors Tverdikov and Pogorelov were in fact in England in 1568.

The Dutch had their own office in Novgorod and traded there without paying duties; after some illegal actions they lost their tax immunities, but regained them on payment of thirty thousand rubles. From discussions of the tsar with the English ambassador Bowes[6] we learn that French merchants and a merchant from Antwerp, Ivan Beloborod (John de Wale), arrived in the famous northern harbors.

We have most information about English trade during the time of Ivan IV. Elsewhere we investigated its origins and treated the final discussions between the tsar and Bowes, the Queen Elizabeth's ambassador. Here we consider it useful to introduce some details to demonstrate the spirit of operation and aims of the Russia Company[7] sanctioned in 1555 by King Philip and Queen Mary. The agents sent to Russia by the Company were obliged to study the character of the Russian population in all estates. The agents were to be on their guard lest they, their men, the sailors or any other Englishman violate any Russian law, either religious or civil. They were to see to it that all duties be paid correctly so that they would not suffer confiscation of their wares and so that everything might transpire peacefully without disruption of order wherever the English went to trade. In Moscow, or some other town or in several towns suitable for trading, the agents were to erect one or several houses for themselves and for their men with shops, cellars and other outbuildings, and see to it that none of the lower servants dared spend the night outside the agent's house without permission.

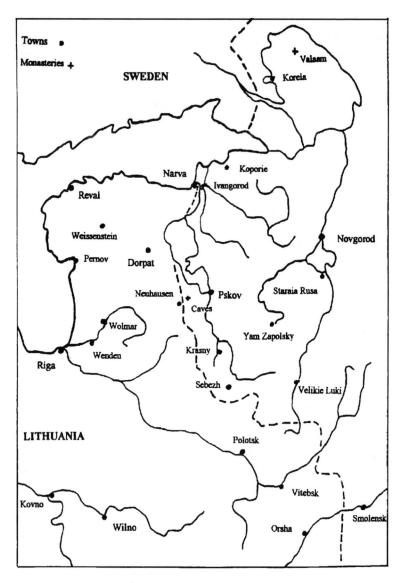

Muscovy's Baltic Neighbors

All lower ranks had to obey the agents, and in case of disobedience were to be punished at their discretion. The agents and factors must assemble daily to consult about what would be most proper and profitable for the Company. No Company employee might enter on his own initiative into any business arrangement, only on behalf of and by order of the agents. The agents were to take careful note of all types of wares which could be sold for profit in Russia, and they must have constantly in mind how they could by any means possible discover the route to China, by sea or overland. They must take care to learn about the Russian people, their character, morals, customs, taxes, money, weights, measures, accounting, goods, whatever was useful or not useful to them, lest the Company suffer harm or loss from ignorance, for such ignorance would not be accepted as an excuse.

Later the Company informed its agents which Russian goods had the readiest market in England, namely wax, tallow, oil, hemp and flax. They were to seek cheap furs only since there was no need to send many expensive ones. Nor were they to send raw hemp because it would be too costly; instead the Company would send to Russia seven rope-makers whom the agents were to set immediately to work, providing them with laborers. This was a matter of prime necessity because the Company considered it cheaper than ordering rope from Danzig.

The Company directed the agents to send samples of iron and copper because it heard there were large quantities of those metals in Russia and Tatary. They were to inform the Company about the kind of wool cloth imported into Russia from Riga, Reval, Poland and Lithuania, with a precise description of the breadth, length, color and price, and what quantity would be for sale in a year, so that they could procure the same in England. They were to send every variety of leather, for it was rumored that the Germans and Dutch were buying large amounts of it in Russia. They also were to send for testing a specified amount of soils or grasses or whatever else the Russians used to dye their wool and linen cloth, leathers and the like, together with the dyestuffs which the Turks and the Tatars imported into Russia, including a description of how to use them for dyeing.

The Russian ambassador agreed to the Company's request that its agents purchase goods from Russians on credit. As a result, the Company required its agents to buy up as much wax as possible by this or any other means so that they hold it all and with their stockpile supply not only their own but foreign countries as well.

What type of profits the Company made from its trade with Russia is evident from the report of its agent Christopher Hoddesdon.[8] In Nizhny Novgorod he sold cloth, which at home cost six pounds sterling, for seventeen rubles per bolt which, in his own words, amounted to almost three times its value. In Moscow goods which cost £6,608 were sold for £13,644. The government of Moscow explained to Bowes its reasons for restricting the tax immunity of the English merchants. Bowes provided other reasons. According to him, the Dutch won the favor of the tsar's three leading advisers, Nikita Romanovich, Bogdan Belsky and Andrei Shchelkalov, for in addition to the constant gifts the Dutch had borrowed from them so much money at twenty-five percent that they paid each of them five thousand marks annually, whereas at the same time the English merchants had not a single patron at court.

Great Novgorod continued in this period to be the most important city with respect to trade. Although the sovereign maintained his throne in Moscow, the English wrote, nonetheless the convenience of waterways and proximity to the sea forced the merchants to frequent Novgorod in preference to Moscow. The most important goods with which Novgorod conducted trade were superior quality flax and hemp, leather, honey and wax. Pskov traded in the latter two goods as well. After Novgorod and Pskov the most important trading towns were Yaroslavl and Vologda. The country between Yaroslavl and Moscow was heavily populated and was considered to be quite productive. In winter on the road from Yaroslavl to Moscow trains of seven hundred to eight hundred sleighs loaded with grain or fish sometimes were encountered. Northerners living within a thousand verst radius came to Moscow to purchase grain, bringing salted fish, furs and leather. Vologda traded principally in flax; besides this, a large share of the vessels sailing on the Northern Dvina, decked boats and flat plank boats, carrying salt from the seashore to Vologda, belonged to Vologda merchants.

The English established a factory in Vologda on the basis of a report by their agent Gass in 1554. He wrote that Vologda was a large city in the heart of Russia, surrounded by many large and fine towns. There was a surplus of grain, and in general an overabundance of vital supplies and all Russian goods. There was not a town in Russia that did not trade with Vologda. All items were half the price they were in Moscow or Novgorod. For the fur trade the most important place was Kholmogory where the furs were transported on reindeer from Pechora, Pinega, Lampas (Lampozhnia, eighteen versts from Mezen) and Pustozersk. The inhabitants of these places bought them from the Samoyed and bartered with the Kholmogory merchants for cloth, tin and copper. For the purposes of this barter a large annual fair was held on the winter St. Nicholas Day [December 6] in Kholmogory, to which seal oil was brought in addition to the furs. Kholmogory merchants took the oil to Novgorod where they sold it to Germans; the furs they took to Novgorod, Vologda or Moscow. In addition Kholmogory supplied neighboring countries with salt and salted fish. We have noted that the salt travelled along the Northern Dvina to Vologda; another route went to the southwest, thanks to merchants from Kargopol, Onega, Turchasov, Porozhie, Ustmoshe and Mekhrenzhe who travelled to the sea, bought salt from the White Sea littoral and sold it in Kargopol to buyers from Beloozero, Vologda and other towns. These merchants did not conduct an honest business, for they added foreign substances to the salt and cheated the merchants of Beloozero and Vologda. Complaining about them to the government, the men of Beloozero pointed out that there were no additives in the salt which the Dvina traders themselves extracted from the river.

Having discussed the distribution of Russian trade during the reign of Ivan the Terrible, we must mention the obstacles it encountered at this time. First of all the immense distances hindered trade, as well as the inconvenience, and in some places the impossibility of summer travel. Despite all efforts, no harbors on the Baltic were obtained. The lengthy route across the White Sea and the Arctic Ocean was open, but the journey by water from the harbor of St. Nicholas [Kholmogory], where the English put in, to Vologda took fourteen days. In summer it was impossible to travel here overland because of the bogs. In winter the White Sea could be crossed and Vologda reached on sleighs in eight days. It was two days' travel on dry land from Vologda to Yaroslavl, and by sail thirty days from Yaroslavl to Astrakhan. Thus from the harbor of St. Nicholas to the Caspian Sea by this route linking Europe and Asia was a forty-six day journey.

Moscow had for some time a Baltic port at Narva but neighboring countries, especially Poland, strove to eliminate trade through Narva. In 1567 the agent Hoddesdon of the English Company sailed to Narva with a cargo of cloth, leather goods and salt worth £11,000. When they were sold the Company received forty percent of the profit. In 1569 the same Hoddesdon sailed from London to Narva with three ships, and wrote the Company that the following spring they should send thirteen ships, all of which he hoped to load down with goods. He then wrote that the ships must be well equipped with firearms in case of an encounter with corsairs. In fact the English ships met six ships of Polish corsairs. The battle was unequal, for one corsair ship fled, a second was set on fire, the remaining four were taken to Narva, and eighty-two prisoners were sold to the Muscovite governor.

A second obstacle was provided by the fact that desolate routes were not without danger. Along the Volga every summer there passed five hundred large and small boats, from the upper reaches of the river to Astrakhan, in search of salt and fish, but these boats had to sail from Kazan to Astrakhan through deserted country. The spot at Perevolok, where the Volga was closest to the Don, was renowned for its brigands. The English wrote that since Astrakhan and Kazan fell under the rule of the Russian tsar there were fewer brigands, but then we encounter Russian information about cossack brigandage on the Volga and the harm they did to commerce. In the Southwest, Ukrainian cossacks, also known as Cherkas, robbed Turkish and Crimean merchants on their way to or from Moscow.

As of old we meet the constant complaints of Lithuanian merchants about oppression and brigandage in Muscovite regions and the complaints of Muscovite merchants about oppression in Lithuania. Lithuanian merchants complained that near Mozhaisk bandits attacked them. Close to the city itself, Mogilev burghers traveling in a large wagon train to Starodub to trade were beaten to death, and six hundred rubles were stolen. Some Lithuanian merchants stopped in the suburb of the Selizharovsk monastery where the monastery servitor Okulov invited them to his place, entertained them and sent them off to the forecourt[9] with four men as escorts. These escorts attacked the merchants on the road, beat them and took twenty-three rubles from them. The merchants petitioned the abbot, but he did not recompense them.

In both Lithuania and Muscovy merchants were detained because they were buying or attempting to smuggle contraband. A Lithuanian merchant brought cloth to Moscow and bought wax. From the silversmiths he bought silver ladles, a cup and silver ingots, fifteen grivenkas[10] of silver in all. All these goods were confiscated, but at the complaint of the ambassador the boyars agreed to return all goods to the merchant except the silver which was purchased. A Pskov merchant journeyed from Constantinople and brought with his other goods some naphtha. The merchant was seized in Kiev, his goods taken and he was held for three years. In answer to the complaint of the Moscow government the king stated that both countries forbade the transportation of naphtha. In 1555 in Moscow it was forbidden to export wax and tallow to Livonia and, similarly, trade with Sweden was restricted. The tsar ordered border dwellers to travel to Vyborg with small goods only, and prohibited travel with wax, tallow, flax and hemp.

The number of domestic tariffs not only did not decrease but actually increased as a result of the establishment of the crown estates. Thus in a Novgorod commercial charter of 1571 we read "Any wholesale merchants and traders of Novgorod from the Sophia Side who travel into the sovereign's crown estates, the Merchants' Side, with goods, must present themselves to the customs agents, who shall collect from them the show tax, and from their goods the tariff and all duties just as they did from suburban and district inhabitants of the Novgorod land."

The ongoing custom of granting monasteries the right to enjoy duty-free trade must be included in the number of rulings injurious to trade. For example the Astrakhan monastery of the Trinity obtained the right to set up a shop in the town, to buy and sell goods without duty for the monastery's use, and the right to keep a "belozerka" or barque thirty sazhens in length from stem to stern. The monastery further enjoyed the right to transport in that boat salt or fish from Astrakhan up the Volga to Yaroslavl and up the Oka to Kaluga, and to sell those goods and buy others without paying duties.

In 1582 a charter was confirmed for the Trinity-St. Sergius monastery according to which the monastery enjoyed the right to send four decked boats with barrels from Vologda on the Dvina to Kholmogory and overseas, to carry in them all types of grain, honey, hops, and goods, to sell and buy salt duty-free in Kholmogory, along the Dvina, in Kargopol, Uglich, Totma and overseas. In addition the monastery might buy one hundred cartloads of fish and bring salt and fish duty-free to the monastery and to Moscow. Having brought goods to Moscow, the monastery could sell and buy duty-free.

To avoid domestic tariffs the merchants chose new places for their fairs where there were as yet no customs agents. The customs agents found out and informed Moscow. As a result merchants were strictly prohibited from trading anywhere but in the designated places, under threat of having their goods confiscated. Sometimes landowners of a famous fair site formally requested that there be no fairs anywhere in the surrounding areas except for their patrimony, for they had purchased the right to collect the tariffs and customs duties. At other times a landowner asked for removal of a fair from his land because his peasants incurred more losses than gains, owing to the contemporary state of morals and the police. The abbot of the Trinity-St. Sergius monastery and the brethren complained that below their monastery of the Virgin in Kirzhacha many gathered three times a year to trade in all types of goods, and because of this their monastery peasants suffered great injuries. The peasants were beaten and robbed, and the grain and hay were trampled, and they were assessed stiff fines by the rural district chief and his tax collectors for selling alongside the traders. The tsar granted their request and ordered the fair moved from Kirzhacha.

NATURAL CALAMITIES

In general, although we do not possess sufficient facts to determine the level of material prosperity of the inhabitants of Muscovy during the reign of Ivan IV in comparison with preceding and following ages, nevertheless from the information which has come down to us we can in no way conclude that the level of prosperity was high. The eastern regions of the realm were set at ease with the subjugation of Kazan, but the southern regions suffered as of old from the Crimeans. The devastating invasion of Devlet-Girey[11] left long-lasting traces in Moscow and in the southern regions, which lost the flower of their population. In the West the prolonged, burdensome Livonian war continued, to which were added wars with Lithuania and Sweden, and in the East untamed peoples rebelled. All of this required strong efforts from the young principality with its sparse population. Ivan was compelled to borrow money from his subjects, and these debts were paid off only by False Dmitry.[12] The right to have elected officials and to reduce violence and willfulness of the vicegerents and rural district chiefs could have contributed to the tranquility and material prosperity of the populace in many places. Still, we recall the complaints of nationals and foreigners against the crown estates and Ivan's cruelty. Foreigners gave first place in trade relations to Novgorod, but we know what Ivan did to Novgorod, and not only to Novgorod, for he began his devastating campaign in Tver.[13]

To this state of affairs were coupled natural calamities. In the autumn of 1552 pestilence, in which 279,594 people perished, raged in Novgorod and its rural districts. In 1553 there was a great pestilence in Pskov. Twenty-five thousand were buried in the paupers' cemetery, and how many ended up in gullies is unknown. In the autumn of 1565 pestilence raged in Polotsk and continued until December 6. In the spring of the following year it was unleashed on Velikie Luki, Toropets, Smolensk, and in the fall it raged in Novgorod, Staraia Rusa and Pskov, reaching Mozhaisk and Moscow. In 1567 small mice from the forests swarmed in areas of Kazan, Sviiazhsk and Cheboksary and left not a single ear of grain, which they devoured in the granaries and corn bins. In 1570 a severe famine and pestilence raged throughout the realm. Mentioned among the measures taken against the spread of the infection were barricades and guards. In the Novgorod chronicle for the year 1551 we read that there was an outcry for all people of Pskov and wholesale merchants to leave Novgorod immediately with their goods. If a wholesaler or man from Pskov was found with goods the next day in Novgorod, they took him out of the city and burned him together with his goods. If they found a visitor from Pskov in a house, they beat the doorkeeper with the knout and burned the man from Pskov. There were barricades on the road to Pskov so that wholesale merchants with goods could not travel from Pskov to Novgorod, or from Novgorod to Pskov.

Under the year 1571 we read that it was forbidden to bury near a church anyone on whom the fatal mark[14] was discovered; they were to be interred six versts outside Novgorod. The people erected gates and set up guards in the streets. If on the street someone with the mark died, they bolted shut the houses with the people inside, and fed them from the street. Spiritual fathers were forbidden to hear their confessions, and if a priest did in fact hear their confession without the approval of the boyars he was burned along with the plague victim. When the dreadful epidemic appeared in Mozhaisk in 1566 the tsar ordered the construction of a fortified gate. During the plague of 1571, according to English information, the roads were barricaded, and anyone who attempted to travel by forbidden routes was burned. In the Pskov chronicle for the year 1568 we read that the guards on the Cheresky bridge saw a light at night, and a great multitude of people armed in military fashion heading for Pskov, but the guards were positioned to protect against the pestilence.

TOWNS IN WESTERN RUSSIA

In the towns of Western Russia the former situation with respect to daily life continued. There was contention between the citizens and the mayors, councillors, palatines, princes, lords and boyars because perhaps nowhere at that time had disregard by the powerful for authority and law attained such a level as in Poland and Lithuania. In their strife with their mayors and councillors the people of Wilno demanded a change in the ancient town statute. King Sigismund I[15] refused, and left everything as it was, but the dissatisfied citizens found a way to attract Queen Bona[16] to their side. In 1536 at her insistence, as the king himself said, he instructed the council and citizens at large to choose from their midst faithful, thoughtful men versed in the German Magdeburg Law[17] who could settle the disputes. Points on which they could not agree they were to refer to the king's judgment. As a result a new town statute with the following composition was drawn up and confirmed.

As of old there must be in the town twenty-four councillors and twelve burgomasters, one half Roman Catholic and the other half Greek Orthodox. From these officials each year two burgomasters, one Roman Catholic, one Orthodox, and four councillors, two Roman Catholics and two Orthodox, were to be in office holding sessions, and they received a salary. The burgomasters each received twenty kopa grosh and the councillors ten kopa grosh. Four stewards managed the town property, its income and disbursements. The council elected two of them from its own members. The other two were chosen by the council from the citizens at large who selected eight men and put them before the council, which then chose two. The stewards were obliged to prepare the accounts annually, supervised by two members of the council. The others could attend as they wished. Likewise one master chosen by the council from each of the guilds had to be present. The citizens chose eighteen men from among the merchants and other Wilno residents who lived there continually, and from these the council chose six. These officials elected from the commoners and the guilds swore an oath at the reading of the financial report that they would not divulge information about the town's property or its secret business.

There must be four locks and four sets of keys for the treasury and town privileges, two sets of keys kept by the presiding burgomaster of the Roman faith, and two by the presiding burgomaster of the Greek faith. This treasury could be used only for general town needs. The council discussed its own affairs with the burgomasters in one chancery, whereas the court assessors sat and judged with the king's prefect[18] in another chancery unless the council summoned the assessors for some common affairs, in which case the assessors would come to the council. The assessors had their own seal which the king gave them in perpetuity. In this fashion, sitting in different chanceries, the council and the assessors would not interfere with each other. A father and son or two brothers could not be elected together to the office of burgomaster, councillor or assessor. Similarly, a father could not sit in the council when his son was in the assessor's court, nor could one brother be in the council and another in the assessor's court.

Every Thursday at the appointed hour the council convened in the town hall, and if anyone did not appear, he paid a fine. If a common man did not obtain justice because someone was absent, the offender was punished according to the law. Envoys who went from the town to the sovereign at the town's expense could not concern themselves at that time with their own or with anyone else's affairs other than the general town business. When the envoys returned from the sovereign to the town the council summoned the citizens at large and the envoys were to relate to the council and the citizens at large what they had brought from the sovereign. The council and the citizens at large were to endeavor as far as possible to have everything ready to defend the town against enemies, including cannons, guns and the like. They were to see to it that each burgher had his own gun, boar spears, buckets and axes.

If a fire broke out, every burgher was obligated to run to put out the fire, and the presiding burgomasters were duty bound to force the people to take part. During epidemics respected people were to take care that no one died without a will. The council was to concern itself with supplying the town with water, it had to see to it that butchers did not slaughter unhealthy animals and sell the meat, it had to purchase grain with civic funds in case of famine or siege, and supervise the merchants' weights and measures. The council must keep all town gates under its own lock and surveillance. Anyone who wished to leave the Magdeburg Law and submit himself to a different law must first sell his real estate to a burgher subject to the town hall. Without the citizens at large the council could not impose any new taxes. Someone coming from elsewhere, having lived in Wilno for six years, could not be deported, nor could he be harassed by any government official, under penalty of five hundred kopa grosh.

Similar financial motives forced the governments of Eastern and Western Russia to ensure that townsmen or burghers did not depart the status of taxpayers with their real estate because this deprived the treasury of income, and the remaining citizens would feel a heavier burden satisfying various public duties. Information reached King Sigismund that many households in Wilno were circumventing the municipal government. Some left through secret agreements and contracts not revealed to the government, others through marriage to noble widows and young noblewomen, or to the widows and daughters of lords' servants. Artisans left by placing themselves under the patronage of council lords and other government officials. All of this resulted in a significant decrease in the incomes of the king and the municipality.

In 1553 the king instructed his prefect and the councillors to guard carefully against anyone avoiding town law under any pretext, and to inform him under oath about this. He would confiscate the households and farmsteads of those disobeying, and hand the properties to the town for its needs. The same year the prefect, burgomasters, councillors and all the burghers complained to the king that many noblemen, boyars and lords' servitors who took burghers' homes as dowries for their wives did not want to share the burden of public duties with the burghers. The king wrote to his Wilno palatine that all manor owners, no matter what they might call themselves, must perform various municipal duties. Within ten years the royal order was forgotten and Sigismund Augustus had to reiterate it to the council lords, lest they take Wilno burghers with their houses into their own estates.

In 1568 Sigismund Augustus, as a reward for their fidelity demonstrated particularly during times of war, granted gentry rights to all Wilno burghers holding government positions in the town. These rights were transferred to their children, provided they did not humiliate themselves by pursuing menial professions. From the new charter based on Magdeburg Law given to Polotsk in 1580 by Bathory, we learn that the prefect was normally the palatine there.

Several times the prefect, burgomasters, councillors and the entire Wilno citizenry complained to the king about the strains placed upon them by the allocation of quarters to lodgers, royal nobles and servants, council lords and officials, their own and foreign envoys (when all these visited Wilno while the king was in residence). They took the best rooms, drove out the proprietor and his wife and children, seized their belongings and livestock. The proprietor, his wife and children were housed in one front room, and lodgers often showed up there too. All this happened not because the lodger needed quarters but in order to extract money from the owner. If he was unwilling to buy them off, he must simply put up with the inconvenience. In 1568 the king ordered that all lodgings be registered in the presence of two town councillors, and that no lodgings be let to anyone having his own domicile in the town.

In 1539 as a result of the complaints of the residents of Cherkasy against their elder it was determined that they were obliged to pay the town watchman two groshas each for every man who ate his own bread. Every year they must give the elder a cartload of hay from each homestead. They were not permitted to take honey to sell in Kiev, but must sell it locally to the elder for eighty-five groshas a pail[19] whether this was above or below the current price. They could prepare mead eight times annually, each time making two pails each, on the vigils of the Nativity of Christ [December

25], Easter, the feast of St. Elijah [July 20], the Transfiguration [August 6], the Dormition of the Virgin [August 15], the Nativity of the Virgin [September 8], the feast of St. Michael the Archangel [November 8] and St. Nicholas Day [December 6]. They gave the elder nothing for the apiaries. The elder gave them permission to harvest the beaver and fish ponds along the Dnieper river out of the portion he had agreed upon with them. In the fall, when they were setting the beaver traps, they gave the town one beaver each. They could catch and sell fish freely, and must give only a part to the town. If a cossack died or the Tatars captured him and he had neither wife nor children surviving, the elder took half of his possessions for the town, and the other half was donated as a memorial for his soul. The Zvonets burghers kept for themselves the Dnieper river rapids, and the elder might not enter there. At Christmastide the burghers and cossacks must give the elder presents of one fox or one marten fur each, but if there were no fox or marten furs they gave six groshas each. The elder collected the transportation fee from every two men for the journey to Kanev. If an envoy or Tatar courier happened along the burghers must provide him quarters and the elder give him honey. As for the steppe and waterway guards and the relocation of the Tatar gentry, the burghers were obligated to serve as guards, and the gentry were to be relocated together with the elder's servants.

In 1538 the king permitted the residents of Wilno to build a bridge using town money, with the right to collect a toll of one peniaz per cart from travelers. The same year the people of Wilno were required to pay five hundred kopa grosh as tribute to the Horde, but they declared that according to the privilege they would pay only eighty kopa grosh, and the king left this privilege in force. Later, when the people of Wilno, relying on their privileges, sought to avoid the new toll levied on all exported goods for three years because of war with Muscovy, the king denied their request and ordered them to pay this toll together with the others.

In 1540 a statute charter was given to the citizens of Svisloch and the rural districts. We take special note of it because it preserves the terms for the oldest requisitions in Rus. It says "but the circuit tax[20] of one and a half groshas per hearth in autumn." In the Mogilev statute charter of 1561 the taxes are enumerated which the citizens must pay on each parcel of land bringing in a certain income, and on houses and shops. Houses situated on the marketplace were distinguished from houses built on streets, and more tax was collected from the former than from the latter. Meadows above the Dnieper river were distinguished from meadows in swamps, and here too more tax was collected from the former than from the latter.

This charter is made especially interesting by the fact that it defines when the citizens could prepare alcoholic beverages at home, for in these stipulations the statute charters for towns of East and West Russia agreed. "Lords are permitted to make mead seven times a year, that is, at Easter, Ascension, Trinity Sunday, Dormition [August 15], St. Nicholas [December 6], St. Peter and St. Paul [June 29] and St. Elijah [July 20], and each time they can purchase mead for no more than two rubles of large groshas.[21] Mogilev burghers are permitted to have twelve banquets a year on holidays, although they cannot make mead worth more than two rubles of broad groshas. In addition, every burgher is free to keep mead and beer for his own use, but not for sale. With the knowledge of the tax collector he can distill spirits for his son's or daughter's wedding and for caroling. In addition to this the burghers can distill spirits five times a year: at Christmas, in Cheesefare week,[22] on Easter, Trinity Sunday and autumnal St. Nicholas Day [December 6]; they cannot, however, use more than four chetverts of malt each time for the spirits."

In this same charter it says that on the strength of a new resolution the office of royal prefect was entrusted to the Mogilev burgher Josifowicz. For better order and administration four hundredmen were prescribed, each having jurisdiction over a certain segment of the population. The prefects could not decide any municipal cases without the advice of the hundredmen and the other principal burghers.

Concerning guilds, in 1552 Sigismund Augustus granted the Wilno prefect, burgomasters and councillors the right to reform the old artisan associations (collegia opificum) and to establish new ones, giving them privileges, prescribing laws and customs. No one in the town might practice any trade without enrollment in a known association; otherwise he was subject to imprisonment, seizure of the tools of his trade and confiscation of his movable property. In 1578 following a petition of the Jews Stefan Bathory ordered the prefects, burgomasters and councillors of every town to judge the Jews according to national law, and not Magdeburg Law.

As early as the reign of Grand Prince Alexander[23] it was decreed that a landowner in Bielsk who wished to institute a lighter workload and tribute on his estate with the aim of enticing more peasants was subject to a fine of one hundred kopa grosh. In 1551 the landowners of Vitebsk district agreed among themselves and decreed the conditions for free peasants to live on their land. Each landowner was obliged to house them according to the accepted custom in Polotsk territory, that is, the peasant had to give the lord every fourth sheaf which was threshed in the presence of the lord's messenger. The peasants also must feed the lord's messengers and deliver the lord's share to the appointed place, and they gave the lords one half of the honey from the bees. Every summer they worked on the lord's grain, eight days of labor service for the lord. For two days they must plow the fallow, for two days they hacked brushwood, they cut hay for two days, and they harvested rye and other grain for two days. In the spring over the course of a week they built new barns on the lord's manor or repaired old ones, and in the winter they went hunting and fishing.

When a free peasant did not wish to live on a quarter lot he must work two days each week for an entire year with a scythe, a plow, a sickle, an axe or with whatever he was ordered, and in addition he was to serve out eight days of labor service in the summer. If a free peasant wished to move to another landowner he was obliged to cede the fallow field to the lord in good time in the summer. Having appeared at the communal gathering in the first week of Great Lent and made his petition and paid the departure fee of twelve broad groshas, he could depart.

Should a free peasant living in the village permit his house or barn to fall into disrepair, before leaving he had to restore and rebuild it so that it was just as he found it. When anyone settled a free man on damp soil where previously there was no settlement nor prepared and plowed land, the settler must be granted a tax immunity of ten years, on the expiration of which he must likewise give the quarter sheaf and perform all the above mentioned services. When they established these conditions the landowners declared that if any of them, being content with less onerous obligations, housed free peasants out of desire to populate his estate, or in any way violated the statute and was convicted, he must pay the king a fine of fifty kopa grosh. In 1553 King Sigismund Augustus confirmed this resolution and adopted it for his own peasants.

In the 1557 statute dealing with plowlands for the royal rural districts of the grand principality of Lithuania, ministerial boyars of ancient and unpurchased right were to be housed on two plowlands, from which they paid their entire obligations with cash, based on land appraisal, but when they were about the king's business they paid nothing. Without the king's order the village constable could not send them anywhere. From these boyars the inspectors selected attendants who must be found in every castle or royal manor in the necessary number. They travelled with the king's writs to the manors subject to constables, and brought the cash tax payments to Wilno. When they made inquests following complaints of peasants, they kept one horse for every two plowlands free of all taxation. Forest beekeepers paid with cash from their plowland based on the value of the land, as did new settlers. When the king ordered them to go to war they were exempt from all taxes that year. They likewise were obliged to repair bridges. Honor guard or court coachmen each had two exempt plowlands. Musketeers likewise enjoyed two exempt plowlands. Their service consisted in hunting and going to war, following the order of the king. Other manorial servants likewise possessed two exempt plowlands; among these were the beaters whom the inspectors chose from the forest wardens.

The prefects in the villages possessed one plowland each and performed a number of service-related tasks. At the instruction of the constable they compelled the peasants to perform labor services or pay quitrent and taxes. They attended payment of taxes, presented peasants to the constable for punishment, supervised their work, handed over oats and hay in Wilno, as well as people transported there from the prefecture. They adjusted the boundary marks annually, and informed the constable about any defacement. The constable tried peasants on market day for all charges except bloodshed and rape, for which two offenses the prefect presented the peasant in the court determined by the constable. The prefect was present in court to assist the peasant, kept a register of the fines received in the treasury and informed the inspectors. He saw to it that the constable did not collect fines greater than what was lawful. The constable tried the prefect for each misdemeanor but only in concert with the inspector could he deprive him of office. Having dismissed one prefect, another must be appointed from the men of the same district who demonstrated behavior above suspicion. The peasants were to agree with the selection.

In every prefecture there were to be about one hundred plowlands although two, three or more villages could be combined to reach this size. To survey the plowlands the prefect needed to have an accurate measuring cord of standard length. Two, three or more assessors were to be appointed in the villages, depending on the size of the village. Their office entailed the prosecution of damage done to fields by pasturing cattle and other causes. For their labor they received for each case one grosh. For false testimony they incurred the death penalty.

We have noticed how much land tax or quitrent royal peasants or taxpaying people paid. They worked each plowland two days every week, but were free from work during Christmas week, Cheesefare week, and Easter week. Work by peasants on Sundays was to be prohibited by the prefect. When a peasant did not work he paid for the first day one grosh, for the second day a ram, for the third day he was punished with the lash on the bench and must make up for the missed days. If for some reason the peasant was unable to work he was to inform the constable through a neighbor or assessor. If the cause indicated was lawful the peasant was not subjected to punishment, but the next day he was to make up for the work he missed. No one could buy himself out of work.

Peasants began their labor with the rising sun and finished at sunset. Those who worked with livestock were given an hour's rest in the morning, one hour at midday and one hour in the afternoon. Whoever worked on foot was given only one half hour of rest.

The peasants in all the castles and districts of the king must begin payment of the land quitrent and other taxes on St. Michael's Day [November 8] and could continue payment until St. Martin's Day [April 13]. Should anyone not meet these payments and the constable found it was simple negligence, the guilty was imprisoned and kept confined until he paid, although his oxen and horses never could be seized for the land quitrent or for any other tax. If a man was unable to pay the tax because of fire, the death or illness of his entire family, famine, hail damage or poverty, the prefect was to present him to the constable. After questioning by the prefect, assessors and neighbors, and examination of the peasant's home, the constable entered his name in a register. When the treasurer received the account, he was to confirm the case again through the inspector.

The inspectors were under oath, good and pious men of fixed address and fully knowing the measurements of plowlands and farms. The inspectors must take care that no one cut the king's forests. They made reports on careless constables, saw to it that places for settlement be marked by the land surveyors in the third middle field, while the constable required the peasants to settle in the designated places. The inspector chose the land surveyors. In every castle and royal manor where land was divided into plowlands the constable received all taxes from the tenth plowland, excluding oats and hay, every third sheaf of grain from the barns, all customs and weight duties from the butchers on market days, the tenth fish when the ponds were drained, fines from the peasants who did not appear for labor, and the like.

Peasants enjoyed the right to go a short distance into the king's forests for firewood, brushwood, timber and bast for their own requirements, but not for sale. Their children and wives were not forbidden to gather mushrooms, wild vegetables, berries and hops in all royal forests. On his own plowlands the peasant could kill wolves, foxes, lynx, wolverines, hares, squirrels and every other small wild animal, as well as every bird, and could sell this game to anyone without declaring it to the constable, but he could not kill chamois or other large wild animals, even on his own plowlands. Peasants were particularly forbidden on pain of death to bear arms or hunt any game in virgin forests or royal hunting preserves. Peasants might fish the king's rivers and lakes with small nets, but they could not construct weirs. In April, May and June they could not fish in the lakes, leaving the fish for spawning, though they could fish at any time in the rivers. During a famine a poor peasant who had sowed his fields could leave in the winter in search of food, provided that he revealed his destitution to the constable in the presence of the prefect. Neither his farm nor his crops could be seized until St. John's Day [June 24]. If he did not return by that date he lost his crops, and his entire farm was turned over to someone else.

When a peasant went away without informing the constable in the presence of the prefect all his land, together with his entire farm, was turned over to another peasant, and the constable searched for the fugitive. If a peasant who left with the knowledge of the constable returned after St. John's Day, and if a fugitive was summoned or returned on his own, they were settled on empty plowlands. When a peasant left as a result of injury inflicted on him by the constable or prefect and later returned, the inspector was to investigate the case and decide whether or not to let him have his crops and farmstead. A peasant could sell his buildings and farm before the constable in the presence of the prefect and assessors. After he settled the buyer, who must be capable of fulfilling the obligations, on the farm, he could move to town or to a deserted plowland, provided it was on the king's estates.

Deserted plowlands were settled with good men who in the course of two or three years were required to pay no more than forty-two grosh for all their obligations. To assemble carriage teams for a distant journey or build castles and manors the peasants pooled three or four plowlands for one cartload or for one laborer, which released the peasants from taxes. Peasants were obliged to build bridges and stand guard in the castles and royal manors. Artisans of every kind were to be housed by the inspector on one free plowland at every castle and royal manor.

With respect to industry there is an interesting charter given by Sigismund Augustus to the Wilno glass factory owner and nobleman Martin Paletsky. He was obliged to give to the royal treasury annually two hundred large and two hundred small phials, in return for which he received the privilege that all glass imported into Wilno, except Venetian glass, be sold only to him, and that in Wilno no one else was permitted to set up glass factories.

Relating to trade is an interesting charter of Sigismund Augustus forbidding speculation in food supplies, thus avoiding high prices for foodstuffs in Wilno. The burgomasters and councillors were charged with ensuring that the king's decree was carried out. In an agreement signed with the Crimean khan in 1540, by the way, it was stipulated that Polish and Lithuanian merchants could take salt freely to Kachi-bey (Odessa). When they paid the toll as of old they could transport salt under the protection of the khan's men to Kiev, Lutsk and other towns. If the king's subjects suffered losses at the hands of the khan's men in Kachi-bey, the khan would pay compensation. Likewise Polish and Lithuanian merchants might travel freely with their goods to Perekop and Kaffa and trade there, paying the ancient tolls. Conversely Tatar merchants might trade freely in royal domains. In 1540 two trade routes were established between Lithuania and Prussia. One went to Memel on the Gorzhdy, where the toll was collected, and the other went to Jurburg where markets were held on Fridays. From the goods stockpiled there salt is mentioned above all else.

At the Wilno Sejm in 1547 the king consulted with the lords and gentry about the fact that his Roman Catholic and Greek Orthodox subjects were taking all types of forestry products in the virgin forests, woods and pine forests of the grand duchy of Lithuania, and were selling them to Prussian and Livonian merchants, and even to their own Lithuanian Jews. Yet at the initial sale of the goods, at their outlet, at the sorting and selling, these merchants and the Jews were deceiving them to such a degree that they made very little profit. The virgin forests, woods and pine forests, the eternal property of the nation, were being laid waste, and only foreign merchants and Jews were getting rich. To avoid this the Sejm resolved to establish at the borders depots to which all Lithuanian subjects must bring their forestry products. Here the king's officials purchased them for a fixed price and then endeavored to dispose of them abroad in a manner most advantageous for the treasury. These depots were set up in Kovno, Brest, Drissa below Polotsk and at Salat in Zhmud.

Information about the commercial importance of Kiev and its rural district during our period has reached us. "Kiev abounds in foreign goods because for everything transported from Asia Minor, Persia, India, Arabia and Northern Syria to Muscovy, Sweden and Denmark—precious gems, silk and goldspun cloth, incense, thyme, saffron, pepper and other spices— there is no more trustworthy, direct and famous route than the one from Kaffa by way of Perekop, the Tavan ferry on the Dnieper river and Kiev. Foreign merchants often set out on this route in caravans numbering close to a thousand, with many wagons and saddled camels. When they leave the old highway and head out from Perekop for Putivl, passing directly into Muscovy in order to avoid the double Dnieper river crossing and the payment of tolls, they often are plundered. Kievan palatines, franchise holders, merchants, money-changers, ferrymen, carters, and innkeepers make a big profit from these caravans even when they pass in the winter across fields and are covered in piles of snow. In the same way it happens that Kievan shacks which, by the way, abound in fruit, milk, honey, meat and fish, and are usually filthy, are filled with precious silken cloth, costly gems, sables and other furs, spices and so on, so that silk is sometimes cheaper there than linen is in Wilno, and pepper is sometimes cheaper than salt."

VI

THE CHURCH IN EASTERN AND WESTERN RUSSIA

EXPANSION OF ORTHODOXY

During the reign of Ivan IV the Russian church saw its limits expand eastwards along with the limits of the realm, thanks to the pacification of Kazan and Astrakhan. Having become Russian towns, they now had to become Christian. In keeping with Kazan's importance as a town and in line with the important consequences for church and state which the conversion of the surrounding population to Christianity could have, it was resolved to erect a special diocese there. Gury, the first archbishop of Kazan and Sviiazhsk, set out from Moscow for his diocese in the spring of 1555. His departure was unusual, a first in the history of Russia. An archbishop travelled to a conquered infidel realm to spread Christianity there and consolidate moral order. He took with him clergy and articles necessary for the church, icons and the like. Gury's spiritual campaign into Kazan corresponded to the departure of the Greek clergy from Byzantium and Kherson to enlighten Rus with Christianity at the time of Vladimir. It was the finale to Kazan's subjugation, that mighty victory accomplished for the triumph of Christianity over Islam. Obviously it was consummated with great solemnity.

On the seventh Sunday after Easter, Metropolitan Makary and the new archbishop Gury officiated at a solemn prayer service in the Dormition cathedral. Bishop Nifont of Krutitsa,[1] assisted by the archimandrite and abbots, consecrated water on top of the relics. After the prayer service the clergy proceeded to the Frolov bridge with the cross, the Gospel book and icons; behind them walked the tsar with his brother and cousin, princes, boyars and a crowd of people. In front of the Kremlin there was another prayer service, after which the tsar and the metropolitan took their leave of Gury. At that time the foundation for the renowned Intercession cathedral, commemorating the taking of Kazan, was laid outside the Frolov gates. Here Gury said a litany and blessed and sprinkled the foundations with holy water. Walking out onto the Zhivoy bridge from New Town, he read the Gospel and a litany, gave a blessing and spoke a prayer for the tsar and all Orthodox Christians, a composition by Metropolitan Hilarion of Rus.[2] Then came the dismissal. Gury blessed with the cross and gave a benediction to the populace following him, sprinkled them and the town with holy water and got into a boat, where the chanting and reading of the Gospel continued.

Below St. Simon's monastery the Kazan clergy left the boat, and were met by the archimandrite with crosses. Here Gury celebrated the liturgy, dined and spent the night. Early the next day he set out on the long journey along the Moscow river, the Oka and the Volga. On the way he sent priests among the riverbank hamlets and large villages to sprinkle the churches, homes and people with holy water. The bishop of Kolomna had to give the order in his own town to summon everyone at market to go to the prayer services and to greet the archbishop of Kazan. Met by the bishop with a procession and all the people, Gury celebrated the liturgy and dined with the bishop. In all the other towns he received the same reception.

Upon his arrival in Kazan the new archbishop was obliged to instruct the people every Sunday. He was to teach continuously the newly baptized the fear of God, instruct them in his home, give them food and drink, favor and take care of them in all things so that the infidels, seeing such solicitousness and mercy, would grow envious of the righteous Christian faith and become enlightened by holy baptism. Gury's instructions stated that should any Tatars desire to be baptized of their own volition and not from compulsion, he was to command them to be baptized. He was to keep the best of them in the bishop's residence, instruct them in the Christian faith and shelter them as far as possible. The others were to be distributed among the monasteries for baptism. When the newly baptized finished instruction, the archbishop was to invite them to dine with him frequently, to give them kvas to drink at table, and after dinner send them mead to drink at the forecourt.[3]

Should Tatars approach him with a petition he must feed and give them kvas in his residence, but was to give them mead to drink in the forecourt. He must lead them to the Christian religion by gentle and calm conversation and kindness, not with harsh words. If a Tatar ran up a debt, fled from his disgrace to the archbishop and desired to be baptized, on no grounds might he be sent back to the commanders. Instead he should be baptized and given shelter in the residence of the archbishop, who was to consult with the vicegerents and commanders. If they so decided, he was to be kept in Kazan on his old field and held to his tribute. Could he not be kept in Kazan because of the danger of renewed treachery, the archbishop was to baptize him and send him off to the sovereign. If the commanders ordered the execution of a Tatar for some crime, and other Tatars approached the archbishop to petition for mercy, the archbishop was to intercede for the release of the accused and, on the advice of the vicegerent and the commanders, transfer him from the vicegerent and commanders to his own household. If possible he was to keep him in Kazan; failing this, the Tatar must be sent to the sovereign.

The archbishop must take counsel with the vicegerent and commanders. Let them inform the archbishop about those Tatars for whom they have a minor censure in store and whom they wish to frighten with punishment but without carrying out the punishment. The archbishop shall intercede for their release from punishment even though he had no petition from them. Using every means at his disposal the archbishop must instruct the Tatars and lead them to desire baptism, but under no circumstances should he frighten them into baptism.

Were the archbishop to learn of any misconduct with respect to the Christian religion among the commanders of Kazan and Sviiazhsk, among the junior boyars and servitors or among the vicegerents themselves, he was to admonish them with tenderness. If they did not listen, he was to sound a threat and if this availed nothing he must write to the tsar about their misconduct. The archbishop must hold the Kazan and Sviiazhsk vicegerents in esteem. If the vicegerent and commanders of Kazan happened to dine at the archbishop's, he must seat the vicegerent at the end of the table, and the commanders near him on the opposite side at the high table, leaving two spaces between them and himself. He must seat the archimandrites, abbots and archpriests at the curved table. After the meal he should pass the tsar's cup to the archbishop, the archbishop's cup to the vicegerent, the vicegerent's cup to the archimandrite or great abbot, and if he was not present, to the archbishop's boyar. If the vicegerent and commanders sought advice from the archbishop about matters of state he must consult with them and give them his thoughts concerning all matters except cases of murder, but he should not tell anyone the thoughts of the vicegerent and commanders.

The archbishop was to exercise great caution against fire in his manor, and have his kitchen and bakery in the yard. He should not keep either mead or beer in his cellar in town, but might keep kvas. He should keep his wine, mead and beer in a cellar outside the town. He should speak rather often to the vicegerent and commanders, urging them to take exceeding care against fire and taverns lest the junior boyars and the servitors sit about with fire at night drinking at their gatherings. Guards must be posted about the town and at the gates and exercise extreme caution so that the junior boyars and servitors not carouse throughout the day as well. If the archbishop learned that the vicegerent and commanders were negligent in their town residences, or that they did violence to their servants, he should speak twice or even three times concerning this to the vicegerent and commanders that they no longer act in this manner. If they did not listen, he must write to the sovereign.

A large salary for those days was prescribed for the new archbishop. He received 865 rubles in cash and a tenth of the customs duties from Kazan, Sviiazhsk and Cheboksary, or one hundred and fifty-five rubles and eleven altyns. In addition to this came the larder provisions in kind, from rye to spice roots. The directive concerning the conversion of the Tatars to Christianity was implemented with unimagined success by Gury and two of his assistants, Archimandrites German and Varsonofy, the former succeeding Gury as archbishop of Kazan. Several thousand Muslims and pagans were converted to Christianity. In Astrakhan there were also conversions. Circassian princes visited Moscow to be baptized themselves, or to have their sons baptized. Priests from Moscow were sent to them in the mountains to restore Christianity, which had lapsed there.

In the Far North the conversion of the Lapps continued. Under Ivan IV, Feodorit[4] finished his heroic struggles for the conversion of the Kola

Lapps, and Trifon[5] did the same for the Pechenga Lapps. A native of the Novgorod district, Trifon was keen on the hermit's life from his youth. Wandering about the forests of his homeland, he heard a voice which told him not to look for Christ in those woods because an unpromising, impenetrable, uninhabited and thirsting land awaited him. Trifon headed for the ocean shores and settled in deserted country on the Pechenga river. Homeless and without a roof over his head, he began to instruct the neighboring Lapps in the new faith. The work was difficult. Lapp sorcerers, not knowing how to refute Trifon with words, beat and tormented him and were about to kill him, but in the crowd of savages defenders appeared and their voices were heard. "Of what is he guilty? He tells us about good things, about the kingdom of God," they cried. "He calls our death a sleep, and says that we shall rise from the dead. Let us leave him now, but if we find some fault in him, we shall kill him." They drove Trifon away, but he returned and catechized many Lapps. The priest whom he brought from Kola baptized the catechumens and consecrated a church for them.

While zealous preachers were spreading Christianity on the barren shores of the Arctic Ocean the bishops of Novgorod had to do battle with the paganism holding on stubbornly in the Votskaia fifth.[6] In 1534 Archbishop Makary of Novgorod had to send to the local clergy in Votskaia fifth, in Chud and in all districts of Koporie, Yam, Ivangorod, Korela and Orekhov. "They informed me here," he wrote, "that in your areas many Christians have strayed from the true faith. They do not go to church or visit their spiritual fathers, they pray in their foul wooden and stone prayer huts. Many eat meat and milk products during St. Peter's fast, and they offer sacrifice and drink libations to the vile demons. They summon the Chud shamans to their foul prayer huts of apostasy. They put their dead in barrows and mounds in the villages with the help of those same shamans rather than bring them to church for burial in the churchyards. When a child is being born they first call the shamans to the women in labor. The shamans call the children by names of their own persuasion, and only then do they call for you abbots and priests. On the eves of festivals they summon the same shamans who conjure vile demons. Yet you neither put a stop to these wicked rites, nor do you preach against them. In your areas many men are living apart from their wives illicitly with women and maidens, and their wives live apart from them with other men illicitly, with neither crowning[7] nor prayer."

To eradicate these disorders the archbishop sent a priest and two of his junior boyars to the Votskaia fifth with orders to tear down, destroy and put to the torch the foul prayer huts, to instruct the Christians in the true faith, to correct the repentant shamans according to church laws and to seize the recalcitrant and send them off to him in Novgorod.

Makary's instructions remained ineffectual, in as much as thirteen years later his successor Archbishop Feodosy[8] had to repeat the same admonitions and instructions, pointing out the very same disorders with the addition of yet another. "In your localities," said he, "in the Chud land, married women and widows shave their heads, wearing shawls on their heads and cloths on their shoulders which resemble shrouds for the dead. In their misconduct they cause great profanation to the female gender."

As of old, monasteries continued to promote the settlement of empty expanses. Abbot Fedor built a hermitage in the dark, wild forest between the districts of Vologda, Kargopol and Vazhsk. In keeping with his petition, the sovereign showed his favor in 1546 and ordered him to clear the forest on all sides of the monastery for twelve versts, plow under the clearing, and invite peasants. According to custom, the newcomers received the usual tax exemptions. Sometimes a monastery was founded because the populace of an entire area petitioned. For example, in 1580 the elected judges and the local people of the town of Khlynov in Viatka sent a petition to the tsar from the whole land saying that Viatka towns were far from Moscow towns, and in the whole land of Viatka there was no monastery. There was no place for the aged or disabled to be tonsured, nor for others who wanted to be tonsured before death. For this reason they wanted to build their own monastery. They chose Brother Trifon, a monk of the Pyskorsk monastery, to be the founder. They had the land, which was untilled because vicegerent's villages were standing empty.

The northern hermitages continued to demand of their monks steadfastness of spirit in the battle against un-Christian happenings. In a fearful epoch marked by bloody battle and the brute force of triumphant authority, the most remote monastery of the North, the Solovetsk monastery,[9] sent to the metropolitan throne in Moscow an abbot who did not hesitate to raise his voice for the cause of mercy. The series of illustrious Moscow hierarchs who contributed so much to the strengthening of Moscow and to the establishment of autocracy, and who are recognized as saints by the church, came to a close with the great martyr for the sacred right of interceding for the fallen and the weak.

Ivan complained in his missives to Moscow from Alexandrov Village that the clergy were pleading for those who in his opinion were unworthy. It is interesting that here the tsar did not mention the metropolitan. Ivan extracted a promise from Metropolitan Philip[10] that he would not meddle in the crown estates or the tsar's household customs, but he uttered not a word about interceding. For Archbishop Gury of Kazan intercession was prescribed as the means to attract Tatars to accept Christianity. Metropolitan Makary's petitioning was received by the tsar with respect, and was put forward frankly as a motive for demonstrating some act of mercy or fulfilling some request. "Our father Makary, metropolitan of all Russia," the tsar wrote to his Novgorod clerks, "has reminded us about the wife of Prince Bogdan Koretsky so that we might favor her and order that she be given some land from her husband's estate for subsistence. For the sake of our father Metropolitan Makary I have favored her and ordered that fifteen areals be separated from her husband's estate for her use."

Owing to the metropolitan, the Novgorod estate holder Kurtsov was favored in that it was forbidden to take away from him his old estate. At the request of Archbishop Pimen of Novgorod and Metropolitan Makary the monetary penalty against Prince Ivan Buinosov-Rostovsky was reduced. Although to the requests of the Lithuanian lords that he mediate the conclusion of a peace treaty the metropolitan usually responded by saying that he did not get involved in such matters because he was competent only in ecclesiastical affairs, we nevertheless find information that the sovereign consulted with him about matters having nothing at all to do with the church. In 1550 the sovereign decided the service placement of boyars and commanders in the regiments with the aid of the metropolitan, his brother and cousin, and the boyars.

THE HIERARCHY

The overthrow of Metropolitan Philip which resulted from his clash with the crown estates was not the first example in the sixteenth century. Grand Prince Vasily deposed a metropolitan, and during Ivan's minority two metropolitans were overthrown.[11] The order for the installation of Metropolitan Joseph[12] has come down to us. "Grand Prince Ivan Vasilievich of all Russia," it states first, "together with his intercessors Archbishop Makary of Novgorod and Pskov, the bishops, the entire consecrated assembly, the spiritual elders and all the boyars, chose for the office of metropolitan the spiritual elder of the Trinity-St. Sergius monastery, Abbot Joseph, and named him metropolitan of all Russia."

After this nomination the sovereign went to the cathedral church of the Dormition with the metropolitan-elect and with the clergy and boyars. Two bishops escorted the nominee into the tsar's presence. After venerating the icons and relics, the sovereign went to the metropolitan's palace, where the archbishop and bishops seated the nominee in the prepared place. Then it says in the record that on the same day (February 6, 1539), in keeping with the counsel of Archbishop Makary, the bishops of Riazan, Tver, Saray and Perm sat in the cathedral church of the Dormition, in the side-chapel dedicated to the Praise of the Mother of God, and elected the metropolitan following the book.

The error in the date is rectified by another record which speaks of the form of the election. On February 5 the bishops, being of one mind and heart with the other Russian bishops, chose three candidates for the office of metropolitan of Kiev, Vladimir and all Russia, namely Archimandrite Jonas of the Miracles monastery, Abbot Joseph of the Trinity monastery and Abbot Feodosy of the Novgorod Khutyn monastery. After sealing the names they handed them to Archbishop Makary who prayed briefly, unsealed one name and pronounced Joseph the metropolitan.

On February 9 the installation of the metropolitan-elect took place. Before the liturgy began he had to read aloud a confession of Orthodox belief. During the liturgy at the third "Holy God"[13] they led the candidate to the royal doors and into the sanctuary[14] where the archbishop and bishops installed him as metropolitan. He himself celebrated the liturgy, but the subdeacons did not hold the metropolitan's crozier. After the liturgy, when the new metropolitan was seated on his stone episcopal throne, the sovereign approached him and after a speech presented the crozier. Upon leaving the church the metropolitan, a cross in his hands, sat on a donkey and rode to the grand prince's palace to bless the sovereign. The grand prince's master of the horse and the metropolitan's boyar led the donkey. After a visit with the sovereign the metropolitan went to his own palace for breakfast with the archbishop and bishops. After breakfast he set out again on the donkey riding around the stone town to bless the people and the entire town, after which he supped with the archbishop and bishops in his palace.

In his written confession the metropolitan swore, among other things, to preserve the Orthodox faith in harmony with the universal patriarchs and not in the way that Isidore brought the faith from the recent irreverently flourishing and unholy Latin council.[15] He confessed that he gave no one anything on his installation, nor promised to give anything, and would not give anything to anyone; he promised to preserve everything following ancient tradition, and that he would do nothing under duress, neither from the tsar or grand prince, nor from the many princes, even if they threatened him with death while commanding him to do something contrary to the divine and holy canons. He promised not to allow any Orthodox to join the

Armenians, Latins and other heterodox groups through marriage, godparentage or fraternity. Joseph was installed on February 9, and only on March 26 did his predecessor Daniel[16] submit, or rather was forced to submit, his letter of resignation.

On the death of Metropolitan Makary in 1564 the tsar and the archbishops gathered to elect a new metropolitan decided that, although the metropolitan was head of the archbishops and all the bishops, nothing indicated the dignity of his exalted rank. He wore the same black kamelaukion[17] as all the bishops except the archbishop of Novgorod, who wore a white kamelaukion. From that time on the metropolitan was to wear a white kamelaukion with bead piping and cherubim, and would seal charters with red wax. The archbishop of Novgorod was to wear a white kamelaukion and to seal charters with red wax, and the archbishop of Kazan was to seal with red wax. Then a new "Order for the Installation of a Metropolitan" was written up, containing a few insignificant changes compared with the old.

Concerning the election of bishops we encounter the expressions in the chronicles "by the command of the tsar and the election of the metropolitan and the council" or "by the command of the tsar, through the blessing and consecration of the metropolitan, on advice of the consecrated assembly." In the chronicle account about the installation of Archbishop Alexander of Novgorod in 1576 we run across the words "but the sovereign himself elected him for the episcopacy." It is said about Archbishop Feodosy of Novgorod that he was installed in 1541 by Metropolitan Makary and brought to the archdiocese by the Moscow boyar Grigory Manuilov. After he arrived in the principal town of his diocese the newly installed archbishop ordered a public reading of his letter of enthronement[18] given him by the metropolitan.

For the year 1572 the Novgorod chronicler relates that Archbishop Leonid sang solemn prayers with all monastic and parochial councils at the Holy Wisdom cathedral, and after the solemn prayers ordered Yakov his priest-sacristan to read his letter of enthronement in front of the entire assembly so that all the people could hear. At the same time the archbishop said to Archimandrite Feoktist of St. George's monastery, "Why do you not show me your letter of enthronement? By what right do you function as archimandrite?" "Sire," the archimandrite replied, "I have not managed to do so. I had to travel to Moscow and so I have not brought the letter to you." "If I did not have a letter of enthronement," retorted the archbishop, "I would not serve for three days." To this the archimandrite responded,

"You want to skin money from me, but I have nothing to give you. You can have the office of archimandrite and the letter of enthronement. If you want to strip the cassock off me, I won't lose any sleep over it." Then the archbishop said, "Abbots and all priests! Listen in the assembly and afterwards do not deny it. The archimandrite contradicts me in the assembly in front of you." Then he told all the priests, "Until now you have not brought me your sacerdotal letters to sign, and I shall not sign them now. God will forgive whichever priests are far away." The fate of Archbishop Pimen of Novgorod is well known.[19] The tsar ordered his successor Leonid sewn in a bear skin and hunted down by dogs or, as another account has it, he ordered him strangled.

REFORMING THE LOWER CLERGY AND MONKS

We have learned that the inhabitants of Khlynov, asking the tsar directly for establishment of a monastery, reported that they already had chosen a founder. Sometimes the abbot of a certain monastery petitioned the tsar that because he was old the tsar should favor him and put in his place such and such an elder, and sometimes the brethren begged the tsar to name such and such an elder as their abbot. In 1551, as a result of the complaint of Novgorod priests, a synodal judgment was promulgated concerning the election of priests. "In all the churches and wards," it stipulated, "the elders and wardens shall select experienced priests and deacons who are good at letters and blameless in life. They shall take no money from them for the church nor a reward for themselves. Having made the selection, they shall go with the priests and deacons to the archbishop. After he has taught and instructed them the archbishop will bless them and will not take anything from them except the fee for the blessing. The priests and parish wardens shall take no bribes from deacons, altar bread bakers[20] and sextons, but for the sake of God all shall elect the priests together so that they be experienced and blameless. Should a priest or deacon becomes a widower and is left with a son or brother, with a son-in-law or other male relative who is suitable for his position, good at letters and experienced, he shall be installed as priest instead, but no fee may be charged."

During the reign of Ivan the Terrible's grandfather the church had turned its attention to improving the morality of the clergy, resulting in the famous resolution about widowed parish priests.[21] During the reign of Ivan IV the yearning to heal the moral wounds from which Russian society was suffering was displayed still more forcefully. This yearning, this awareness of failings and the unwillingness to be reconciled to them, revealed the strength of society and its capacity for further prospering. Yet as in our period, so too for a long time afterwards society's yearning had to be confined largely to pointing out moral wounds, to expressions of desire to heal them and to exhortations to such a healing process. The evil was not extirpated because circumstances hindered the effective application of the principal means of eliminating the evil, although the necessity was readily admitted by the best people. This means was enlightenment. Because of the lack of enlightenment progress was made gropingly, and superficial measures were adopted which did not lead to the goal, and which were insulting to the moral dignity of an individual as, for example, the resolution concerning widowed parish priests. Owing to the lack of enlightenment objectives could not be sufficiently defined and real moral failings were confused with customs having not the slightest relationship with morality.

In 1545 tithe collectors complained to Archbishop Feodosy of Novgorod that the abbots and priests of Ustiuzhna Zhelezopolskaia were neglecting church order and the liturgy in that they celebrated the ritual for first-time marriages for digamists[22], were saying prayers for third marriages without the tithe collector's fee and certificate, and paid no taxes to the tithe collectors. Others, ignoring the canons, said prayers for many people for their fourth and fifth marriages, representing them as digamists and trigamists. They performed marriages for people who were close relations, godparents, in-laws and legally divorced. Husbands, not knowing any better, dismissed their legal wives and took other wives, and the dismissed women were married other husbands. The abbots and priests uncanonically sanctioned such marriages with crowning and prayers because they had no fear of God. Many abbots and priests arrived from the metropolitan see and from other bishops and served in the Novgorod archdiocese, in the Ustiug deanery, without the knowledge or blessing of the Novgorod archbishop. Others again were ordained as priests and deacons for the Ustiug deanery by the metropolitan and other bishops without the advice, order or ordination certificate of the Novgorod archbishop. They were made priests and deacons under false pretenses, and fraudulently obtained their letters of commendation[23] from the metropolitan and bishops, not showing these ordination and commendation letters to the Novgorod archbishop or his tithe collectors. Still others officiated with neither ordination nor commendation letters. Were a priest or deacon widowed, after being tonsured he served the liturgy in churches of his own volition, without the archbishop's affidavit, inquest, knowledge or blessing. If for similar reasons the tithe collector placed abbots, priests and deacons under a surety bond and set the date for their appearance at the archbishop's tribunal, they would not appear in court or post bond. They beat the tithe collectors and cursed with unseemly swearing.

REFORMS OF THE COUNCIL OF 1551

At the church council in 1551[24] the tsar gave the bishops a list of irregularities and demanded their cooperation in putting a stop to them. "In the churches," it was stated, "bells shall be rung and the singing will be according to the typikon.[25] Deans shall be placed over all priests. The bestowal of antimensia[26] is turning into a large sale. Icons are painted improperly. There should not be a large fee when marriage certificates are issued to Christians. Scribes copied divine books from incorrect translations without correcting the copies. Teachers teach letters carelessly. At the episcopal tribunals boyars, secretaries, agents, tithe collectors and constables do not judge or administer justice uprightly. They prolong trials and impose fines together with the court heralds. The tithe collectors impose fines on priests in the villages without pity and they invent cases with the heralds. Women and maidens plotting with the judge falsely accuse monks, priests and laymen of rape and abuse. In the monasteries some are tonsured for their bodily comfort so that they may always carouse. Archimandrites and some abbots are strangers to the divine service, the refectory and the brotherhood; they take refuge in their cells with guests, they accommodate their relatives in the monastery and satisfy them with the monastery's things. The same occurs in the villages, where they bring women and girls into their cells, young boys live in all the cells, but poor brethren go hungry and thirsty and find no refuge. The authorities keep all the monastery wealth with their relatives, boyars, guests, acquaintances and friends.

"Monks and nuns roam about the world, nuns live like parish altar bread bakers, and monks live in parish churches like priests. The altar bread bakers speak incantations over the altar breads. Alms and the annual maintenance, bread, salt, money and clothing are distributed from the tsar's treasury to the hospices in all the towns, and Christ-lovers likewise donate alms yet freemen and their wives buy their way into the hospices from the stewards while the truly poor, sick and disabled go about the world neglected.

"Monks and nuns, priests and laymen, men and women go in procession with images and collect for building a church, to the marvel of foreigners.

Should there indeed be charters of legal exemption?[27] Possessions are handed over to monasteries yet there is never any construction in the monasteries, and old foundations become derelict. Who is making a profit? It must be decided whether it is proper for monasteries to lend money at interest. Monks and priests become drunkards. Widowed priests lead others into sin by their behavior, they remain in the churches and conduct all the occasional rituals but do not serve the liturgy. An elder monk erects a cell or builds a log church in the forest, and he walks about the world with an icon begging on behalf of his building. He asks the tsar for land and benefice, but what he collects he drinks.

"We must elect worthy abbots and priests. People stand in churches in their skull-caps and headgear with their walking canes, there is talk and murmuring and all sorts of swearing and conversations and shameful words. The priests and deacons drink to excess, the minor clergy[28] are always drunk, and they stand without fear and quarrel. The priests scuffle among themselves in the churches and also in the monasteries. The priests and deacons celebrate the liturgy without their vestments. Sextons and cantors who are twice or thrice married enter the sanctuary and touch the holy objects. They shave their heads and beards and wear the clothing of non-Orthodox lands. They make the sign of the cross without rhyme or reason. They swear oaths lightly and quarrel with churlish words. Even among the non-Orthodox such outrages are not committed. They swear falsely, using God's name. Beneficed priests do not fulfill their obligations. Strangled animals are sold.[29] Christians bring kutia[30] to church on a vigil and on Easter they bring paskhas,[31] cheese, eggs, baked fish while on other days they bring fancy bread, pies, pancakes, karavai[32] and all types of vegetables. In Novgorod and Pskov a side table[33] was built in every church for this, but in Moscow these foods are brought to the prothesis in the sanctuary itself.[34] In monasteries monks, nuns and laity live together. Captives must be ransomed from Muslim hands."

In order to satisfy the tsar's demands the council passed the following resolution concerning deans in Moscow. "One hundred priests, or as the number warrants," it read, "will elect one priest who is filled with spiritual understanding, is zealous for the divine writings and adorned with every virtue. He shall choose his own assistants. There shall be one dean for the churches in an area so that the priests more opportunely can assemble to deliberate about church ceremonies, spiritual matters and every devotional ceremony. Seven collegiate churches and seven deans are to be established in Moscow. The elected deans shall be brought to the metropolitan, who will examine and instruct them. The deans and the priests shall keep in the collegiate church a complete collection of canon law, which the deans are to consult constantly, and hold meetings about all spiritual matters in the presence of the priests and deacons assembled in their collegiate church. They shall settle all cases according to the canons of the Holy Fathers and if there be some doubt they shall inform the common pastor and teacher, the metropolitan."

Regarding church decorum and the morality of the clergy, the council decreed that the church building and altar furnishings must be beautiful, clean and unsullied. No comestibles or any other objects may be brought to the altar and sanctuary except icons, crosses, sacred vessels, chasubles, veils, candles, incense, altar breads, oil and liturgical wine. Care shall be taken that the third veil or aer[35] covers the sacred vessels without fail. The altar shall not be without a cover nor the royal doors be without curtains.

Among the simple lay folk children are born in cauls and it was the custom to bring these cauls to the priests, who placed them on the altar until the sixth week.[36] The council decreed that henceforth such impurity and abomination must not be brought into the holy church.

The council decreed that "altar bread bakers must be widows of one husband, at least fifty years old and with a reputation for good works. They must on no account pronounce any words over the altar breads. Nuns could not live as altar bread bakers in parish churches. The council decreed that the church bell must be rung according to the typikon. Priests must urge their spiritual children to go to church more often, especially on Sundays and the Lord's holidays. In the churches the priests must show themselves an example of every virtue, piety and sobriety. Likewise at banquets, at public gatherings and in all worldly conversations priests must converse in a spiritual way and instruct in every virtue, using the divine writings. On no account shall they engage in vain words, blasphemy, cursing and telling jokes, and they are to forbid their spiritual children to do the same. Where there are psalteries, pipers and rowdy amusements priests must keep their distance, go home and on no account dare partake of such things themselves. Priests must conduct the church services in an orderly fashion, wearing their vestments.

"All the town priests and deacons are obliged to show their charters of privileges and letters of ordination, blessing and commendation to each new tithe collector in the presence of the deans and local elders and the sworn officials who sit with the tithe collectors in court, but they pay no fees for these documents. When a priest or deacon does not have such documents he shall be sent to the spiritual authorities for surety. Assistant priests and local elders shall examine the documents of village priests and deacons. For greater support of the faith all bishops will send to the clergy and to all Orthodox Christians in all towns and villages good and experienced collegiate priests so that the church ceremonies and divine singing be performed according to the typikon. The bishops likewise must send documents to the archimandrites, abbots and archpriests, commissioning them to observe the behavior of the deans and assistants and all the clergy."

Relating to our observations about the fulfillment of the council's prescriptions, we have a copy of a document from 1552 issued to Bersenev and Tiutin. "In keeping with the sacred canons and the council's code," it states, "those in the priestly and monastic ranks are forbidden to enter taverns, get drunk, use idle talk, and quarrel. If any priests, deacons and monks go to taverns, get drunk, stumble about inebriated in the courtyards and streets, curse, quarrel using obscene language and scuffle, you are to seize such disorderly clerics and impose the tsar's penalty on them according to local custom, as is imposed on ordinary carousers. Send the monks to the archimandrites and abbots in their monasteries, who shall discipline them according to the monastery's rule. Send the priests and deacons to their deans, who will inform the bishops. These shall correct them according to the sacred canons. If you cannot collect the penalty from a monk, collect the penalty from whoever made him drunk. Order it proclaimed in the marketplaces that Orthodox Christians, from the small to the great, must not swear falsely using God's name, falsely kiss the cross or quarrel using obscene words. They must not upbraid father or mother with filthy words, neither shall they shave their beards and crop them, or trim their mustaches. They must not go to soothsayers, sorcerers and astrologers, and there must be no sorcerers at duels."

The kinds of measures used to correct church ministers forgetful of their duties are likewise evident from the following tale of the Novgorod chronicler under the year 1572. Archbishop Leonid commanded the clerks to put his cantors in the stocks and ordered the collection of one Moscow poltina[37] from each because they did not come to church at the beginning of the service.

Concerning the painting of icons the council resolved that iconographers must paint icons following ancient models, just as Greek iconographers, Andrei Rublev[38] and other prestigious iconographers painted, and they were to alter nothing of the model's concept. "Archbishops and bishops shall test master iconographers in all the towns, villages and monasteries, and shall examine their paintings personally. Each will select a few iconographers in his own district who are acclaimed masters, and will instruct them to supervise all iconographers, that there are no bad and tasteless painters among them. The archbishops and bishops personally shall observe the chosen iconographers and keep a strict watch, and they shall protect the iconographers and honor them more than simple people. Magnates and simple people likewise must honor the iconographers in everything."

Concerning the depiction of the saints there was a curious occurrence in Pskov in 1540. Around the feast of the Dormition some monks, travelers from another land, brought an image of St. Nicholas and St. Piatnitsa[39] carved on icon cases. Such carved icons never were seen in Pskov before, and many ignorant people held this for idolatrous veneration. There was loud clamor and commotion among the people. The simple people told the priests, and the priests went to the vicegerents and clerks of council because of the great commotion among the people. They seized the monks and sent the icons to the archbishop in Novgorod. Archbishop Makary himself prayed before these holy icons, sang a solemn prayer service for them with many priests and showed them honor. He accompanied them personally to the boat and ordered the people of Pskov to barter for the icons from the monks, and greet them with a church procession.

To the tsar's complaint that pupils were careless about learning to read and write, the council responded, "The bishops interrogate candidates severely about why they know how to read and write so poorly. They answer, 'We learn how from our fathers or our masters, but there is nowhere for us to go to learn more.' Yet their fathers and masters themselves barely know how to read and write, whereas formerly in Moscow, Novgorod and in the other towns there were many schools where letters, writing, singing and reading were taught. Following the tsar's advice we as a council have legislated that we must select good priests, deacons and minor clerics who are married, pious and literate, versed in reading and writing, and set up schools in their homes. They shall teach children using every spiritual admonition, and most of all they must guard and protect their charges in all purity and preserve them from every corruption, but especially from the disgusting sin of sodomy and from masturbation."

In Novgorod priests, deacons, minor clerics, sextons, altar bread bakers and wardens accepted their church posts for large sums. For a sexton about fifteen rubles were collected, and sometimes twenty or thirty rubles. If someone gave money the people went with him to the archbishop as one street and presented him for the post. When the bishop sent to a church a priest of good behavior who was versed in reading and writing but who gave no substantial money to the wardens, they would not accept him. As a result of these abuses, the regulation about the election of parish priests was enacted.

Concerning ecclesiastical courts the council decreed, "The bishops themselves shall try in council according to the sacred canons the entire priestly and monastic order in all ecclesiastical matters and other cases except murder and flagrant robbery, using torture and investigation. Those whom the bishops appoint as judges may try them, but these judges cannot be laymen. If in the monasteries the archimandrites, abbots and founders have charters from the tsar where it is recorded that bishops may not judge archimandrites, abbots, priests, monks or any minor ecclesiastic, these charters were issued contrary to the sacred canons and no longer shall be valid. If members of the priestly or monastic rank happen to sue laymen for damages, they shall file suit before civil judges with whom there must be episcopal judges, decade priests[40] and local elders. Kissing the cross and the judicial duel shall not be admitted in the court, which shall use only the judicial inquiry. When there are no witnesses and an inquiry proves impossible, lots are to be drawn. He who draws the longest straw wins the case. Kissing the cross and duels shall not be used to ascertain guilt or innocence of a priest or monk in any cases except murder and flagrant robbery. For such accusations the civil judges will judge according to civil laws.

"The tsar's majordomos and clerks will manage the monasteries and monastic treasuries and make a record for all monasteries. They will instruct the archimandrites, abbots and founders with the council elders, and they will audit the archimandrites, abbots and founders with respect to all income and expenditures, so that the episcopal court remains blameless. If the metropolitan is sick he will order the bishop of Saray and the Don to judge in his place, together with all the archimandrites and abbots, but the metropolitan's boyars shall not sit on this episcopal tribunal, except for the scribes whose business is to record the proceedings. After he has judged in council and investigated with trustworthy witnesses, the bishop will place the court record before the metropolitan and present both plaintiffs to him. After he has listened to the record and asked the plaintiffs if this was their suit, the metropolitan will decide the case in council according to the sacred canons.

"If those lodging a complaint about the legal proceedings submit a petition against spiritual pastors, archimandrites and abbots of great and respected monasteries, the bishops shall not send their constables for them nor put them under surety bond. They will send to them their personal charters with their own seals, along with these plaintiffs, that they may settle with them, taking from each plaintiff a surety bond so that they appear on time if they do not settle. The archimandrites and abbots shall determine the time limits in their commissioning charters in keeping with the tsar's statute charters and charters of privilege, excepting spiritual matters. The plaintiffs must return the commissioning charters to the archimandrites and abbots in front of the brethren in assembly. Should the archimandrites and abbots not settle with the plaintiffs let them send their servants in their stead to the defense, but if they wish to defend themselves, they are free to do so.

"In spiritual matters the archimandrites and abbots will attend the defense as the bishops order them. In the event of disobedience the bailiff shall be sent after them with subpoenas, and present them before the bishop. The tsar's boyars and majordomos and the metropolitan's and bishop's boyars shall not prosecute abbots, abbesses and founders for any charges. The bishops themselves will judge them according to the sacred canons, except that bishops shall instruct their boyars to prosecute priests, deacons and all the parish clergy and laymen on charges pertaining to goods and chattels, altercations, robberies and all other matters except spiritual concerns on the basis of contracts, testaments and indentures. The deans, two fiftymen and three tenmen on weekly rotation, and the town elders, sworn officials and the local crown secretary whom the sovereign so orders shall sit on the boyar's tribunal. The boyars shall lay the court record before the bishops and arraign both petitioners. The bishops, having heard the record, shall ask both petitioners if this was their suit. When they say that it was so, the bishops, having discussed the record with experienced men, shall order that justice be administered and fines collected from the guilty party.

"Where previously during the time of the great miracle workers Peter, Alexis and Jonas[41] there used to be tithe collectors who managed and tried the entire priestly and monastic rank, all parish clergy and other people in every matter except the spiritual, now let the tithe collectors continue to judge,but with them on the tribunal there shall be deans, tenmen, local elders, sworn officials and local crown secretaries. They will mete justice according to the trial and investigation, without bribes and without delays.

They will not set the times for priests and deacons to appear at duels or cross-kissings without the bishop's knowledge. If unable to decide a given case they shall set a date for both petitioners to appear before the bishop. Tithe collectors may not manage taverns, but they may keep drink for themselves. Local elders, sworn officials, deans and decade priests must oversee the behavior of tithe collectors and in the event of abuse they must write to the bishop. If the bishop does not admonish them, they shall write to the tsar. Then the tithe collector shall suffer extreme disfavor from the tsar, and he will make threefold restitution for what he wrongly took. The tithe collectors may release an accused on bail only with the deans and decade priests or the local elders and sworn officials, taking nothing of the surety or tribute. Church or crown clerks shall record the investigations in the presence of the tenmen, elders and sworn officials. The local elders, deans and the decade priests must collect the bishop's tribute, the tithe collector's duties, the maintenance, the visitation tax and marriage fees according to the books which the bishop sends them. They collect one altyn as the marriage fee for the first wedding, two altyns for the second wedding, and three or four for the third wedding."

Concerning disorder in the hospices, the council answered, "Let the pious tsar command that all the sick and aged in every town be listed separately from the healthy poor, and let there be erected in every town hospices for men and for women where the sick, the aged and the homeless may be satisfied with food and clothing. Let the lovers of God bring them alms and all needful things. Appoint as many healthy poor and nurses as are suitable to look after them. Good priests, sworn officials or good townsmen are to see to it that they suffer neither violence nor injury from the nurses. The priests must come to visit them in the hospices and instruct them in the fear of God, so that they live in purity and repentance. They shall perform all the liturgical services there. Healthy beggars and their wives are not to live in the hospices, but be fed by the lovers of God as they pass from manor to manor. If any are able to work, they should work."

Concerning the ransoming of captives the council answered, "If the tsar's envoys to the Golden Horde, to Constantinople, the Crimea, Kazan or Astrakhan ransom captives or themselves are ransomed, all these captives are to be ransomed using the tsar's treasury. When Greeks, Turks, Armenians or other wholesale merchants ransom any captive Orthodox Christians, bring them to Moscow but then wish to take them out of Moscow, they shall not be allowed to do so. Stand firm and ransom the captives from the tsar's treasury. The amount of ransom paid out of the tsar's treasury must be recouped from the plow tax throughout the land, and what anyone pays is all the same because such ransoming is known as common almsgiving." When the articles of the council resolutions were sent to the Trinity-St. Sergius monastery, to Joseph the former metropolitan, Alexis the former archbishop of Rostov, Vassian the former archimandrite of the Miracles monastery, Jonas the former abbot of the Trinity monastery and all the members of the consecrated assembly, they confirmed the articles, but wrote concerning the ransom of captives, "Do not collect the ransom from the plow taxes, but from the archbishops and monasteries rather than have the peasants, sovereign tsar, shoulder the burden. In your taxes, Sire, show them mercy."

Having prohibited without specific details the remaining irregularities mentioned by the tsar, the council turned its attention to certain improprieties and superstitions. "Minstrels play at weddings. When the wedding party drives to the church to be wed the priest rides with the cross but in front of him the minstrels rove with their satanic games. Some do not litigate properly and, having borne false witness, they kiss the cross or the holy icons, fight a duel and shed blood. During this time sorcerers and magicians render them assistance. They beat tambourines, look at *Aristotle's Gates*[42] and astrology books, gaze among the stars and planets and observe days and hours. Hoping in such sorcery, the slanderers and defamers are not reconciled; instead they kiss the cross, and fight duels and kill. Men and women, monks and nuns are forbidden to wash themselves in a common bath. This observance is decreed in Pskov. Minstrels travel around remote areas, gathering into large throngs of sixty, seventy and one hundred. They travel from village to village extorting food and drink at peasants' homes, stealing property from storerooms and badly injuring people on the roads.

"Junior boyars and boyar servants and all revelers play dice and drink away their earnings. They do not serve their duty, they do not earn their living, and every sort of evil is done by them. They steal, assault and murder. Wandering about hamlets and villages are false prophets, peasant men, women and maidens and old peasant women, naked and barefoot, who let their hair grow long and unkempt. They shake and beat themselves, and they say that St. Piatnitsa and St. Anastasia appeared to them and ordered them to tell Christians to keep vigils. They command Christians not to perform manual labor on Wednesdays and Fridays and order women not to spin, wash clothes or kindle fire with stones." The council forbade people to devote themselves to wicked heresies and listed them as astrology books, *The Six Wings*,[43] augury, astronomy, zodiacs, almanacs, astrology, Aristotle, *Aristotle's Gates* and other fabrications, and

heretical wisdom and demonic deceptions. It armed itself against superstitions, already well-known to us, to which the people yielded on Trinity
Saturday, St. John's Day, Holy Thursday and so on.

MONASTIC IRREGULARITIES

The type of violence against the weak which the powerful permitted
themselves is evident in the day-to-day life of the landowner and peasant.
The complaint of the abbot and brethren of the monastery of St. Cyril of
Beloozero sent to the tsar against the monk Alexander shows what liberties
a bold man could take, even in a monastery. "Sire," it read, "this Alexander
does not live in keeping with the monastery typikon. He does not go to
church, but builds a hermitage where he lives more than in the monastery,
depletes the monastery, takes all manner of supplies from the treasury,
cellars and drying rooms, flour and malt from the mills and grains from the
villages, and sends it to his hermitage. When he arrives at the monastery,
he berates the abbot and brethren as sons of b. . . .[44] He has driven other
monks out of church and sent them to the sea. He stabs with a pick and beats
with a lash the remaining brotherhood of priests and choir monks without
the advice of the abbot or elders, and he puts them in fetters and irons.

"He was a superior in Moscow without a servant for seven years, but
gave no account in the monastery's treasury. After the Great Canon[45] he
drinks with gusto in the cellar with those whom he invites to the hermitage.
He threatens to put the brothers in fetters and irons until death. To you, Sire,
he will bear false testimony against the elders and the whole brotherhood,
and the brethren run away from his blows and threats. O Orthodox sovereign tsar! Instruct us how to put up with Alexander.

"Order an inquiry into his hermitage and way of life. He is ruining the
common life at St. Cyril's. He keeps his own servants and horses, and
carries with him quivers, sabers and guns. He trades in salt for his own gain,
and his boats sail separately from the monastery boats."

For his part Tsar Ivan rebuked the monks for paying far too much
attention to noble monastics, saying that in order to please them they were
destroying the ancient and strict monastic rules. "It behooves you," he
writes in his famous missive[46] to the monastery of St. Cyril of Beloozero,
"to follow diligently the great miracle worker St. Cyril, to adhere firmly to
his tradition, to struggle bravely for truth and not to be fugitives. Do not
throw down the shield, but take up the whole armor of God. Do not
surrender the miracle worker's tradition for the sake of voluptuousness, as
Judas surrendered Christ for the sake of silver. You have your own Annas

and Caiaphas,[47] Sheremetev and Khabarov,[48] your own Pilate, Varlaam Sobakin[49] and you even have Christ crucified, the scorned tradition of the miracle worker. Holy fathers! If you admit relaxation in a small thing, great evil results. Thus, owing to the laxity of Sheremetev and Khabarov the miracle worker's tradition has been ruined among you. If God favors our being tonsured in your midst, the monastery will no longer exist, but in its place will be the tsar's court!

"Why therefore become a monk, why say you renounce the world and everything in the world? He who is tonsured makes a vow to obey the abbot, to listen to the brothers and to love them. As for Sheremetev, how can he call the monks his brothers? He even has a tenth slave[50] who lives in his cell and eats better than the brothers who eat in the refectory. Great luminaries such as Sergius and Cyril, Varlaam, Dmitry, Pafnuty[51] and many other saints in the Russian land established firm rules for monastic life and taught the way of salvation. Then the boyars who come to you introduced their own voluptuous rules as though it were not they who were tonsured by you, but you who have been tonsured by them. It is not you who are their teachers and lawgivers, they are yours. Indeed, Sheremetev's typikon is good, so keep it, and Cyril's typikon is bad, so abandon it! Today one boyar introduces a certain passion, tomorrow another introduces yet another weakness, and thus little by little the whole monastic way of life becomes empty, and there will be worldly customs.

"The founders originally established a solid life in all the monasteries, but after them voluptuaries have destroyed it. St. Cyril the miracle worker was in St. Simon's monastery, and after him St. Sergius, and the rule was what kind? Read it in the life of the miracle worker! Then someone introduced a minor vice, others introduced new vices and now what do we see in St. Simon's? Except for some secret servants of God, the rest are monks merely by virtue of their clothing, and everything is done in a worldly way. You have built a church over Vorotynsky.[52] Good! A church over Vorotynsky, but there is no church over the miracle worker. Vorotynsky is in the church but the miracle worker is outside. At the Savior's dread judgment Vorotynsky and Sheremetev shall be more exalted, Vorotynsky by reason of the church, Sheremetev by reason of the rule, since his rule is more powerful than Cyril's.

"Look! As far as we can see boyars are not tonsured at the monastery of St. Dionisy Glushitsky[53] or at the monastery of the great miracle worker St. Alexander Svirsky,[54] yet those monasteries are flourishing with ascetical feats. For behold, first you gave pewter vessels to Joseph the Wise for his cell, and you gave the same to Serapion Sitsky and Jonas Ruchkin, but to Sheremetev you gave a table and kitchen. If you are going to give free rein to the tsar, then give free rein to the huntsman as well; if you are going to show indulgence to the magnate, show it to the simple peasant too. Vassian Sheremetev has subverted ascetical life at the Trinity-St. Sergius monastery; so now his son Jonas is trying to extinguish the last lamp which shines equal to the sun. He wants to uproot the ascetical life in his own hermitage at St. Cyril's monastery as well. In the world this same Sheremetev and Viskovaty[55] were the first to stop walking in solemn processions. Observing them, others all stopped taking part in processions, whereas previously all Orthodox Christians with their wives and children walked in the processions and did not do any trading except in foodstuffs. If anyone traded, a fine was collected from him.

"Previously when we visited St. Cyril's monastery as a youth and came late to dinner, the monk in charge of our table asked the sub-cellarer for sterlet and other fish. The sub-cellarer answered, 'There are no instructions for me concerning this, but I have prepared food according to the instruction. It is now nightfall and there is nowhere to get these fish. I fear my sovereign but I must fear God more.' Such was your fortitude, in keeping with the prophet's word, 'Even before kings I shall not be ashamed for justice's sake.' Now you have Sheremetev who sits in his cell like a tsar, Khabarov comes to him with other monks, and they eat and drink as if they were in the world.

"God only knows from which wedding or relatives he gets them, but Sheremetev sends pastilles, honey cakes and other spicy foods from cell to cell. Instead of a monastery he has a court, and in his court are sundry supplies for a year. Yet you watch such outrageous conduct in silence! Certain people say that they even brought distilled spirits into Sheremetev's cell on the sly, yet in monasteries it is shameful to keep even Frankish wines, to say nothing of distilled spirits! Is this the path of salvation, is this the monastic sojourn? Or is it that you had nothing with which to feed Sheremetev, so that he has his own supplies for a year?

"My dear friends! Previously St. Cyril's monastery fed many regions during famines but now even in time of plenty you would all die of hunger if Sheremetev did not provide for you! Is it proper that you feast in St. Cyril's as Metropolitan Joseph feasted with the choir monks in the Trinity monastery, or that you live like magnates as Misail Sukin lived in Nikitsk monastery and in other places, or as Jonas Motiakin and many others are living? Is this the path of salvation, that the boyar does not tonsure away his boyar status and the slave is not rid of his slavery? During our father's time the cellarer at the Trinity monastery was Nifont, a slave of Riapolovsky, but he ate from the same plate as Belsky. Now the boyars in all the monasteries have rendered the brotherhood meaningless through their voluptuousness.

"I will tell you something even more frightful. When Peter the fisherman and the village farmer John the Theologian and all twelve paupers stand to judge on behalf of the all-powerful tsars who ruled the universe, will you present your Cyril as if he were equal with Sheremetev? Which is greater? Sheremetev was tonsured from the boyar status, but Cyril was not even in the sovereign's chancellery! Do you see where your laxity has led you? Sergius, Cyril, Varlaam, Dmitry and many other saints did not pursue boyars; boyars sought them out and their monasteries expanded. The reason is that monasteries stand on their virtue and do not fall into decline. Virtue ran dry at the Trinity-St. Sergius monastery and the monastery is in decline. No one will be tonsured there and no one will donate anything. Furthermore to what state have they come at St. Sabbas the Guardian monastery?[56] There is already no one to lock up the monastery, grass is growing about the refectory, but we previously saw up to eighty brothers there and eleven choir monks used to stand on either side of the choir.

"If someone says that Sheremetev is genuinely ill and that he needs a dispensation, let him eat alone in his cell with his cell-monk,[57] but why the gatherings, why the feasting, why the vegetables in his cell? Until now you did not even keep extra needles and thread in St. Cyril's monastery, to say nothing of other things. Why the residence outside the monastery and the supplies? All of that is lawlessness, not necessity; but if there is need, let him eat in his cell like a poor man. In addition to bread, let him have a fish steak and a cup of kvas. Beyond this (if you are lenient) give as much as you want, but he should eat alone, and there should be no meetings and feasts, so that everything will be as it was before in your monastery.

"Let no one go to him for spiritual conversation during refectory time, and let there be no food or drink; in this way it will indeed be a spiritual conversation. If his brothers send memorial gifts, he should send them away to the monastery liturgies and not keep any objects in his cell. He should divide whatever they send him among all the brethren, not among two or three on the basis of friendship and partiality. You shall satisfy him with everything in the monastery cell, provided that it does not arouse the passions.

"His servitors should not live near the monastery for they will come from his brothers with charters, supplies and memorial gifts. Let them depart after they have spent two or three days and received a charter in reply. Thus shall he have peace, and the monastery will be freed from disturbance. Now you have sent letters and we have no rest from you over Sheremetev. I wrote to you that Sheremetev and Khabarov should eat in the refectory with the brothers. I commanded this for the sake of the monastery's discipline, but Sheremetev pretends to be in disgrace. Perhaps you have such pity for Sheremetev and you stand up for him so forcefully because his brothers still correspond with the Crimea and direct Islam against Christianity?

"Yet Khabarov orders me to transfer him to another monastery. I shall not be an advocate for him or his disgusting way of life; I am utterly sick of him. The monastic life is not a little game. Three days a monk, and he changes to his seventh monastery! When he was in the world he knew only too well what it was to frame icons, to bind books in velvet with silver clasps and scarab-like embossing, to adorn lecterns, to live in seclusion, set up a cell, beads in his hands. Yet now he does not want to eat with the brethren. Beads are needed not on tablets of stone, but on the tablets of human hearts. I myself have seen how they revile each other with filthy words on the beads. What is in those beads? There is nothing for me to write about Khabarov. Let him be a fool if that is what he wants. Sheremetev says that I am familiar with his illness! You cannot violate the holy canons for the sake of every malingerer!

"I have written to you a little of many things, out of love for you and the monastic life. There is nothing more to write. Do not bore us any more with Sheremetev and other such nonsense for we shall give no reply. You know yourself that if virtue is not necessary and vice is pleasant, then even if you forge golden vessels for Sheremetev and set him up like a king you know what will result. Establish with Sheremetev your own traditions, but set aside those of the miracle worker and all will be well. Do whatever is better. You know yourselves what you want with him, but it is none of my business one way or the other. Stop pestering us with this. I tell you that I shall answer nothing. May God and peace, and the mercy of the most holy Mother of God and the prayers of the miracle worker St. Cyril be with all of you and with us! Amen. We bow our heads before you, my lords and fathers, to the very face of the earth!"

In the monasteries of Novgorod, throughout the period we are describing, the common life continued to be introduced at the insistence of the bishops. The phrase "to occupy a community" was the current phrase, meaning "to establish the common life."

The metropolitan and bishops had their own boyars to whom they entrusted the ecclesiastical tribunal. The council of 1551 resolved that without the tsar's knowledge the metropolitans and bishops were not to dismiss their boyars and majordomos and put others in their place, except when these boyars and majordomos repeatedly were accused of bribery, for then they were to be deprived of their offices and estates. Were boyars and majordomos transferred away from any bishop, he should choose new ones from the same families. When there was no one to choose from those families, he was to choose replacements from other families having informed the tsar. If the bishop could not find anyone capable he was to petition the tsar so that the sovereign might favor and choose someone from his own household; likewise bishops would keep clerics with the tsar's knowledge. As for their maintenance, the bishop's boyars evidently received service estates from the tsar as well, for Archbishop Leonid of Novgorod, having given an estate to his boyar Fomin in 1574 writes in the charter, "This service estate is given for as long as his sovereign pleases and orders to grant an estate here in Great Novgorod."

CHURCH AND MONASTIC PROPERTY

At the council of 1551 the important question about church real estate was raised once again. For the first time it was decided to impose certain limits on the increase of such property. The council decreed that archbishops, bishops and monasteries henceforth not purchase patrimonies from anyone without the tsar's knowledge and validation charter, and that no princes, junior boyars or servitors sell their patrimonies without a validation charter. "If anyone buys or sells without a validation charter the buyer forfeits the money and the seller forfeits his patrimony. The sovereign shall confiscate the patrimony without money changing hands. Patrimonies given then or later to monasteries as a memorial for souls shall not be redeemed by anyone under any circumstances. If on surrendering patrimonies to a monastery a donor writes in his testament, letter of donation or some other charter that his relatives may redeem it for a specific sum of money, let the relatives redeem it according to ancient custom, as was done during the time of the sovereign's father and grandfather."

In some instances the bishops or monasteries evicted junior boyars or peasants from the tsar's service estates or free lands on account of debt. Elsewhere the scribes assigned such lands to the church out of indulgence.

"If bishops or monasteries made woodland settlements on such land belonging to the sovereign there must be an investigation to ascertain the original owners of the land, after which their titles shall be confirmed. Return villages, rural districts, fisheries, profit-making lands and rental villages given by the boyars to bishops and monasteries after the time of Grand Prince Vasily. Do the same with benefices and charitable gifts endowed to monasteries and churches after the time of Grand Prince Vasily. Likewise donations converted from temporary to permanent status must be turned back into temporary ones. In Tver, Mikulin, Torzhok, Obolensk, Beloozero and Riazan the princes of Suzdal, Yaroslavl and Starodub shall not give patrimonies to monasteries as memorials for their souls without the sovereign's validation. If they donate them, take the patrimony from the monastery for the sovereign without cash payment. Seize for the sovereign those patrimonies surrendered without the sovereign's validation before the present stipulation, but pay cash for them in keeping with their measurement and give them over as service estates."

In 1573 following the sovereign's instruction, Metropolitan Anthony,[58] the entire consecrated assembly and all the boyars stipulated that "henceforth no patrimonies shall be donated to great monasteries where there are many patrimonies. If a patrimony has been bequeathed already, do not register it in the Chancellery of Military Tenures, but return it to the family and clan for their servitors, so that there is no loss in service, and the land does not leave service. Henceforth patrimony owners shall not redeem monastery patrimonies. If someone gives a patrimony to small monasteries which have little land, those patrimonies must be registered after the circumstances have been explained to the sovereign."

In 1580 a more decisive step was taken in the conciliar resolution reached on January 15. "Because of the impending barbarian menace," it said, "from the Turks, the Crimean and Nogay Tatars and from the Lithuanian king with whom Poland, the Hungarians and foreigners in Livonia and Sweden[59] have allied themselves in violent fashion, have united like ferocious beasts, puffed themselves up haughtily and intend to extirpate Orthodoxy. In order that the churches of God and the holy places be without disturbance, and the military rank take up arms mightily for the battle against the enemies of the cross of Christ we, Anthony, metropolitan of all Russia and Ivan Vasilievich, pious tsar and grand prince of all Russia, together with his son Grand Prince Ivan Ivanovich, the entire consecrated assembly and the tsar's council have decreed that the metropolitan, dioceses and monasteries shall not be required to withdraw from any lands and profit-making possessions they have been given up until now. These properties shall not be seized or redeemed on the basis of any judgement or lawsuit. What has not been confirmed by deeds cannot be redeemed, and monasteries no longer may be sued over patrimonies.

"From this day forward, January 15 and subsequently, patrimony holders shall not hand over their patrimonies as a memorial for their souls. Instead they shall give the monasteries money for their memorials, and their heirs shall take the villages even if they are only distantly related. If someone does not have even a distant relative, take the patrimony for the sovereign and pay money from the treasury for it.

"The metropolitan, the bishops and the monasteries shall not buy lands or hold them in mortgage, but if anyone after this statute buys land or keeps a mortgage for himself, take the land for the sovereign. If any mortgaged properties are held now by the metropolitan, bishops and monasteries, seize them for the sovereign. How he will favor his intercessors in money, God and the sovereign know. If any princely patrimonies were donated previously, God and the sovereign are at liberty to determine how to favor his intercessors. Henceforth no one may take princely patrimonies. If someone takes such property without the sovereign's knowledge, seize those patrimonies for the sovereign without payment. If anyone has bought princely patrimonies, seize these as well for the sovereign, and God and the sovereign know how he will favor his intercessors with money. If any poor monastery has little land or none at all, let the monastery petition the sovereign who, deciding conjointly with the metropolitan and boyars, may furnish the monastery with such land as shall be suitable."

Concerning the taxes from the clergy for the use of the bishops the council of 1551, in answer to a complaint of the Novgorod priests, abolished the holiday tax of one altyn per priest and three dengas per deacon. The Novgorod archbishop was permitted to take no more than the previous amount from the monasteries and town priests for the transportation tax. Evidently the clergy also assisted the bishops in the construction and repair of their homes. The Pskov chronicler says under the year 1535 that "they began to build the bishop's palace in Pskov, but the priests did not offer any assistance at all, whereas the monasteries, covered the upper rooms with moss and built the summer bedroom." The Pskov clergy gave the Novgorod archbishop maintenance when he travelled to Pskov. For this reason the chronicler relates for the year 1544 that "Bishop Feodosy came to Pskov and the village and bytown priests were separated from the town priests in all seven deaneries because the town priests were collecting a larger maintenance than they themselves paid, and there was a great commotion. The bishop gave them their own dean."

In the "Hundred Chapters," that is, in the decrees of the council of 1551, we read "In Moscow at the metropolitan's manor a perpetual administrative tax is collected, called a 'crossing.'[60] The archimandrites, abbots, archpriests, monks, priests and deacons from all the towns arrive on business. While living in Moscow they meet for the 'crossing' at the marketplace in Ilyinsk street and are hired by Moscow priests to perform the liturgy in the many churches. They are presented to the metropolitan's agent and receive a license from him for one month, two months or more, and give him the fee, for a month ten dengas, and for each additional month, two altyns. If clerics do not inform the agent and begin to celebrate the liturgy, he shall collect a fine of two rubles apiece from them, but he need not investigate to see if they have installation and commendation letters." The council determined that henceforth such letters be examined.

Just as the government granted tax exemptions to the settlers and freed them from tribute during their settlement of wilderness, so too did the bishop free his parish clergy from their dues during the construction of a new church. In 1547 Bishop Cyprian of Perm and Vologda gave a charter to the abbot and brethren of St. Cyril's monastery. "They have built a new church in my diocese of Vologda," it read. "Those who serve the liturgy in their church, whether abbot, priest or deacon, need not pay my Christmas tribute, nor the donations, nor the tithe collectors' tax, nor the constables' tax, nor the stable, cook, or servitor duty, nor the tithe on the charter. They shall not be subordinate to the priest's dean with the taxpaying priests in any matter. My tithe collectors shall not judge them in anything, nor will bailiffs be sent after them, neither will our constables approach them for anything. If anyone seeks damages of any kind from them, I myself shall judge them. Abbot Afanasy and the brethren will inform me, Bishop Cyprian, themselves." From the last words it is evident that St. Cyril's monastery was obliged to give the bishop a specific recompense for the loss of income caused by the newly constructed church. Bishop Alexis of Rostov granted the same kind of charter to the Trinity-St. Sergius monastery concerning a church in the village of Berliukovo, even though evidently the church was not completely rebuilt.

In general it was advantageous for monasteries to free the clergy in the villages belonging to them from archiepiscopal taxes. In exchange they committed themselves to supply the bishop with the incomes owing him. Thus in 1542 Bishop Dionisy of Rostov sent a charter to the same Abbot

Afanasy of St. Cyril's monastery. "Priests in St. Cyril's monastery villages may perform marriages for peasants in their own parishes without the marriage license fees of our notary priest, but they shall collect the licenses in St. Cyril's monastery from the treasurer and pay the tax to the treasurer. Having collected the marriage fees, the treasurer will pay our notary priest in Beloozero." Also in 1542 the Pesnosh monastery freed the clergy of its villages in the Dmitrov district from the tribunal of the metropolitan tenmen and the bureau of priest deans. In his charter the metropolitan promised to judge the priests of these villages himself, provided they paid the specified annual quitrent to him, to his tithe collector and the diocesan tax officer. This quitrent the priests themselves brought to the metropolitan's treasury in Moscow. The tithe collectors and tax officers did not go to them, nor did they send for anything, nor did they collect the taxes for cartage or drivers.

We encounter charters of bishops concerning service obligations from their own monasteries. Archbishop Leonid of Novgorod gave such a charter to the Staraia Rusa monastery of St. Cosmas and St. Damian in 1574. "They shall give the house of the Holy Wisdom and me, for my visitation and for the tithe and for all the tithe collectors' fees, one Moscow ruble each annually in keeping with the new fixed rate. If I happen to go to Moscow at the sovereign's command, that year the monastery shall give me the visitation fee and tithe in full according to the schedule." Under the year 1571 the chronicler related an argument of Bishop Leonid of Novgorod with his priests over alms. "After his departure Bishop Leonid ordered all the priests, elders, tenmen and fiftymen of Novgorod to remove their vestments and told them, 'Dogs, thieves, traitors, and all Novgorod with you! You have slandered me to the grand prince, you submit petitions for alms money and you get six Moscow dengas each, the deacons get four Moscow dengas each. You shall not have my blessing in this world or the next!'"

MONASTERIES

Concerning the upkeep of monasteries we continue to encounter the tsar's benefice charters, private memorial requests[61] and those of the tsar, by which land parcels for the memory of souls were given to monasteries prior to the last council decision. In 1575 the tsar himself gave to his favorite monastery of St. Cyril of Beloozero two patrimonies of Boyar Prince Ivan Dmitrievich Belsky in the Rostov and Moscow districts for the repose of the prince's soul. Ivan's father gave this same monastery one thousand rubles for purchasing villages, and Ivan himself gave three hundred rubles in memory of his daughters Anna and Maria who died in infancy. Since at the council of 1551 it was stipulated that monasteries not buy patrimonies without validation certificates the abbot and brethren of St. Cyril's petitioned in 1556 for permission to purchase a patrimony with these money donations. The tsar allowed them to buy land but not for more than two thousand rubles. They could purchase land only outside the boundaries of Novgorod, Pskov, Riazan, Tver and Smolensk, and not from patrimonial princes, who were forbidden to sell their lands without the tsar's knowledge. If it turned out that the monastery paid more than two thousand rubles for a patrimony the lands must be seized for the tsar, and the monastery lose its money. Should the monastery buy empty lands or wilderness and plow them under, clear them of forest and populate them but the old patrimony owners wished to redeem these lands, they could redeem them after paying the monastery for the buildings and plowed fields. From this same charter we learn that during the reign of Ivan IV's father and early in his own reign the St. Cyril monastery held the right to trade ten thousand puds of salt, which brought it an annual income of six hundred rubles. Later Ivan took this privilege away from them.

From this period a number of statute charters have come down to us which the monasteries gave to their peasants. For example we have from the year 1548 a statute charter of the Solovetsk abbot St. Philip to the peasants of the Viremsk district and to other monastery peasants. "By the mercy of our Lord Jesus Christ and his holy Transfiguration," it begins, "of his Most Pure Mother and her Honorable and Glorious Dormition and of the miracle worker St. Nicholas and the miracle workers St. Zosima and St. Savvaty, I Abbot Philip Kolychev, having consulted with the priests, cellarer, treasurer, council elders and all the brothers, have blessed and favored our peasants. We have given them their own statute charter which details the duties of the monastic manager and cellarer and our servant the bailiff, and how to collect their own memorial dues from year to year."

For collection of these fees the peasants were divided into three ranks, those living on taxable homesteads, cotters who lived in their own dwellings, and cossacks. The first rank paid for the amount of profitable land belonging to them according to the calculation per bow.[62] If an unknown cossack or even one who formerly lived there returned and wanted to reside and earn a living in the monastic districts, he and his host must go to the manager and bailiff to present him and pay the presentation fee to both officials. If the cossack wished to depart the monastic districts his former landlord must go with him again to the manager and bailiff, present him, but pay nothing. If a cossack departed without being presented and his host did not report his departure, the manager collected from him the monastery's and his own fees. If the cossack went away, but during that time there was no manager or bailiff in the district, the landlord must show the cossack to his neighbors. If the cossack ran away without a trace the manager interrogated the landlord under oath, and if he believed him he collected nothing from him."

The manager performed the duties of judge and collected the court fees. The bailiff received a travel allowance if he had to travel for an inquest. In the event that monastery peasants took legal action against other peasants the bailiff attended court, where he must strive to protect the monastery peasants. He could not collect fees or travel money from them, but the peasant whose case was being handled must bring him and provide maintenance for him. When a peasant woman was sent to be married in a different district he who sent her away must pay the manager two altyns for the fee. When marriage was contracted between peasants of the monastery districts the manager collected one altyn from the prince and princess (from the bridal couple),[63] and when a bride was brought into the monastery district from elsewhere, he collected four Moscow dengas from the bridal couple.

If wine merchants traveled from district to district, the manager must forbid their being received in the forecourt. Neither he himself, nor the peasants nor the cossacks might buy wine from them, nor could they ferment their own. When a peasant or cossack bought some wine he paid a fine to the monastery and to the manager and bailiff. If peasants or cossacks played dice among themselves or with transient cossacks the manager collected from them a fine for the monastery, for himself and the bailiff, and ran them out of the district when any cossack played dice the manager banished him and settled the matter of the fine with whoever sheltered him in the forecourt. If the manager or bailiff injured a peasant or cossack he received due punishment from the abbot, and double the fine was exacted from him to the benefit of the injured party.

In 1561 the peasants of Puzyrev, a village of the Solovetsk monastery in the district of Bezhetsky Verkh, petitioned the same abbot because the monastery managers collected quitrent and taxes and ordered them to perform tasks not in line with the charters nor according to the fixed rate. They complained that when the manager lent out grain he took gifts and two thirds on the measure and tributes, and if grain prices were high he sold grain for cash at market value, not as a loan. As a result of the petition St. Philip granted them a statute charter in which the quitrent was defined. "For each plowland the peasants shall pay four chetverts of rye and the same amount of oats, on Lady Day [August 15] a dry cheese, on the feast of the Intercession [October 1] fifty eggs, a loaf of bread and a fancy loaf. For the manager, servant and bailiff the peasants must grind the rye for bread and prepare malt for brewing kvas. They shall bring to the monastery manor three cartloads of firewood for each plowland, and drive carts to different towns with one horse per plowland. They will pay the bailiff one Moscow grivna per plowland and three dengas per house for the visitation. The manager shall act as judge. With him at court shall be a priest and five or six good and middle-rank peasants. They shall collect their fees from the guilty party."

The charter also defined what the peasants must pay the manager and bailiff for weddings, for the sale of horses, cows and log huts. The peasants were bound also to repair the monastery manor and barn, and rebuild dwellings. They had to obey the manager in all things and go to their monastic chores at sunrise, when the tenman gave the signal. "Anyone who does not go to work shall pay the manager a fine of two dengas, and two dengas to the bailiff and tenman. If the manager summons peasants for monastery labor above and beyond the prescribed amount he must feed those who come with the monastery's grain. If any peasants have groves in their fields they are not to cut them for firewood or poles, but must preserve them; if anyone needs a pillar, strut or cross-beam he may cut down trees with the permission of the manager. If anyone cuts down a tree without written permission, he must pay a fine to the monastery. The manager shall lend the peasants grain, rye and oats without interest and not at market value, and shall take from them for the sweepings and for spillage per chetvert annually the following amounts: on rye four Moscow dengas each, and on oats two dengas each. He shall do the same even in bad harvest years.

"Peasants may exchange homesteads and lands freely and sell them, as long as they inform the manager. If anyone sells his lot or exchanges it, the manager is to collect the show tax of twenty-five copecks from both parties for the monastery. When someone sells his lot and then leaves the district the manager shall collect from him the residence tax[64] in full, and he shall collect from the buyer the sales tax, based on the land and profit-making possessions. If anyone fares poorly and wants to move out of the district but there is no buyer for his lot the manager shall collect from him the residence tax in full and release him at the appointed time."

In 1564 the elders and sworn officials and all the rural residents of the Solovetsk monastery's rural district of Suma, the village peasants and all the district and village cossacks petitioned St. Philip because of a lively disturbance among them in Suma regarding the apportionment of the tax burden and all fiscal service obligations. The abbot, having consulted with his brethren, wrote them this edict. "When you conduct the apportionment of the tax burden in the district you shall elect two of the best men, from the middle men two, from the lower men two, and from the cossacks two men. These eight men shall sit on your assessment board and assess the peasants and the cossacks in divine justice, determining what is suitable for whom and who is deserving of what. They must not favor their friends or seek vengeance on their enemies, neither may these elected assessors take bribes. Should any of them accept a bribe or refuses to be an assessor, place a high bail on him and set a date for appearing at court before them in the monastery.

"Those peasants and cossacks on whom the assessors impose a tax must pay the tax without any conversion.[65] If anyone is obstinate and will not pay, you shall request a bailiff from the agent and order him to recover the debt without delay. They must pay the surtax and areal taxes according to the tsar's charter. You peasants shall pay on the basis of the areal, not on the basis of livestock or head count, but cossacks shall not pay this tax. When the military service obligation falls due, you peasants and cossacks without exception must pay the dues on the basis of the areal and livestock, cottage industries and head count, in keeping with your assessment of each man's worth.

"In the taxation schedules various taxes are recorded: the vicegerent's tax, the crown secretaries' tax, the town elders' tax, the sworn officials' tax, taxes for ransom and armaments, the plowland tax, taxes for public works, bridges and road construction, and grain taxes. You peasants and cossacks must pay all these different levies according to your assessment based on livestock, cottage industries and head count for the year when there is no military service levy. If the military service levy is in effect the peasants shall pay all these different taxes based on the areal, livestock, cottage industries and head count, but the cossacks will not pay any taxes that year; they will pay only the military levy. When customs duties are collected on the land the peasants and the cossacks will pay them based on their trading activities and head count, not on livestock. He who trades more shall pay more duties.

"The maintenance for the Vygoozersky rural district chief is paid on the areal. The peasants shall apportion the courier taxes and transportation duties on the basis of the areal and the saltpan.[66] If cossacks have their own homesteads where they keep horses and cattle, impose on them the partial plowland levy according to the assessment of each man's worth. If peasants have children or adult relatives who are able to beat game, catch birds and fish and gather berries and mushrooms, impose on them the tax in conformity with the tax on cossacks, according to the assessment of each man's worth. If on account of our sins homicide occurs, you peasants and cossacks shall apportion the burden according to the head count on the basis of your assessment.

"Concerning saltpans we have decreed that in all our villages salt shall be boiled in saltpans on one hundred and sixty nights in winter and summer. Each year six hundred sazhens of firewood for the saltpans shall be cut. Store only enough firewood for one year and no more. If anyone boils salt on additional nights or cuts extra firewood, or stores more wood than is needed for one year, you shall collect a fine for the monastery from them."

Further on in the charter follow definitions of what the peasants were to pay to the agent, bailiff, elder and town crier. Everyone, peasants and cossacks, paid the elder and town crier one Moscow denga per head, excluding only those under fifteen. In the village of Sobolev belonging to the Trinity-St. Sergius monastery the peasants paid the monastery three rubles per plowland annually, giving the manager twenty chetverts of rye for the whole district and the same amount of oats. Four times a year, at Easter, on St. Peter's feast, in the autumn, and at Christmas they gave him one altyn per plowland. Then on the entire district they gave one ruble in cash annually and were obliged to mow sixty hay stooks for the monastery. The "Hundred Chapters" stated that "Archimandrites, abbots and hieromonks shall not make the rounds, and monks shall not be sent as rural managers. Send instead good servants as managers but for monastic land cases, for grain inspection or for peasant justice send good elders for a time. Should elders be unable to administer justice, archimandrites, abbots and hieromonks are not prohibited from going once or twice a year themselves for supervision, but they must not make the rounds in the villages, attend feasts or receive gifts." The "Hundred Chapters" likewise forbade bishops and monasteries from lending money and seed grain for interest to their own peasants or those belonging to others.

The sovereign assigned bailiffs to the monasteries and peasants to protect them against crime. In 1540 the abbot of the Dormition-St. Zosima hermitage complained that he and the brethren were annoyed with the former bailiff, who neglected the monastery's affairs and even offered for sale elders, servants and monastery peasants. The sovereign favored the abbot and brotherhood and gave them a bailiff-extraordinary who would please them. The duties of the bailiff consisted in the following. If the abbot, the brotherhood, monastery servitors and peasants sought damages from someone, or if someone sought damages from the abbot, brotherhood and monastery servitors and peasants, the bailiff-extraordinary put both the plaintiffs and the defendants on bail, and set the date for their appearance in court, although the constables would not go after the abbot, brotherhood, their men and peasants. The bailiff-extraordinary also must take care that no one dared fell timber in monastic forests, must arrest the accused, impose bail on them and present them to court. From other charters it appears that these bailiffs-extraordinary were appointed from among the scriveners and the crown choir clerics.

HERETICAL MOVEMENTS

Earlier Metropolitan Cyprian[67] complained about the distortion of sacred and liturgical books by copyists owing to their lack of education. This complaint was raised once again before Tsar Ivan at the 1551 council. Yet how could the ill be remedied without the removal of its principal cause, lack of education, when even from priests the only thing required was the basic ability to read and write? Apart from unintentional distortions arising from unseparated words in the original and from slips of the pen, there were willful distortions arising from the false interpretation of words and entire expressions.

Religious interest was strong. The literate man who sensed a need for intellectual nourishment was obliged to turn exclusively to religious subjects, to ecclesiastical books. He dwelled on certain passages and began to explain them for himself; but how could he explain them when he lacked education? From whom could he find guidance and correction should his opinions be erroneous? From a priest not unlike those about whom Archbishop Gennady of Novgorod wrote?[68] It was easy for teachers, self-appointed interpreters, to crop up, for who was able to verify the legitimacy of their title? Anyone who could read and write, was well-versed in Scripture or was a gabbler unfailingly acquired indisputable authority in the midst of a crowd of the illiterate and poorly-read. He often spoke absurdly, obscurely, but he was speaking about lofty things which commanded general reverence, and he constantly cited words from Sacred Scripture and the church fathers. The more incomprehensibly and obscurely he spoke, the greater the admiration he inspired. This was called "speaking loftily." Sometimes such a savant did not restrict himself to conversations alone. He would write a small book, and the book was vouchsafed the same honorable reception, especially if the author himself or the copyist inscribed it with the name of a renowned church father.

Naturally in the absence of education the juvenile thought of our ancient literate figures did not appeal to the spirit but to the flesh, to the external, more accessible aspect pertaining to the daily routine of human life. With the revelation and consolidation of Christianity the educated Graeco-Roman world turned its attention to the principal substantial subjects of the new teaching, the result of which was a gradual resolution of questions, a gradual affirmation of dogmas at ecumenical councils. What kinds of questions occupied ancient Russian people and sometimes violently disturbed the peace of the church? The question about which food could be used on certain holy days if these fell on fasting days, a question which was resumed with equal vigor in both the South and the North. Then during the reign of Ivan III the ecclesiastical and civil governments became deeply concerned with the question about how to walk in procession at the consecration of a church, with the sun or against it? Social calamities were attributed to the incorrect resolution of this question.

In the first quarter of the fifteenth century in Pskov district the question arose about the number of alleluias in the refrain "Alleluia, alleluia, alleluia, glory to you, O God." Should there be two or three? At the end of the century Archbishop Gennady of Novgorod inquired of the learned interpreter Dmitry the Greek, renowned in his day, how to settle the question correctly. Dmitry answered him from Rome that he examined books and found nothing in them about the matter. "I remember," he continued, "that there was among us an argument about this matter between great men, and they decided that both were permissible. A triple alleluia followed by "glory to you O God" signifies the consubstantiality of the trihypostatic Godhead, and the double alleluia signifies the one person of Christ our God in two natures." Great men reasoned thus, and even Gennady was reassured.

Others did not want to be set at ease and in 1547 the *Life of Venerable Evfrosin, the Miracle Worker of Pskov* appeared, composed by the cleric Vasily (Varlaam) about seventy years after the death of the saint.[69] In this Life it was proclaimed that the sign of the cross must be made with two fingers just as priests did when they blessed, and this opinion was expounded in a composition attributed to blessed Theodoret,[70] a fifth century writer. That the pastors of the Russian church had so little opportunity to verify similar opinions and compositions is evident from the fact that pseudo-Theodoret's opinion about the two-fingered sign of the cross crops up in the sermons of Metropolitan Daniel.[71] In the Code of Canon Law of Metropolitan Makary we find excerpts from the book of Enoch the Righteous.[72] Abbots of monasteries wrote in their charters "By the divine mercy of our Lord Jesus Christ and of his godly Transfiguration and his Pure Mother of her honorable and glorious Dormition." Opinions about the two-fingered sign of the cross and the double alleluia, together with the prohibition of shaving beards and cutting off mustaches, were intermingled in the resolutions of the council of 1551 and disseminated together with them.

In this way opinions were amassed and elucidated which ultimately appeared as the fundamental opinions of the Schismatics.[73] Alongside these opinions we meet those about more important religious subjects, having a link with the old teaching of the Judaizers,[74] renewed by adherents of the teachings of the new western Reformers.

After the great Moscow fire when the Kremlin churches burned down[75] the sovereign sent for icons from Novgorod, Smolensk, Dmitrov and Zvenigorod. Icons were brought to Moscow from these and other towns and were set up in the Annunciation cathedral, where iconographers copied new images from them. The famous Sylvester,[76] having reported to the sovereign, ordered the following icons to be painted: "The life-giving Trinity in vignettes," "I believe in one God the Father," "Praise the Lord from the Heavens," "Sophia the Divine Wisdom," "It is worthy," "And God rested from all his works on the seventh day," "O Only-begotten Son and Word of God," "Let the people come and bow down before the trihypostatic Godhead," "In the grave in the flesh," and others. When the famous crown secretary Ivan Viskovaty saw these new icons he was led astray and said loudly before the people that icons should not be painted in that way, that the invisible Godhead and the incorporeal beings ought not be depicted. "I believe in one God the Father almighty, Creator of heaven and earth, of all things visible and invisible," should be written in words. The rest of the creed from " . . . and in our Lord Jesus Christ" to the end then could be depicted in keeping with the dispensation in the flesh. Viskovaty even wrote to the metropolitan that Sylvester removed the ancient icons from Annunciation cathedral and set up new ones of his own invention.

Sylvester justified himself before the metropolitan saying that if "It is worthy" and "I believe in one God" were proclaimed at a holy ecumenical council iconographers could paint this on icons, that the painters all painted from his old models, from ancient tradition going back to the times of St. Vladimir, and that he, Sylvester, added not a single line from his own mind. Sylvester demanded that the matter be discussed at a council. At the beginning of 1554 a council was convoked and the case was settled in Sylvester's favor. A penance was imposed on Viskovaty because he had doubts about some holy icons and was clamoring and stirring up the people, Orthodox Christians, and because he transgressed the canon of the sixth ecumenical council[77] which forbade the laity from assuming the rank of teacher. The metropolitan, by the way, told Viskovaty, "You stood up against heretics, and now you speak and philosophize incompetently about the holy icons. Do not fall in with the heretics yourself. You should know the matters which have been laid against you, do not throw away the lists."

The council was not convoked for this case only. Writing to the metropolitan a complaint against Sylvester regarding icons Viskovaty wrote, "Bashkin and Artemy and Simeon are in agreement, and the priest Simeon is spiritual father to Bashkin and praises their works."[78] Although Sylvester is not mentioned here by name, he nonetheless considered it necessary to deflect any suspicion from himself, so he wrote to the metropolitan, "The priest Simeon (of Annunciation cathedral) spoke to me about Matiusha (Bashkin) at orthros during the fast of St. Peter. 'An extraordinary spiritual son approached me, and with great imprecations he implored me to welcome him in spirit during Great Lent. He laid before me many bewildering questions and demanded from me instruction, and sometimes he himself instructed me.' I became greatly perplexed by all this. 'Simeon,' I replied, 'what kind of spiritual son will you have when his ill repute precedes him?' When the sovereign arrived from the monastery of St. Cyril, Simeon and I recounted everything about Bashkin to him in the presence of Archpriest Andrei (the tsar's confessor) and Alexis Adashev.[79] Simeon said that Matiusha was asking him to explain to him many things in the Epistle[80] and that he himself interpreted the texts not according to their real meaning but in a distorted fashion. 'Even I,' Simeon told him, 'did not know about what you were inquiring,' but he answered him, 'Ask Sylvester. He will tell you.' We told the sovereign even about this and he ordered Simeon to tell Matiusha to indicate all his own words in the Epistle. Matiusha marked the whole Epistle with wax and Simeon brought the book to church where the sovereign saw it, and they listened to Matiusha's entire gloss and invention. Then the sovereign went to Kolomna, and the case was set aside. If you wish to ask Simeon about this case, and he remembers something, he will tell you everything. I have never communicated with Matiusha, neither was there any agreement between us."

"Matvey Bashkin," the priest Simeon wrote to the metropolitan, "came to me during Great Lent for confession and said in his confession, 'I am a Christian, I believe in the Father and the Son and the Holy Spirit, and I venerate the image of our Lord God and Savior Jesus Christ and the Most Pure Virgin, the great miracle workers and all the saints depicted on an icon.' He said, 'Great is your task! It is written, "There is no greater love than this, that you lay down your life for your friends,"[81] and you lay down your life for us and keep vigil for our souls. As the saying goes, you will be rewarded on Judgment Day.' After this he came to me and said, 'For the sake of God, be of benefit to me spiritually. We must read what is written in the Gospel discourses, and not hope in the word but do the work; the initiative lies with you. Previously you priests had to teach us the rudiments and instruct us.' Then he sent after me a man and when I came to him he told me, 'In the Apostle it is written, "The whole law is fulfilled in the words, you shall love your neighbor as yourself; if you bite and devour yourself, take care that you are not devoured by each other."[82] Yet we keep for ourselves Christ's slaves. Christ calls everyone his brother, but we have on some people limited service contracts, on others fugitive contracts, on others labor contracts and on others full slavery contracts. I give thanks to God. I tore to shreds all the service contracts of the full slaves, and I keep my servants on a voluntary basis. If anyone is happy, he stays; if anyone is unhappy, he goes where he wants. It befits you, fathers, to visit us often, to instruct us how we should live and keep servants without wearing them out. I saw this in the canons and this seemed good to me.'"

Having investigated the case, the council found that Matvey Bashkin and his kindred spirits were guilty of the following. (1) They do not acknowledge that Jesus Christ is equal to God the Father, and some even indoctrinate others in this disrespect. (2) They consider the body and blood of Christ to be simple bread and wine. (3) They deny the one, holy, catholic and apostolic church, saying that the assembly of believers is the only church, whereas these created things are nothing. (4) They call the depiction of Christ, the Theotokos and all the saints idols. (5) They consider confession of no avail, saying that when anyone stops sinning there is no sin for him even though he did not confess to a priest. (6) They call the Traditions of the Fathers and the Lives of Saints fables. They accuse the seven ecumenical councils of pride, saying that they wrote all this for themselves so that they could control everything, both secular and episcopal matters. In a word, they call the whole of Sacred Scripture a fable, and they interpret the Epistle and Gospel incorrectly.

Bashkin accused Artemy, the former abbot of Trinity-St. Sergius monastery, of sharing the same opinions. Confronted face to face with Bashkin, Artemy denied that he was guilty of anything that Bashkin brought against him. In addition to Bashkin the former abbot of St. Ferapont's monastery, Nektary, likewise accused Artemy. Once Artemy told him, "In a book of Joseph of Volokolamsk it is written in ignorance that God sent two angels to Sodom, that is the Son and the Holy Spirit."[83] According to Nektary, Artemy did not curse the Novgorod heretics, praised the Latins, did not keep the fast, ate fish throughout Lent and at the tsar's table on the feast of the Exaltation of the Holy Cross [September 14]. At the personal confrontation[84] Nektary also accused Artemy of traveling from the Pskov Monastery of the Caves to the German town of Novy Gorodok (Neuhausen)[85] where he extolled the German faith. To this Artemy replied that he indeed had travelled to Novy Gorodok and spoken with German princes and asked whether or not they had anyone with whom he could discuss books, but they did not point out to him any such scholar.

Another accuser appeared, namely the cellarer of the Trinity-St. Sergius monastery, Adrian Angelov, who revealed that while in the abbot's cell in the St. Cornelius monastery[86] Artemy expounded on the commemoration of the deceased in this fashion. "You will not assist them with Offices for the Dead[87] and liturgies, they will not escape their torments by these." Artemy confessed that he said this about people who were corrupted in life, and about robbers. The Holy Trinity monk Kurachov wrote that he heard from Artemy unseemly words about the Jesus Canon and the Akathist of the Theotokos.[88] Concerning this Artemy himself told the council, "They say in the Canon, 'Sweet Jesus!' Yet when they hear Jesus's word about his commandments, how he commanded us to be, they become bitter because they have to fulfill them. In the Akathist they repeat, 'Rejoice, yes rejoice, O pure one!' Yet they themselves do not rejoice over purity, and they pass the time in idle chatter. Thus what they say, they do so by habit and not in truth."

Abbot Simeon of the St. Cyril monastery wrote to the tsar that when he revealed to Artemy that Bashkin was found guilty of heresy, Artemy replied, "I do not know what the heresy might be! Kuritsyn and Rukavy were burned,[89] and now they do not know why." "I do not recall," Artemy told the council, "whether or not I spoke like that about the Novgorod heretics. I do not remember the Novgorod heretics, and I do not know myself why they were burned. If I said that I do not know why they were burned and who judged them, I said this about myself, not about anyone else."

The metropolitan, addressing Artemy at the council, told him, "Matvey Bashkin was preaching heresies, he separated the only-begotten Son from the Father, stated that the Son was not equal to the Father and said, 'If I commit some vulgarity with respect to the Son, the Father can deliver me from torment at the dread Second Coming, but if I commit some vulgarity with respect to the Father, the Son will not deliver me.' Matvey prayed to God the Father alone and left out the Son and Holy Spirit. Matvey now repents of everything and he has laid bare all his deeds at the council."

"Matvey acted like a child," Artemy answered the metropolitan, "and does not himself know what he did through his cleverness, for he does not discover this in scripture and it is not written in heresies." "The former heretics," said the metropolitan, "did not repent and the bishops cursed them, but the tsars condemned them and imprisoned them and handed them over for execution." "They sent for me to judge heretics," Artemy replied, "but I cannot judge heretics to be handed over to execution. So now there are no heretics and no one argues."

"Matvey wrote a prayer," said the metropolitan, "to the one principle, writing God the Father alone, but he left out the Son and the Holy Spirit." "Why was he satisfied to keep on lying," retorted Artemy, "since there is a prayer to the Almighty prepared by Manasseh?"[90] "That was before the coming of Christ," the metropolitan replied, "but whoever writes to the one principle now is a heretic." "The prayer of Manasseh," Artemy answered, "is written in the Great Canon and it is recited." The metropolitan said to Artemy, "If you are guilty of anything, repent." "I do not philosophize in the way that has been reported against me," he replied. "They all have lied about me. I believe in the Father, the Son and the Holy Spirit, the consubstantial Trinity."

Nektary, former abbot of St. Ferapont's monastery, accused Artemy of many blasphemous words against the Christian religion and the divine scripture, and sent for witnesses, namely, for three hermits from Nil's hermitage and for one monk from the Solovetsk monastery. At the council these witnesses revealed that they did not hear Artemy reviling the Christian religion or the divine writings. Because the witnesses did not corroborate Nektary's accusations, the tsar released Artemy from punishment, but since the council found that Artemy was not exonerated of the other charges he was sentenced to imprisonment in the Solovetsk monastery. There he was confined in a silentiary cell so that the soul-damaging and blasphemous illness could not spread from him to anyone else. He could not talk with anyone nor write to anyone, nor receive letters or anything else from anyone, and had to sit in silence and repent. He was assigned a spiritual father who was to inform the abbot whether his repentance was sincere. The abbot himself was to instruct him and in the event of reform must permit him to receive communion in mortal sickness. He could have only those books which the council allowed. According to some information one of the fathers of the council, Bishop Kassian of Riazan, allowed himself to speak out in an ill manner about the book of Joseph of Volokolamsk. He was struck with paralysis, lost the use of his arms and legs, left the episcopacy and retired to a monastery, but even there he did not repent and refused to call Christ "the Almighty."

From Artemy's replies about the book of Joseph of Volokolamsk and about the Novgorod heretics it is clear that he together with other contemporary educated people, as for example the famous Prince Andrei Kurbsky,[91] did not share Joseph's convictions regarding heretics and the justice of the measures taken against them. The Transvolga Elders[92] inveighed against the measures taken by Joseph of Volokolamsk. According to evidence in the chronicle, Bashkin also said that the Transvolga Elders did not revile his anger but affirmed him in it.

Maxim the Greek, who was still among the living when the case about Bashkin's heresy was raised, was in contact with the most famous of the Transvolga Elders, Vassian Kosoy.[93] Together with others he was invited to the council, but the council members informed the tsar that Maxim took offense at the invitation. Maxim thought that they called him to the council because he was suspected of sharing Bashkin's opinions and that, based on his opinions and statements about heresy, they intended to make a finding about whether or not he was an enemy or a secret well-wisher of the heretics. In order to set Maxim at ease, the tsar wrote to him. "I have sent for you," he assured him, "so that you too may be a defender of Orthodoxy equal to the ancient God-bearing fathers and appear as a zealot for piety so that the same heavenly dwellings will welcome you which welcomed previous champions of virtue. We have heard that you take offense, thinking that we link you with Matvey and thus have sent for you. Never have we reckoned a faithful man with the impious. Set aside your doubt and increase the talent given to you by God. Send to me a missive against the current wickedness." From this letter it is clear that the tsar released

Maxim from attending the council, asking of him only a missive denouncing heresy.

Bashkin and his confederates were imprisoned in various monasteries. Of his followers, Feodosy Kosoy, a monk from Beloozero, and a certain Ignaty were caught in 1555 and imprisoned in a monastery in Moscow, but they fled to Lithuania, got married there and continued to preach Feodosy's doctrine in freedom. This doctrine held that the Godhead was not a Trinity, that Christ was a simple man and that the whole visible organization of the church was unnecessary. Artemy also managed to escape from Solovki to Lithuania despite the strict surveillance.

There is more news of the council in connection with the heresy of David, archbishop of Rostov in 1582. This David was made out to be a fellow schemer of Antonio Possevino,[94] who himself was brought to the council, where he set forth his strange doctrine completely like that of David's, and was refuted by Tsar Ivan. The information about Possevino, however, is obviously fabricated. The tsar could not have talked with him the way he was presented as speaking at the council. Moreover, had something like this occurred, information about it would have been preserved in the official protocol. This composition is not unlike the correspondence of Tsar Ivan with the Turkish sultan that has turned up in certain collections.[95]

RELATIONS WITH EASTERN ORTHODOXY

Steady relations with the Orthodox East carried on as before. In 1543 the monks of St. Panteleimon monastery on Mount Athos received a charter which granted them free passage everywhere in the regions of Muscovy including maintenance and transportation without their having to pay any duties. In 1547 Metropolitan Makary wrote an encyclical letter concerning relief for the monks of the St. Panteleimon monastery travelling to Moscow for alms. Likewise Paisy, abbot of the Bulgarian monastery of Chilandari on Mount Athos petitioned the tsar that they were being exhausted by the tribute to the sultan, and were suffering grave injuries at the hands of the Greeks. They asked the sovereign to favor them and send his personal letter to the sultan, requesting a reduction in the tribute and defence against the Greeks. The tsar fulfilled their request and sent a letter to the sultan. In 1545 Patriarch Joachim of Alexandria wrote to Ivan pleading for the release of Maxim the Greek who was imprisoned unjustly. "Orthodox Christians," he wrote, "do not treat poor people this way, especially monks, and it is unfair to detain a man by force and offend him. It is not good to believe every word, every writing without an investigation. I have never written to you, nor have I ever asked anything of you. So do not offend me now, do not force me to write a second time, for I shall not cease writing to you until my request has been fulfilled."

In 1556 Metropolitan Joseph of Euripus[96] arrived in Moscow with a letter from the Byzantine patriarch. Giving him leave the following year, the tsar sent with him a letter to Patriarch Joseph[97] in which he asked for a synodal blessing of his coronation as tsar. The patriarch was sent sables worth two thousand gold pieces. The requested document was sent in 1562. In it the synod of Eastern bishops acknowledged that Ivan was worthy of the imperial title because he traced his lineage from Princess Anna, the sister of the autocrat Basil Porphyrogennetos, and because Emperor Constantine Monomachos sent the imperial insignia with the metropolitan of Ephesus to Prince Vladimir, who was crowned tsar.[98]

After the deaths of Tsaritsa Anastasia, of the tsar's brother Prince Yury Vasilievich and of Tsarevich Ivan, abundant alms were sent to the patriarchs, to Mount Sinai and Mount Athos and to the poor of Constantinople. Young men from Moscow were sent to the patriarch of Constantinople to learn Greek. The boy Obriuta Mikhailov Grekov was sent to Patriarch Dionysios in 1551. "You should order him," the tsar wrote to the patriarch, "to learn from you Greek writing and language. If you are unable to teach him, send him to Holy Mount Athos to our monastery of St. Panteleimon." After Obriuta two more boys, Ushakov and Vnukov, were sent to study. The patriarch complained that it was very difficult to teach them because they were already grown, and it was impossible to discipline them, for they might run off to the Turks.

THE ORTHODOX CHURCH IN LITHUANIA

At the same time that the Russian church in the East, that is, in Muscovy, was expanding together with the expansion of the borders of this state, in the West, in Lithuanian-Russian regions the opposite phenomenon was occurring. Here the Russian church, instead of acquiring new, was losing old members, at first as a result of the dissemination of Protestant doctrines, and then as a result of Catholic counteraction, the principle motive force of which was the Jesuit order. In addition, being under the control of a het-erodox government which, if not openly hostile, was indifferent to the interests of the Russian church, could not assure its tranquility and order.

After the elimination of the Galician metropolitanate[99] the title of metropolitan of Galicia was attached to the title of the Kievan metropolitan, and the diocese of Galicia found itself under the immediate jurisdiction of the metropolitan, who appointed his own vicar general. At the same time the Catholic archbishop of Lvov held the right to appoint a vicar for the management of the Galician Orthodox church on the strength of a charter granted in 1509 by King Sigismund I. Thus the Galician vicar must receive the consent of both the Orthodox metropolitan of Kiev and the Catholic archbishop of Lvov, as well as royal confirmation, in order to exercise his duties. In the 1540s the metropolitan vicar in Galicia was Sikora, whose behavior roused the indignation of the diocese.

The Galicians sent a request to Metropolitan Makary asking him to place them under the guardianship of Lavrenty, the bishop of Peremyshl. The metropolitan appointed the priest Goshevsky to be their vicar, and wrote to the Galicians that if he did not please them they might refuse to accept him. In fact the Galicians did not like the new vicar and sent another petition to the metropolitan. "We the inhabitants of Rus (Galicia) and Podolia," they wrote, "conjointly did not send to your eminence the priest Goshevksy, and we did not choose him, and now none of us, great or small, rich or poor, want to have him as our vicar, just as was the case with Sikora, because under Sikora your eminence was subjected to great disorder, burdens and disobedience. The same or still worse happened under the priest Goshevsky. Since your eminence wrote to us that we must choose a good man and send him to you, all of us, the clergy, the nobility, the estate owners and the whole people from the greatest to the least, have chosen Makary Tuchapsky, a citizen of Lvov, and we humbly beg your eminence to bless him as our vicar." The metropolitan fulfilled their request and the new vicar began to function to general satisfaction.

The old vicar Sikora, having insinuated himself into the confidence of the Catholic archbishop of Lvov, began to prompt him against Makary, who was elected without his archiepiscopal consent. The archbishop pressed the king to appoint a commission to review Makary's actions and with letters royal they summoned him to the commissioner's court. Makary had to appear at this court accompanied by a large number of inhabitants of Galicia and Podolia, who were to testify on his behalf. As usually happened, Makary and his witnesses spent a lot of money, but to no avail, and Makary transferred the case before the king in the Sejm. The king decided the case in favor of the archbishop. On the basis of old Jagiellonian privileges he placed the Orthodox clergy of Galicia under his control, removing them from the management of the Kievan metropolitan and his vicar.

Perpetual confinement threatened Makary but the Galicians, with the assistance of two lords, gained access to Queen Bona, who had great influence over her husband. The king and queen were not above accepting a bribe of two hundred bullocks from the Galician clergy. The privilege granted to the Catholic archbishop would be torn up and a privilege promised Makary as soon as the two hundred bullocks were received.

The matter did not end there. When the king arrived in Lvov, Makary gave him fifty bullocks, for which he received the order to travel to Cracow for the privilege. But before the king left Lvov the archbishop once again prevailed upon him to return the Rus Galician clergy to his jurisdiction. As a result, Makary once again was forced to concern himself with bullocks, of which he distributed one hundred and ten to the king, queen and lords, and received a second time the order to go to Cracow for his privilege.

Makary went, and spent a long time in Cracow, but did not receive his privilege. The king deferred the matter to the Sejm, which Makary had to attend. Makary proceeded, having spent just short of a year in Cracow, and he finally obtained his privilege "with great trouble, expense and effort." The Galician clergy had to pay another one hundred forty bullocks. Even then the matter was not settled. When Makary returned from Cracow the Catholic archbishop sent him his secretary, ordering him with threats to appear before him with his privileges. Makary himself did not go, neither did he send his privileges. "While I am alive," the archbishop said, "I will not let this matter rest. Rus must be in my control; the king cannot settle this without me otherwise." He sent the king a complaint against Makary and wanted to cite him to the Sejm. Then the Galicians hurriedly sent Makary to Kiev to the metropolitan with the request that he consecrate him bishop, for as bishop he would have nothing more to fear from the archbishop or Catholic bishops. Makary went to Kiev accompanied by a considerable crowd of his own Rus who feared for his life, for the archbishop several times ordered him killed.

Later, between 1569 and 1576 a similar occurrence appeared in Galicia. Before his death the Galician bishop Mark Balaban handed over the episcopacy to his son Grigory Balaban, with the permission of the king. The Catholic archbishop of Lvov, Shlomovsky, declared to the king that he had the right to appoint Orthodox bishops, already having named Ivan Lopatka Ostalovsky. Sigismund Augustus, in spite of the permission previously given to Balaban, confirmed the appointment of Lopatka. Balaban and his side, basing themselves on the prior permission of the king, refused to recognize Lopatka's rights although the king confirmed them several times afterwards, and when Lopatka died Balaban was confirmed in the episcopacy.

Sigismund Augustus was indifferent towards Catholicism, hence during his reign it was easy for the lords of the Greek faith to obtain for the Orthodox nobility equal rights with the Catholics. This equalization occurred at the Wilno Sejm in 1563.

Under Bathory the Russian church in Lithuania strongly sensed what to expect from the Catholic counter-reformation and its principal champions, the Jesuits. In 1583 the king ordered land seized from all Polotsk churches and monasteries except those belonging to the bishop, and handed it over to the Jesuits. In Lvov on Christmas Eve of 1584 the Catholics, following the orders of their archbishop, with weapons in their hands attacked Orthodox churches and monasteries, dragged priests from the altars, some of them at the consecration of the gifts, others just before communion. They sealed up the churches and strictly prohibited divine services to be conducted.

While bishops were still living the kings sometimes appointed boyar laymen as their successors, "having looked affectionately at their faithful service, following the wish of the governor and boyars." Sometimes an aged bishop surrendered the administration of diocesan affairs to some layman, keeping for himself only the title and seniority. The new administrator approached the king with a petition to have himself confirmed in the episcopal throne on the death of the old archbishop. Having appointed a metropolitan in Kiev, the king informed the patriarch of Constantinople so that he might bless the new metropolitan. In this case, the royal charter to the patriarch had the this formula. "We are informing your worthiness that among our lords of the grand principality of Lithuania the metropolitan of Kiev, Galicia and all Rus is no longer among the living. In his place we present from the inhabitants of the Greek religion as being suitable for this honor the humble bishop so-and-so. Bless him as metropolitan according to your law for the service of the holy Christian church and for the instruction and administration of everything which belongs to this dignity, for which he will receive from us such thankfulness as previous metropolitans have received from our predecessors. In respect of which we wish you every blessing."

The strife between the bishop of Polotsk and the metropolitan over a title, and the strife between the same bishop of Polotsk and the bishop of Vladimir-in-Volhynia, were settled by the king and the lords of the council. In 1548 when Simeon, archbishop of Polotsk, together with the princes, lords and boyars of his region presented the king with a complaint against Metropolitan Makary because once again he ranked him lower than the bishop of Vladimir, the metropolitan declared to the king that this was an ecclesiastical judgment with which the king could not interfere, in accordance with the privilege given to Metropolitan Joseph. The matter must be settled at a synod in keeping with Greek law. The king agreed to the calling of a synod, stipulating that if any of the litigants found the synodal decision unfair that party had the right to transfer the case to the decision of the king.

That same year the Wilno burgomasters, councillors and burghers of the Greek faith solicited the metropolitan for a charter which handed the Wilno clergy over to their jurisdiction and, should a priest not wish to obey them, they might remove him from the church and replace him with another priest with the permission of the metropolitan. The archpriest and all the priests presented to the king a petition against such action by the metropolitan. "We are greatly surprised," wrote the king in 1542 to the metropolitan, "that the Wilno burghers have bypassed us and turned to you with such a matter and have obtained such improper charters according to which they have appropriated to their own town's jurisdiction our sovereign authority, which they had no right to do. You had no right to assign the priests, our intercessors, to the authority of anyone with your charters. You cannot remove from under our sovereign jurisdiction the churches of God of our capital city and entrust them to the administration of subjects, which never happened under our predecessors. We have ordered this your charter brought to our chancellery, and we command that if the priest of any church dies, the burgomaster or one of the good people together with your vicar, the Wilno archpriest, shall go to that church, make a list of the church property in it and seal it up. The church keys shall be surrendered to the cathedral church of the Mother of God. Then, having selected some good and learned man, they shall inform you. After ascertaining his suitability, you shall ordain him to the priesthood and order that the church and all its property be handed over to him." To the burghers the king wrote that they must not dare regulate the priests, under threat of a fine of one thousand kopa grosh, and that henceforth they not accept any similar charters from the metropolitan. These charters had no force whatsoever, for the metropolitan held authority over the clergy only in spiritual matters, and in all other matters he could not force them to do anything.

The matter did not end there. The priests did not stop petitioning the king about the burghers, and the burghers did the same about the priests. Then in 1544 the king, acknowledging his right to issue decrees for the churches of God, granted them a statute charter in which he determined the means of selecting priests, deacons and minor clerics. "When a priest becomes seriously incapacitated," it read, "the archpriest must inform the burgomaster of the Greek faith. The burgomaster will go himself, or send two councillors and the clerk, to make a list of all church objects together with the archpriest and priests. When the priest dies, the burgomaster shall lock the church and keep the keys himself until a new priest is installed. The burgomasters and councillors together with the archpriest and two priests will choose the priest, deacon, precentor[100] and sexton." The charter defined how much to pay the priest for funerals and for anointing the sick. Concerning confession it was decreed that the burghers approach their spiritual fathers of their own volition, not by compulsion, and should confess their sins wherever they wanted. The priests must not summon anyone who is unwilling. Priests did not have the right to meddle in the spiritual affairs of laymen. Anyone dissatisfied with the judgment of the bishop might petition the king, and he would instruct the metropolitan to reexamine the case.

As for the relations of monasteries with secular authority, conflicts between monks and archimandrites were judged by the governors. Thus in 1534 the governor of Polotsk tried the case of the monks of St. John the Forerunner monastery and their archimandrite. The monks complained that the archimandrite was taking for himself half of the income owing them. The archimandrite replied that when the Polotsk governor or his village constables came to the monastery the archimandrite and the monks used to entertain and give them presents. Now the monks did not help him bestow presents on the lord governor, for which reason he deducted the amount from their half of the income. The monks objected that the monastery had tonsure money to pay for the needs of the church and for gifts to the commanders. When anyone became a monk he paid a ruble in cash into the monastery treasury.

In 1540 the complaint of the monks of Unevsk monastery against Bishop Makary of Lvov was submitted to the king and metropolitan. The case was examined before ten nobles, four burghers and a court investigator. Makary was acquitted, then wrote that the case cost him twenty bullocks which he had to give to Lord Krakovsky. The monks confessed that they complained about the bishop's rapacity merely in order to be released from Makary's control, notwithstanding the royal charter according to which their monastery was entrusted to him. Fifteen years later, in 1555, the case recommenced. The archimandrite of the Unevsk monastery petitioned Metropolitan Makary against Arseny, bishop of Lvov, because he plundered the monastery each time he visited and summoned the archimandrite to court before the king and the council lords, wishing to bring the monastery under his authority. The king ordered the metropolitan to examine the complaint. The metropolitan set a date for the bishop and archimandrite to appear before him and decided the case in favor of the archimandrite, released the monastery from the control of the bishop and disregarded King Sigismund's charter. Thereupon the bishop complained to the king about the injustice of the metropolitan's decision, and the metropolitan was summoned to a royal trial.

Sometimes powerful lords used their constables to interfere even in the ecclesiastical court of the metropolitan and other clergy. Relying upon the patronage of some powerful grandee, they permitted themselves to disregard the authority of the metropolitan. In 1554 Metropolitan Makary complained to the king that Princess Slutskaia was ordering her deputies to handle church cases, to judge priests, to imprison them and to divorce husbands and wives. When the metropolitan forbade the Slutsk archimandrite Nikandr from performing the service because he twice failed to appear in court, the archimandrite disdained even reading the metropolitan's letter. He beat the servant sent with the letter and sought recourse in the patronage of Princess Slutskaia, who interceded on his behalf. The king forbade the princess similar actions.

On the basis of their right of donation kings continued to grant Orthodox monasteries to laymen for administration. Thus in 1562 Sigismund Augustus handed over the Polotsk monastery of St. John the Forerunner to the nobleman Korsak, with the proviso that he keep in the monastery a deputy, a learned clergyman capable of managing ecclesiastical affairs according to Greek law. At the Grodno Sejm in 1568 Metropolitan Jonas, among his other letters of petition, made representation to the king that ecclesiastical dignities not be distributed among the laity. Should the king delegate an ecclesiastical office to a layman, and over the course of three months he did not take orders, the bishop was within his rights to remove the dignity and the clerical salary from such men, and redistribute it among the clergy. The king replied that the request was just, adding that if a grant recipient did not wish to enter the clerical state the bishop did not have the right to remove the grant from him and give it to another. Instead he must inform the king, who would withdraw the grant and give it to another whom he deemed worthy. It is obvious that this reply was made in order to avoid fulfilling a request when this proved necessary.

In 1571 Sigismund Augustus gave the clerk of the crown chancellery Vysotsky the Kievan Mezhigorsk monastery, unconditionally, in return for his faithful service, wishing thereby to strengthen all the more his zeal for service. Clearly the clerk, who had to continue his chancellery service, could not be tonsured as a monk. In other situations the royal reply given at the Grodno diet was called to mind. King Stefan gave the Ascension monastery in Minsk to the nobleman Nevelsky, who had no desire to enter the clerical state. With the king's leave he turned the monastery over to the noble landowner Dostoevsky who was not even Orthodox. Metropolitan Ilia and the Minsk castellan Yan Glebovich complained to the king that Dostoevsky was using the monastery merely for profit, and was generally unconcerned with the management of the monastery. They requested that he entrust the monastery to the Minsk landowner Mikhail Ragoza,[101] a devout man who knew Sacred Scripture and who soon would be tonsured as a monk. The king fulfilled their requests in accordance with the reply of Sigismund Augustus given to the metropolitan at the Grodno Sejm. This was in 1579. In 1581 we see a charter to the nobleman Levonovich for the Bratslav monastery specifically with the proviso that he enter the clerical state.

Sometimes a monastery was handed over to the control of a layman and his sons. For example Sigismund Augustus gave the monastery of St. Savva at Vladimir-in-Volhynia to the Oranskys, the father and his three sons, who were to manage it one after the other. The father and his sons were released from the obligation of being tonsured as monks, but had to keep a cleric as vicar in the monastery. Sometimes such owners mortgaged their monasteries.

The Wilno Trinity monastery also was among those monasteries of which the kings disposed. It was given by the king to Metropolitan Onisifor Devochka.[102] While he was still alive the burgomasters, councillors and Wilno shopkeepers of the Greek religion petitioned the king in 1584 that as a result of the rare visitations by the metropolitan and the great distance from Kiev the Trinity monastery was impoverished and in disrepair. Lest it fall into complete decay, they asked the king to transfer it to the municipal administration after the death of Metropolitan Onisifor.

The king fulfilled their request and entrusted the monastery to them with a view to collecting revenues and using them for the monastery's needs, for the maintenance of buildings, for the support of the archimandrite, priests, monks, poor nuns and church servants and for establishment of schools where the children of servitors who lived in and around the monastery were to be educated. The burgomasters, councillors and shop-keepers received the right to choose for the monastery its archimandrites, who did not have the right to dispose of monastic property without their leave. The burgomasters, councillors and shopkeepers elected one or two good men themselves or together with the Orthodox burghers of Wilno. These elected good men oversaw the monastery's revenues and rendered an annual accounting to the burgomasters, councillors and shopkeepers. With royal consent, monasteries elected their own trustees who were obliged to protect their amenities.

In 1522 there was a petition submitted to King Sigismund I by the monks of the Kiev Caves monastery, who restored the monastic community after it's decline because of impoverishment after the Tatar raids. The restored community existed only since Archimandrite Ignaty, whose successors destroyed it for their own advantage, distributing the monastery revenues to their children and relatives. The monastery entered into decline, and at mid-century the monks turned once again to King Sigismund Augustus with a request concerning the restoration of the community. The king entrusted this matter to the Kievan governor Prince Fridrikh Glebovich Pronsky and the nobleman Oransky, who wrote a statute for the community. It determined which revenues must go to the monastery treasury and which to the archimandrite and clerics. For funerals the monks must take what they were given and not barter; they must bury their brethren and commemorate them individually, whether or not the monk left property reverting to the monastery after his death.

The archimandrite and monks were to eat and drink in the same place, and reading was to accompany the meal. Monks must not dare leave the monastery without permission of the archimandrite and steward. The archimandrite and the brethren were to punish the disobedient according to their ecclesiastical law, and to expel them from the monastery. The cells and gardens were to be held in common use. A monk who wished to leave the monastery could not sell his cell and might take only movable property. Clothing and firewood were to be given to the monks from the church treasury.

Monastic clergy could not keep white clergy, youths or any living creature in their cells. The archimandrite alone might keep a servant and a slave. The church seal was to be kept in the treasury. The archimandrite was to manage the ecclesiastical government only. Revenues and expenditures and management of properties were placed under the supervision of the steward, a member of the town council and the brethren. Twice a year the steward and councillor must render account of the revenues and expenditures to the archimandrite and brethren. The archimandrite and elders could not receive monks from Moscow or Wallachia. Nonetheless in Moscow the Kiev Caves monastery was not forgotten. Tsarevich Ivan sent there alms worth one hundred rubles.

It is known that in 1509 Metropolitan Joseph summoned in Wilno a council at which measures were instituted to forestall disturbances arising from the conflict of ecclesiastical with secular authority. In 1546 Metropolitan Makary summoned a council in Wilno at the behest of King Sigismund Augustus. "We have heard from many princes and lords," wrote the king, "about disturbances arising among your clergy of the Greek religion, likewise among the princes, lords and commoners, especially among bishops, as for example in Volhynia, yet you, your grace, their senior pastor, do not wish to know about this or suppress them." The archbishop's sermons to the priests after ordination in Southwestern Rus were similar to those sermons we have seen used in Muscovite Rus.

The change to the calendar made by Pope Gregory XIII provoked a powerful agitation among both the Protestant and Orthodox inhabitants of Poland-Lithuania who did not wish to adopt the novelty issuing from Rome. In 1583 Patriarch Jeremiah II of Constantinople forbade the Orthodox clergy from conforming to the new Gregorian calendar, in consequence of which in 1584 Stefan Bathory forbade government officials to force the Orthodox to adjust their holidays in keeping with the new calendar.

VII

LEGAL REFORMS

CONFRATERNITIES

Since time immemorial the custom of confraternities or festive associations was widespread in ancient Russia. An ancient chronicle mentions the confraternities, an ancient song sings about them, ancient statutes and charters constantly speak about them. Language itself testifies to the antiquity and importance of confraternities in the life of our people. In a well-known saying the confraternity appears as the representative of every common cause, of every union. About the man whose querulous and unsociable nature renders him incapable of joining in a common cause it is said, "You can't brew beer with him." Another proverb says, "You want to run when there is beer, you want to talk when there is talk," and thus testifies to how people loved to frequent confraternities and their free beer.

Some respectable figures were invited to confraternities. Officials, rural district chiefs and agents received from the confraternities specific incomes. Apart from invited guests or those who owing to their position rightfully attended the confraternities, many uninvited guests and those "with whom it was difficult to brew beer" showed up. For this reason diverse rural districts and villages obtained charters prohibiting uninvited guests from coming to their confraternities. It is understandable that after drinking beer it was far from difficult for arguments and brawls to start even among the members of the confraternity and their invited guests. It was easy to argue and pick a fight, and it was easy to be reconciled through the mediation of the other members. It was impossible to look at the arguments and brawls produced by beer in the same way as disturbances caused by those who were completely sober, and it was impossible to exact the usual monetary fines from someone who quarreled after too much beer, but hastened to be reconciled once he sobered up. Hence in certain statute charters it stated that "if anyone quarrel or fight at a banquet or confraternity, and without leaving the banquet be reconciled with his opponent, he shall pay nothing; even should he leave the banquet and then be reconciled before the constable, he shall pay nothing except the judicial escort fee."

In a few regions the confraternities tried to free themselves completely from the interference of government officials and obtain the right to try their own members causing disturbance during a banquet. It is easy to guess that the confraternities obtained this great degree of independence primarily in Novgorod and its possessions and in Pskov on the basis of the well-known forms of their way of life. Thus in a Pskov legal charter it says "Confraternities shall judge as judges." The same right was enjoyed by the confraternities or brotherhoods in Western or Lithuanian Russia, where the urban way of life closely resembled that of Novgorod and Pskov, and where the guild structure was more strongly developed. We must now turn to these very same brotherhoods of Western Russia because detailed information relative to this time about their structure has come down to us.

From the dossiers for the period under examination and later it can be observed that in certain places, for example Wilno, brotherhoods received their constitution rather early, namely in the middle of the fifteenth century. In 1579 three burghers of Mstislav petitioned Stefan Bathory in the name of all their brethren that since time immemorial they held fraternity banquets three times a year, on Trinity Sunday and on the autumn and spring St. Nicholas days [December 6, May 9]. For each of these holidays they fermented ten puds of mead and sold it. They distributed wax for candles to the church, and the money earned from the mead they likewise donated for church facilities. Yet the Mstislav elders would not permit them to sell the banquet meads for more than the three days, and if they had any unsold mead left the elders seized it for the castle. Because of this they suffered losses, while the churches of God grew impoverished and fell into disrepair. The king ordered the elders not to seize the stores of mead, and to permit the burghers to sell all of the mead, even after the three days had elapsed.

In 1582 the Wilno burghers of a merchant's brotherhood declared in a petition to the king that they had a special brotherhood house in Wilno built at their own expense. In that brotherhood house the Wilno merchants of the Greek faith assembled to discuss the needs of the church and hospital, and following ancient custom they purchased honey eight times annually: on Easter Sunday, on the Saturday after Pentecost, St. Peter's Day [June 29], the feast of the Dormition of the Virgin [August 15], the feast of the Intercession [October 1], St. Nicholas Day [December 6], Christmas and the feast of the Annunciation [March 25]. They fermented the honey and drank it, meeting for three days in the brotherhood house. They gave to the church wax for candles, and the money earned from the mead they donated for church facilities, for church servants, hospitals and alms for the poor.

So that the business of the brotherhood be conducted with greater order, they asked the king to confirm this statute. "The senior and junior brothers of the merchants' fraternity," it said, "shall elect annually from their midst elders to whom they entrust the entire funds of the brotherhood, all its property and all business. At the end of the year the elders shall give an account to the senior and junior brethren. During brotherhood meetings these annual elders personally and through their stewards diligently will see to it that the registered brothers and invited guests sit decorously in the brotherhood house and speak no unseemly words among themselves, that they not lie on the tables or spill the brotherhood mead, and that they drink in moderation and cause no damage whatsoever.

"Should anyone become drunk through overindulgence and cause damages of any kind, utter unbecoming words, lie down on the table and spill drinks, the elders must restrain him first of all verbally and, in case of stubbornness on his part, collect the fine which the brothers impose on him.

Should anyone incite an argument in the brotherhood house the offended party shall report his injury immediately to the elders. After hearing the complaint the elders will postpone the matter to the following day, when the brothers assembled in the brotherhood house shall judge and decide who is right and who is at fault. The offender shall pay a fine to the brotherhood. No one injured in the brotherhood house shall complain to any other authority, neither spiritual, secular, local or municipal, nor to any authority of the Roman or Greek faith. He must have his complaint tried before the elders and brothers of the house where the argument occurred.

"Should anyone in the brotherhood house gives the elder a dressing-down, or scolds or strikes the steward, he will be punished with the brotherhood fine. A steward who is insubordinate to the elder will be restrained first verbally and then punished with a brotherhood fine. If an elder wrongs a brother, the senior and junior brothers will reprimand him the first time, but the next time they will punish with the brotherhood fine. If ecclesiastical servitors of the Roman or Greek faith, either enrolled in the brotherhood, or invited by one of the brothers, or enrolled for one day only, incite a quarrel with anyone they must not petition the prince bishop if they are of the Roman faith, or the metropolitan if they are of the Greek faith, but be tried by the brotherhood and abide by its decision. A member of the gentry or nobility, or some other stranger invited to a fraternity supper, or who has joined the brotherhood for one day, must not make a fuss about place, but is bound to take his seat where assigned by the elders, knowing the title of each.

"No one shall dare enter the brotherhood front room with a weapon, or bring his servant with him. Should an enrolled member desire to transfer into another brotherhood he is bound to declare his intentions to the elders and brethren and to make a copy from their register. If his name stands in the brotherhood list, but he desires to fulfill his brotherhood obligations elsewhere, he no longer is considered a brother, and the brotherhood is not obliged to bury him. If an enrolled brother dies, the brothers are obliged to give velvet and candles for the funeral and act as pallbearers. The burgo-masters and councillors of Wilno, of the Roman or Greek side, must not take servitors enrolled in the merchants' brotherhood to serve in their own fraternities, because each brotherhood chooses and retains its own special servants." The king confirmed the statute.

NEW CODE OF LAW IN EASTERN RUSSIA

The reign of Ivan IV, remarkable for its enunciation of new crown require-ments, also was marked by issuance of a more complete judicial charter.

In 1550 the tsar and grand prince Ivan Vasilievich, together with his brother, cousin and boyars, promulgated the Code of Law which explained how boyars, lords-in-waiting, palace officials, treasurers, crown secretaries and various government officials, the vicegerents in the towns, the rural district chiefs, their agents and various judges were to judge. Since throughout the sixteenth century there was strong demand for measures against abuse by government figures and judges, this demand could not help but be expressed in the Code of Law of Ivan IV, one of the features which distinguished the tsar's Code of Law from the former grand princely Code of Law[1] of Ivan III.

Like the Code of Law of Ivan III the new code prohibited judges from showing favoritism or seeking vengeance, or taking bribes. It was not limited solely to general prohibitions, but threatened definite punishments for cases of disobedience. The Code of Law of Ivan III says about incidents of unjust verdicts by judges that "if a boyar accuses anyone not on the basis of the trial, and with the crown secretary issues a record of the trial against him, this document is considered null and void. He must return what was received, but the boyar and secretary shall pay no fine." The new Code of Law stipulated, "If a judge pronounces an erroneous verdict or *without ulterior motives* convicts someone contrary to the trial and this is duly investigated, there is no fine for the judge. When a judge accepts a bribe and convicts someone contrary to the trial and this is duly investigated, collect the court costs of the plaintiffs, triple the tsar's fees from the judge, and as a penalty collect what the sovereign shall indicate. If a crown secretary who accepted a bribe draws up a register or records a case not in keeping with the trial, take half the costs from him before the boyar, and throw him into prison. Should a scribe as a result of bribery record a complaint not in keeping with the trial, beat him with the knout. If an accused lies to the judge, beat him with the knout and put him in prison."

According to the Code of Law of Ivan III a judge must not dismiss plaintiffs without having answered their petitions. The new Code of Law speaks more precisely about this as well. "If a judge sends away a plaintiff, does not receive his complaint and pronounces neither a verdict nor a refusal, and if the plaintiff petitions the sovereign, the sovereign shall return his complaint to the same judge and order him to pronounce sentence; if after this the judge still does not pronounce sentence, he shall be in disgrace. If the plaintiff submits a petition not relevant to the case, the judges refuses him and he proceeds to petition and weary the sovereign, throw him into prison."

The judge received eleven dengas, the secretary seven and the scribe two, when it was a case concerning money. To this regulation in the former Code of Law was added an article concerning the penalty for taking an excessive fee. "He who takes such a fee pays triple the amount. If in one town there are two vicegerents, or in one rural district there are two rural district chiefs, but they do not have separate courts, both shall collect the fees for one vicegerent on the basis of the fee schedule. Their agents will collect the fees for one agent and they will divide the fees in half. If any towns or rural districts which are administratively distinct have a common court, both officials shall take the fees jointly, and divide them evenly between themselves. If two vicegerents or two rural district chiefs or two agents collect two fees for one case and they are found guilty of this, he who paid the fees will collect twice the fee from them. Should anyone petition that the court officials took too much from him at court and it turns out that the plaintiff lied, punish him with public flogging and throw him into prison."

Precautions against abuse by crown secretaries and scribes and the punishments in the event of their detection were enacted. "The secretary," it was stipulated, "shall keep any undecided cases to himself for his own seal until it is settled. Secretaries who distribute complaints among the scribes for them to transcribe a fair copy must affix their signature to complaints and cases after the gluings, and when a scribe is copying the secretary himself shall collate the copy with the original, affix his signature and keep the cases to himself for his seal. Scribes must not keep to themselves any cases. If a case is taken from a scribe or a register without the seal and signature of the secretary, collect from the secretary the petition fees, tariffs and travel allowance and beat the scribe with the knout. If someone takes a register or complaint from a scribe outside the town or to the forecourt, collect the petition fees from the secretary but punish the scribe with public flogging and expel him from the ranks of the scribes. The constable must not request bribes for judges nor accept any himself. When otherwise punish him with public flogging, pay back the bribe twofold and dismiss him from his duties."

In addition, guarantor documents were given for each constable in which about ten guarantors pledged "He shall perform his duties duly, on our guarantee. He shall exert neither coercion nor distraint against anyone. He shall not be moved by animosity to instruct brigands and thieves to slander servitors nor to release convicts in the stocks and thieves. He shall issue documents pertaining to judgments by default and trial records and he shall not cause delay for the plaintiffs or defendants. He shall not send his own servitors or relatives with records, nor send unregistered riders with bailiffs. He shall not keep innkeepers, dice players, forgers, fornicators and various criminal types in his home, nor shall he commit any type of criminal acts. He shall settle the court costs and the tsar's fees for completed cases without delay, return the court costs to the plaintiffs, and shall not steal the fees for court cases. Having recovered the fees, he shall not keep them on his person, but surrender them to the tsar's treasury. When he does not act in keeping with what is written in this bond note collect from us, his guarantors, the tsar's penalty as the sovereign indicates, the court costs and crown fees, and take our heads for his head, our property for his property."

Threatening corrupt judges with punishment, the new Code of Law also included measures against malice. In the towns the vicegerents judged the townsmen, investigating them with respect to their possessions, their trades and according to the apportionments or how many rubles each gave as tribute to the tsar. On the basis of this information they made judgements and administered justice. The elders, hundredmen, tenmen and all town dwellers were to send their apportionment books annually to Moscow to the boyars, palace officials, treasurers and crown secretaries whose chancellery looked after their towns, and others were to give their apportionment books to the elders and sworn officials who sat in court with the vicegerents. When townsmen sued each other for large amounts not in keeping with their property value, the officials were to investigate on behalf of plaintiffs, using the apportionment books to establish how many rubles in tribute a given plaintiff paid on his property. When he had as much property as he was seeking, he was to be granted a trial. If not, he was to be prosecuted, the fees collected from him and he must be sent to the sovereign in Moscow.

Townsmen also might bring suit against vicegerents and their servitors in keeping with their possessions, trades and apportionments although if in some year the elder and sworn officials had not sent the apportionment books to Moscow a trail might not be granted against the vicegerent that year. Rural district chiefs were to judge the taxpaying peasants on the basis of their complaints and must administer justice without delay. When someone sued for a large sum not in keeping with his own possessions, and the defendant petitioned that the plaintiff was suing for a large amount and did not have as much as he was suing for, the rural district chiefs must select from their rural districts some of the worthiest men and one or two sworn officials, as the matter warranted. They must send them to investigate thoroughly whether or not the plaintiff had as much property as he was suing for, and after the investigation they should proceed as in the previous instance. If the plaintiff said that he had property belonging to someone else, they must investigate whether or not this was true, how much such property he had, and how it came into his possession.

In 1582 it was reported to the sovereign that many boyar slaves were giving evidence for their masters and hiring themselves out at trials of other people, bringing them to ruin through slander and sedition. "They write in the complaints large court costs, lie in court and do not speak to the case, dragging out the trial. Or they instigate sedition, mentioning other former cases and invective. Those who are hired by a plaintiff or defendant stand for him at court and, making a secret deal with the opponent, they sell out their employer. They utter irrelevant things in court or do not testify what is necessary and in this way they accuse him. Others compose complaints and judgments in return for money, instill sedition in the people and multiply the improper lawsuits. Such wicked men, junior boyars and slaves and men of other ranks go unpunished."

The sovereign decreed with all his boyars that, in keeping with the former codes, they must not spare slanderers, plotters and false accusers. "If someone appears in court for himself or for his master, or for someone else, and writes in the complaint a large claim, and the defendant proves that the claim is falsely signed, the plaintiff is to be prosecuted. What he sought in excess but did not exact is to be given back to the defendant, and he is subject to fees and distraint. If at the trial he does not speak to the case neither is he to be listened to, nor is his testimony to be recorded. After being beaten with the knout he shall be dismissed from court and not admitted to court again. If he defamed someone in a previous case, this shall not be recorded either, and if he does not prove his allegation he shall be beaten with the knout and the defamation penalty be exacted without a trial.

"If anyone calls another a thief or fails to report murder, sedition and treason against the sovereign tsar, he shall be punished with death. There is no disgrace in a complaint and a trial, but anyone who lies in a complaint and at a trial and concocts slander shall be punished by public flogging and enlistment in the cossack regiment in the borderland towns of Sevsk and Kursk. When any criminal, having taken money, sells out him whom he represents, a mistrial shall be declared. The hired witness shall be punished with the death penalty, and from whoever bribed him shall be exacted everything written in the complaint, including the fees and all damages, and he shall be punished with public flogging. If under torture the witness does not say that he was bribed, refer the matter to a lower court. If any junior boyars, fleeing their service, go to court for others, or maliciously petition for large claims yet settle for a lesser amount because in the complaints they do not write their claim in keeping with the case, charge such plaintiffs for the whole claim and do not admit them to court again, neither accept complaints from them in any chancellery. When anyone is found guilty of false accusation and sedition, punish such a criminal with public flogging and exile him to the cossacks in the borderland towns. After seizing his service estate and patrimony, distribute it to his family; if he has no family, give it to servitors who have no estates and whom the sovereign favors. If a judge assists any false accuser or slanderer or conceals a plotter, does not condemn slander or accepts a complaint not according to the case, or permits testimony in court that does not pertain to the case, from this a judge collect the claim of the plaintiffs, the fees and damages and the penalty as the sovereign indicates."

Sworn officials appeared in Novgorod in the reign of Grand Prince Vasily. In his son's Code of Law we read that at the trial of boyars, junior boyars and their agents where there was a majordomo there must be an elder and the worthiest men, *sworn officials*. In those districts where previously there were no elders or sworn officials, there now shall be elders and sworn officials everywhere. "Should someone from these rural districts bring a lawsuit or defend himself before the vicegerent or rural district chief or before their agents, the elders and sworn officials of the district from which he is making a claim or answering charges must be present at the trial. Should the vicegerent or rural district chief or their agent send the court record for final review and validation, and the plaintiff or defendant denies the record at its review, send it to be verified by the majordomo, elder and sworn officials who sat in court on this complaint. If these judicial men say that the judgment was just as it was recorded, if their signatures are on the record, if the copy was written by the vicegerent's secretary, and if it agrees word for word with the court record written by the local secretary, he who declared the record to be false is guilty. In the opposite case, if the judicial men say that the judgment was not as recorded, that the record was not written by the hand of the local secretary, that their signatures are not those on the record, and that the copy is not identical to the original record, collect the claims of the plaintiffs from the judge, and in addition impose on him the penalty which the sovereign shall decide.

When the majordomo and those judicial men, the elders and sworn officials who know how to read and write say that the judgment was indeed as recorded, and that their signatures are on the record, but those judicial men who do not know how to read and write differ with them, and say that there was a trial but not as the record shows, and that the copy does not agree word for word with the trial record, the judge and the judicial men who came to an arrangement on the basis of the record are guilty. Collect from them the claim of the plaintiffs and the penalty which the sovereign indicates.

"If servitors of the vicegerent or rural district chief place a bond on someone before and after the trial and there is no bond on him, they must inform the town managers, the majordomo, the elders and sworn officials about these servitors in the town. In the rural districts they must inform the elders and sworn officials who sit in court. If the servitors of the vicegerent or rural district chief, without informing the manager, majordomo, elder and sworn officials, take someone on whom there is no surety to their house and they chain him there, and his family and relatives approach the managers, majordomo, elder and sworn officials in order to petition, then the manager, majordomo, elder and sworn officials must take this man from the servitors of the vicegerent or rural district chief, and collect from them the compensation for his dishonor, and whatever he exacts from them, take twice the claim."

With regard to criminal offenses we find in the new Code of Law more precautionary measures directed against renewed occurrences and greater attention paid to the interests of society as a whole than in the old Code of Law. For example the old Code of Law decreed that someone apprehended while committing theft first be beaten with the knout, then compensation for the plaintiff and distraint for the court would be exacted from him, after which he would be released. If he had no property he would be beaten with the knout and then handed over to the plaintiff as a slave in distraint. In the new Code of Law the government no longer so readily released anyone found guilty of some transgression who might repeat the offense immediately after the trial and punishment.

The new Code of Law stipulated that a thief arrested the first time be placed on strict surety bond after being beaten with the knout and after the claims of the plaintiff were exacted from him. "If no strict surety bond is placed on him, throw him into prison until there is a surety bond. If a thief has no property with which to pay back the plaintiff, then after beating him with the knout hand him over to the plaintiff as a slave in the stocks until his redemption, but place the plaintiff on a bond so that he will deliver the transgressor to the boyars after he has exacted his own claim. When the plaintiff does not wish to post bond on himself that he will bring the criminal to the judge, throw the thief into prison until a bond is posted on him, and then in exchange for this bond exact from him the plaintiff's claim."

Concerning the stocks, the sovereign decreed with his boyars in 1555 that a criminal spend one month in the stocks for a claim of one hundred rubles. If the claim were more or less, he should spend the appropriate period according to the schedule. Those convicts for whom even one month was not enough to exact the plaintiff's claim must be handed over to the plaintiff until their redemption. If anyone petitioned for a commutation, a deadline of up to two months was to be imposed for the money to be paid, but a more generous deadline must not be granted for pernicious delay.

An important difference between the new and old Codes of Law consists in the attention paid by the new code to the personal confession of the transgressor. "If he is caught red-handed the first time," it specifies, "he shall be tried and sent for interrogation. If during the investigation the witnesses call him a felon, he shall be tortured. If he incriminates himself, punish him with the death penalty; if he does not incriminate himself, throw him into prison for life, and pay the plaintiff's costs from his possessions. If in the investigation the witnesses say that he is a good man, decide the case on the basis of the trial. Likewise for a second arrest for a felony it is commanded to torture the felon, and if he incriminates himself punish him with the death penalty and if he does not confess, investigate. Where the witnesses say that he is a disreputable man, incarcerate him for life. If they declare him a good man, put a strict surety bond on him. Likewise should the felon accuse someone, and in the investigation it turns out that the accused is a disreputable man, torture him and if he confesses, punish him. If there is no evidence of guilt, and in the investigation he is accused of no crime, do not trust the words of the felon, but put the accused only on a surety bond."

In cases of robbery personal confession was not given such weight. In an instruction to district criminal judges in 1571 it says that "if during the investigation any individuals are accused of being criminals, felons and robbers, and witnesses state that the robbers approached them to fence the stolen goods, and if the accused openly admit their disreputable deeds, naming those they assaulted and robbed, the elders shall order the criminal court secretaries to write their testimony down accurately. They shall order the archimandrites, abbots, priests, deacons and investigation officers who know how to read and write to affix their signature to the testimony, and whoever does not know how to read and write, in their stead their spiritual fathers shall affix their signatures.

"When in an investigation it is said that some individuals are criminals, but there are no plaintiffs against them, the elders will send for them and order them to appear. Their property will be inventoried and sealed until conclusion of the case, and they will be tortured. If they accuse themselves of robbery and make accusations against others, the elders shall send for those so accused and place them under visual confrontation with their accusers. Their property also shall be inventoried. If in the visual confrontation the informer does not retract his testimony, the elders will interrogate many concerning them. If after the investigation it turns out that they are good men, the elders shall surrender them on cash bonds to those involved in the investigation who found them blameless, but by reason of the criminal testimony they shall collect from them a fine for the plaintiff's claims in keeping with the investigation and the new sentence, amounting to one half of the plaintiff's claim.

"When anyone confesses to robbery, punish him with the death penalty, but concerning his property write to Moscow to the boyars in the Chancellery for Criminal Affairs. If an informer accuses someone of robbery after a single torture, but in the visual confrontation retracts his testimony and in the investigation he is declared blameless, give him on cash bonds without penalty to those involved in the investigation. If an informer accuses someone after two tortures and in the visual confrontation or third torture or, going to punishment, he retracts his testimony and they declare him blameless in the investigation, place him on a cash bond but collect a fine from him, and do not believe his testimony.

"Should an informer accuse someone of robbery but in the investigation both parties are declared criminals, torture them. If a robber has confessed under torture and is a boyar's man, collect from his master a fine for one half of the plaintiff's claim. If an informer accuses some individuals of robbery and in the investigations they are declared criminals, but they themselves do not confess under torture, punish them with the death penalty after investigation. If plaintiffs sue someone for robbery, but the informers do not accuse them of robbery and the plaintiffs, except for judicial duel, introduce no evidence of any sort, investigate. If they say in the investigation that they are criminals but do not say precisely what crime they have committed, torture them. When they do not confess under torture, imprison them for life. If they themselves do not confess but if in the investigation the witnesses accuse them of robbery by name, punish them with death.

"If an informer accuses someone and half the investigators call him blameless and the other half declare him a criminal, torture him. Should he not confess, surrender him on surety bond to the investigators who found him blameless, but according to the criminal testimony collect on him a share. If it happens that in the half which said he was a criminal there is a majority of fifteen or twenty men, but he does not confess under torture, imprison him for life, and if at a later date a second charge of robbery is brought against him, punish him with death but collect the fines from the investigators who found him blameless. When two or three informers accuse someone of robbery but in the investigation one half declares him blameless, and the other half a criminal, torture him. If he confesses, imprison him for life, and if later a new charge is brought against him, punish him with death, and from the investigators who found him blameless collect a fine. In addition to this, beat the two or three worthiest men with the knout. If informers accuse anyone of robbery and change their minds in the visual confrontation, but in the investigation they declare him proven a criminal, torture and punish him with death, even though he did not confess under torture."

The Code of Law defined that "if anyone sues for assault or plundering and the defendant says that he assaulted but did not plunder, find the defendant guilty of assault and collect from him the fine for dishonor, but as a penalty take what the sovereign decides, based on the person. A trial and justice are for cases of plundering; do not bring accusations there for everything. Proceed in the same manner if the defendant says that he plundered but did not assault. In other cases judge in the same way. If anyone is declared guilty of something, collect the penalty from him, but for the rest there is the trial and justice and cross-kissing. According to the old Code of Law, if five or six blameless junior boyars accuse someone after kissing the cross of the grand prince, or if five taxpaying peasants or six blameless Christian sworn officials say that he is a felon, but there is no evidence that he committed felonies previously, collect from him compensation for the plaintiff without trial." In the new Code of Law the number of witnesses in this circumstance was increased to ten or fifteen.

In the new Code of Law we meet the following kinds of stipulations dealing with judicial duels. "The lord-in-waiting and crown secretary will come to the duel and ask the plaintiff and defendant who are serving as their attendants and guarantors. Whoever they say are their attendants and guarantors, order them to attend the duel but the attendants and guarantors shall not bear armor, cudgels or clubs. The duelists shall do fair battle; but if outsiders come to the duel the lord-in-waiting and crown secretary shall send them away. Anyone who does not obey and does not go shall be sent to prison. In a duel a fighting man will do battle with a fighting man, or a noncombatant with a noncombatant, but a fighting man will not do battle with a noncombatant. If a noncombatant wishes to fight with a fighting man, that is his choice.

"If anyone sends for character witnesses[2] but the character witnesses disagree among themselves, some taking the plaintiff's side, others not, and if the former request a duel with the latter, they are to be permitted to do battle. If the character witnesses who testified on behalf the plaintiff defeat the character witnesses who testified against him, collect the plaintiff's claim and the fees from the defendant and the character witnesses who testified against the plaintiff, and conversely. If the character witnesses do not request a duel, having testified in agreement with the plaintiff, or if the character witnesses do not reach an understanding about the plaintiff's testimony, the plaintiff shall be prosecuted. If they are tried for any matter up to the duel, and the defendant petitions that he is unable to stand for duel, with the result that they are ordered to kiss the cross, he shall abandon the duel. In this event the plaintiff may choose whether he wishes to kiss the cross himself or let the defendant kiss the cross, and conversely if the plaintiff petitions." The Novgorod chronicler says under the year 1572 that the tsar installed the vicegerent in Novgorod according to ancient tradition, and ordered that there be duels according to ancient tradition.

In 1556 it was stipulated concerning investigations that "if plaintiffs and defendants litigating before boyars and in all the chancelleries anonymously call many as witnesses for the investigation, the boyars will send for the elders and sworn officials to investigate. The elders and sworn officials will command many and all the worthiest men, the princes and junior boyars, their bailiffs and the peasants, archimandrites, abbots, priests and deacons to come to the investigation. The elders and sworn officials will command that the investigation be conducted face to face by the worthiest men from the trading quarter of the towns, but these men shall not record testimony in the absence of the investigation witnesses. The investigation witnesses shall write their own testimony themselves. If any of them are illiterate they may make their mark, and their spiritual fathers shall affix their signatures to the testimony.

"When the investigation witnesses do not give the same testimony, with some speaking in favor of the plaintiff and others in favor of the defendant, then if more witnesses, fifty or sixty men, speak in favor of one litigant, give the verdict in his favor on the basis of the majority's evidence and convict the other litigant on the basis of less evidence, without resorting to a duel or kissing of the cross. After this the sovereign shall order the bishop or archimandrite or the abbot to find out truthfully which half lied, and to punish the liars. If in the investigation they speak equally, one half for the plaintiff and one half for the defendant, do not settle the case on the basis of such investigations, but order a second investigation, to be conducted with many others for the purpose of learning which half lied. When it is proved which half lied, select from it from every hundred men some bailiffs and peasants, and five or six of the worthiest men, and beat them with the knout, and send abbots, priests and deacons to the bishop. Exact all losses which the just party suffers, except the court costs, from those proven to have lied. If any individuals were tortured on the basis of the false investigation, let them collect the fine for dishonor twofold from the false witnesses, so that they do not tell lies again. Witnesses who give double testimony for one and the same case during an investigation will be subject to the same penalty.

"If a plaintiff or defendant does not call many as witnesses to the investigation, but calls only five or six men, and it is impossible to believe them, do not conduct an investigation with them, but settle the case on the basis of the trial and the charge that is presented in court. If a plaintiff or defendant summons as witnesses a boyar or a crown secretary or a chancellery official who can be believed in light of the case at hand, accept their testimony and settle the case on the basis of what they say without a duel or kissing of the cross. When a plaintiff or defendant calls as witness an individual or individuals from the accused, accept this evidence too, even if only one, and prosecute on the basis of what he says. Even if he brings little evidence against the plaintiff or defendant, prosecute.

"Boyars, crown secretaries, all chancellery officials and courtiers must give strict orders that at investigations in their villages their slaves and peasants not tell lies, but speak the truth. If it is discovered that their slaves and peasants have lied during interrogation the boyars themselves and the junior boyars will be held at great disgrace by the sovereign, and they are to punish their slaves and peasants as in criminal cases. Should a boyar, crown secretary, chancellery official, noble or junior boyar learn that in the interrogation their slaves and peasants lied, they shall tell the truth to the sovereign. In such circumstances they will not be held in disgrace by the sovereign but they are to settle the case, having investigated it correctly. The elders shall investigate correctly felony, robbery and various complaints on the basis of cross-kissing and must not favor a friend or take revenge on an enemy. They must take care to investigate strictly, so that in the interrogation they do not speak vainly, through collusion with family groups and conspiracies. The elders must write about such people to the sovereign. In the event of non-compliance with these duties, punish the elders without mercy."

The new Code of Law differed from the old in the detailed regulations for payment for dishonor. "Dishonor compensation paid to junior boyars who receive maintenance shall be set against their income on the basis of the books, and for their wives it shall be twice the amount. The payment of the dishonor compensation to those junior boyars who receive a salary is equal to the salary; the payment to their wives is double the amount. Crown secretaries at the palace and court receive the dishonor compensation assigned by the sovereign; their wives receive double the amount. Leading merchants receive a dishonor compensation of fifty rubles and their wives receive double the amount. Traders and urban merchants and all the middle ranks receive as dishonor compensation five rubles; their wives receive double the amount. A boyar's good man receives a dishonor compensation of five rubles, except for his agents and exactors who receive payment for the dishonor matching the amount of their income; their wives receive double. An agricultural or non-agricultural peasant receives a dishonor compensation of one ruble, and their wives receive two rubles. A boyar's lesser man or a taxpaying townsman of the lowest rank likewise receives a ruble dishonor compensation, the wife receives double. For injury impose a penalty proportionate to the person and the injury."

A case has reached us from our period involving the famous secretary Vasily Shchelkalov, against whom the scribe Aigustov brought many criminal charges. Under torture the accuser confessed that he compiled many charges against Shchelkalov at the instigation of Prince Mikhail Cherkassky. The sovereign ordered that six hundred rubles be collected from Aigustov as compensation for the dishonor to Shchelkalov and his wife. Since Aigustov did not have sufficient funds to pay the fine, his patrimony was seized.

An addition was made to the regulation in the old Code of Law relating to foreigners. "When a subject of the crown seeks a claim against a foreigner, or if a foreigner seeks a claim against a native subject, give them lots. He whose lot is drawn, having kissed the cross, receives or renounces the claim." The Englishman Lane describes for us this drawing of lots. "Two wax beads with the names of the litigants are placed in a cap, and he whose name is drawn out first wins."

Concerning loans, the tsar considered it necessary in 1557 to make the following decree. "Recover cash and grain loans to servitors on the basis of the loan documents, promissory notes and testaments over the course of five years (up to 1562), exacting the *true* sum, money without interest and grain in level measure, calculated in five portions. The sovereign has cancelled all interest payments based on old loan documents up until Christmas Day of 1557, but if the servitors borrow money or grain on interest during those five loan-recovery years, and in the appointed years do not repay the new debts, then from Christmas Day 1562 and henceforth recover the new debts from the servitors entirely in their true amount, and in addition collect money with half interest (ten percent) and grain with interest. If during this five-year period a given borrower does not pay each year, being in service or on an official mission for a year or two, when he returns immediately recover what was not paid for all those years in which he did not pay. When anyone is in service or on an official mission for the entire five years of the loan term, upon his return settle with him the entire debt immediately, but without interest. Set the collection of a debt of one hundred rubles from a servitor at two months, but if the debt is greater or less then according to calculation, but place non-servitors in the stocks for a month for a debt of one hundred rubles.

"Always settle accounts in full against all slaves on the basis of their contracts. Collect in its entirety the debt from non-servitors in the fixed five-year loan term according to the ancient loan documents, but without interest. If they borrow money or grain on interest during those loan recovery years, always impose the stocks on them for the new debts, but command that the interest on money and grain be recovered at one half the sum (ten percent). When they do not repay the new debts during the fixed five-year term, collect from them the full interest on money and grain (twenty percent).

"If anyone borrows money without a loan document and without a promissory note, or if anyone takes any type of loan and does not deny it in court, order that it be recovered from him in full and always impose the stocks. He who borrowed money and mortgaged his patrimony to the lender to farm for interest can repay the debt in the five-year term in the following manner. In the first year he yields a fifth portion of the debt according to the calculation, and takes back his patrimony, but the lender continues to farm it for interest. The debtor cannot mortgage it or sell it, nor exchange it nor give it as a dowry or a memorial until he repays all the money; if he does not repay, he must return the patrimony to the lender. If the debtor, not having paid all the money in installments in five years, sells his patrimony, and even after selling it does not repay the debt, collect from him the debt in full. If the debtor is not present, collect from him who bought the mortgaged patrimony from him. If it is impossible to settle the account with him, take the patrimony from him and hand it over to the lender to whom it was mortgaged, and let him impose the stocks on him from whom he purchased it. If it is impossible to recover the money from him, turn him over as a slave until he is redeemed. If he is not present, he who purchased the mortgaged patrimony forfeits the money because he who purchases a patrimony ought to investigate whether or not it is free of encumbrances. If the seller appears afterwards, let the purchaser seek justice from him."

In 1558 the sovereign ordered that "if anyone borrowed money and issued a loan document on himself according to which he would perform service instead of paying interest, but when the matter comes to litigation he denies the loan document and says that he is the son of a junior service boyar, investigate the matter. If he has been a debtor for more than fifteen years, was not about the sovereign's service, was not enlisted in the military roll, and the loan document was written out more than fifteen years ago, grant a trial against him. If he was a debtor for less than fifteen years, do not grant a trial on the basis of the loan document." In 1560, because of a fire, it was stipulated that "if anyone losing his household through fire proceeds on the basis of loan documents to make a claim against those whose households also burned, do not send the bailiffs, but suspend payment of the debts for five years."

The old Code of Law, in all probability as a result of the influence of Mosaic laws which were inserted into the Code of Canon Law, stipulated that the property of a deceased who had no son was to be handed over to the daughter, and if there were no daughter, the property went to the next of kin. Ivan IV deemed it necessary to restrict the right of inheriting ancient princely hereditary estates to the male descendants of the deceased. At the same time, in 1562, Ivan decided with respect to inheritance after the death of childless boyars and childless junior boyars that if they had no close relative or testament the patrimony escheated to the sovereign, but the sovereign ordered that the wife be granted enough from this patrimony for her to live on, and likewise a memorial for the repose of the deceased's soul be endowed out of his own treasury.

In 1572, with respect to patrimonies bestowed by the sovereign, it was defined that in the event of the owner dying childless the sense of the charter must be taken into account in order to determine whether it stated that the patrimony was granted to him, his wife, his children or his family. Matters should proceed on the basis of what was written. If it was written in the charter that the patrimony was granted to one person only, after his death the estate escheated to the sovereign. If he did not have a charter from the sovereign the patrimonies were to be seized for the sovereign after his death, even though he had children. Even the right of collateral relatives to inherit hereditary estates awarded for service was restricted to specific degrees, namely the brothers, nephews and great-nephews inherited the property of him who died childless. If one of these nephews or great-nephews died childless, the portions of the deceased's estate were handed over to their brothers, uncles, nephews and great-nephews, but the patrimony might not be handed over to relatives more distant than great-nephews.

In the new Code of Law we find a regulation concerning the right to redeem patrimonies, which in all probability arose out of strong familial ties and common familial possession of land property. "If anyone sells a patrimony," said the law, "his children and grandchildren have no claim on it, nor may they redeem it. If the brothers or nephews of the seller sign the deeds of purchase as witnesses they, their children and grandchildren, also have no claim on the sold patrimony. Were the brothers or nephews not witnesses, the brothers, sisters and nephews might redeem the patrimony. If the seller wishes to redeem his patrimony he can do this amicably with the agreement of the purchaser but he cannot compel him to do so. When forty years pass after the sale of the patrimony the former owners no longer hold any claim to it, nor do they have a claim on the purchases. If anyone sells his purchase, his children, brothers and nephews may not redeem it.

"If anyone reserves his purchase as an inheritance for his children it becomes his patrimony, and henceforth he may redeem it. Should anyone redeems his own patrimony within the forty-year limit he must keep it for himself, and may not sell it to a different clan or mortgage it. He must hand it over in his own clan, namely to relations who did not sign their names as witnesses in the earlier deeds of purchase. If an individual redeems his patrimony with money not his own, or mortgages it, or if he sells it, and a relative who has sold it before proves that he who redeemed it did so with someone else's money and is not holding it for himself, the patrimony belongs to the prior seller without cost. When anyone except the owner wishes to mortgage his patrimony to a third party, these third parties must take as a mortgage for the patrimony only the sum which the patrimony is in fact worth. If the third party assumes the patrimony in mortgage at a higher value, and the patrimony owner proceeds to petition, he can take this patrimony in mortgage for the amount it is worth, but he forfeits that money which the third party gave as a loan in excess. If anyone exchanges his own patrimony for another and accepts money in the exchange, and if one of the owners wishes to redeem it, he can do so, but to him from whom he is redeeming the estate he must leave lands worth the same amount for which he exchanged his own lands."

In one copy of the Code of Law the following supplementary regulation is found. "If childless princes, boyars and junior boyars and men of various ranks wish to sell their lands or mortgage them, or donate them to a monastery as a memorial for their souls, they are free to do so with all their purchases. As for the patrimonies, they may alienate only half. If anyone alienates more than half and the owner petitions about this, give the excess sale to the owner. He who purchased more than the half or took it under mortgage without having tried to learn the details forfeits his money."[3]

In 1556 a decree concerning testaments stated that "if a wife who is dying writes in her testament the name of her husband as the executor he shall not be the executor and this testament is null and void because the wife is obedient to her husband, writing what he orders her to write." In 1561 the metropolitan's boyars were ordered to copy from the metropolitan's decree how to act in the following instances. "Children bring before court the testaments of their fathers and mothers, others present the testaments of their brothers and sisters, their nephews and wives. The brothers or third parties are designated as executors and wives have their husbands or spiritual fathers. The wills are not signed and carry no seal, the signature of the testator is absent because he did not know how to write, or died suddenly. On some wills there is only the hand of the executors and spiritual fathers, and on others only that of the spiritual fathers. The respondents at court denounce these wills and they call them pro forma testaments[4] but they do not show who drew them up. Their only defect is that they are not signed and carry no seals. Should these wills be believed or not? The metropolitan's boyars wrote that these wills should be trusted even though they were not signed and had no seals, since they did have the signatures of the spiritual fathers, executors and third parties, and there was no proof that they were falsely composed. If in the will the wife named her husband as executor, and in addition to him the wife's relatives are named as executors, such wills may also be believed. Where in the will only the wife's husband is named as executor and there are no third parties, this will is not to be believed."

The expression in the foregoing decree, "The wife is obedient to her husband, writing what he orders her to write" clearly indicates the position of the wife in the period under examination. According to the concepts of that age, a wife must share the lot of her husband in cases of transgressions he committed. Prince Ivan Pronsky stated in a written oath given to the tsar that in the event of his withdrawal from service the tsar was free to punish him and his wife.

From the different juridical charters, conveyances, allocation and transferal documents we see the notion of common clan ownership and of apportionments for close relatives, that is, for first and second cousins, as well as imperfect apportionments. The form of the conveyances is remarkable, supporting what we said concerning the origin of landownership in Muscovy. "We such-and-such (brothers) transferred the lands belonging the grand prince but in our possession to such-and-such (brothers). We have not evaded service for the grand prince or tribute and various local apportionments, we have taken so much for ourselves for a land parcel." Entire communes possessed land. Thus in 1583 Nikita Stroganov allotted his village to the elders and sworn men and all the peasants in the rural district in Davidov settlement. For division of lands, the brothers involved in the division had recourse to third parties as intermediaries. The third party was divide the land into portions after which those sharing the land cast lots in his presence. Whoever's lot was drawn first could take the portion he wished, the second lot drawn did the same, and the last took what was left.

NEW STATUTE IN WESTERN RUSSIA

Concerning legislative activity in Western Russia, a new statute was issued there in 1556. Its first section, concerning the person of the sovereign, decreed that "if anyone conspires or incites rebellion against the sovereign, even though the intention was not carried out, he who is found guilty in the face of clear evidence loses honor and life. If anyone incites rebellion against the sovereign with intent to harm the state, mints coins without the sovereign's permission, raises an army with the intention of usurping the throne on the death of the sovereign, enters into relations with the enemy, shows him assistance, surrenders to him a castle, or leads a hostile army into Lithuania, he shall lose his honor and life, his sons shall be considered disgraced and his property shall be seized for the sovereign. The wives of such traitors, if they swear they knew nothing of their husband's intention, do not lose their paternal or maternal chattels, or the marriage settlement recorded for them by their husbands before the treason.

"If anyone causes dishonor to the sovereign majesty he shall be punished in accordance with the seriousness of the act or words, but not with loss of honor, life or chattels. Whoever denounces a transgression against the sovereign must support the truth of his statement by his own oath and the oath of a nobleman, worthy of belief and beyond suspicion. Counterfeiters, as well as goldsmiths who adulterate gold and silver by admixing zinc or tin, shall be burned to death without mercy. In cases involving chattels the grand princes will litigate in one court with all Lithuanian subjects.

"Writs of adjournment, which postpone the date for court appearances, shall be granted by the crown only in three circumstances. (1) If he who is summoned to court was held captive by the enemy. (2) If someone is on a diplomatic mission outside the country or has been dispatched on some other assignment for the sovereign. (3) If someone is genuinely ill, which he must afterwards corroborate under oath.

"If anyone assaults an envoy of the sovereign bearing letters royal, likewise if anyone assaults the envoys of council lords, magistrates and local judges travelling with their letters, and tears up the letters, he must spend twelve weeks in prison and compensate the court official for the dishonor. A court official at the presenting of writs must always have with him two nobles as witnesses in the event something happens to him. Safe conducts shall not be granted by the sovereign to such debtors who by their own fault have lost their estate and are unable to pay their debts. These writs shall be issued solely for such as have fallen into destitution by an act of God, by fire, flood, hostile attack and also if the individual has come to ruin in performing crown service. They shall not be given more than a thirty-year limit to pay the debt. Safe conducts shall not be granted to commoners, merchants, and Jews against the nobility. No one shall dare to introduce new tolls under pain of losing the property on which the new toll was introduced. The nobility's carts laden with grain from their own barns and not with purchased grain do not pay a toll."

In the third section, concerning the freedoms of the nobility, we find a regulation concerning dietines and local delegates. "Four weeks prior to the Great Sejm the dietines are assembled. In them are gathered the provincial governors, castellans, rural village constables, princes, lords and nobles and they consult on all local needs. Then after a unanimous decision they elect delegates, two men from each land court and for as many courts as there are in each province. They send these delegates to the Great Sejm, entrusting to them all regional affairs and investing them with plenary powers. The king is bound to keep everything as of old and when it becomes necessary to issue a new decree this is possible only at the Great Sejm. The king shall be bound not to elevate commoners over the nobility, nor induct them into dignities, nor give them service rank."

In the fourth section, concerning judges and courts, it was decreed that "in every region there must be a judge, an assistant judge and a clerk elected in this fashion. At the time appointed by the sovereign all landowners of the region assemble at the court located in the middle of the region. From all the nobility they shall select four good men for the office of judge, four good men for the office of assistant judge and four good men for the office of clerk. From these twelve the sovereign will choose three men to serve as judge, assistant judge and clerk. The land clerk is bound to write all writs and summonses in Russian and not in any other language. For each region the governors shall choose judiciary agents from the good nobles who live permanently in the region.

"The duty of the judiciary agent consists in the following. He must take the writs and summon people to court with them, indicate the time limit, swear witnesses in at court, carry out court decisions, conduct investigations and enter the findings in books. For abuse of office the judiciary agent is punished with death. The judges and assistant judges must render judgement themselves, and not through their representatives. Neither clerical figures nor crown constables may be chosen as judges. The judges try civil cases whereas criminal cases they present to the court of governors, elders and prefects. In addition, the governors, elders and all castle wardens and wardens of the sovereign's regional manors, each in his rank, must choose a good nobleman who, together with the castle constable, shall judge all cases relating to the castle.

"The land court will sit three times a year, on Trinity Sunday, on the feast of St. Michael [September 29] and on the feast of the Epiphany [January 6]. At that time the judges, assistant judges and the clerk will travel to the appointed place and hold court for two weeks if there are many cases, and if few cases then until they get through with them." Afterwards, under Bathory, the session was extended to three weeks.

"If anyone attending court rails against his opponent," the decree continued, "confine him in the nearest castle for six weeks. If he elbows or strikes his opponent with his hand, he must pay him twelve rubles in cash. If he draws a weapon he shall lose a hand, and if he inflicts a wound he shall be deprived of his life. The same punishment shall be meted out if the accused acts in the same way with the judge, the assistant judge, the clerk or any of the village constables. Conversely, the same punishment shall be meted out to the judge, the assistant judge, the clerk and the village constables if they act in the same way with the accused. No one shall judge the sovereign's village constables except the sovereign, but in cases concerning chattels they are obliged to appear before the land court.

"Witnesses at court must be Christians, good people, worthy of belief and above suspicion. Involuntary slaves cannot be witnesses either for or against their masters; the insane cannot be witnesses; those who are accused together for the same crime cannot testify on each other's behalf. If the judgment of the court seems unjust to any of those standing trial, he may appeal the case to the sovereign's court, but he may not say to the judge any vulgar words. All he may say is, 'My lord judge! Your judgment seems to me unlawful. I am appealing the case to the sovereign for his mercy.'

"In each region there must be a property magistrate appointed by the sovereign for life. In all disputes concerning land or boundaries the land court shall inform the property magistrate, who has the right to issue summonses for both litigating parties under his own name and seal, to fix the date of inspection of the disputed land for four weeks. When he has visited and examined the charters and boundary markers and has heard the witnesses, he shall admit for testimony that party which has the best charters and evidence and the clearest survey markers. Having heard the argument, the property magistrate shall make his decision, establish the boundaries and prepare the charters of his judgment for his own signature and seal. In every region the property magistrate shall choose as his assistants one or two stewards, noblemen who have a permanent residence in the region and are suitable men."

In the fifth section marriage contracts are discussed. "The father giving his daughter in marriage and providing a dowry for her must take from his son-in-law a charter in exchange for his seal, and for the seals of good men, attesting that he has signed over to his future wife a third portion of his real estate. When he does not do so, on the death of her husband the daughter loses her dowry even if she brought a great sum of money with her, but the children and relatives of the deceased are bound to give her thirty kopa grosh as a wedding gift if she remarries. If she does not wish to remarry, she receives from the estate of her husband an equal portion with his descendants, and it remains in her use until her death. If the estate of the deceased is not worth thirty kopa grosh, the wife receives a quarter of the chattels which he owned before his death, even if she remarries."

Then follows an article concerning the recording of a marriage settlement similar to the same article in the old Statute. "If some permanent or temporary resident of the grand principality marries in Lithuania and settles real estate on his wife as part of the marriage settlement, he is obliged to perform military service in wartime from the estate of his wife and from others if he obtains them, without excusing himself on the grounds that his wife did not transfer anything to him; otherwise he and his wife lose their estate to the benefit of the crown. When a noblewoman, a maiden or a widow marries a commoner, she forfeits her estate, both paternal and maternal, which passes to another descendant, who nevertheless is obliged to hand over to her a sum of money determined by the statute, for each service unit of men five kopa grosh, and so forth. Noble widows who marry commoners lose their recorded marriage settlement. A widowed noblewoman cannot marry a second time earlier than six months after the death of the first husband. Otherwise she loses her recorded marriage settlement, and if she has no marriage settlement she pays twelve ruble groshas into the treasury. In divorce, if the ecclesiastical court recognizes the husband as guilty the wife shall keep her marriage settlement; if the wife is guilty, she loses both the marriage settlement and the dowry. Should they be divorced by reason of consanguinity or other causes where neither the husband nor the wife are at fault, the marriage settlement remains with the husband, and the dowry with the wife."

The sixth section included a regulation concerning guardianship. "The age of majority is set at eighteen for men and fifteen for women. The father may be the guardian of minor sons to whom the mother's estate was left. If during the guardianship the father alienates this property permanently or temporarily, when the sons attain the age of majority they have the right to initiate a lawsuit for the property against him who acquired it, provided they did not exceed the limitation. Should the father spend on himself the chattels of his son and then dies, leaving several other sons, before the equal division of the estate they must all share among themselves their father's debt, not excluding even that brother in whose debt the father was. When each has paid back his share of the debt they may proceed with the equal division of the inheritance.

"Those who may be trustees are, first of all, he whom the father names in the will. When no trustee is named in the will the eldest brother, who must have reached the age of majority, shall act as trustee for his younger brothers and sisters. If no brother has reached the age of majority, the paternal uncle shall act as trustee. If there are no natural uncles, the nearest paternal relative shall act as trustee; and if there are none, the maternal relatives shall serve. If there are no maternal relatives, a trustee shall be named by the sovereign or the governors, or by the land court. He may not be a foreigner, and his estate must be equivalent to the estate held in trusteeship. The trustee from the relatives must be of substantial estate as well, except those trustees named by the father in his will."

In the seventh section promissory notes and sales are discussed. Here it was decreed that everyone was at liberty to alienate, bestow, sell and otherwise divest himself of his own estates, paternal or maternal, which were obtained through service, purchased or acquired by any means whatsoever. He might do so *without regard for the old statute with its reservation of two thirds of an estate for relatives,* and without regard for his children and relatives. From the family estates only one third could be alienated in perpetuity, and two thirds could be redeemed by the children and relatives. For this reason whoever sold the two thirds could not take more money for them than they are valued, lest he who redeemed them afterwards must pay more than the value.

In the eighth section wills are regulated. Concerning movable property or acquired immovable property, everyone might make a will, whether healthy or ill, being only sound mind. He might bequeath to whom he desired, having summoned the local village constable, the judge, the assistant judge, clerk or chaplain. Where these were not found a will might be drawn up before three credible witnesses. If the testator died thereafter the testament still had force even if he did not affix his seal. Those who themselves could not make a will could not be witnesses to wills, among them women, executors, trustees indicated by the testator, and finally any beneficiaries of the will. No one might bequeath in his will anything to his slave without first giving him his freedom. An administrative servitor, a burgher of a non-privileged town or a commoner could bequeath a third of their movable property to whom they wished, but two thirds they must leave in the house of the son who was obliged to serve from the land on which he was resident. If he had no children these two parts were left in the house for the service of that lord on whose land he resided. Should the children of the deceased, provided they were free, wish to go away, they could leave after they had taken two parts of the paternal movable property but the land with the grain sown, with the barns and with everything present when their father took the land, remained for the lord. The reasons for which a father could deprive his son or daughter of their inheritance consisted of disrespectful treatment, desertion in hardship, stubborn attachment to heresy and immoral conduct on the part of the daughter. A blind man could make a will in the presence of no less than eight witnesses.

The eleventh section deals with acts of violence perpetrated by the nobility. If anyone forcibly married a maiden or widow and it was shown that neither she nor her relatives gave permission, the abductor forfeited his life, and a third part of his estate went to the abducted woman. When a maiden or widow gave her consent to marriage and abduction without the knowledge of her relatives, she forfeited her paternal and maternal estate.

Should one of the spouses take the life of the other and the crime was confirmed under oath by seven noblemen, the transgressor must be punished with death in the same way as a patricide or matricide. If someone deprived another of his hand, foot, eye, lip, teeth or ear he must pay for each such member fifty kopa grosh and spend twenty-four weeks in prison. If he deprived him of both hands or both feet, both ears and eyes, he paid one hundred kopa grosh and spent a year and six weeks in the fortress, and so on.

If a burgher in the service of the burgomaster injured a nobleman, he paid him as indicated above; if a common burgher injured a nobleman, he lost a hand. If a common slave injured a nobleman, he lost a hand; if he deprived the nobleman of his hand or foot or maimed him on some other member, he forfeited his life. If a son or daughter murdered father or mother, the transgressor must be brought to the market place, his body torn with pincers and then, having been tied in a bag together with a dog, a rooster, grass snakes and a cat, he must be drowned. His accomplices were subjected to the same punishment. If a father or mother murdered a son or daughter they must spend a year and six weeks in the fortress and then four times a year in front of the principal church they must do public penance.

Whoever murdered his sister or brother forfeited his life, and the estate which belonged to him and his children went to other heirs. Whoever killed his brother-in-law forfeited his own life but his wife, the sister of the slain man, inherited after the brother, just like her children. A servant who slew his master was punished with the cruel death penalty; if he only drew a weapon, he lost a hand.

In section twelve, concerning murder and compensations for wounds to commoners, by the way, a decree was inserted which prohibited Jews and their wives from wearing gold or silver. A yellow patch on his headgear must distinguish a Jew from a Christian. A Jew, a Tatar and a Muslim could not receive any office, could not have Christian slaves, but they could have debt slaves. If it were proven that one of them persuaded a debt slave to convert to their faith he was to be burned without mercy. Christian women could not be wet-nurses for Jewish and Muslim children, and anyone who forced them to do so forfeited his life.

In the fourteenth section transgressions are treated. "A thief apprehended with goods worth more than a poltina grosh shall be executed. If the stolen goods are worth not more than a poltina grosh, the thief shall be fastened to a pillar and beaten with canes. The stolen goods shall be returned to the owner, who shall be compensated from the chattels of the thief. If the thief has no property, cut off his ear. When a thief is caught a second time with stolen goods, even though the goods are not worth even ten groshas, hand him over to death."

INTERNATIONAL LAW

With respect to international law, Grand Prince Vasily issued a regulation relating to ambassadors from the Christian sovereigns of Europe. "According to custom," he asserted, "ambassadors travel between sovereign majesties and perform the business between them in accordance with an agreement on both sides, but no coercion of any kind holds sway over them." His son Ivan, owing to his character, often could not refrain from violent actions regardless of circumstances and thus he allowed himself to detain ambassadors if their words did not please him. For this reason the Swedish and Lithuanian ambassadors were detained.

Beginning with the reign of Ivan IV ambassadors to Moscow were rather more strictly confined than previously, and this restriction subsequent by was maintained. The reason was the disclosure of relations between Prince Simeon of Rostov and the Lithuanian ambassador Dowojna, which were deleterious to the crown. When the new Lithuanian ambassador Prince Zbarazhsky arrived, he was ordered to be kept completely cordoned off. Bailiffs received the order "to take good care that junior boyars, boyar servitors and merchants do not pass the embassy nor enter the courtyard and do not talk with any embassy officials. Water their horses at the embassy and do not let them go to the river. If they say that previously they watered their horses at the river, and that the water in the wells is foul and the horses do not drink, the bailiffs are to answer that the wells are good, better than river water. Previously when they watered at the river and at the public trough the embassy servitors always fought with the locals and lost the horses. If the embassy servitors do not want to water the horses at the embassy, send them to the river with bailiffs to their own ice hole, and take care that no one talks with them."

In addition to detention the ambassadors experienced other signs of the tsar's displeasure if negotiations did not lead to the desired goal. For example, when the Lithuanian ambassadors Kishka and companions rejected the tsar's demands and asked to be dismissed, the tsar and the boyars decided that "if the matter is not settled by the ambassadors, they should be dismissed. At their leavetaking order them to make a bow to their king, but not to shake hands, because in the tsar's answer an angry word was pronounced against the ambassadors." When the Swedish ambassador from Gustav Vasa arrived after the war, the tsar did not summon him to his hand or to dine because he was first to arrive after the war, and it was still not known what type of charters he brought with him.

Special customs were observed for the reception of Crimean ambassadors. The ambassador gave thanks for the sovereign's favor, knelt down and removed his cap. After he kissed his hand the ambassador and his entourage were given mead, and then gifts were distributed to them. During the years of Ivan's minority we encounter information concerning the protection of the sovereign's hand during the presentation of ambassadors. "He (the grand prince) summoned him (the ambassador) to his hand, but Prince Vasily Vasilievich Shuisky and Prince Ivan Ovchina protected his hands." Regarding the presents which ambassadors received, there is some curious information concerning the mission of Prince Romodanovsky to Denmark. The ambassadors gave presents to the king from themselves, and the king presented them with gifts in return, but the ambassadors declared to the royal council that the king's presents were not worth even half the value of their presents, and that the tsar did not favor the Danish ambassadors in that way. The grandees answered that they would report this to the king, adding that the king granted his ambassadors favors, not trade goods. He favored them with whatever he happened to have. "We have brought the king grand gifts," the ambassadors answered, "and given him great honor, so that he might look more favorably on our mission. The gifts are not for trade, for we do not wish a profit from the king's favor." The king sent part of their gifts back, at which they were told, "You spoke about your gifts as if you wanted to market them, but our sovereign does not wish to barter. He took what pleased him, and what he did not like he sent back to you."

In Moscow the custom was to show attention to foreign ambassadors by sending them a part of the bag from the tsar's hunt as a gift. In connection with this, a curious instance was entered in the embassy records. Coming from the sovereign the kennelman arrived at the Lithuanian ambassadors' court with the sovereign's gift of hares from the hunt. The ambassadors entertained the kennelman with wine, but gave him nothing in return. The bailiffs considered it their duty to send to inquire of the ambassadors why they had not given gifts to the kennelman in return for the sovereign's favor. The ambassadors then forwarded to the kennelman four gold coins from their own purse, and two gold coins from their court officials. The one sent with the money told the kennelman, "The ambassadors favor you, but the officials petition you." The kennelman took the two gold coins from the officials but did not take the four coins sent by the ambassador, since he was offended by the expression "they favor."

In 1537 the grand prince ordered all gifts returned which were presented to him by the Lithuanian ambassador Jan Glebowicz and his companions, and instead he sent to him his own favor. The ambassadors took the gifts and the sovereign's favor, but told the bailiff, "We came to the grand sovereign for a good cause and brought gifts as befit his realm. We thought that in this way we were showing respect to him and our lord, but the sovereign has offended us because he refused our presents. What good is his grant to us? Take this grant away. We did not come for our own profit, but on the king's business." The bailiff reported this to the grand prince who ordered him to tell the ambassadors, as if it were the treasurer speaking, "Even we cannot speak to the sovereign about what is unprecedented. Their uncles and brothers used to visit the sovereign. Anything that the sovereign liked from their gifts he took, and what he did not like he ordered sent back. In addition, he favored the ambassadors with his own presents. Whether the business was settled or not, the sovereign showed his favor, for such is the sovereign's practice. Now the sovereign has favored them, and in our opinion they do not speak well when they tell us to take back the favor." In 1554 the Moscow ambassador Boyar Yuriev and his companions brought presents to King Sigismund Augustus, but the king ordered all the presents sent back. They brought goblets, gerfalcons and tambourines, but the gerfalcons were sick, and there was not a single red one among them.

Also of interest is the information about the conduct of the Lithuanian ambassadors Jan Krotoszewski (Skrotoshin in the sources) and his companions, both in Moscow and on the road. Their servitors picked a quarrel in more than one place. In Viazma their servitors beat the junior boyars; at the reception in Moscow they did the same. Riding about the mercantile quarter they sounded the trumpet, dishonored the bailiffs, threw stones at one and broke his nose, and railed against the crown secretary. They gave a junior boyar a potion to drink, from which he died, and they cut the tail off a horse. After liturgy the tsar's confessor Archpriest Evstraty was riding from Annunciation cathedral and the kings' men dishonored him, swore at him and beat him, but the ambassadors did not initiate an investigation or offer protection. When he learned of this, the tsar ordered that the ambassadors be told, "Did they come here with the embassy or are they to carry on as they see fit?" The tsar ordered that he who dishonored the archpriest be exposed publicly as a rogue, and that all gear be stripped from his horse. The sovereign refused to receive the ambassadors because owing to their misconduct it was impossible for them to be in the sovereign's presence.

The ambassadors made excuses, saying that in Viazma it was the Muscovites who beat their men, that they sounded the trumpet according to Polish custom, and the bailiffs said nothing about not sounding the trumpet, nor had the bailiffs complained to them about the other instances of misconduct. They said that it was impossible to find out who cut off the horse's tail, that they did not give the sick man an evil potion but medicine, and he died according to God's judgment, and that the king's merchant struck the archpriest with a cane unintentionally. When the tsar himself repeated the same complaints to the ambassadors, saying that they beat the archpriest after pulling him from his horse, the ambassadors said nothing in their defense. Then for their part the ambassadors presented a writ on which were enumerated their losses, everything that was stolen from them on the road. The ambassadors also complained that in Moscow wares were taken from Lithuanian merchants, but nothing was given in return. "We have inquired about all these articles," the boyars replied, "and the treasurer and clerk told us that the horses and wares were taken as the tsar's penalty from Armenians and Greeks whereas, according to previous customs never did Armenians and Greeks travel with Lithuanian ambassadors. Indeed we know very well that Armenians and Greeks do not live in your sovereign's realm yet now this novelty has been brought to us, that men from different lands arrive with Lithuanian ambassadors. Men of the Turkish sultan were with you, they travelled under the name of your sovereign, and they were with you for the sake of espionage. They were seeking to perpetrate some wicked deed against our sovereign's land yet such is still the mercy of the tsar's majesty that they were not punished." In the order to the Muscovite ambassadors sent to Lithuania to confirm a treaty it was said, "If they say that the king's ambassadors suffered dishonor in Moscow, answer that this occurred because your sovereign sent to our sovereign Polish and Lithuanian ambassadors together; the Poles were known in Moscow before, and they brought their haughty manners with them across the border."

Those sent with the Russian ambassadors sometimes did not understand that their principal duty was to remain silent. Thus the tsar wrote to Naumov, who was ambassador in the Crimea, "You released your servants to Moscow but on the way they told all the information. You know yourself that such matters must be kept secret. You did this unwittingly, for you dismissed your servitors, but they divulged the entire message. Henceforth you should write your messages to us and not dismiss your servitors prematurely, so that such secret information might reach us, and there be no rumor among the people without our knowledge." The crown secretary accompanying the ambassador had to kiss the cross that he would conduct business in keeping with the sovereign's order, not utter a word to anyone until death, and not conceal anything from the sovereign.

From the description of the siege of Pskov in the sources we run across information about the treachery by which Zamoyski sought to deprive Prince Shuisky of his life. A Russian captive from the Polish encampment appeared before Shuisky with a large chest and a letter from the German Moller who previously was in the tsar's service. Moller wrote that he wished to surrender to the Russians, had sent on ahead his treasure, and asked Shuisky to unlock the chest, take out the gold, and guard it. The chest appeared suspicious to Shuisky, who ordered it carefully opened by a skilled locksmith. He found loaded muskets covered with gunpowder. Heidenstein,[5] the historian of Bathory, says that Zamoyski permitted himself this action in revenge against the Russians who attacked the subsequently famous Zolkiewski[6] during a truce concluded to allow burial of the dead.

Regarding prisoners, in the relations of the Moscow court with the Lithuanian, each of the two realms normally demanded that prisoners on either side be set free when they considered this advantageous for themselves, that is when one side had fewer prisoners than the other. Every time one side would not agree to the liberation the affair ended in exchange and redemption. If they could not agree on the price of the redemption, prisoners were left to die in captivity. Sometimes prisoners were allowed to return to their homeland in order to collect ransom for themselves and their companions. The Smolensk vicegerent wrote in 1580 to the elder of Orsha that Junior Boyar Satin left Lithuania for ransom, in trust of his sovereign the grand prince, but his companion Odoevtsov remained a prisoner of the Wilno governor. Now Satin arrived in Smolensk with the ransom, bringing two hundred fifty rubles for himself, and for Odoevstov forty marten pelts, a black fox pelt and two black beaver pelts.

In campaigns against Lithuanian districts prisoners occasionally were released because of religious convictions. Thus the chronicler says for the year 1535 that the grand prince sent his generals against Lithuania and they took many prisoners, they showed mercy to many on account of their Orthodox faith and released them. Likewise they ordered the entire army to hold the churches of God in honor, to cause them no harm, nor to remove anything from a church. On the conclusion of peace with Sweden the Moscow government stipulated that the Swedes redeem their own captives, but return the Russian captives without compensation.

Concerning the fate of Tatar captives in the period under discussion we find frightful information in the chronicles during both the minority and the majority of Ivan IV. Under the year 1535 is said that "they imprisoned for life seventy-three Tatar men of Khan Shah Ali in Pskov, in which number figured seven small boys, and in Novgorod they imprisoned eighty-four men. Over a twenty-four hour period they died. Only eight men remained alive in the tower, and they were not given either water or food for many days. They killed these and imprisoned their wives in another tower, under easier conditions. The following year Archbishop Makary assumed responsibility for these women and distributed them among the priests, who were instructed to baptize them into the Christian faith; the priests began to marry them off, and they were very sincere in their Christian faith." For the year 1555 we read that "the crown secretaries gave the monasteries Tatars who were in prison and desired to be baptized, but those who did not desire to be baptized they drowned."

In 1581, during the war with Sweden, the tsar gave the order to execute Swedes taken among the informants. The tsar permitted Lithuanian captives taken in Polotsk to be seen by Lithuanian ambassadors, but on condition that they speak Russian during their meeting, and not Polish. Prisoners of little significance were given as presents or sold. In 1556 the tsar forbade the sale of Swedish captives in Livonia and Lithuania, and permitted their being sold only in Muscovite towns. Once the tsar sent the khan as a gift a red gerfalcon and two captive Lithuanians, royal officials.

We learn from dealings with the Crimea that upon arriving in Moscow the khan's courier and merchants purchased fifteen or twenty Lithuanian and German captives. Owing to their inattentiveness these captives escaped on the road. They importuned the sovereign concerning this, and petitioned the chancellery officials to hunt down the fugitives. "Your couriers have bought a Lithuanian and a German prisoner in Moscow," the tsar once wrote to the khan. "We ordered them to be given our charter for the governor in Putivl regarding the free passage of these prisoners. But the governor detained seventeen Lithuanian and German prisoners and a woman who claimed to be Russian because in the letter of free passage these fifteen were not listed. Your couriers acted improperly because they took an extra captive without accepting our charter of free passage." The Nogay Tatars also bought prisoners in Moscow. The tsar wrote to Prince Ismail, "We gave your man fifty rubles to buy what you need, and we permitted him to buy German prisoners, as many as you need."

If the Tatars bought many captive Lithuanians or Germans in Moscow, on the other hand during their attacks on Muscovite districts they led away many Russian prisoners of war. A contemporary account of the Lithuanian Mikhalon concerning the condition of these unfortunate men in the Crimea has come down to us. "Ships from across the sea, from Asia, sailed frequently to the Crimean Tatars and brought them weapons, clothing and horses, and then departed laden with slaves. All their markets are renowned solely for this one commodity which they always have on hand for sale, for a pledge and for gifts. Any one of them who has at the very least one horse will promise, on the basis of a contract, to pay his creditors for clothing, weapons and horses with livestock. Not with horses, mind you, but with slaves, men of our own blood. He will do this even if in fact he does not have a single slave, but on the assumption that he can acquire a certain number of them. These promises are fulfilled to the letter as though they always had our countrymen in their backyards. For that reason a Jewish money changer, seeing the continual shipment of an innumerable multitude of our captives to Taurida, inquired of us whether or not there were still people left in our countries, and whence came such great numbers?

"Thus they always have slaves in supply, not only for trading with other peoples, but also for their pleasure at home, and to satisfy their tendencies to cruelty. The stronger of those unfortunate men, if they were not made into eunuchs, often were branded on the forehead and cheek. Bound or fettered, they suffered during the day in slave labor and at night in the dungeons. They kept alive on small quantities of food consisting of meat from putrid animals, covered in worms and repulsive even to dogs. The women who were more delicate were kept otherwise. Some had to entertain at banquets if they knew how to sing or play an instrument. Beautiful women, those belonging to the more noble blood of our race, were led away to the khan. When slaves were transported for sale they were put on a platform in single file, in groups of ten, bound to each other around the shoulder, and they were auctioned off in tens, during which time the auctioneer shouted loudly that these slaves were quite new, simple, not cunning, just brought in from the king's people, not from Moscow. They considered the Muscovite tribe to be cheap, crafty and deceptive. The value of this commodity was estimated with considerable knowledge in Taurida, and was purchased at a high price by foreign merchants who sold it at an even higher price to remote peoples."

According to the same Mikhalon's information, Christian captives who were led away from Taurida to distant countries suffered all the more from the fact that they were separated from the temples of God. Hence the ransom of captive Christians from Tatar hands became necessarily a holy, religious duty, and from an act of private generosity it turned into an act of the crown, for the government possessed the means to arrange more satisfactory ransoms. The chronicle states under the year 1535 that Grand Prince Ivan Vasilievich and his mother Elena sent such a charter to the bishop of Novgorod. "In former years," it stated, "the Tatars marched against the tsar's borderlands and, because of our sins, took into captivity junior boyars, men, women and maidens. The Lord God did not despise His creation nor allow Orthodox Christians to live among foreigners, whose hearts He has softened. They returned the captives but they asked for silver from the sovereign. The grand prince ordered his boyars to give silver, and he instructed his intercessor Bishop Makary to collect from all the monasteries of his archdiocese seven hundred rubles on the basis of the areal reckoning." Makary ordered the money collected as quickly as possible, recalling the Lord's word, "If we hand over gold, we shall find more to replace it, but for a human soul there is nothing which can be given in exchange."[7]

Certain arrangements regarding the ransoming of captives were formulated at the council of 1551. The ransom of captives became a very lucrative industry for the Crimean couriers. "The Crimean couriers do not

travel for reasons of crown affairs," complained the Muscovite ambassadors in the Crimea. "They buy the office of courier from the princes and
murzas and travel for their own debts. They purchase captives in Crimea
cheaply and collect on them surety notes, not in accordance with the
sovereign's edict, but for large sums of money, and not in keeping with
their ancestry." An instruction given to Prince Mosalsky, who was sent to
the Crimea as an ambassador, states that "if Crimean princes and couriers
after arriving in Moscow say that they brought ransomed prisoners with
them but were not given full payment in Moscow, answer that they have
paid ransom for young junior boyars not on the basis of their ancestry.
They have paid ransom for cossacks and boyar servitors in the same way.
For any junior boyars taken in battle the sovereign gave the ransom money
based on each man's worth. This is a business matter, since they are trading
in a scarce commodity, but henceforth our sovereign shall not pay a price
which they are not worth. The treasurers and sovereign's crown secretaries
have told your couriers more than once that they would buy at market
value, but would not write any additional boundless price. For now,
whatever type of surety notes the couriers might have, our sovereign has
ordered that a large amount of money be paid out, even if the individual
was not worth the amount, because the khan and kalghay[8] have written
about this, but henceforth let them ransom captives for what they are
worth." "Henceforth if your couriers wish to ransom captives," the tsar
himself wrote to the khan, "let them do so, ascertaining who costs what and
making inquiries of our ambassadors. But if in future your ambassadors
and couriers bring back ransomed prisoners and have neither our
ambassador's bond nor a surety note for them, we shall send them back.
There shall be no reduction in the payment for any captive whom our
ambassador redeems, having taken out a surety note on himself."

VIII

MORALS AND CUSTOMS IN EASTERN
AND WESTERN RUSSIA

EASTERN RUSSIA

That the reign of Ivan the Terrible could effect a refinement of morals and
the introduction of better customs in Muscovy is impossible to imagine.

The phenomenon of Ivan the Terrible, agreeing as it did with the state of contemporary morality, had a yet more harmful influence, inculcating cruelty, violence and disdain for the life and welfare of one's neighbor. The church armed itself against itinerant minstrels and bear trainers because of their immoral conduct; monasteries ordered them driven out of their domains, but Ivan set the example of a predilection for the coarse amusements offered by bears and minstrels. Ivan loved to set bears on people, and servants imitated their lord.

"On the Sophia Side in the Land domains," relates the Novgorod chronicler under the year 1572, "Subbota Osetr bloodied the crown secretary Danilo Bartenev and had him torn apart by a bear, and the crown secretary was with the bear in his office. Scribes were tossed out of upper-story windows of the office. The bear tore to shreds the clothing worn by a crown secretary who was brought to the forecourt wearing only a caftan. At that time in Novgorod and in all towns and rural districts they rounded up jesters and bears for the sovereign, and sent them to the sovereign. Subbota left Novgorod with the minstrels in carts, and they brought the bears with them in carts to Moscow."

It is clear that for the crown estates henchmen nothing was sacred. Thus during the sovereign's devastation of the Novgorod region they broke open the grave of the miracle worker St. Savva Vishersky.[1] In the missives of church pastors we run across strictures against the expansion of deplorable unnatural vice; we will not repeat what foreigners were saying. In addition the state was still weak and did not have sufficient means to keep public order. Therefore antisocial tendencies, the tendency to live at the expense of one's neighbor, was given wide scope as before. The young society displayed its vitality, its strength, in the fact that it did not regard this with indifference, did not want to put up with similar phenomena, and sought all possible means to establish better order. The historian cannot help but recognize this fact, but also must admit that the good efforts of society for taming public order met with powerful obstacles.

Raids were still a fact of life for society. For example in 1579 the tsar's commissioner of St. Daniel's monastery, with his own men and the sovereign's peasants, raided the monastery's village of Khrepelevo. The criminal statutes clearly reveal how far lawlessness advanced during this period. "You have petitioned us because robbers attack your many villages and hamlets and steal your property. They burn the villages and hamlets, rob and attack many people on the roads, and beat many people to death but many others harbor criminals, and to these the robbers bring their stolen goods."

Of some interest in this regard is the order sent by Prince Fedor Obolensky from Lithuanian captivity to his son Prince Dmitry. "If you lived in keeping with your father's instruction," he writes, "you would not stir up sedition. You would forbid your father's servitors and your own to steal, attack and commit various crimes, and you would stop them from committing any crime. You would order your servitors to cultivate grain in the hamlets and to be satisfied with that. If you cannot restrain your father's or your own servitors from evil, petition Boyar Prince Ivan Fedorovich Obolensky (Telepnev) that he order them restrained, so that you incur no shame from the sovereign grand prince on account of your father's or your own servitors."

It was unfortunate that homicides occurred even among those who did not belong to gangs of robbers. In 1568 a certain Koval from Vologda complained against Mamin, a servitor of the Buturlin family. "Mamin gave my little son Trenka a thrashing on the square in front of court, but my little son did nothing to deserve it, and now lies close to death." Conciliation writs dealing with criminal complaints serve as proof of how weakly rooted were notions of statehood, how in this regard society still had not advanced very far from the time of the *Russian Justice*.[2]

"I Mikhailo Leontiev," runs a conciliation writ in 1560, "a servant of the Novinsk metropolitan monastery, have petitioned the sovereign instead of the abbot and the brethren, against the peasants of St. Cyril's monastery, who killed a servant of the Novinsk monastery. Instead of going to court before the criminal judges Prince Gnezdilovsky and his companions, appointed in accordance with the sovereign's charter, we have been reconciled with the servant of St. Cyril's monastery Istoma Vasiliev, who settled with us on behalf of those murderers. I collected from Istoma the debt of the slain man and forty rubles of treasury funds as compensation for the monastery's losses resulting from the charters, for maintenance expenses and for the delay. Henceforth I and other monastery servants will not pursue this case against the murderers; otherwise take from the abbot and steward of Novinsk monastery one hundred rubles for St. Cyril's monastery."

Another conciliation writ has come down to us, concluded by the relatives of the victim with his murderers. "We, Mikhaila Kondratiev, Danila Lukianov and Stepan Skomorokhov have put a surety note on ourselves for Uliana Skorniakova and Vasily Skorniakov owing to the fact that the murder of Uliana's husband and Vasily's brother-in-law, the notary public Grigory Ivanov, was perpetrated because of sins. We shall pay the murder compensation for the slain man, but Uliana and Vasily shall incur no loss for this compensation."

Of course conciliation writs with known robbers who committed homicides for theft were not permitted, but there is a curious tolerance of such antisocial habits such as murder in a fit of rage or in a quarrel. If a homicide was committed "because of sins" the killer paid the murder compensation to the relatives of the slain man, and he was exonerated. Curious too are these expressions in the cited writs. "He gave my little son a thrashing but he has done nothing to deserve it," as if to say that if he did something the killer would have some kind of justification. In the second writ the conciliation is concluded with people who are called by their real name, murderers. These conciliation writs clarify for us the conduct of the Shuiskys and of Ivan himself, as well as the propensity to violent acts in a moment of anger and the lack of respect for the life of one's neighbor. Ivan because of sins also gave a thrashing to his son,[3] which clearly he did not wish to do, and afterwards he repented intensely. As before, the chroniclers complained about looting during fires.

The government considered itself duty-bound to restrain infringements on the property of a neighbor by means of legal forms. Beginning in 1577 and continuing for five years, debtors were granted a tax exemption to pay off their apportionment without interest. This obviously put creditors at a disadvantage and gave rise to the expected petitions. Liapun Nekrasov, son of Miakinin, and in the name of his brothers, petitioned against Fedor and Vasily Volynsky. He and his brothers borrowed from the Volynskys, on the basis of two debt agreements, one ruble on one agreement and two rubles on a second agreement. The debt agreements were written in the name of their servitors. He tried to pay the Volynskys the money according to the agreement, but they would not take it. The money grew in buying power and they wished to keep the notes for the five-year term, as in the sovereign's edict. We also meet a petition that creditors would not take money from their debtors, desiring to keep the mortgage. When real estate was mortgaged, the creditor used it for interest. "For the sake of the interest cultivate the hamlets, manage the various pasturages and control the peasants." We have seen that interest ran at twenty percent.

As in the past the church guarded against the strengthening of antisocial phenomena. "For the sake of God, sire," wrote Archbishop Feodosy of Novgorod to the tsar, "make haste and be solicitous for your patrimony Novgorod the Great because of what now occurs there. Without repentance and communion souls perish continually in taverns and houses, on roads and in marketplaces. In town and about the churchyard hamlets there are homicides and lootings, and there is no safe passage or thoroughfare. Except for you, sire, there is no one to put a stop to this spiritual harm and domestic trouble. I am writing to you not because I wanted to instruct and admonish your keen mind and noble wisdom, for it would be improper for us to forget our place and dare such a thing, but as a pupil to his teacher, as a slave to his master do I remind you and beg you incessantly. Because the king of heaven has given you, who are like unto the heavenly powers, a scepter of might for the earthly kingdom, so may you instruct your people to preserve the truth, and may you banish the devil's desire from them. As the sun with its rays illumines the whole of creation, it is a matter for the tsar's virtue to show mercy to the poor and wronged. The tsar is greater than the sun, for the sun sets, but the tsar exposes secret wrongs with the light of truth. As much as you exceed everyone in might, so is it fitting for you to shine with deeds," and so forth.

In 1555 the abbot of the Trinity-St. Sergius monastery, speaking with the cellarer and the council elders gave instructions to their Prisetsky peasants (two peasants were named) and the entire rural district in accordance with the decree of the sovereign tsar and metropolitan, forbidding them to harbor minstrels, sorcerers, fortune-tellers, thieves and robbers. "If they harbor any of these, or if a minstrel, sorcerer or fortune-teller is found in one of the hundreds, collect from the hundredman and his hundred a fine of ten rubles in cash. Expel from that rural district any minstrel, sorcerer or fortune-teller who may have assaulted or burgled, and do not allow minstrels passing by to enter the district."

In ancient times no one liked to wage war during Lent, nor did anyone conduct assaults against towns on Sundays. In 1559 the tsar gave a memorandum to the treasurers ordering that whenever a major memorial for the dead was served, when the metropolitan is at the side of the sovereign's throne and the sovereign stands in front of him, they must not impose the death penalty or public flogging on anyone. Before the start of important undertakings alms were distributed to the monasteries with the request for prayers. Seven rubles were sent to the Solovetsk monastery before the Kazan campaign with the request "that you pray to the Lord God for the health and tranquility of all Orthodox Christians and for the sovereign's transgressions and health, that you sing a liturgy and perform solemn prayers asking the Lord God to grant victory to our sovereign, his commanders and the army, and to forgive the sovereign all his sins."

In 1562 the tsar wrote to the Trinity-St. Sergius monastery "that you favor us and pray the Lord God for our transgression which I as a man have committed. For there is no man who can live without sinning even for a single hour. Hence I ask your holiness that you strive assiduously in prayer so that, because of your prayers, God will examine our great acts of lawlessness and grant remission of our sins, bestow upon us understanding, judgment and wisdom for the governing and multiplying of the flock of Christian rational sheep entrusted to me by God. Our enemies are also the enemies of Christianity. The Crimean khan is an ancient apostate of God and raving barbarian who is always ready to shed Christian blood. The Lithuanian king blasphemes the names of God and His Most Pure Mother and all the saints. He tramples on sacred icons and dishonors the holy cross. The German race was seduced by the devil from of old. All of them have raged violently against the whole of Orthodoxy wanting to devour it, trusting only in their demonic sorcery," and so on.

In 1567 the metropolitan sent St. Cyril's monastery a charter. "On account of our sins," it read, "the godless Crimean khan Devlet-Girey, together with the whole Muslim and Latin world, and the Lithuanian king Sigismund Augustus, and the pagan Germans have fallen into different heresies, in particular into the Lutheran deception. They have ravaged the holy churches, desecrated venerable icons and continue to spread evil counsel against our pious Christian faith of the Greek dispensation. Hearing of this, the divinely anointed tsar and sovereign became outraged. He lamented over the holy churches and the venerable icons and, taking God as his help, he marched with his army against these enemies," and so on.

In 1571 on the occasion of war with Sweden the metropolitan wrote to St. Cyril's monastery that the monks not only should offer prayers for the success of the tsar's forces, but also should observe a fast. That during the fast of St. Philip, the great meat-eating period and in Great Lent they should not drink themselves into a stupor. Intercessory letters were sent to the monasteries when the tsar was ill. During a famine, in keeping with the prescription of the metropolitan, the clergy sang solemn prayer services and blessed water, and the archbishop sent encyclicals around the eparchy, admonishing to moral correction. In the event of victory bells rang the entire day until midnight, and all the churches offered solemn thanksgivings.

It was customary in towns to lead a procession of the cross around the citadel and merchant quarter, to sing solemn prayers and bless water three times annually, on the second Sunday after Easter, on the first Sunday of the fast of St. Peter and during the fast of the Dormition. At Epiphany and on August 1 water was blessed in the river. On September 1, New Year's Day,[4] *the changing of the year* was celebrated in front of the church. On

June 21, 1548 with the blessing of the metropolitan the tsar established until the end of the world a general memorial for pious princes, boyars and the Christ-loving army, the priestly and monastic rank and all Orthodox Christians slain by foreigners in battles and bloody skirmishes and led off into captivity, who succumbed to hunger, thirst, nakedness, cold and every hardship, who were killed in conflagrations and perished in fire or drowned.

One of the characteristic features of ancient Russian society were holy fools who, by taking advantage of the profound respect felt for them by the government and people, were emboldened to expose moral misconduct in the name of religion. The most famous fools for Christ for the period were Nicholas of Pskov, Vasily (the Blessed or Naked) and Ivan (Big Cap) of Moscow.[5]

Among those customs not pertaining to religion we note that of writing marriage contracts before the wedding and the handing over of the wife to her husband. In 1542 Princess Sogorskaia gave her daughter in marriage to Prince Khovansky. The daughter was a widow, but the marriage contract was written in the name of the mother alone. The contract itemizes the dowry given to the son-in-law and not to the daughter, consisting of icons, lands, service chiefs, ordinary slaves and money which, it is stated, was to be spent on clothing and various feminine adornments. Bridegrooms gave written guarantees that they would marry without delay in the time appointed, otherwise they must pay the relatives of the bride the sum of money shown in the marriage contract for the wedding deposit. Sometimes the bridegroom added to the marriage contract that after his death his entire property would pass to his wife; should any member of his clan demand the estate from her, he must pay her the sum of money indicated in the marriage contract.

One peasant-widower who had three sons took as his wife a widow who had one son and four daughters. In the marriage contract the property brought by the groom and the bride was listed, and they jointly would marry off their daughters in keeping with their means. If the wife's son (stepson) wished to set up on his own, it was stipulated that he receive a share of his mother's estate. If the husband died, his three sons from the first marriage received half of the estate. In a second similar contract the groom said that if his stepson wished to leave, he was to take the proceeds from the sale of his father's house; if he remained to live with the heir and was obedient to him, he likewise would receive a share of the heir's estate. One peasant married the widow of a Tikhvin townsman and gave a written guarantee to the Tikhvin monastery that he would support his stepsons and nurture them until adulthood, but once they came of age they would be peasants of the Tikhvin monastery like their grandfather and father. While they lived with him the heir must not give them away to any other place, nor contract them as slaves or peasants in a boyar household. The Hundred Chapters council stipulated that a man could not marry before the age of fifteen, or a woman before the age of twelve.

We find the following terms relating to clothes and adornments: a linen smock, a leather smock, exquisite pearls, ear-rings of rubies embedded in silver with pearls, a long-skirted, short-sleeved caftan, a large long-skirted, collarless caftan with cloth-covered buttons, a collarless caftan of motley fabric, a sarafan, sheepskins, a long caftan with a waistband, cloth collarless caftans and coarse-cloth caftans, unbleached linens, housecoats, plain cloth and dyed sarafans, quilted jackets, a fur coat, embroidery, aprons and puffs.

We run across descriptions of residential architecture. There is first the yard, and in the yard mansions. A mansion might consist of an upper story built over a ground floor, an upper story with two rooms over the ground floor, two summer bedchambers, a drying room on the ground floor, a cellar on the street opposite the yard. Or the yard might have two huts, a rectangular log framework on the ground floor, a wash house, two hay sheds on two cattle sheds and a barn. Sometimes a hut is encountered, to which has been added an upper story on two notched logs, and against the upper story there is a warehouse built on two substructures with a ramp. We may find a large upper story built on a substructure, but this upper story has passageways which serve as entrance halls, with their covered space. There is a room in the winter hut. We encounter a formal dining hall built on the substructure with an entrance hall, an upper story with rooms built on the substructure, a drying room with an addition, a cellar and an icehouse. Or we find three huts built on two lean-tos and a door covered with a curtain. Mention is made of town yards having gardens with apple and cherry trees.

WESTERN RUSSIA

With regard to the morals and customs in Western Russia some interesting information has come to us in the composition of Mikhalon Litvin[6] already cited more than once. It must be borne in mind that as he rails against the luxury and the effeminacy of his contemporaries' morals, contrasting these with the morals of their ancestors and neighboring peoples, the author is no stranger to exaggeration. "More and more often," he says, "factories which produce vodka and beer from grain are encountered in Lithuanian towns. The inhabitants take these beverages with them to war and, being accustomed to drinking them at home, they perish from cramps and diarrhoea if they happen to drink water on campaign. Peasants, abandoning their field, go to the inns and carouse there day and night, forcing trained bears to amuse them with dances to bagpipes. The upshot of all this is that, having wasted their wealth, they end up starving. They turn to theft and robbery so that in every Lithuanian province in a single month more people are executed for this crime than have been executed in Tatary and Muscovy for one or two hundred years. Intemperance or arguments during drinking bouts, not the government, kill off our people. The day begins with a drink of vodka; while still in bed they shout, 'Some wine, some wine!' Men, women and young people drink that poison on the streets and in the public squares and, having become drunk, can do nothing but sleep. Once somebody is accustomed to this, his passion for drunkenness grows steadily."

Mikhalon complains about court fees. "The president of the court collects a fee, the servant of the judge collects a fee, the notary collects a fee, the protonotary collects a fee, the court officer who sets the day for court collects a fee, the man-at-arms who brings in the accused collects a fee and the official who calls witnesses collects a fee. A poor man wanting to summon a grandee to trial will not find an advocate for any sum of money. Anyone can be a witness in any complaint except surveying matters, and no one needs an oath to be believed. Because of this many have made a living out of giving false witness. The accused, although an obvious thief of someone else's property, is not obliged to appear in court until a month after the summons. If a horse worth fifty or one hundred grivnas is stolen from me during the most crucial time of field labor I cannot summon the thief to trial before paying for the summons the price of the stolen horse, even though afterwards not only shall I not receive compensation for my losses, but neither will I be able to bring the guilty party to court for a whole month. In this way the injured party either yields everything to the thief or he deposits as much. Although two military governors from the mass of grandees living in close proximity to each other fulfill the office of judge for all of Lithuania, still how can they examine all litigations of such a numerous people and so many provinces, especially when they also must attend to government business? Because they are occupied with a multitude of public and private matters they examine litigations only on holidays when they happen to be relatively free of business. What is more astounding, there are no set locations for their sessions. Often the injured party must travel more than fifty miles to seek justice. We have forty days dedicated to the commemoration of the Lord's passion, to fasting and prayer, which we spend in litigation. These governors have their own representatives. While feeding their bodies they sit in court, normally under the noise of visitors, and are little acquainted with the laws, but are meticulous in levying fees for retrials.

"In our country the Jews, the most evil of all peoples, have congregated and dispersed among all the towns of Podolia, Volhynia and other fertile regions. They are a perfidious, cunning and pernicious people who spoil our wares, counterfeit our money, signatures and seals, who rob Christians of their livelihood in all the markets and who know no other craft except deception and slander.

"We keep in permanent slavery our own people, acquired not in war or by sale. They are not foreigners, but belong to our own race and faith. They include orphans, the impoverished and those who have fallen into the net through marriage with a slave. We exploit our power over them for evil, we torture them, we mutilate them, we kill them with impunity on the least suspicion. Contrary to this, among the Tatars and Muscovites not a single official can kill anyone even in the event of obvious crime, which right is granted solely to the judges in the capital cities. Yet among us death sentences are carried out even in the villages and hamlets. Add to this the fact that for the defense of the land we collect taxes only from our poor subordinate townsmen and from the poorest plowmen, leaving in peace estate owners who receive even more from their domains.

"Neither the Tatars nor the Muscovites give their wives any liberty, saying 'Whoever gives liberty to his wife takes it away from himself.' Their women have no authority whereas among us some women control many men, owning villages, towns and land, some by right of limited use, others by law of succession. In keeping with their passion to dominate they live under the guise of unmarried or widowed status unrestrainedly, a burden to their subjects, persecuting some with hatred and ruining others with blind love.

"Our enemies the Tatars laugh at our nonchalance, attacking us while we are deep in sleep after our revels. 'Ivan, you are sleeping, they say, but I am working, I am tying you up.' Now more of our soldiers die from festivities in taverns where they kill each other, than from our enemies who frequently lay waste to our country. It would be better if our soldiers found the opportunity to demonstrate their courage in battle against sober and effective enemies on the borders of Podolia and Kiev, for there they could make valiant warriors out of the recruits, and we would not need to search for such men outside the homeland.

"The Tatars laugh because our distinguished people rest easily and sleep on benches when the divine liturgy is being celebrated, but forbid people of poor condition to sit down. They arrive at church with many escorts and place them in front of themselves so that they can brag about their numbers. Greek monks refrain from taking wives whereas that priests in former times took wives is evident from many places in Sacred Scripture. If ours did so now they would be more chaste than in that sham monasticism in which they live as effeminate sybarites, always burning with passion and maintaining concubines. The duties which we entrust to them they pass off onto their vicars, and devote themselves to sloth and pleasures, feasting and dressing magnificently."

The Muscovite émigré Prince Kurbsky shared Mikhalon's complaints about the luxury and effeminacy of the men in Western Russia, and against their subordination to the influence of women. Details about the life of Prince Kurbsky in Western Russia also contain some interesting features of contemporary life.[7] We begin with his family relationships. Kurbsky left behind in Muscovy his family, his mother, wife and young son who, as he says in the foreword to *The New Pearl*,[8] were imprisoned in the dungeon and *were poisoned slowly* there. In 1571 Kurbsky entered a marriage with Maria Yurievna Kozinskaia, born Princess Golshanskaia, twice a widow and the mother of two grown sons by her first husband Montolt.

At first Kurbsky lived agreeably with his wife, who signed over to him almost all of her possessions and confirmed this bequest in her testament but relations soon began to change. The princess wrote her testament in March 1576 but in August 1577 judiciary agents were already arrayed with the nobility, with good men, to investigate a complaint of the princess's son Andrei Montolt. The complaint alleged that Prince Kurbsky killed his wife, having tormented her and put her in confinement, and because of these beatings and tortures she was no longer among the living. The judiciary agents found Prince Kurbsky ill in bed, but the princess was healthy and seated beside her husband. "See, lord agent," said Kurbsky. "My wife is sitting there in good health but her children are fabricating stories against me." Turning to the princess he said, "Tell him yourself, princess." "What can I say, gracious prince," she answered, "the agent can see for himself that I am sitting up." "They have had their mother dead for a long time," Kurbsky added, "but she is still very much alive and will bury me." "How are we to know? It is more likely that your grace will bury me, for I am in poor health," the princess remarked.

On the very day that the judiciary agent was entering this scene in the civil books Prince Kurbsky issued a complaint that not long before his wife removed from the storeroom a trunk in which were kept privileges and other important papers, and gave them to her Montolt sons; that one of them, Andrei, rode out near Kurbsky's estates with servants and other assistants, hunting and lying in wait for Kurbsky on the roads, setting up an ambush and plotting against his life. Following this Kurbsky complained that Andrei Montolt raided his estate of Skulinskaia, burned down the lodge, beat, tortured and drowned the wardens, bound some of them and carted them off to his own estate, and burned all the barrel staves. In the trunk Kurbsky found his wife's purse with sand, hairs, and other charms. Rainka, the princess's maid, declared that some old woman gave all those things to the princess, adding that it was not poison but only a drug prepared to awaken love in Kurbsky for his wife. Now, continued Rainka, the princess was trying to meet with the old woman again to obtain a potion which she could use, not for love, but some other purpose.

Finally, on the advice of some friends Kurbsky and his wife decided to separate, though some of the princess's estate had to be left for Kurbsky. The settlement was signed on August 1, 1578 and on August 2 the former Princess Kurbskaia registered a complaint against her husband that he did not treat her as a wife, put her in confinement for no reason at all, caned her and forced her to give him some blank sheets of paper with her seals and autographed signature, and concluded acts to her detriment. She complained that Kurbsky, by separating from her, kept her movable property and forcibly kept her servant Rainka, torturing her and putting her in prison, and that he ordered her to be raped there. For his part Kurbsky registered a complaint that when he sent his former wife to Vladimir with every courtesy in a four-seater carriage, the governor of Minsk, Sapieha, who was a mediator on the side of Maria Yurievna during the divorce, ordered his servants to beat Kurbsky's coachman soundly with a cane on his hands and feet, and to detain the carriage. He abused Kurbsky with shameless words.

In December Maria Yurievna was reconciled with Kurbsky. She announced that he gave legal satisfaction in all her lawsuits, and that she would not initiate new suits against him or against his children and descendants. Under these circumstances her maid Rainka also declared that all her earlier testimony against both Kurbsky and his former wife was false, that she made such testimonies in anger at the instigation of others, that she was never beaten, tortured or raped. When Kurbsky married the young woman Alexandra Semashkovna with whom he was very satisfied, as can be seen from his will, his former wife once again submitted a complaint to the king concerning the unlawful dissolution of the marriage. Then Kurbsky gave a legal reason for the ecclesiastical trial. Three witnesses testified that they saw with their own eyes how the former Princess Kurbskaia violated marital fidelity. The case was concluded once again with a settlement.

Kurbsky was to experience still more unpleasantness. In 1575 Prince Andrzej Wiśniowiecki, the governor of Braslav, assembled a multitude of armed servitors, boyars and peasants, mounted men and infantry armed with muskets and guns, and attacked Kurbsky's lands, seizing two herds and killing four shepherds. When Kurbsky sent his servants and character witnesses to inquire about the reason for the attack, in place of an answer Wiśniowiecki ordered them seized and slain.

Kurbsky hastened to take revenge on him that very day. A few hundred of his servants and subjects fell on Wiśniowiecki's estate, killed his peasants and stole the grain. Nor did townsmen refrain from violence. Kurbsky's favorite servant, the Muscovite Ivan Kelemet, submitted a complaint in 1571. "I was in Vladimir [-in-Volhynia] to answer before the court on business of my lord. As soon as I left town the high bailiff, councillors and burghers of Vladimir ordered that the bells be rung and the town gates closed. They gathered together with a multitude of burghers armed with various weapons intent on depriving me of my life without any reason at all on my part. I scarcely succeeded in getting out of the town. After this the burghers, councillors and high bailiff chased after me and, having driven me out on to a field about a mile from town, they covered me, the servants of my lord who were with me, my own servants and our horses with wounds. They jolted my large coach, harassed my wife and tore the rings from her hands, and they took a trunk and a case from the coach."

In 1575 Prince Kurbsky himself submitted a complaint. "Not long ago, when the Tatars invaded the land of Volhynia, in keeping with my duties as a nobleman I rode with my own detachment as quickly as possible against the enemy, and I instructed my elder Kalinovsky to come after me post haste with money. When he was passing between Berestechko and Nikolaev, the Ostakhovich's, burghers of Berestechko, and their many assistants seized Kalinovsky on the highway, and my boyar Turovitsky who was travelling with him. They beat them cruelly, and like brigands they covered them with wounds, taking everything they had. After this they left them for dead and returned home to Berestechko. When the Berestechko constables learned about the assault they captured the malefactors and put them in jail, but when Kalinovsky was brought into Berestechko barely alive, declaring that he was my servant, the constables took counsel among themselves and pocketed all the property stolen from my servants by the malefactors. They released from jail the same malefactors, who made off who knows where. They detained Kalinovsky in Berestechko for some time, then laid him in a wagon scarcely alive and dressed only in a shirt, and ordered him hauled out of town and thrown in an oak grove at the scene of the crime."

We have referred to Kurbsky's faithful servant Ivan Kelemet and the assault on him by Vladimir townsmen in 1571. The following year a violent death befell him in the same place, Vladimir. While he was there once again on his lord's business some servants of Prince Bulyga came to his quarters at night and the unwelcome guests started settling in. The owner of the house, the burgher Kaplia, showed them the door, but they answered, "Why should we go? For that Muscovite?" One of them took a bottle from the stove and threw it at Kelemet. An argument began, weapons were drawn. Kelemet managed to chase them out of the front room and bar the entrance, but they beat down the doors and windows. Kaplia then ran out of the house and, when he returned, observed that none other than Prince Bulyga stood in the shadows, but Kelemet was lying dead on the floor of the front room. The money and objects which belonged to Kelemet were stolen by his assailants. Bulyga did not appear in court, so the local court sentenced him to pay the murder compensation and all losses, and to send the actual perpetrator to the king's court. Through the mediation of several lords, however, the assailant concluded a settlement with Kurbsky, which bound him to pay Kurbsky the murder compensation for the slain man and all losses, and to spend a year and six weeks in the Vladimir castle. Peter Boronovetsky, another of Kurbsky's servants who fled with him from Moscow, also was slain by an unknown assailant. The wife of the victim at first accused Prince Kurbsky himself of the crime, but later she retracted her accusation.

After these occurrences Kurbsky had the right to complain that he, unjustly exiled, found himself wandering among dour and very inhospitable people. It is clear from all this that he and his Muscovites were disliked in their new homeland. On the other hand let us see how Kurbsky himself proceeded in conflicts with neighbors and subordinates. The Smedinsk peasants who lived next to the districts granted him by the king accused him of taking possession of their land, of driving away the bees, of perpetrating violence, fights and thefts. When the king sent him his memorandum, Kurbsky replied, "I do not give the order to enter the land of Smedinsk, but I do order the defense of my own land. If the people of Smedinsk appropriate my land, considering it their own, I shall order them caught and hanged, but as for the satisfaction which the people of Smedinsk demand from my elders and peasants for offenses and injury, I am not obligated to grant them a trial in this matter or give them justice because if my elders and peasants have done anything, they did it to defend my land."

On the basis of some right Kurbsky controlled the estate of the lords Krasensky. King Sigismund Augustus decided that Kurbsky must return the estate. Kurbsky received a royal injunction when Sigismund Augustus was no longer alive. The king's messenger rode about Kurbsky's estates at length with a royal writ. Kurbsky's servants sent him from one estate to the next, one of them even threatened him with a cane. Finally the messenger found Kurbsky and wanted to serve him the royal writ, but Kurbsky told him in the presence of many notable personages, "You come to me with dead writs because when the king has died, all his writs die with him. Even had you come from a living king I would not cede my estate to you or to anyone else."

In 1572 a complaint against Kurbsky was submitted, stating that he intercepted on his estate a servant of a lord hostile to him, held him up, tortured him and interrogated him concerning his intentions against him. In 1579 a judiciary agent travelling to see Kurbsky to summon him to trial submitted a complaint that the prince's servants attacked him on the road, beat him soundly and hurled him down barely alive. As they beat him they repeated over and over, "Do not bring summonses to his grace our lord prince."

Kurbsky's trusty servant Ivan Kelemet imitated his master. In 1569 some Vladimir Jews submitted a complaint that Kelemet, Kurbsky's constable in Kovel which was entrusted to him by the king, seized as payment of debts two Kovel Jewish men and a Jewish woman on the Sabbath, while they were at prayer in the synagogue. He put them in a pit filled with water, and sealed the shops and beer cellars of their houses and those of other Jews. The judiciary agent detailed to Kovel for this complaint testified that when he and his nobleman witness arrived at the gates of the castle the gatekeeper did not admit them to the castle. Standing at the gates, they heard the screams of the Jews locked in the watery pit, whom leeches were sucking. Finally Kelemet went out and said, "Is not a lord free to punish his subjects not only in prison or with some other type of punishment, but also with death? Anything I do, I do it following the orders of my lord, his grace Prince Kurbsky, because my lord, who controls the estate and subjects of Kovel, is free to punish them as he wishes but the king, his grace and no one else care in the least." The Vladimir Jews who arrived with the judiciary agent replied, "A lord is free to punish his subjects, but only in accordance with the law. You are violating our rights which have been confirmed by royal privileges." Kelemet answered, "I do not want to know about your rights and liberties," and he ordered all Jews expelled from the town. According to a royal decree, Kurbsky had to release the Jews and unseal their synagogue, houses and shops.

The knight boyar of Kovel, Porydubsky, submitted a complaint to the king that Kurbsky attacked his estate and home with an overt force of servants, boyars and peasants, and ordered him taken prisoner, together with his entire family. He was held for six years in cruel confinement, and all his estate was plundered.

Regarding resistance to judicial and royal sentences, the behavior of Kurbsky and his servants was not exceptional. In 1582 a judiciary agent stated that he went to Lord Krasensky, following the instructions of the town deputy of Vladimir, to recover money from him for the benefit of Prince Kurbsky. Krasensky, armored and with several hundred mounted and armed men, blocked his way to his village, saying, "We shall beat you and defend ourselves to the death." In fact they did assault two of Kurbsky's servants. The king was forced to issue a decree that the elders of Kremenets, Vladimir and Lutsk, having enlisted the support of the nobility of the entire province of Volhynia and being armed, should conduct an exaction from Krasensky. Instead of complying with the king's decree, many nobles joined forces with Krasensky. He divided his armed men into three details and blocked the road to two of his estates himself with one detail, while his wife Hanna blocked the road to the Krasny estate with the other two details.

In 1548 Paul, the Catholic bishop of Wilno, complained to the king that in his diocese many women were deserting their husbands and living with Jews, Turks and Tatars, forgetting their Christian faith. Alongside this information, which cannot give us a worthwhile notion of the moral state of Western Russia for this period, we run across information which shows as well the activity of a life-giving source which used to awaken an individual, and point out the higher aims of life. On the road along which a drunken lord with his likewise intoxicated wife travelled returning from a feast, and whether drunk or sober having no respect for the life, honor and property of their lesser brethren; on the road along which a lord with his armed detail of servants and peasants went to attack the estate of his opponent; on the road along which menservants and maidservants walked in order to bear false witness at court or shamelessly to declare false what was correct—on this same road it was possible to meet a young man who, having experienced hardship, recognized it as divine punishment and took upon himself some ascetic feat to purify himself of an infamous sin. He went on foot to collect money for an ecclesiastical institution.

We have seen the morals, the way of life, the mutual relationships of the West Russian lords. Now let us enter their dwellings, those houses where they reveled, argued and made up. A spacious house with large entrance halls was located in the middle of a sizable yard. Off the entrance halls was the doorway into the parlor, and in the parlor were curtained doors, four windows, an oak table on legs and four benches around it, and a green-glazed stove; off the parlor was an entrance to a store room. From the same entrance halls on the opposite side was an doorway into a second parlor in which was the same furniture as in the first, and an entrance to a second store room. From the entrance halls a staircase went to the next level. In addition to the large house there were some other structures in the yard, some parlors with windows set in tin, with multicolored tables of oak and linden, green-glazed stoves, benches at the tables and around the parlors, oak beds, fireplaces, and above the doors a gallery with windows. In the description of lordly manors we meet an old familiar word, "reception hall." In the yard might be a large reception hall, in it a table and four benches. The house was enclosed by a stockade on the side facing the pond and wild forest.

Polish Commonwealth After Treaty of Yam Zapolsky (1582)

IX

LITERATURE AND PRINTING

The moral state of society with all its aspects, both light and dark, inevitably was reflected in literary monuments. The final battle between the new order of things and the remnants of the old, waged to the bitter end, did not occur in silence. Two descendants of Monomakh fought in the last internecine war, and in this final feud they did battle with words. These

were the descendant of the senior line of the Mstislaviches, Prince Andrei
Kurbsky-Smolensky-Yaroslavsky, and the descendant of the junior line,
the line of Yury Dolgoruky, Ivan Vasilievich of Moscow, tsar of all Russia
and autocrat. Yet the extremes of the struggle and the personal character
of the combatants alone do not entirely explain for us this development. It
must be added that these warriors were reared in literary combat and its
traditions. They grew accustomed to acknowledge the importance of this
combat, to esteem this new weapon, the word. The struggle which termi-
nated in the reign of Ivan the Terrible, that of the Moscow sovereigns
against princely-boyar pretensions founded on the past, began under Ivan
III, and even then was linked with literary activity.

The struggle of Sophia Paleologue[1] with the Patrikeevs and Riapolovskys
was intimately linked with the ecclesiastical struggle regarding the heresy
of the Judaizers.[2] The affair could not be limited solely to the actual battle,
persecutions and punishments. Joseph of Volokolamsk,[3] while demanding
strict measures from the government against the heretics, also had to write
a book exposing them. Joseph's enemies did not remain silent, for the
Transvolga Elders[4] refuted Joseph's opinions in writing. Brother Vassian
Kosoy (Prince Patrikeev)[5] was the leader of these elders and was considered in Moscow to be one of the most learned and clever of men. There was
also Maxim the Greek, a luminary of contemporary learning. Russian
scholars gathered around him, and even Prince Kurbsky considered himself one of Maxim's pupils. There also gathered around the Athonite monk
those dissatisfied with the new order introduced by the Greek woman
Sophia, and literary activity once again became closely linked with politics. Maxim the Greek suffered disgrace, as did Vassian Kosoy. Their
enemy Metropolitan Daniel[6] was also one of the most prolific writers of the
age. In the political struggle the word was used constantly as a weapon.
Thus the political and ecclesiastical polemical literature characteristic of
this age clearly took its beginning where the political struggle began, in the
struggle of Sophia and Joseph with the Patrikeevs and the Judaizers.

TSAR IVAN THE WRITER

We already are familiar with the works from Ivan's pen. Whereas earlier
we had chiefly to turn our attention to the subject of these works, now we
shall say a few words about their form, which likewise will serve to explain
the character of this famous historical personality and the means of expression at his disposal. In keeping with his own day's means of intellectual

formation, Ivan was an autodidact who read Scripture by rote, and the same happened to him as can be observed nowadays in those similarly educated. The very forms of the language in which he read, which for him held an important, sacred meaning, crowded densely in his memory. When he wished to use them he did not study the peculiarities of the forms. Guided only by his memory, often he could not control them or the structure of a phrase. He threw together words and clauses without conjunctions, jumped from one subject to another and without completing one thought began another. There was also Ivan's passionate nature, which hindered him from calm consideration of what he was writing.

What Ivan read is clearly evident from his letters. He read Sacred Scripture, translated works of church fathers, Russian chronicles and chronographs, from which he gleaned information about Roman and Byzantine history. Yet he was chiefly under the influence of the first two genres, so that his missives are full of scriptural and patristic citations. Ivan's talent is seen in his skillful use of options. In his correspondence with Kurbsky he cleverly turns to his correspondent's religious sentiments, and thrusts into his view that aspect of his action against which such a sentiment must especially cry out. "Prince, why have you sold your soul for the sake of the body? You have raged against me and have ruined your soul, for you have raised your hands to tear down the church. You think that you will protect yourself from this, don't you? Don't bet on it. If you go with them (the Lithuanians) to war, without fail you will destroy churches, trample on icons, ruin Christians. Imagine how the tender bodies of youths will be trampled on and torn apart by horses' hooves. Thus your wicked design resembles Herod's fury against the Innocents, does it not? Would you call that piety? So for the sake of the body you have ruined your soul, for the sake of passing glory you have acquired infamy, and you have not raged against a man, but you have risen up against God. Understand, unfortunate one, from what a height and into what an abyss you have been precipitated, both soul and body! Even there they can understand who is more sensible and grasp that you did not run from death but left in the hope of fleeting glory and wealth. If you were righteous and pious, why did you dread an innocent death which is not death at all, but gain?" Then Ivan proves with words of Scripture that Kurbsky's very act of desertion is a sin, even without war against his Orthodox homeland. "Why have you despised the Apostle Paul who said, 'He who opposes authority opposes God's will.'[7] Look and think how he who opposes God is called an apostate, and this is the most serious sin."

Kurbsky points to his descent from the sainted prince Fedor Rostislavich Smolensky-Yaroslavsky[8] and entrusts his case to the judgment of his ancestor. Here too Ivan humiliates him. "Gladly do I take as my judge the holy Fedor Rostislavich, even though he is your clansman, because anyone who was righteous here in this earthly life will act all the more righteously after death, and will judge righteously between you and me. This same holy prince Fedor cured our princess Anastasia, whom you likened to Eudoxia.[9] Clearly he has extended his mercy, not to you, but to us though we be unworthy. Thus do we hope even now that he will assist us more than you. If you were a child of Abraham you would perform the works of Abraham,[10] for God can raise children of Abraham out of stones;[11] not all who descend from Abraham are reckoned his seed, but those who live in the faith of Abraham.[12] You write that you wish your letter buried with you in the grave. This means that you already have set aside the last of your Christianity. The Lord has commanded us not to oppose evil, but you reject even final forgiveness. Thus you should not be buried according to Christian rites."

Ivan borrowed his comparisons from Sacred Scripture. "For the sake of temporary glory, love of money and the pleasure of this world," he writes to Kurbsky, "you have trampled on all your spiritual piety, together with its Christian faith and law. You are like the seed which fell on rock and grew up under the heat of the sun,[13] but suddenly because of a false word you sinned, you fell away and produced no fruit."

It is understandable that in the face of the unsatisfactory state of education which prevailed in Russian society of that time the scholar who learned by rote enjoyed all the more admiration the more he displayed his learning and erudition in speeches and writings. Clearly Ivan loved to display his learning, inserting in his letters voluminous historical excerpts. As a rule such men loved to brag about what was rare and new, for the crowd was drawn by quantity and abundance. The validity of the question about propriety or moderation was admitted by the very few intellectually mature. By nature Ivan was incapable of belonging to these few, for he was the least capable of complying with the demands of propriety and moderation. The fecundity of his speech, the inability to restrain or moderate himself which generally flowed out of his passionate nature, also depended to a greater or lesser degree on his particular state of mind. The first letter to Kurbsky, written in intense agitation and anger, is distinguished by a particular garrulousness, whereas the second letter is brief. Among the other reasons for this brevity must be acknowledged the fact that the second letter was written during a period of great tranquility of soul and great satisfaction with his own situation, resulting from military successes.

Ivan's unhealthy moral condition expressed itself all the more in mockery, in the desire to take someone at his word, to place him in a difficult situation and take pleasure in this, as well as in the absence of respect or condescension towards the unfortunate situation of his opponent, in the desire not to console him in misfortune, rather to lay the blame for misfortune on him, to show him that he had no right to complain. It is not surprising that he did not spare Kurbsky his derision. "You yourself wrote," he answered, "that we sent you into distant towns as though holding you in disgrace. Now, by the will of God, we have sent you further than your distant towns. Our horses have traversed all your paths in and out of Lithuania, we have gone on foot and we have drunk water in all these places. So it is now no longer possible to say that our horse's hooves have not been everywhere. Even where you wished to rest from all your labors, in Wolmar, even there to your refuge has God brought us, and wherever you thought you might run, we chased you there by the will of God, and you have gone further away."

It is not surprising that Ivan found satisfaction in irritating the Crimean khan, reminding him of an inopportunely expressed outburst of disinterestedness. "Why do you request gifts from me? Did you not just write that all the riches of the world were like ashes for you?" One of Ivan's closest and most diligent new servants, Vasily Griaznoy,[14] elevated as a consequence of the tsar's disapproval of more high-born men, fell captive to the Crimean Tatars. "You wrote that because of your sins," the tsar wrote to Griaznoy, "they took you prisoner. But Vasiushka, you cannot pass through the midst of Crimean villages without a right of passage. If you insist on passing through, you must not sleep as though on a ride-about. You thought that on a ride-about you could arrive with dogs for hunting hares, but instead the Crimeans have snared you in their net. Or did you think that in the Crimea you could jest as you do in my presence after eating? The Crimeans do not sleep as you do, and they know how to catch you, milksop. If only the Crimeans were softies like you, they would not even be across the river, let alone just outside Moscow! You call yourself a great man. Is it true that you conceal sins? Our father's and our own boyars betrayed us, and we brought you into our confidence, little man, hoping for service and truth from you. If only you recalled your father's greatness and your own at Aleksin.[15] Such men rode even in the cossack squadrons. You yourself lived in the cossack settlement of Peninsk, little better than the houndsmen, and your ancestors served the bishops of Rostov. We do not deny that we had you in our inner circle, and that because of your closeness to us we would give about two thousand rubles for you, but before those days men like you were to be had for fifty rubles."

Ivan, the rhetorician of eloquence, loved to display orally the abundance and beauty of his speech in his answers to envoys. He avoided an argument with Possevino because he feared being shown up as unsound in front of the learned Jesuit, and because he feared offending the head of the Catholic world by speaking against Catholicism, but information concerning an argument with the Protestant Rokyta[16] has reached us, where he was not afraid of offending anyone. "I have told you before and I am telling you now, that I do not want to have an argument with you, because you only wish to find out our opinions without agreeing with us. Thus we must act in keeping with the Lord's command not to give holy things to dogs or cast pearls before swine.[17] Beforehand I shall speak about your teacher Luther who both in life and in name was wild,"[18] and so on.

It needs to be pointed out that everywhere at this time, both in Western Europe and in neighboring Lithuania no decorum at all was observed in bitter arguments, or as they are better called, squabbles, and men loved to give an amusing and offensive meaning to the name of their opponent, especially when there was a similarity of sounds. Thus in Lithuania Catholics came up with "Volan" as the name for a famous Protestant champion.[19] In Germany Thomas Müntzer called Luther "Doctor Lügner" [Doctor Liar] and our Ivan the Terrible found an even closer consonance. That word formations were in full swing is evident from other information. It is related that Ivan the Terrible at one time fawned over the Germans, which is understandable because he wanted to recruit the Livonians, being suspicious of his fellow Russians, and because he wanted to excuse his own behavior by the disreputableness of the Livonians. He bragged of his German descent through Bavarian dukes, and as proof he brought forth the word *boyare* [boyars], which sounded to him like the word *Bayern* [Bavaria]. Fletcher[20] recounts that once while handing over some gold objects and ingots to an English goldsmith for him to make tableware, the tsar ordered him to pay close attention to the weight, adding, "My Russians are all thieves." The Englishman smiled, and when asked for the reason for his smile answered, "Your majesty forgets that he himself is Russian." "I am not Russian," answered the tsar, "my ancestors were Germans."[21]

PRINCE KURBSKY THE WRITER

Kurbsky's letters relating to the account have a different character than Ivan's letters to him, and this for different reasons. First of all, Ivan was a bookish autodidact whereas Kurbsky was Maxim the Greek's pupil and hence must have possessed other, loftier notions about rhetorical eloquence, must have acquired considerable ability in dissecting literary material and constructing his own speech more harmoniously. In his reply to Ivan, Kurbsky reproaches him for his inappropriate wordiness, for his inharmonious speech and for his too extensive citations from Sacred Scripture and patristic writings. "I have received your wide-ranging and obstreperous letter, comprehended and understood that it was belched out of indomitable anger with venomous words that would be unworthy not only of a tsar so great and universally renowned, but also of a simple, wretched soldier. In particular much in it is picked up from Sacred Scripture, and these words are introduced with great fury and ferocity, not in lines or verses as is the custom of the skilled and the learned who enclose much reason in brief phrases, but rather immoderate and entangled, with whole books, liturgical readings,[22] and letters! In it is talk about beds and quilted jackets and odds and ends just like the fables of frantic old women, and everything is so barbaric that not only learned and skilled men but also the simple, yea even children, are surprised and laugh, especially in foreign countries where there are men who are skilled, not only in grammatical and rhetorical learning, but also in dialectics and philosophy."

Indeed if we compare Ivan's letters with those of Kurbsky on the basis of form we cannot help but prefer Kurbsky's. Here, for example, is the beginning of one of his letters to the tsar. "If prophets used to weep and mourn over the city of Jerusalem, over the most beautiful temple built of the fairest stone, and over the ruin of its inhabitants, how can we not but lament over the destruction of the city of the living God or of the temple of your body which the Lord, not man, has created. The Holy Spirit once dwelt in that temple which after praiseworthy repentance was purified and washed clean with pure tears, from which pure prayer like sweet-smelling myrrh or incense rose to the Lord's throne, in which on the solid foundation of the Orthodox faith pious works were created. In this temple the tsar's soul sparkled like a dove with silver-plated wings, more precious and brighter than gold, adorned with works through the grace of the Holy Spirit, fortified and sanctified by the body and blood of Christ. Such was the temple of your body at one time!"

The fact that Kurbsky was more adept at maintaining his composure, was not so petulant and passionate and was not so perverted in his youth as Ivan the Terrible, contributed to the greater harmony, the greater elegance and calm in Kurbsky's speech. Finally the situation in which he appeared as a writer, the situation of an exile, must have exerted a great influence on Kurbsky's form of speech. The feeling of abhorrence for his oppressor, which aroused him to angry words, was abated by another feeling, profound grief over the loss of his homeland, the cheerlessness of his situation.

This is especially palpable in his first letter, which consists of one morbid scream. "Why, O tsar, have you destroyed the strong in Israel and handed over to various forms of death the captains given to you by God and shed their victorious, holy blood in the churches of God during episcopal solemnities, staining the thresholds of the churches with their martyr's blood? Why have you conceived against your well-wishers, who would lay down their lives for you, unheard-of tortures and persecutions and deaths, falsely accusing Orthodox Christians of treachery, sorcery and other unworthy actions, endeavoring zealously to turn light into darkness and call bitter what is sweet? What offense did they commit before you, O tsar? How did they anger you, defender of Christians? Did they not destroy haughty kingdoms with their bravery and subject to you those who formerly enslaved our forbears? Were not the strong German towns given to you by God through their keenness of intellect? What is your reward to us for all of this! You destroy us by whole families! Do you think that you are immortal, or have you been seduced by heresy, thinking that there will be no Jesus as judge? He, my Christ, who is seated on the cherubim throne, is the judge between you and me. What type of evil and persecution have I not endured from you? What misfortunes and disasters have you not raised against me? What vile tissue of lies have you not imputed against me? I am now unable to enumerate in order the various calamities which have befallen me through you owing to their great number, because I am still enveloped by bitterness in my soul, but I will tell it all in one breath. I have been deprived of everything and driven from the land of God for spurious reasons!"

The importance of *The History of the Grand Prince of Moscow* written by Kurbsky in exile is well-known. In this excerpt the author discussed the purpose of this history in general as follows. "The glorious deeds of great men are written in histories by wise men, so that future generations will be jealous of them. The destructive and foul deeds of wicked and cunning men are written so that people will be on guard against them like a poison or epidemic, which brings death not only to the body but also to the soul." As one of the main participants Kurbsky describes the capture of Kazan in detail. It is interesting to observe how he understands the meaning of this event. "With divine assistance against our foes the Christian army was victorious. Against which foes? Against the mighty and terrible race of Ishmael at which the entire universe once trembled, and not only trembled but was laid waste. Not against one tsar alone was the Christian army's support enlisted but simultaneously against three great and powerful tsars, that is, against the tsars of Perekop and Kazan, and the Nogay princes. With the assistance of Christ our God the army repulsed then the attacks of all three, and was adorned with illustrious victories, and in a few years the borders of Christendom were expanded. Where formerly there were Tatar winter camps in the empty border regions of Russia, towns now have been constructed. Not only are the horses of Russian sons watered from the flowing rivers of Asia, but towns have been established there as well." One of the most educated people of Eastern and Western Russia, Kurbsky did not miss a chance to praise the learning and eloquence of others. Thus, speaking of Prince Ivan Belsky he adds that "he was not only courageous but also reasonable and somewhat skilled in the Sacred Scriptures." About the captive Livonian land marshal Philip Bell he says, "He was a man not only courageous and bold, but also full of eloquence and possessing a sharp mind and good memory."

Kurbsky was a pupil of Maxim the Greek, and together with him a zealous protector of the Patrikeev traditions. Hence it is not surprising to find the following comment about Vassian Kosoy. "Forsaking worldly fame, he settled in a desert place and practiced a strict and holy life like the great and glorious Anthony of old and, so that no one might accuse me of boldness, he resembled John the Baptist because he too forbade a marriage contrary to divine law."[23] Kurbsky commented on the deportation of Maxim the Greek by the tsar. "Venerable Maxim," he wrote, "a very wise man, was not only powerful in rhetorical art but also an experienced monk,[24] anointed with old age and adorned with the patience of a confessor." Kurbsky was also closely linked with the famous Artemy,[25] the abbot of the Trinity-St. Sergius monastery, who according to his words was completely innocent of unorthodox opinions. Our church historians are of the opinion that Artemy was not entirely correct before the council. Whether or not Kurbsky was entirely correct in his opinions, and to what degree his sympathy for the enemies of the author-enlightener and all

Josephans exerted an influence on the correctness of his opinions, we do not know. Still it is well known that in Lithuania Kurbsky showed himself to be one of the most zealous defenders of Orthodoxy against Catholicism, and even more against Protestantism. It is clear that the banishment itself, the yearning for the land of Holy Russia, as he expressed it, must have strengthened this zeal for the faith, which more than anything bound him to his lost homeland, which alone forced him to think that he was not in a completely alien land in Lithuania. Understandably, because he suffered from nostalgia for his Holy Russian land, Kurbsky became very diligent in supporting the confession known as the "Russian faith" in Lithuania. Kurbsky experienced what the poet said, "Your native land is the same as your health. You only recognize its full worth when you lose it!" In the heat of anger Kurbsky sometimes called his homeland ungrateful, but even there he vented unwillingly his melancholy at being banished from his *beloved* homeland.

In *The History of the Grand Prince of Moscow* Kurbsky expressed at every opportunity his strong dislike for Protestantism. Thus he ascribed the fall of Livonia to the acceptance of Protestantism. Talking about the capture of Narva by the Russians, Kurbsky adds, "There is the reward for the foul-mouthed who liken Christ's image painted according to the flesh, and the image of his mother, to statues of pagan deities! There is the recompense for the iconoclasts! In truth a sign of judgment before the Judgment has been revealed in them so that others shall fear to blaspheme holy things." The loss of the warring spirit among Poles and Lithuanians Kurbsky likewise attributed to the spread of Lutheran heresies among them. "When they abandoned the way of the Lord and rejected the faith of the church they rushed into the diffuse and broad path, that is, into the abyss of Lutheran heresy and other diverse sects, especially their wealthiest grandees, and then this misfortune overtook them."

After translating John Chrysostom's discourse on faith, hope and love from Latin into Slavonic, Kurbsky sent his work to Prince Konstantin Ostrozhsky,[26] who gave it to a non-Orthodox man to translate into Polish. Kurbsky was angered and wrote Prince Ostrozhsky, "I do not know how it happened that you have handed my translation for examination to a man who is not only inept in knowledge, but also knows nothing about grammar rules, who in addition to this is replete with filthy words, has no shame, and belches impurely the words of Sacred Scripture, for I heard from his own mouth a distortion of the words of the Apostle Paul. You write that you gave it for translation into Polish. Believe me that if a multitude of learned men assembled and broke the grammatical rules of the Slavonic language, transposing into Polish barbarism, they would be unable to explain it precisely." In the face of powerful movements and the flaring of passions at the appearance of new teachings as was then the case in Lithuania, Kurbsky could not avoid heated arguments with promoters of these ideas. Such an argument he had with Prince Koretsky and Lord Chapli, a follower of the Moscow heretics Feodosy Kosoy and his companion Ignaty.

The argument, as is clear from Kurbsky, ended with very heated words on the part of Chapli. Seeing that passion and not reason was operative, Kurbsky refused to answer. Chapli did not leave him in peace, but sent him a written exposition of his teaching. Kurbsky responded that he had nothing to learn, having studied the Sacred Scriptures since his youth. Just as the apostles and their pupils did not ask for explanations from ancient heretics, so neither would Kurbsky demand the explanations of Melanchthon, Luther and his pupils, Zwingli and Calvin, and others who even while still alive did not agree with him. So now Lord Feodosy and Lord Ignaty were following them not for the sake of learning, but for the sake of their lords. "You urge that I write to you about Luther," Kurbsky continues, "because I called him a false prophet. I told you already at length that he not only despised all the saints, but also many books of the Old Testament, and he rejected some of the writings of the apostles. Have you forgotten, or do you wish to wheedle out of me some composition and give it to Lord Ignaty so that he defame our church of God? No, you will not succeed. We are on our guard, as the Lord says, against casting holy things to dogs."

The Protestants loved to expose the wealth of bishops and monks. "With regard to the wealthy bishops," Kurbsky answered Chapli, "and avaricious monks who received properties from our ancestors, not for their own profit, but so that they could welcome strangers, give alms to the poor and beautify the church—God will judge them for their management of those properties, not I, because I have my own heavy burden of sins. We are not talking about such as these, but about true apostle-like bishops and poverty-loving monks whom Luther mixed together with today's trans- gressors of the canons. He reviles them and repudiates their typika, just as your grace repudiated the Damascene.[27] You revile him using others' words, without having read him I think, because the book is not translated into Slavonic. Although some parts have been translated, it was done so poorly that it is unintelligible; but the Greeks and Latins have the whole book. You, your grace, and your teacher Lord Ignaty do not know either

Greek or Latin, I imagine, and you are adept only at reviling and quarreling." Kurbsky was very happy when one of the young Polish nobility, Bokej Pecichwostowski, converted from Protestantism back to Orthodoxy. He wrote him two exhortatory letters so that he would remain firm on his new and true path.

During Kurbsky's times it was necessary for the defenders of Orthodoxy to inveigh against more than Protestantism, for a Catholic Jesuit opposition was following, more dangerous than divided Protestantism. "I have heard," wrote Kurbsky to the Wilno mayor Kuzma Mamonich, "from many worthy men about a Jesuit who spews forth many venomous syllogisms against our holy faith, calling us schismatics, when in fact they themselves are the consummate schismatics, drinking from turbid springs flowing from their newly wise Popes. But if God grants it, we shall converse more extensively about this with our own people and even with the Jesuits if possible. Now I shall recall only how they terrify our people not perfectly versed in Scriptures, saying that anyone who does not obey the Pope is not saved. This false scarecrow of theirs is exposed. Now advise our people that they not do battle with them without Orthodox scholars, nor they attend their sermons. They are not ashamed of reviling and putting to shame right believers who stand on the seven-pillared dogmas,[28] confusing them with heretics, with Lutherans, Zwinglians, Calvinists, and leading them away from Orthodoxy to half-belief, to newly invented and lame theology from true theology.[29] It is praiseworthy to acquire philological aptitude and act to defend what is right but they, having mixed elocution with dialectical sophisms and added to this pronunciation, turn against true believers and endeavor to destroy the truth with oratorical tricks, playing up to their Pope, extolling their terrible grandiose bishop girt with weapons and leading a company of soldiers. They disparage our patriarchs, our needy and poor, those adorned with the humility of Christ, those who suffered like martyrs among the godless Turks and preserved the dogmas of piety unharmed."

In another letter to the same Mamonich Kurbsky wrote, "I already wrote to you about the sly ruses of the Jesuits. Do not be afraid of their sophisms, but stand firm in the Orthodox faith. The enemy shall not destroy utterly the Eastern churches with their sly ruses! What have they published against our church? Booklets decorated with their own pagan syllogisms, sophistically perverting and corrupting apostolic theology? Behold, by the grace of God we have been given a book from the Holy Mountain, transported as it were by the very hand of God owing to the simplicity and profound lack of expertise of the clerics of the Russian church, not to mention the laziness and gluttony of our bishops. I already spoke to you about this book and that Prince Konstantin Ostrozhsky gave it to Lord Haraburda and me to copy. Their present-day fifes and pipes are not in this book, but all the syllogisms which their Pope and all the cardinals and their best theologian Thomas (Aquinas) have belched out against the apostolic theology of the Eastern churches, and which have been refuted by the godly men Gregory and Neilos, metropolitans of Thessalonica.[30] I advise you to read this my letter to the entire Wilno council so that they may become fervent with divine zeal for the sake of our ancestral Orthodoxy and hire a good copyist. When copies of the book have been made, let them read it soberly, having separated themselves from drunkenness. In it are prepared answers of these blessed men. If, having stretched out, we lie in our long-accustomed drunkenness, not only will the Lord Jesuits and the presbyters of the Roman church, mighty in Sacred Scripture, be able to tear you slouches apart, but even the wretched little beasts, that is, the newly-appeared heretics, will be able to tear you apart and drag you off each to his own lair. So do not grow weary, do not despair, do not be afraid of sophisms, but choose one of the presbyters or even someone from the laity who is literate and knowledgeable in Scripture and, having taken the book in hand, resist with this invincible weapon."

Princess Czartoryska[31] wrote to Kurbsky that her son, fortified in the fear of God and in his ancestral Orthodoxy, desired to study Sacred Scripture, and that she wanted to send him to Wilno to study with the Jesuits. "Your intention is praiseworthy," Kurbsky answered, "but as your servant and friend I do not wish to hide from you that many parents have handed over their children to the Jesuits to study the liberal arts, but the Jesuits will not instruct them before they have separated them from Orthodoxy, as they did the sons of Prince Korsinski and others. By the way, Basil the Great, Gregory the Theologian and John Chrysostom travelled to study in Athens with pagan philosophers, yet did not lose their spiritual uprightness and ancestral Orthodoxy. I leave the matter to the wise consideration of your grace and your friends."

Another famous zealot for the cause of Orthodoxy, Prince Konstantin Ostrozhsky, considered it permissible to play one group of enemies of Orthodoxy against another, to use the writings of the Protestants against the Jesuits. Kurbsky did not share this opinion. Once when Ostrozhsky sent him a book by the Jesuit Skarga[32] and a letter of the Arian[33] Motovilo directed against the book, Kurbsky replied, "Who ever has heard or in which chronicle was it written that a ravenous wolf should be summoned to pasture in a flock of sheep? Where was it heard that an Orthodox Christian took delight in epistles from an Arian enemy of Christianity or received from him letters in aid of the church of Christ our God?" When Ostrozhsky sent him Motovilo's book against the Jesuits a second time, Kurbsky replied, "Your grace sent me a book written by the devil's son, compiled by the Antichrist's assistant! Does your grace send me, an Orthodox Christian, your liege brother, this book as a gift? O calamity worthy of weeping! O most accursed poverty! Christian leaders have fallen into such impudence and stupidity that they not only are not ashamed to feed and keep in their homes the venomous dragons, they also consider themselves their defenders and assistants! What is even more amazing is that they instruct them to defend the church of God and order them to write books against the half-believing Latins!"

Kurbsky supposed the cause for such behavior of Prince Ostrozhsky to be laziness and negligence, an unwillingness to occupy himself with the study of Sacred Scripture. "All of this is happening to us because of laziness and reluctance to read Sacred Scripture. I have worn you out with words about this, hoping that you would read Scripture often, even a little at a time, and I shall not stop pestering you until my own death (because of my great love for you) until I see that you are making a greater effort in this regard."

Kurbsky's religious activity was not limited to his class circle. He addressed his exhortations to Mamonich and the entire Wilno citizenry of the Orthodox confession. We find among his letters one to Simeon Sedelnik, a townsman of Lvov, whom he calls a beloved brother adorned with right belief. In answer to Simeon's question about purgatory, Kurbsky sent him Chrysostom's gloss on the apostle Paul, which he translated from Latin. "Accept this my spiritual present," wrote Kurbsky to Simeon, "read it attentively and rejoice with the Orthodox of the Eastern churches, but do not show it to the schismatics nor argue with them. Visit me, and then we shall discuss how best to proceed with them, so that they may not oppose the truth. For they have the habit of opposing Gospel truth with very clever syllogisms of pagan philosophers, which they combine with their own obstinacy. They attack particularly those who are armed with the Sacred Scriptures, but nonetheless do not know how to proceed, being unskilled in countering enemies."

Kurbsky repeatedly spoke about the lack of expertise of Russians in wielding a spiritual weapon, and about the skill of their enemies in this matter. More than once he dissuaded his brethren in the faith from dangerous debates with the cunning Jesuits. Clearly grasping the lack of weapons for the fight, to be sure, he had to endeavor with all his might to acquire them, to acquire books accessible in the language of the majority of the Orthodox. For this the books of the holy fathers of the Eastern church had to be translated.

How much trouble Kurbsky took over this translation is best seen from a letter to Mark, a pupil of Artemy. In all likelihood this was Mark Sarygozin, a Muscovite refugee. Kurbsky says in this letter that Artemy, who was already in Lithuania, asked him to purchase all the works of Basil the Great and to find someone to translate them from Greek or Latin. "Even if I find a man who knows Greek and Latin," Kurbsky replied, "he will probably not know Slavonic." "Although I am old," Artemy answered, "I will come on foot from Lutsk wherever you wish, and help with the translation." "When I heard this from the mouth of the venerable man," Kurbsky's letter continued, "I not only searched for translators, but I myself, though grey-haired, spent a few years learning Latin with great difficulty. Through my entreaties I moved a noble youth, my brother Prince Mikhail Obolensky (likewise an émigré) to pursue higher studies in the Roman tongue, to which he submitted, and spent three years in the Cracow school. Then he went to Italy to complete his studies, and spent two years there, having left behind his house, wife and children. Now he has returned safely without injury to his ancestral piety, like a ship brimming with precious treasures. I not only purchased all the works of Basil the Great, but those of some of our other writers such as St. John Chrysostom, Gregory the Theologian, Cyril of Alexandria, John of Damascus, and a chronicle translated from modern Greek into Latin, which is very useful and full of wisdom. It was written by Nicephoros Kallistos.[34] For the sake of the union of our beloved Christ, and also of his servant, your elder and my father, the holy and venerable Artemy, show your love for the single family of Russia, for the entire Slavic tribe! Do not delay visiting us for a few months to assist our coarseness and lack of expertise, because we are unable to master perfectly the Slavonic language the way you and Prince Obolensky can and I am afraid of setting out alone on such a great and praiseworthy task without help.

"I am sending you the foreword of one book of our translation, not so that we might be extolled or become conceited thereby, but to demonstrate to you our deficiencies and ignorance. I have searched for assistance, have turned here and there and nowhere did I find any. If God brings you to us,

I would sit with a baccalaureate behind a book of Pauline epistles interpreted by Chrysostom, and your grace would sit behind another book with
Prince Mikhail. I am sending your grace as a spiritual present a speech by
Gregory the Theologian and a sermon by Basil the Great which we have
translated."

The preface to his translation of some sermons of Chrysostom, which
he called *The New Pearl*, Kurbsky began with complaints about his
unfortunate situation, his unjust banishment, and his sojourn among gloomy
and inhospitable people perverted by various heresies, whereas in his
homeland the fire of martyrdom was burning cruelly. "Hearing this I am
overcome with pity and from all directions I am being constrained with
despondency, unbearable misfortunes are eating up my heart like a moth.
In my grief I turn to the Lord and am consoled by my scholarly affairs,
studying the thoughts of ancient exalted men. I read through Aristotle. I
often returned to read my familiar Sacred Scripture with which my fore-
fathers were raised spiritually. I happened thereby to recall how venerable
Maxim the New Confessor[35] once told me that the books of the great
Eastern teachers were not translated into Slavonic, but after the fall of
Constantinople they were translated into Latin.

"Remembering this, I began to learn Latin so that I could translate into
my own language what was not yet translated. Foreigners delight in our
teachers while we waste away from spiritual hunger, looking only at
ourselves. For this purpose I spent several years learning grammar, dialectics and other sciences. Having mastered the language, I bought some
books and begged a youth named Ambrose, who was skilled in Scripture
and attained the summit of natural philosophy, to participate in the translation. Before all else he and I translated from Latin into Slavonic the table
of contents for Chrysostom's books, first so that all would know how many
were translated into Slavonic and what a large number were not yet
translated; secondly, so that devout men become zealous for God and
translate the remaining works; thirdly because certain poets and many
heretics ascribed their compositions to Chrysostom in order to gain a more
favorable reception thanks to his name. Thus let our register show what
belongs to Chrysostom and what does not.

"On examining these chapters I wanted to begin translating the epistles
of the Apostle Paul as explained by Chrysostom, and I looked for some
men who had a good command of the Slavonic language but I could find
none. Those I did find from among monks and secular clergy did not want
to help me. The monks declined, not out of commendable self-abnegation,

but from hypocritical humility and laziness. The secular clergy did not want to join us because they were caught up in the vanities of this world, stifling the seed of grace with thorns. I was afraid because in my youth I did not master the Slavonic language, constantly having to address myself to fulfilling the tsar's orders. In the rank of a commander, and then a senator I managed my affairs, sometimes judicial, sometimes advisory, and I often took up arms with the army against the enemies of Christ's cross. Once I arrived here I was coerced by the king into military service, and when I was released from service, hateful and crafty neighbors prevented me from devoting myself to this task, wanting to snatch from me the estate the king gave me for subsistence, even desiring to satiate themselves with my blood. In spite of this I attempted to translate with the aforesaid youth Ambrose a few of the sermons of Chrysostom which up until then were not translated into Slavonic."

In the preface to his translation of a book by John of Damascus, *The Heavens,*[36] Kurbsky drew attention to the importance of education and defended himself against those in Muscovy who did not grasp this. "Let us accept the finest words and, for the sake of God, let us not indulge the senseless, or rather, the sly deceivers who flaunt themselves for their teachers' benefit. I myself have heard from them while I still was in Russia under the dominion of the Moscow tsar. They seduce our disciplined youth who desire to learn Scripture, telling them, 'Do not read many books,' and they point out, 'See, this man lost his mind on books, and that man fell into heresy.' O misfortune! They deprive us of that weapon from which demons flee and by which heretics are exposed, and some are corrected, and they call medicine a death-dealing poison!"

"Among us," he wrote elsewhere, "even one tenth of the books of our ancient teachers have not been translated, owing to the laziness and the negligence of our rulers, because the supposed teachers of the present age are more engrossed in Bulgarian fables and the ravings of old women, reading and extolling them, than in finding enjoyment in the thought of our illustrious teachers. Lord Christ our God, open for us our mental eyes and deliver us from the likes of these!" Finally, in order to lend support to the Orthodox in their battle with Catholicism, Kurbsky wrote a history of the Council of Florence.

DISCIPLES OF MAXIM THE GREEK

Thus one of the first men of letters of the land of Moscow, a pupil of Maxim the Greek, strove to uphold the faith of his ancestors in Western Russia.

This honorable name "pupil of Maxim the Greek" belongs not only to Kurbsky, for it is encountered as well among other writers of the second half of the sixteenth century and demonstrates for us best of all the importance of the famous Athonite monk. In his *History of the Grand Prince of Moscow,* Kurbsky says that in his own home Metropolitan Daniel cruelly put to death the venerable Selivan,[37] Maxim's pupil, who was well-versed in both natural and spiritual philosophy. This Selivan, Maxim's fellow-worker on translations, was renowned as a grammarian. In a seventeenth century collection the following entry is found. "No one can write correctly who does not know the grammatical construction, the genders, numbers, cases, tenses, declensions, the endings according to gender in all the cases, especially in the possessive nouns, as says Brother Selivan, pupil of Maxim the Greek the venerable elder."

The third pupil of Maxim the Greek, Zinovy Otensky,[38] was famous in the East for the same reason as Kurbsky was in the West, for his battle against newly-appeared heresies, namely against the heresy of Feodosy Kosoy. In the beginning of his book written to expose this heresy, Zinovy relates that one day three men came to visit him in the monastery, two monks and a layman. To Zinovy's question of who they were and where they came from the monks replied that they were clerics in the Savior monastery of Staraia Rusa. One was called Gerasim and the other Afanasy; the layman was an iconographer by trade and was called Fedor. "For the sake of God," they said to Zinovy, "do not reject us, do not conceal what is useful for being saved."

Zinovy. You call yourselves clerics, so it follows that you are continually reading the Sacred Scriptures which instruct us on how to be saved.

Clerics. The books are written in a hidden way.

Zinovy. The divine Gospels are open, and the Fathers' sermons are ready for the comprehension of any who so desire.

Clerics. The Scripture is open to the educated, but to the uneducated it is very closed indeed.

Zinovy. The divine Gospel and the Fathers' writings can be understood by everyone, even by the unlearned.

Clerics. There is now a doctrine going around, and many are extolling this current doctrine because it is open, but the Fathers' doctrine is closed, and for that reason there is no profit to be had from reading the Fathers' doctrine. We beg you, tell us the truth and for God's sake do not reject us.

Zinovy. I know well the Fathers' doctrine, and I also know the divine Basil's book on asceticism, but I have not heard of this current doctrine about which you speak.

Clerics. For God's sake tell us the truth. What is your opinion of the current doctrine? Is it divine, is it of God? Surely the current doctrine is good because it prohibits following human traditions and orders us to follow the Scripture, the pillar-like books. For God's sake tell us the truth, for the new doctrine is praised and accepted by many, and many love it.

Zinovy answered that his evaluation of the new doctrine already existed thanks to its very name "It is new," he said, "and therefore, unlawful, for the apostle Paul said, 'Even if an angel from heaven proclaimed a Gospel other than the one you have received, let him be anathema.'[39] Tell me, who is this new teacher?" "The teacher of the new doctrine," answered the clerics, "is called Feodosy, with the surname Kosoy." "Right from the start," said Zinovy, "when you revealed the name of the teacher you showed the depravity of the doctrine. Can the crooked ever be straight?[40] Tell me, who is this teacher and whence does he come?"

The clerics told of Kosoy's fate and then they explained his doctrine. Zinovy then set about refuting that doctrine. We shall leave aside the theological side of his refutation as not pertaining to us, and turn our attention to the scientific means which the most educated people of the time possessed. Demonstrating the necessity of the first cause Zinovy said, "Nowhere has it been written that a bird was ever produced without an egg, or that an egg does not come from a bird, except for the so-called solitary phoenix. It is the same with fish; there is not one fish which is not from roes, nor are there roes which are not from fish. Where then is the progenitor for all of these? An adherent of an original heresy might say that the progenitors appeared out of air because from the clouds of the air it once rained grain, sometimes it has rained ashes, sometimes silvery fragments, as is written in the chronicles, and once within our own memory dead fish were found on waterless ground after a heavy rain. It is not the air which is the parent of all these things, rather the clouds draw up a fish with water from below, and then they let it fall back to earth with the rain. Neither the earth nor the sky in 7074[41] [1566] produced from themselves anew any progenitors, but they nurture what already exists."

Especially important for us in Zinovy's book are the indications of a link between the new heresy and an old heresy, that of the Judaizers,[42] and the desire of Kosoy's followers to be established firmly on the authority of the elder Vassian (Prince Patrikeev) and Maxim the Greek. "Monasteries," the clerics told Zinovy, "transgressing the commandment of non-possession, own villages. Prince Vassian wrote very well about this, and Maxim the Greek also spoke a great deal about it, for he wrote a conversation between a lover of possessions and a non-possessor."

"With respect to fulfilling the Lord's commandments," Zinovy responded, "towns and villages are no different than monasteries. Why do Vassian and Maxim condemn monasteries for transgressing evangelical precepts but cast no shame on towns and villages? Every country has its own custom in keeping with its climate (according to its particular features derived from the sun's path and air currents). How is it possible to bring every country into line with the custom of a single realm? Basil the Great said that the clothing and food of an ascetic must be in keeping with the custom of each land. It would appear that your pious Maxim forgot about these words of Basil the Great! I am a coarse man and cannot understand the thought of the wise Maxim, but I think that he wrote arbitrarily (he was carried away by flights of fancy). He condemned Russian monasteries for their love of possessions but unlike Daniel and the three youths[43] he himself could not leave the grand prince's table. As a monk he laid down the law concerning non-possession for the Russian monasteries, yet he himself came from a monastery owning many possessions. Both Latin and Russian monasteries once were supported by alms. They differ only in that the brethren of a Latin monastery went twice each week into town to get food and wine, whereas Russian monasteries, going once a year into the village given to them as alms, collect fruit. The rest of the time they spend in silence in the monastery, fasting and praying.

"Although the good Maxim philosophized loftily about non-possession, it was nonetheless improper for him to hold up as an example before Russian monasteries a monastery of the Latin region and heresy. He has not shown what non-possession and possession mean in one or another country, because different countries do not have the same system from God. He only wrote for the sake of reproach, since he did not bring forth as an example the Egyptian monasteries, which shone forth with powers and signs like the heavens with stars, and instead brought forth as his example a Latin monastery. Had he presented an Egyptian monastery as an example, it is well known that Egypt is not the same as Russia. Tears well in the eyes when you remember how those monks used to live who are condemned because they owned villages. The skin on their arms became cracked from their labor, their faces grew haggard, their hair in disarray, their feet turned blue and swollen. Tax collectors wrung taxes from them mercilessly; they had no more money than the poor who came to them for alms. Well, indeed, on the rare monk could be found five or six silver coins. Their food was bread from unwinnowed oats and ground ears of rye, their drink was water, their hot dish made of cabbage leaves, the rich had one of beets and turnips, their dessert was made of rowan berry and guelder rose. Yet how did Prince Kassian live in St. Simon's monastery? It did not suit him to eat the St. Simon's dishes—rye bread, cabbage soup, beet-tops, kasha. He did not drink the soured milk and the monastery beer which purifies the stomach, because this food and drink came from the villages. Instead of this he dined on meals brought to him from the grand prince's table, and the non-possessor drank Romaneia,[44] schnapps, muscatel and Rhenish wine."

Hatred for the first exposer of the heresy, Joseph of Volokolamsk, spewed forth from Feodosy Kosoy and his followers. "Kosoy says," the clerics told Zinovy, "that it no longer befits anyone after the seventh council to write books whereas Joseph of Volokolamsk wrote his books after the seventh council contrary to the canons, and for this reason they must not be read." Obviously Zinovy easily could respond, and in passing remarked, "Kosoy reproaches Joseph's book because his heresy was laid bare in it as in a mirror." We find an even more important indication of the heresy of the Judaizers and its continuation. The clerics said, "Some people say in the creed, 'I expect the resurrection of the dead.' Even Maxim the Greek ordered it said thus, because the word 'to hope for' is not strong enough. We hope for something that may or may not happen, but we expect something that will undoubtedly happen."[45]

"Maxim the Greek was very learned," Zinovy answered, "and skilled at translating from Greek into Latin. When he arrived from the Holy Mountain and Grand Prince Vasily ordered him to translate the exposited Psalter[46] from Greek into Russian, he sought out Latin interpreters and translated the Psalter from Greek into Latin, and the Latin interpreters translated from Latin into Russian because Maxim the Greek did not understand Russian well. During the time of Grand Prince Ivan and his son Vasily a godless heresy arose and many grandees and officials were led astray. The grand princes, especially Grand Prince Vasily, convened the court against the impiety and exterminated the blasphemers with fire. Then many grandees, because of fear before the autocrat, renounced their impiety but only superficially, not in their hearts. They then planned a deceit against the holy confession of faith. They upset popular speech and introduced something new, saying that the meaning of the word 'expect' was imprecise. Maxim adopted this from the grandees. I think that this deceitful design of the enemies of Christ or of men with crude intentions was to introduce into learned speech a word chosen from common popular words, whereas in my opinion it is more appropriate to correct popular speech with learned speech and not dishonor learned with common words."

After being fixed on polemical compositions with a religious and political content in which Ivan's stormy century was narrated, a century of motion, of various undertakings and protests, our attention now turns to two monuments in which society endeavored to assemble and then present its moral options. In one collection are the rules of worldly wisdom, in the other a treasure trove of church doctrines and exemplars of the higher spiritual life. The first monument is the *Household Manager*,[47] the second Makary's *Menology*.[48]

THE HOUSEHOLD MANAGER

It is not surprising that the name of Sylvester, the young tsar's famous instructor of morals and founder of good behavior in the tsar's family, is linked with the *Household Manager*, a collection of regulations of worldly wisdom and household family discipline. In the *Household Manager* the following chapter belongs unquestionably to Sylvester, beginning thus, "The benediction of Sylvester, priest at Annunciation cathedral, to my beloved son Anfim." This instruction to his son, corroborated by personal example, and strongly reminiscent of the Instruction of Monomakh,[49] could easily be taken for a completely separate composition having nothing to do with the *Household Manager* properly so called, and added to it by some later compiler or copyist by reason of similar subject matter. Thus we must first turn to Sylvester's own instruction and then to the more extensive *Household Manager*, which also is of great significance for us by reason of its exposition of the ideas and customs of the time.

"My son!" says Sylvester, "you have received the benediction of the bishop and the favor of the sovereign tsar, the sovereign tsaritsa, the tsar's brother and cousin and all the boyars, you associate with good people, and with many foreigners you have great commerce and friendship. You have received every good thing. Know therefore how to complete it in God as it was begun under our care. Have faith in God, set all your hopes on the Lord, always hasten with faith to God's churches. Do not sleep through orthros, do not miss liturgy, do not drink through vespers. You must sing compline, the midnight office and the hours every day in your home. If possible, and time permitting, add the canons; this depends on you. You will receive great mercy from God. In church and at home you, your wife, your children and domestic servants shall stand in prayer with fear, not chattering, not looking about. Read in unison in one tone, not in two. Respect the priestly and monastic orders, obey your spiritual father, invite priests into your home to perform solemn prayer services. Come to church with alms and an offering. Invite ecclesiastics, the poor, the young, the unfortunate, the grieving and wanderers into your house. Feed them as you are able, give them drink, warm them and give alms at home, in the marketplace and on the road. Remember, my son, how we used to live. No one ever left our house empty or doleful. Have sincere love for all, do not condemn anyone, do not do to another what you yourself do not like, and above all preserve bodily purity and despise alcoholic beverages. For the Lord's sake cast away all drunkenness, for every evil habit is born of it. If the Lord preserves you from this, you will receive from God every good and needful thing, you will be honored by men and you will create in every good deed a ray of hope for your soul.

"Love your wife and live with her according to the canons. What you yourself do, teach your wife, namely the fear of God, every type of knowledge and industry, needlework, housekeeping and orderliness. She herself should know how to bake and cook, she should know the household procedures and every type of womanly handicraft. She should have no love at all for alcoholic beverages, nor should her children or servants. A wife must not be even a minute without some handicraft, likewise her servants. With guests in your house or as a guest elsewhere she must never get drunk. She should conduct conversation with guests about her needlework, her household, about a lawful Christian life, but she should not make fun of or gossip about anyone. When visiting or at home she should not permit herself or her servants any devilish songs or vulgarities. She should have nothing to do with sorcerers, magicians or any type of incantation. Should your wife not obey, do not fail to punish her with dread but do not get angry. Punish her in private, and having punished her, speak gently to her, favor and love her.

"Likewise teach your children and the domestics the fear of God and every good deed. Clothe and give sufficient food to your domestics. You saw how I lived in piety and the fear of God, in simplicity of heart, in the church's employ, always profiting from the divine Scripture with fear. You saw how I was respected and loved by all. I tried to please everyone. I did not vaunt myself before anyone, I never crossed anyone, I did not condemn, make fun of, reproach or quarrel with anyone. If an offense came from someone, I bore it and took the guilt upon myself. In this way enemies were made into friends. I never omitted any church hymn. I never scorned a poor stranger or one grieving. I ransomed prisoners, captives and debtors, and I fed the hungry. I released all my slaves and provided for them, and I redeemed others' slaves. All our slaves are free; they live in good homes and pray to God for us and they always wish us well. Now all our domestics are free, they live with us of their own choice.

"You saw how many orphans, slaves and destitute, both male and female, in Novgorod and Moscow, to whom I gave food and drink until they grew up, how I taught the skill befitting the abilities of each. Many were able to read, write and sing, others were adept at icon painting, others at book illumination, some could learn silversmithing, others some other type of fine handicraft, and others I taught how to trade. Your mother as well reared many young girls, orphans and unfortunates. She instructed them and having provided for them, married them off. For the men we found wives from good people. Many of them are in priestly or monastic ranks, or are crown secretaries, scribes, or are in other offices for which they were born and in which God has blessed them. Among all those whom we reared or who were in our service there was never any disgrace or loss, none were sued by others nor have we sued others, nor have there been litigations with anyone. If from any of them there were vexations or great losses, they took it all on themselves, no one heard of it and God accomplished it for us. You, my son, must do the same. Take every type of offense upon yourself and suffer patiently, for God will complete your work twofold. Feed merchants who visit you, and live in love in your neighborhood and with your acquaintances for the sake of hospitality, good transactions and every type of loan.

"If you travel somewhere as a visitor take some inexpensive gifts for friendship. While travelling give from your table to householders and wayfarers, seat them at your table, do the same for innkeepers, and give alms to the weak. If you act in this way they will attend you everywhere and come to meet you, they will accompany you on your way and protect you from all ill. They will not assault you in the encampment, they will not rob you on the road. See, this is why they give provisions. They provision a good man in return for his goodness, but the evil man because of his evil so that he might return to the good. In all of this there is no loss. Among good people hospitality is an obligation. So too are presents, but the result is eternal friendship and a good reputation.

"Do not start a fight on the road, at a banquet or during a transaction, but if someone berates you, bear it for God's sake. If your servitors are involved in a quarrel with someone, reprove your own men, and if the matter grows worrisome, strike your man even though he is in the right. In this way you keep the peace and there will be neither loss nor hostility. Give your enemy food and drink, for instead of hostility there will be friendship. Remember God's great mercy towards us and His intercession. From my youth until the present day I never put anyone on bond, nor has anyone posted me on bond, neither was I ever in court with anyone.

"You yourself have seen that there were many types of master crafts-men. I gave them money for their handicraft in advance and many of them were trouble-makers and carousers. For forty years I bade them farewell on good terms, without a bailiff, without any grief. All this was done peaceably with hospitality, drink, tribute and my own patience. If I myself bought something from anyone, the seller received from me tender affec-tion, payment without delay and hospitality above and beyond the usual. For this reason friendship lasts forever; they do not sell without me and they do not give poor goods. If ever I sold something to someone, all was done in love, not deception. If someone does not like my wares, I take them back and return the money, and I have never had a quarrel or litigation with anyone over purchases or sales.

"Wherefore good people, both foreigners and locals, have believed me in everything. No one was ever lied to, or lured into anything, or had the time limit altered. I issued no service contracts or bills against myself, nor was there ever a lie about anything. You yourself have seen what serious entanglements there were with many people, yet everything ended without hostility, thank God. You yourself know that you don't win honor with good men by means of wealth. Rather, it is by means of justice, tenderness, and love and not with pride and without any kind of lie."

In this exhortation, in this instruction on his own manner of thought and life, Sylvester completely reveals himself to us. We understand the impres-sion which such a man must have made on his contemporaries. A pious, sober, meek, merciful, tender, obliging, superb lord who loved to arrange his domestics' fate, a man with whom it was both pleasant and advanta-geous to do business—this is Sylvester! In fact this man had to be thus, for otherwise we cannot understand his moral influence on the young tsar, or how a simple priest attracted the remainder of the boyar class.

How then, might it be asked, did Sylvester manage to irritate the tsar and tsaritsa, given all his meekness and tractability? This is very easily ac-counted for by the same thought and actions which find expression in the *Household Manager*. Sylvester found himself in the role of preceptor and instructor with respect to Ivan. He considered it his duty to act strictly, to demand the literal fulfillment of what was prescribed. Sylvester ordered his son to strike his domestic servant even though he was in the right, as long as hostility and loss could be averted. For Sylvester, Ivan was his own son and pupil. Just as Sylvester himself in a conflict with others considered it his duty to yield, to back off, thereby averting hostility, so too did he demand the same from the tsar in his conflicts with the boyars. This explains Ivan's complaints about sacrificing his own advantages to those of the boyars. Taking advantage of his moral influence, Sylvester forgot the tsar in Ivan, and saw in him only a young man who was obliged to be meek, patient and obedient. In the boyars he saw men of counsel and valor. Thus when the young tsar decided to contradict them and to insist on his own way, as for example regarding the Livonian war, Sylvester considered this to be a sin, and he threatened the young man with heavenly retaliation for his willfulness.

In spite of the fact that Sylvester's exhortation to his son has to all appearances a religious, Christian character, we cannot help noticing that its purpose is to impart worldly wisdom. Meekness, patience and the other Christian virtues are presented as means of acquiring worldly advantages and other people's benevolence. Good deeds are prescribed, and immediately the material advantage to be gained from them is brought to the fore. By prescribing tractability and avoidance of animosity, all the while basing this on a seemingly Christian commandment, Sylvester ended up by prescribing something quite contrary to Christianity, namely servility to other human beings. "Strike your own servant even though he be in the right, for in this way you will quell the fracas and avoid loss and animosity."

Here is the result of Christianity understood not in spirit but in the flesh. Sylvester considered it a good act to set slaves free, and he boasts that all his domestics are free and dwell with him of their own choice, yet at the same time he considers it permissible to beat a domestic even though he be right. He wants to fulfill the form but does not understand the spirit. He did not understand that Christianity, a divine and eternal doctrine, has no truck with transitory forms. It acts on the spirit for its purification and by means of this purification it has an effect on the improvement of the forms.

That an individual derives little worldly benefit from the confusion of the pure with the impure, of the rules of heavenly wisdom with the rules of worldly wisdom is best of all evident in Sylvester's example. He told his son, "Imitate me! See how I am respected by all, loved by all, because I pleased everyone." Yet at the end it emerged that he did not please everyone, for such a thing is impossible. True wisdom commands us to serve the Lord alone. In all likelihood during the tsar's illness Sylvester wanted to please everyone, as a result of which he gave way. Initially his voice was not heard, but then he wanted to reconcile Prince Vladimir with the sick Ivan and he said to the sworn boyars, "Why do you not admit Prince Vladimir to the sovereign? He only wishes the sovereign well."

The extensive *Household Manager* treats one's obligations towards God, one's spiritual shepherds, one's neighbor in general and the tsar. Among the religious prescriptions common to all times, some in particular hold our attention. For example, "Having made the sign of the cross you shall kiss the holy cross, icons and relics while holding your breath and not opening wide your mouth. You shall not bite the altar bread with your teeth as though it were ordinary bread, but shall break it into little pieces and place it in the mouth. Eat it with your lips, do not champ with your mouth. If you wish to kiss someone in Christ you must also hold your breath and not make a smacking noise with the lips. Consider human weakness. We shun insensible vapor such as the stench of garlic, hops, sickness and various other things. How much more loathsome before the Lord are our stench and smell."

Concerning parental obligations towards children it states, "The father and mother shall have concern for their children. They shall provide for them and raise them in good instruction, teaching them the fear of God, decent behavior and all discipline. Taking into account time, the children and their maturity, teach them a trade according to the ability which God gave each of them. Love and protect them and save them with fear, and in teaching and punishing, inflict wounds with deliberation. Punish your son from his youth and he will look after you in old age. Do not slacken when beating a boy. If you beat him with a rod he will not die but be healthy. By beating him on his body you will deliver his soul from death, and so on. If a daughter is born to anyone, sensible people set aside something for her from the harvest and newly born livestock. They also place linens and other items for her in a special trunk every year, and they continually add to it a little at a time, not all at once. The daughters grow up, they learn the fear of God and good behavior, and they have their dowry with them, so that when a marriage contract is formalized everything is prepared."

With regard to children's obligations towards their parents we find nothing particular beyond general moral norms. The *Household Manager* defines a husband's obligations towards his wife as follows. "She goes to church whenever possible, after consulting with her husband. Husbands must teach their wives with love and easily understood instruction. If a wife does not live according to her husband's instruction, the husband must admonish her in private, and having done so he must favor her and speak tenderly; they must not be cross at each other. He must also admonish the servants and children, examine them for guilt and inflict wounds, but having punished them he must show favor. The master must be solicitous for his servants, so that the servants will be reliable. When the servant does not accept the word or instruction of his wife, son or daughter, let him whip the servant with a lash, though he should not beat him in front of the other servants, but in private. He must not beat on the ears or face, nor strike below the heart with his fist, or kick or strike with a staff or any iron or wooden object. If the guilt is great, strip him to the waist, bind his hands and beat him with a lash.

"Wives shall ask their husbands about various proprieties and submit to them in everything. Having risen and said her prayers, the mistress must assign the maidservants their daily task. She herself must know how to prepare every type of dish, both meat and fish, and various dishes using meat and dairy products and Lenten foods. She must be able to perform the various handicrafts so that she can teach her maidservant. If she knows everything through her husband's instruction, threats and good judgment, all will be successful, and there will be plenty of everything. The mistress herself should never be without work, for by observing her the maidservants will work out of habit. If her husband or a guest comes, she must always be seated at some needlework, for this is her honor and glory and her husband's praise. Never must the servants awaken the mistress, she must awaken the servants.

"The mistress must not exchange empty and mocking words with the servants. Do not let market women, idle women or sorcerers visit her, because much evil is caused by them. Each day a wife should ask permission of her husband and consult with him about each routine. She should be acquainted only with those whom her husband permits. With merchants let her converse about her handicrafts and about the household management, taking note where she sees something good. Let her inquire courteously about what she does not know. If anyone shows her something, let her bow her head low and, having returned home, let her tell everything to her husband. It is useful to associate with good women, not for food or for drink, but for good conversation and knowledge; let her pay heed to what is to her own benefit. She shall not gossip or talk about anyone. If others ask about something concerning someone else she shall answer, 'I do not know. I have heard nothing, nor do I inquire about the unnecessary. I do not gossip about princesses and boyars' wives or neighbors.' She at all costs must be preserved from intoxicating beverages, and must drink non-alcoholic home-brewed beer and kvas at home and in the company of others. She should not eat or drink in secret from her husband. She must not keep a stranger in the house without her husband's knowledge. Let her consult with her husband about everything, not with a man-slave or a female slave. She should not inform her husband about domestic nonsense. She must tell her husband truthfully about anything she is unable to correct herself."

The *Household Manager* talks about relations towards servants. "Masters must reward their slaves, give them food, drink and clothing, keep them warm, content and happy. But if a master keeps more slaves in his household than he can afford and does not satisfy them with food, drink or clothing, or if he keeps unskilled slaves who themselves are unable to produce anything, such slaves inevitably will lie, steal and lead a debauched and lamentable life, for the men will fight and steal and drink in taverns. Such thoughtless masters are a sin in the eyes of God and the laughing stock of their slaves. Compared with their neighbors they lead a vain and foolish life.

"Command your servants not to gossip. At home they must not tell where they were in public and what wickedness they observed, nor should they discuss in public what happens at home. Should they remember for what reason they were sent and others inquire about something else, they shall not reply. Instead they must finish their business all the more quickly and come home. Thus there will be no disputes among masters.

"If a servant is sent somewhere to good people, he must knock gently on the gate. When he goes about the yard and someone asks him what his business is, he must answer, 'I was not sent to you, I will speak only with him to whom I was sent.' He need only say who sent him. Let them inform their master. In entrance halls, an office or a cell a servant must wipe off his dirty feet, blow his nose, clear his throat and artfully perform a prayer. If no 'amen' is given in response, he must say the prayer a second and even a third time, a little longer than the first time. If even then no response is given, the servant shall knock gently on the door. When he is let in, he shall bow before the holy icons and present the petition and commission from his master. During that time the servant must not pick his nose, cough, blow his nose, hawk up or spit. If any of this is necessary, the servant shall go off to the side and take care of it in a genteel fashion. The servant shall wait and not look to the side, he shall complete what was ordered without conversing about anything else, and return quickly home. Wherever a servant happens to be, in the master's presence or without the master, he shall not turn over any object, inspect it or shift it from its place, nor may he taste the food or drink. Neither shall he examine or taste anything which is being sent somewhere."

Here is the ideal of family life as it was created by ancient Russian society! A woman was put in a visible spot. Her activity was broad-ranging, she was the mistress. That means that she rose earlier than all others, awakened the servants and toiled incessantly until night, instructing and giving orders. She could not be idle for a minute. The husband must go to church every day to all the services, the wife went whenever possible, as often as her household affairs permitted. Although a woman, she was not first and foremost a mother.

Briefly and in general terms, a woman and her husband together must raise the children in the fear of God and piety and she must teach her daughter handicrafts. The *Household Manager* describes in considerable detail how she must accumulate a dowry for her daughter from the day of her birth. Material and household cares must absorb the entire being of a woman, beginning with her twelfth year when she can be married legally. Yet when she crosses the threshold of the house or goes visiting, what does the *Household Manager* demand of her? She must converse with guests about handicrafts and the household, how to keep things orderly and at what handicraft to work.

According to social conditions there were not, nor could there be, diversions necessary for restoration of spirits, for a change of occupation or even a change of conversation topic. The *Household Manager* was entirely correct to prescribe that women busy themselves solely with the household and talk only about the household, for there was no other suitable occupation or conversation for them. If she did not talk about the household, she would quip and prattle. At home she must always be seated at some kind of work or directing the work of others. Such diversions to which she might abandon herself were shameful and harmful, such as empty small talk with the servants, exchanges with market women, idle women and sorceresses.

I repeat that we have no right to chide the *Household Manager* for cruelty towards women. There were no suitable, innocent pleasures it could offer her, and hence it was compelled to prohibit any pleasure at all, compelled to demand that she not have a free moment which might arouse in her a desire for some unsuitable pleasure or, what was worse, a desire to cheer herself up with alcohol. How many women of good will were able to approach the ideal delineated by the *Household Manager?* How many had to be coerced to approximate it and how many could not be coerced by any force at all? How many women succumbed to unbecoming pleasures? We have decided not to answer these questions.

Many chapters in the *Household Manager* are dedicated to household details such as how to cut out clothes, to save remainders and scraps, how to organize the tableware and work tools so that the householder owned everything, and there was no need to go to someone else's home for anything; how to wear each article of clothing carefully, how to purchase the year's supplies and every type of ware; how to buy what was inexpensive from a load; how to plant a vegetable plot and a garden, and so on. In the chapter on how to keep a building clean and in good repair we see only a list of implements to be kept clean and in order. It is laid down how to wash the building, the walls, shelves, benches, floor, windows and doors and to put straw for wiping one's feet in the lower wing, and hopsack or thick felt in front of the doors. It says that icons must be hung on the walls, arranged attractively with various types of ornamentation, lamps and a curtain.

Each day the husband and wife, his children and domestics sing vespers, compline and the midnight office at home. After the canon they may not drink, eat or talk. At midnight they must get up quietly and pray to God with tears.

When a banquet is offered, at first the priests glorify the Father and the Son and the Holy Spirit, and then they glorify the Virgin and bring forth the panagia.[50] At the conclusion of the meal they elevate the panagia and when they have sung the hymn "It is meet and right,"[51] they eat it and drink a cup in honor of the Virgin. They then drink a second cup for health and another for rest. When food is placed in front of you do not dare disparage but eat with thanksgiving.

There is a very curious instruction on how to behave at a wedding which reveals the morals and customs of the time. "When you are invited to a wedding," it says, "do not drink yourself to the point of inebriation and do not remain seated until late, because in inebriation and lengthy sitting are quarrels, brawls and shedding of blood. I do not say that you should not drink at all! No. I do say that you should not get drunk. I do not disparage God's gifts, but I do berate those who drink without self-control."

THE GREAT MENOLOGY

To gain some concept of that famous collection known under the name of Makary's *Menology* we do best to look at the preface written by the compiler himself. "In November 1553 I presented this holy and great book, the menology for the month of November and the remaining twelve great books. In these menologies are collected all revered books. The holy Gospels, the four Evangelists are exposited, the Holy Apostle and all the holy Apostolic letters and Acts with expositions, three great Psalters of different commentators, books by Chrysostom, the *Zlatostrui* [Golden-mouth] and *Margarit* [Pearl], the Great Chrysostom, Basil the Great and Gregory the Theologian with commentaries and the great book of Nikon[52] with his other letters. All other holy books have been collected and copied in them, including sermons of the prophets, apostles and fathers, festal sermons and laudatory sermons, the lives of all the holy fathers, the acts of the holy men and women martyrs, the lives and ascetical feats of the venerable and God-bearing fathers and the trials and ascetical feats of holy women. All paterikons[53] have been copied, the Alphabetical, Jerusalem, Egyptian, Sinaitic, Sketic and Kiev Caves paterikons. All holy books have been collected and copied which are found in the Russian land and which deal with the new holy miracle workers. I copied these holy books in Novgorod the Great when I was archbishop there, and I wrote and collected them in one place for twelve years at much expense and with many different scribes, not sparing any money or honor. I endured especially many labors and ascetical feats while correcting foreign and ancient expressions, translating them into Russian, and I was able to correct as many as God granted us to understand."

Details about how Makary labored at assembling his menologies and the names of scholars to whom he entrusted the writing of saints' lives have come down to us. Under the year 1537 the chronicler says that Vasily Mikhailovich Tuchkov, a junior boyar and valiant soldier, arrived in Novgorod from Moscow to muster soldiers. Having discovered that Tuchkov was acquainted with Sacred Scripture from his youth, Makary blessed him for a spiritual undertaking, to write a life of Mikhail Klopsky, for although one already was written it was very simplistic, because at the time the people of Novgorod were not skilled in writing.

With the benediction of Makary, by then metropolitan, the monk Varlaam (in the world Vasily) wrote the *Passion of Isidore the New Presbyter and Seventy-Two Russians* who were tortured by the Germans in Livonian Yuriev (Dorpat) during the reign of Ivan III and the tenure of Metropolitan Philip and Bishop Jonas of Novgorod. Isidore was a priest in the church of St. Nicholas and St. George the Cappadocian in the Russian section of Yuriev. He aroused the Germans against him through his denunciation of their faith, was seized with his parishioners at Epiphany during the procession to the Omovzha river, and was locked in prison. He responded to the exhortation to accept Latin Christianity with the most forceful denunciations and was drowned in the same Omovzha river along with seventy-two Russians. The same Vasily wrote a few lives of other saints, including that of Evfrosin of Pskov. The chronicler says that in 1536, in accordance with the instruction of Bishop Makary, an exposited Psalter was translated from Latin into Russian by the very old Dmitry the Translator.

CHRONICLES, FOLKLORE, EDUCATION

Pertaining to our period is the composition of the *Book of Generations of the Tsar's Genealogy,*[54] an exposition of ecclesiastical and civil events of Russian history from a religious perspective. During this period the need to write in florid language was evident. Makary was not satisfied with the ancient life of St. Mikhail Klopsky because it was written very artlessly. The *Book of Generations* presents a model of the style considered beautiful, for example, in the praise of Grand Prince Vladimir. "For you are truly named tsar," it reads, "who reign over passions and are able to conquer voluptuousness, who are crowned with the crown of chastity and clothed in the porphyry of truth. For such a one are you, an earnest, high-minded ruler, an all-valorous instructor, a true steersman, an excellent champion, a mighty intercessor, a lover of purity, an image of chastity, a pillar of patience, a firm advocate of piety for Russian princes, boyars, grandees and all men, a benevolent interlocutor for bishops and the entire consecrated assembly," and so on.

The composition of chronicles continued as before. It is easy to detect in some of the extant copies two types of composition, the governmental and the private. There can be no doubt that the chronicles of the period were composed by crown officials under closest supervision. "Taxation registers," we read in the description of the tsar's archives. "He wrote a memorandum about what to write in the chronicle of recent years, which was taken from Alexis." Or, "In Box 224 are lists concerning what to write in the chronicle, recent entries gathered from the year 7068 [1560] until 7074 [1566] and 7076 [1568]." At the same time different varieties of chronicles were being compiled by private individuals in Moscow and other towns, in which we find disapproval of executions and the crown estates. These references of chronicles composed evidently in Moscow, were cited in their own place.

The Pskov chronicler took strong issue against Muscovite decrees. Speaking about the deportation of Germans from Yuriev to Muscovite towns he added, "Why they led them away we do not know, only God knows. The commanders broke their solemn word which they gave when they liberated Yuriev, that they would not exile them from the town." The Pskov chronicler also explained the reason for Ivan's anger with the boyars. "Tsar and Grand Prince Ivan Vasilievich" it reads, "arrived with great displeasure in Novgorod and he killed many esteemed men, and a great multitude were beaten in the stocks, including monks, priests and nuns. There was grave tribulation and grief among the people; holy monasteries and God's churches and villages were desolated. In addition the tsar gave orders to collect the plow tax under the guise of a military detail and to build bridges into Livonian territory and to mine gunpowder ore. From this tax and the forced collection all the inhabitants of Novgorod and Pskov grew impoverished and they performed labor service because they could not afford to pay the plow tax, for there was nothing to give. There in a foreign land they perished from cold and hunger, from the bridges and military labor.

"In Pskov they towed longboats and large boats with auxiliary recruits up to Livonian towns, and having towed them a little, they abandoned them in the forests where they rotted, and the people were killed. After taking twenty-four towns from the Germans, he settled his own people with soldiers and provisions. Supplies were transported from distant towns beyond Moscow. He filled foreign towns with Russians, and left his own empty. When the tsar returned to Russia, the Germans gathered from across the sea and Lithuanians came from Poland, and they captured for themselves all those towns and killed the Russians in them. They sent to the tsar a German, an evil magician named Eleazar (Bomelius), whom the tsar took into his confidence as a favorite. Eleazar induced timidity in the tsar, so that he ran from the attacks of the infidels. He almost managed to lead the tsar away from the faith. He filled the tsar with ferocity towards the Russian people, but towards the Germans he instilled love.

"The godless Germans knew in their craft that they could ruin him utterly. For this purpose they sent such a wicked heretic to the tsar because the Russian people have a weakness for sorcery. Eleazar incited the tsar to murder many families of princes and boyars and in the end inspired him to flee to England and marry there, but to kill the remaining boyars. Eleazar did not succeed. He was handed over to death and the Russian tsardom and Christian faith were not utterly ruined. Such was the reign of the terrifying Tsar Ivan Vasilievich." Bomelius was a doctor, by birth a Dutchman. According to foreign testimonies, he was a rogue who incited Ivan to murder and concocted poisons, then was accused of dealings with Bathory, and was burned publicly in Moscow.[55]

In some of our chronicle collections the tale about the beginning of Constantinople and its capture by the Turks is encountered. It is thought that this tale, by an unknown author, could have been introduced soon after the event by Greeks who were arriving in Moscow seeking alms. Naturally linked with it is a narrative about the ordinances of Sultan Mehmet,[56] a narrative which had been located separately and ascribed to Ivan Peresvetov.[57] This narrative has political significance and an immediate bearing on the circumstances of Ivan's era.

The ordinances of Mehmet II, who drew his wisdom from Christian books, are presented as a model. "Tsar Sultan Mehmet ordered all revenues from his entire kingdom to be brought to his treasury. He did not give his grandees in a single town a service rank lest they be tempted to judge unjustly, but he gave them an annual salary from his treasury according to each man's worth, and in the entire kingdom he gave fair judgment." There follows a description of the cruel punishment reserved for corrupt judges for their injustice, who were flayed alive. "Sultan Mehmet said that a tsar cannot keep his realm without intimidation. Emperor Constantine (Paleologue) gave free rein to his grandees, and God vented his anger against him, against his grandees and the entire empire because they disdained justice. Mehmet ordered brought to him the full and limited contract service books and had them burned. He stipulated that a slave must serve only seven years, but if he was purchased at some expense, then for ten years. Tsar Mehmet copied from the Christian books the wisdom that there are no valiant men in a kingdom whose people are enslaved.... The Greeks boast about the sovereign realm of the faithful Russian tsar, for there is no other free Christian realm of the Greek faith. In disputes with the Latins the Greeks point to the Russian realm. If Turkish justice were added to this true Christian faith, the angels would converse with the Russians."

The narrative of the Pskov chronicler and the testimonies of foreign contemporaries about Doctor Bomelius were introduced above. In this connection there is the tale of a certain God-loving man. There once was an Orthodox, God-loving and merciful tsar who walked in the commandments of God, but through the devil's influence one of the senators appeared before him, an evil magician who came to him in mercy and slandered innocent men. The tsar brought suffering upon the innocent through various hostile actions, and he himself incurred their enmity and dread, but the time drew near for God's vengeance. The surrounding towns rose up and captured his lands, they destroyed his towns, defeated his men and reached the capital city. The tsar, seeing the calamity, repented and burned the magician together with his companions.

The events of Ivan's reign have entered into popular traditions as well. In old Russian verse we find a song about the capture of the tsardom of Kazan. In agreement with actual fact the song talks of how the town was taken by undermining its walls. It says that only after the conquest of the kingdom of Kazan did the grand prince of Moscow ascend to the imperial throne and settle in the Moscow tsardom, that only then was Moscow founded and from that time enjoyed great glory. Ivan himself considered the subjugation of the kingdom of Kazan to be one of his rights to the title "tsar." In a song about how Yermak[58] took Siberia it is said that three Don Cossack leaders assembled at the mouth of the Volga and the eldest of them, Yermak, told his companions, "Not for self-interest was this joke played by us. We roamed the blue sea, we killed a Persian envoy, and how we will have to answer for that! We cannot live in Astrakhan, to live on the Volga is to be known as thieves, to go to Yaik is a big journey. We could go to Kazan, but the dread tsar is there, and if we go to Moscow we will be apprehended. Let us go to Usolie to the Stroganovs!" The song differs from the chronicle in that it sends Yermak himself to Moscow to petition the tsar for Siberia.

In a song about Mamstriuk Temriukovich, Ivan's brother-in-law, the battle of the Cherkas prince Mamstriuk with two Moscow heroes is described, and the Muscovites emerge the victors. As in this song, so too in the song about Yermak the figure who is closest to the tsar is the grand boyar Nikita Romanovich. The traditions about the reign of terror rich in punishments, about the favorite crown estates henchman Maliuta Skuratov, the swift executor of bloody orders, about the Romanovs' hatred for the Godunovs, about the murder of a son followed by bitter repentance of the murderer—all these traditions, confused and distorted in the popular memory, are recalled in the song *Nikita Romanovich Was Given the Village of Preobrazhenskoe.*

Ivan appears in the popular memory as a terrifying tsar, subjugator of Kazan, Astrakhan, and Riazan, the extirpator of treason in Kiev and Novgorod. It is curious to see how popular stories and songs, though distorting the important events, faithfully preserve some small details. It is known that in a fit of rage Ivan, spying a man unpleasing to him, plunged his sharp scepter into his foot. That is how he acted with Kurbsky's servant who was presenting him a letter from his master. In a song Ivan does the same thing to Nikita Romanovich, on whom the Godunovs informed because he rejoiced during the tsar's grief at the loss of his son. We mentioned the Don Cossack leader Mishka Cherkashenin who was a menace for Azov. A song preserved a tradition about a steppe cossack leader. "From beyond the town of Zaraisk, beyond Riazan the Ancient, far away from the pure steppe, from the broad expanse, as though he were a bay aurochs, they brought the slain, they brought the slain cossack leader of the steppe, the steppe cossack leader, and his name is Mikhail Cherkashenin."

Concerning the general state of education in Muscovy during the reign of Ivan the Terrible, we could not help but notice vibrant literary activity as compared with the former era. Movements both political and religious awakened intellectual activity, summoned to the struggle with words which could not be entered upon without preparation, without erudition. The example of the tsar as a rhetorician of eloquence could not help but have an influence on those close to him. Moral weapons were being gathered and stockpiled in one place, so that they could be used more conveniently. Metropolitan Makary collected all known religious books in Russia in twelve enormous folios. Monasteries continued to collect books, and the importance they gave to their libraries is evident in that they each had their own librarian. There were more than one thousand books in the monastery of Joseph of Volokolamsk. Nevertheless, in spite of the strengthening of literary activity and the expansion of literacy, society, all the while admiring learning, was far from convinced of its necessity, even for those occupying the primary positions in the realm.

If in the boyar Prince Kurbsky we see a remarkable writer, given the then available means, we must also note that two grandees, Ivan Sheremetev the Lesser and Ivan Chebotov did not sign their names to the charter of 1566 because they did not know how to read or write. In the bond note for boyar Ivan Petrovich Yakovlev we find the addition, "Some princes and junior boyars are written in this note, but their signature is not on the note. Those princes and junior boyars stood before the crown secretary and said that they guaranteed Ivan Petrovich, but their signatures are not on the note because they do not know how to write." There were some who turned young men away from studies by threatening them with the prospect of insanity or heresy charges. In the *Household Manager* we find no exhortation to fathers to teach their children reading and writing, which is recognized as a necessity only for the clerical estate and officials. We have seen what means were used by the council of 1557 to disseminate literacy in Muscovy. In the life of St. Gury of Kazan it is said that his master put him in prison, a friend brought him some paper and ink and the saint wrote some pamphlets for instructing children, sold them and distributed to the poor the money so earned. In Western Russia there were schools attached to churches. In 1572 Dmitry Miturich asked Prince Konstantin Ostrozhsky for a parcel of empty land on condition that he take no taxes from it, but only serve in the church, keep a school and be the ecclesiarch. Possevino writes that Princes Ostrozhsky and Slutsky had a printing press and schools with which the schism was nourished.

THE PRINTING PRESS

To the reign of Ivan IV belongs the introduction of that powerful means which lent wings to human thought, the printing press. Already in the fifteenth century book printing appeared in the Slavic world, namely in 1491 in Cracow. In 1525 we see a press in Wilno. In 1548 Tsar Ivan wrote to have typographers among the other experts sent from Germany, but they were not permitted to enter Russia. In 1552 the Danish king Christian III sent Hans Missenheim to Moscow with the proposition that the tsar accept Protestantism. Missenheim brought with him a bible and two other books which contained the essence of the Christian faith according to the new doctrine. If the tsar agreed to the king's proposition, Missenheim was to print several thousand copies of the books after translating them into Russian. It is not known how Missenheim was received by Ivan, but it is unlikely that the tsar would entrust the construction of a printing press to a man clearly sent to spread Protestantism.

According to Russian information the tsar, needing church books for the many new churches being constructed, ordered them bought up in the markets, but there turned out to be very few in good repair. This brought Ivan to the idea of the necessity of a printing press. Metropolitan Makary approved of the idea, and in 1553 they set to work building a house with funds from the tsar's treasury. Not until 1563 did two experts begin printing operations there, namely Ivan Fedorov the deacon from the church of St. Nicholas of Gostun,[59] and Peter Timofeev Mstislavets. In addition the name of a master of printed books, Marusha Nefediev, was encountered earlier under the year 1556. On March 1, 1564 was completed the printing of the first book, containing the Acts of the Apostles and the Catholic Epistles,[60] with the Letters of the Apostle Paul. In the seventeenth century the rumor spread that these first masters of printing learned their art from the Germans. Some said that at first Russian masters printed books in small and inexpert characters but afterwards they learned from the Germans (or Franks) how to print better.

ꙗꙗсꙗпꙗꙗꙗꙗсꙋꙗпꙗꙗнетꙋꙗꙗꙗ

Пѣрвое ꙋбѡ слово сотвⷬⷯих҃ъ ѡбсⷯⷯъ .
ѡ деѡфиле . ѡн҃же начаⷮⷯ іс , тѣѡ
рⷯнⷮⷯже ноⷣⷯинⷮⷯи . дꙗнⷮⷯсѡⷤⷯ дн҃і ,
заповѣдаⷡⷯ апⷯлоⷨⷯ дⷯхⷯѡмъ ст҃ⷯⷯ .
иⷯхⷯже изⷣⷯбраⷡⷯ вознⷮесеⷮⷯсⷯⷯ . прⷣⷯннⷣⷯнꙗⷤⷯ
иⷯпⷯѡⷮⷯставниⷤⷯбⷯиⷤⷯива пⷣⷯстраданⷯиⷯ

скⷣⷯемъ . вⷯ мноꙁⷯⷯхъ иⷣстинныхъ ꙁнⷯамⷣⷯ
нⷣⷯиⷯхъ . днⷯьⷯми четырⷯндⷣⷯсⷯⷯатⷯⷯ явлⷯⷯ
нⷯиⷯⷯⷯ имⷯⷯ гл҃ⷯⷯⷯⷯⷯⷯⷯ ꙗⷯⷯⷯⷯⷯⷯⷯⷯⷯⷯⷯⷯⷯⷯⷯⷯ ѡⷯцⷯⷯрⷯⷯⷯ

From the First Book Printed in Russia

The Acts of the Apostles, 1564

Even though book printing was introduced with the aim of staving off the corruption of books, nonetheless given the contemporary state of education there were no means of verifying the Slavonic text with the Greek or of choosing the best of the Slavonic versions. The fact that the publishers called the text of the New Testament a text of seventy expositors serves as evidence of the lack of education. The orthography in the first printed book was very poor, but the physical appearance was for the time quite satisfactory. The first master printers, who printed a *Book of Hours*[61] in 1565, were compelled to flee abroad from Moscow, accused of heresy. They themselves explained afterwards that they were expelled because of the envy of many superiors, bishops and teachers who falsely charged them with many heresies, desiring to convert the good into evil, not because they acquired grammatical acumen or were filled with religious understanding, but because they inadvertently let pass an evil word.

It is said that the printing house was burned down by malicious people. In 1568 a Psalter was printed by Andronik Nevezha in Moscow, and in 1578 it was printed in Alexandrov Village, but in information from the seventeenth century about book printing it is said that Andronik Nevezha and his companions printed Books of Hours, Psalters, Apostles and Gospels, Triodions, Oktoikhs[62] and other liturgical books. The Moscow exiles Ivan Fedorov and Peter Timofeev, having fled to Lithuania, printed many books there. Both worked in Zabludov under Hetman Chodkiewicz.[63] Then Ivan Fedorov printed in Lvov, and Peter Timofeev in Wilno. Finally Ivan Fedorov moved to Ostrog to Prince Konstantin and in 1581 he printed there the entire Slavonic bible. Although this important edition seemingly was undertaken with sufficient preparation, nonetheless the Ostrog Bible contains some significant errors. Prince Konstantin lamented that he did not have enough assistants, but even one of these few assistants confessed that he never saw the inside of a school.

The first book, the Apostle, was printed on thick Dutch paper. Chroniclers have left us information about the exorbitant cost of paper, which naturally must have concerned them. In the Novgorod chronicle for the year 1545 we find the information that "in that year paper was expensive, that is, two altyns for book paper." Under the year 1555 we read that "paper was expensive, a sheet cost half the scribe's fee."

We consider it appropriate to conclude our survey of the domestic conditions of Russian society under Ivan IV with the words of a foreign observer. "What will become of the Russian people if they unite military prowess to their abilities to endure a harsh life and to be satisfied with a little? If they recognized their might, no one would be able to compete with them, and their neighbors would have no rest from them." Foreigners observed only one side. To them it all seemed as though learning would increase only the material means of the Russian people, who then would employ these means against their neighbors. Learning, however, lends awareness not only of material but also of moral strengths. It enables men to moderate their material strengths and direct them to their own good and that of other peoples.

NOTES

INTRODUCTION

1. Corresponding to Volume 9, Chapters IV-V, and Volumes 10-11 of this series.

2. *Chteniia v Obshchestve Istorii i Drevnostei Rossiskikh* (Readings at the Society for Russian History and Antiquities), Vol. 4 (Moscow, 1846).

3. Konstantin Alexandrovich Nevolin (1806-1855) was born in Orlov, the son of a priest. He did not follow his father's footsteps, but embarked on a distinguished career as a scholar of jurisprudence. His dissertation entitled *On the Philosophy of Legislation among the Ancients* earned him the title of doctor in 1835, and he assumed teaching duties at Kiev the same year. In 1839-1840 he published the *Entsiklopediia zakonovedeniia* (Encyclopedia of Jurisprudence) which earned international acclaim. In 1843 he took a position as professor of civil law at the University of St. Petersburg, and continued to work on his *History of Russian Civil Laws*, which appeared in 1851. Poor health forced him to retire in 1855 to Brixen, Tyrol, where he died the same year.

4. This is particularly true of the sections where he provides information about Lithuania. For example, when discussing the situation of the church Soloviev goes into some detail concerning the status of Orthodox Christianity in Poland-Lithuania. While what he says is in itself interesting, it has no obvious relation to his remarks concerning the church in Muscovy. As is the case elsewhere in this volume, čontemporary circumstances may have influenced Soloviev in his selection of source material. Thus the reader should know that in 1839 Eastern Rite Catholics throughout the Russian empire were suppressed in favor of the Orthodox church. Only in Galicia, controlled by Austria, did large numbers of Ukrainian (Ruthenian) Catholics survive.

5. See p. 180, below.

6. Horace W. Dewey, "The 1550 *Sudebnik* as an Instrument of Reform," *Jahrbücher für Geschichte Osteuropas*, 10 (1962), pp. 161-180.

7. See pp. 182-183, below.

8. Likhachev points out that Ivan IV was one of the best educated men of the day and cannot be accused of breaking stylistic convention out of ignorance. Ivan wrote extemporaneously, in response to the issue at hand. His writing, says Likhachev, has the vitality of oral speech, where repetition and sudden shifts of subject and mood are frequent. See D.S. Likhachev, "Stil' proizvedenii Groznogo i stil' proizvedenii Kurbskogo (tsar' i «gosudarev izmennik») (The Style of Ivan the Terrible's and Kurbsky's Works. The Tsar and the Traitor Against the Sovereign)," *Perepiska Ivana Groznogo s Andreem Kurbskim* (The Correspondence Between Ivan the Terrible and Andrei Kurbsky), ed. Ya. S. Lur'e and Yu. D. Rykov (Leningrad, 1979), pp. 184-187.

9. I quote from Volume VI at length for the benefit of those not in possession of this segment of the History. "Ivan's character and conduct are explained historically by the struggle of the old with the new, by events arising in his childhood and youth, during his sickness and later, but can they be morally justified by this struggle and these events? Can we excuse a man on the basis of his moral weakness, his inability to resist temptations or control the wanton inclinations of his nature? It is incontestable that a dreadful sickness nested in Ivan, but why was it permitted to develop? [...other historians] would excuse his cruelty on the grounds that his times were severe. Indeed, the moral state of society in the time of Ivan IV does not present itself in an attractive fashion at all [...] but the possibility of finding an explanation in contemporary society is not a justification for the historical person. Neither dare we lay the blame for Ivan's deeds on sixteenth-century Russian society, for it was founded on a different principle than the society over which Sultan Mehmet ruled; it was capable of producing a man who pointed out to Ivan the requirements of this fundamental principle. Russian society, by producing a St. Philip, by uttering through the mouth of this pastor the demands of its fundamental spirit, and by expressing its disapproval of Ivan the Terrible's conduct, showed that it had a law and a prophet, and thus is purified and justified before history. For this reason Ivan, who ignored Philip's admonition, cannot be excused." Soloviev, *Istoriia rossii s drevneishikh vremen*, Book 3, pp. 712-713. See also Volume 11 of this series.

10. Josef Glazik, m.s.c., *Die Islammission der Russisch-Orthodoxen Kirche* (The Mission to Islam of the Russian Orthodox Church) (Münster, 1959), pp. 44-61.

11. Glazik, p. 137.

12. Glazik, p. 134.

13. For a fascinating presentation, see Richard Stites, *The Women's Liberation Movement in Russia. Feminism, Nihilism and Bolshevism, 1860-1930* (Princeton, 1978, 1990).

CHAPTER I

1. Sigismund Freiherr von Herberstein (1486-1566), renowned diplomat and statesman, left the world an invaluable source of information about Muscovy in his

Rerum Moscoviticarum Comentarii (Commentary on Muscovite Affairs) which he published in Vienna in 1549. Well trained in European languages, law and philosophy, and from an early age exposed to Slavic culture, Herberstein was an obvious choice for two diplomatic missions to Moscow, in 1517 and 1526, with the aim of negotiating a peace treaty between Muscovy and Poland to the benefit of the Holy Roman empire. While the missions proved to be largely unsuccessful, Herberstein was able to write down for posterity his perceptive observations on life in the Muscovite state. The *Commentary* presents the reader with invaluable information about Vasily III, his coronation as grand prince, his divorce and remarriage and about religion, law, daily life and war in Muscovy. See Hugh F. Graham, "Herberstein, Sigismund Freiherr von," *Modern Encyclopedia of Russian and Soviet History*, (Academic International Press, 1976-) (hereafter MERSH), Vol. 14, pp. 6-10.

2.   The chiliarch or thousandman (tysiatskii) led a unit of soldiers notionally numbering one thousand men. Tsarevich Ivan Ivanovich (1554-1581) was very close to his father, sharing his energy and political goals, as well as his cruel nature. He participated in the brutal subjugation of Novgorod in 1570. As the tsarevich matured, the close father-son relationship suffered from Tsar Ivan's meddling in his son's personal life. He arranged all three of the tsarevich's marriages and broke the first two. The tsarevich's ties to the Romanov family further clouded the court atmosphere. According to one report, family strife may have been the cause of the tsarevich's untimely death. On November 9, 1581 Ivan Ivanovich rushed to defend his third wife Elena Ivanovna Sheremeteva from Ivan IV's chastisements and was mortally wounded when the enraged tsar struck him on the head with a metal-tipped staff.

3.   At the time of his father's third wedding Ivan Ivanovich (1554-1581) was betrothed to Evdokia Saburova whom he married in November 1571. When in 1580 Ivan IV married his sixth wife, Maria Fedorovna Nagaia, Ivan Ivanovich was remarried twice. He sent in succession Evdokia and his second wife Praskovia Solovaia to a convent, and married Elena Sheremeteva.

4.   Magnus of Livonia was a Danish prince enlisted by Ivan IV in 1570 to rule over a united Livonia as his vassal. Magnus was unable to bring under control those parts of Livonia which were not yet subdued by Russia. The assault which he led in 1570 against Reval, Sweden's most important fortress in Livonia, ended in a twofold failure. Sweden was drawn into war with Muscovy and Magnus lost his Muscovite patron. Princess Maria was one of two surviving daughters of Prince Vladimir Andreevich, the last prince of Staritsa, who fell victim to Ivan's ruthless annihilation of any suspected threats to his person or rule. Robert O. Crummey, *The Formation of Muscovy, 1304-1613* (London, 1987), p. 171.

5.   It is most unlikely that the Protestant King Magnus would be married by a Roman Catholic priest. The chronicler was either unaware of the religious climate in Western Europe or from long tradition simply considered any Western clergyman to be a Roman Catholic.

6.   Metropolitan Makary (1481-1563) began his religious career as a monk in the monastery of St. Pafnuty of Borovsk. He showed great managerial aptitude and

was named archbishop of Novgorod in 1526 by Grand Prince Vasily III Ivanovich, restoring that city to prosperity for the first time since its annexation to Moscow in 1478. In 1542 he was installed as metropolitan of Moscow and became a patron of Ivan IV, whom he crowned tsar in 1547. Makary worked towards the centralization of church and state and was a strong supporter of the notion of autocracy. In two major councils of the Russian church, in 1547 and 1549, Makary canonized a large number of Russian saints, and had many lives written in their honor. He also convoked the reform council known as the Hundred Chapters in 1551. Of immense importance was the impressive *Great Menology*, a collection of saints' lives for the twelve months of the church year, which Makary compiled from 1529-1541 and then again during his tenure as metropolitan. He is also credited with the compilation of the *Book of Degrees of Imperial Genealogy* in which he traced the history of the Russian tsars from Vladimir of Kiev down to Ivan IV. See David B. Miller, "Makarii," MERSH, Vol. 21, pp. 1-4; N.F. Droblenkova, "Makarii," *Slovar' knizhnikov i knizhnosti drevnei Rusi. Vtoraia polovina XIV-XVI v.* (Dictionary of the Bookmen and Literature of Old Rus. Second Half. XIV-XVI Centuries), ed. D.S. Likhachev (Leningrad, 1989) (hereafter *Slovar' knizhnikov*), No. 2, Part 1, pp. 76-88.

7. The monastery of the Miracles of St. Michael (Chudov monastery) was founded in 1365 by Metropolitan Alexis and Sergius of Radonezh. It was built inside the Moscow Kremlin on the site of the former residence of the Mongol khanate representative, donated in 1357 to Metropolitan Alexis in thanksgiving for his having cured Taidula, wife of Khan Janibeg. At first constructed of wood the monastery was rebuilt in stone in 1501-1504. In the 1930s the monastery was torn down by the Soviet government to make room for an administration building. David Goldfrank, "Chudov Monastery," MERSH, Vol. 7, pp. 97-98.

8. Anna (1548-1550) was the first child of Ivan IV and Anastasia Romanovna. This happiest of Ivan's numerous marriages produced five children, only two of which survived into adulthood, Ivan Ivanovich (1554-1581) and Fedor Ivanovich (1557-1598). The other offspring were Maria (1551) and Dmitry (1552-1553).

9. The service known as orthros (utrenia) in the Orthodox church loosely corresponds to the Latin rite offices of mattins and lauds. Though intended to be celebrated at the beginning of the day, orthros frequently is anticipated on the preceding evening, following the all-night vigil service (vsenochnaia), as is the case here. The office comprises a number of prayers, litanies, psalms, antiphons and hymns. The most important part of the service is the lengthy poetic composition known as the canon. See Robert Taft, *The Liturgy of the Hours in East and West* (Collegeville, Minn., 1986), pp. 273-291.

10. Alexander of Kazan (1547-1566) was the son of Khan Safa-Girey of Kazan. Only two years old when his father died, Utemysh-Girey was installed on the throne under the regency of his mother Sumbeka; he was replaced shortly afterwards by Shah Ali, an ally of Moscow, and was taken to Moscow himself. There Utemysh was baptized in 1553 and took the name Alexander. He became versed in law and letters and received a pension from from the tsar from 1560 onwards.

11. Ivan Fedorovich Obolensky-Ovchina (died 1538) was the son of the boyar Fedor Vasilievich Telepnia. Between 1512 and 1519 he served intermittently as military governor of Starodub. After a distinguished service record he was promoted to boyar in 1532 and began to play a leading role in Moscow society. Owing to his romantic involvement with Elena Glinskaia, his position changed dramatically. Using her protection, Obolensky-Ovchina manoeuvred himself into the supreme position among the boyars during the minority of Ivan IV. He removed those boyars who opposed his ambitions. Mikhail Glinsky was imprisoned, Ivan Liatsky and Semen Belsky fled to Lithuania, Ivan Belsky and Ivan Vorotynsky were charged with aiding and abetting their flight. Obolensky-Ovchina controlled the future tsar Ivan IV through his sister Agrafena Cheliadnina, whom he appointed as nurse and guardian of the young Ivan. His rise to power earned him many enemies, and when his patron Elena Glinskaia died in 1538 he was arrested by Vasily Shuisky and starved to death in prison. Herberstein claims that Obolensky-Ovchina was hacked to pieces.

12. Ivan Ivanovich Andreevich Cheliadnin was the son of Master of the Horse Boyar Ivan Andreevich (died 1516) and the brother-in-law of Yury Vasilievich Glinsky. He inherited the title and rank of boyar master of the horse only in 1539, and died around 1541. A.A. Zimin, *Oprichnina Ivana Groznogo* (The Crown Estates System of Ivan the Terrible) (Moscow, 1964), p. 276.

13. The Russian term is *diadka*, the diminutive of *diadia*, meaning "uncle."

14. Soloviev names the following articles of clothing: sashes; *ferezi*—long male garments with long sleeves, no collar or waist; *terliki*—a type of long caftan with a waistband and short sleeves; *armiaki*—an unpleated peasant's coat of heavy woolen cloth; caftans; *kaftantsy*—a foppish caftan; caps; *chugi*—a long caftan; *opoiaski*—a belt or cincture for the outer garment, sometimes with tassels; *nauruzi*; *opashni*—a male summer outer garment or a broad, long-skirted caftan like a ferez but with short, broad sleeves; *odnoriadki*—a long-skirted caftan without a collar, with a straight wrap-around and small buttons; a smock; *tegiliai*—a caftan with a stand-up collar and short sleeves; *epanchi*—a long mantle, or cloak; *taf'i*—a calotte or skull-cap; fur coats; *kolpaki*—sleeping caps; *zipuny*—homespun coats; Morocco stockings embroidered with gold, silver and silks; shoes; *choboty*—ankle-boots with turned up pointed toes; chains and necklaces.

15. Ivan IV called an assembly of the land on June 28, 1566 to reach a decision concerning a proposed peace treaty with Lithuania and Sweden. The Lithuanians were willing to yield Polotsk, Yuriev and Narva to Moscow, whereas Ivan insisted on obtaining territories around Polotsk west of the Dvina river. In particular Ivan IV insisted that Lithuania cede Riga to Muscovy. Because the negotiations were at a standstill, Ivan sought the support of his government and army in the Assembly of the Land. With the support of the assembly Ivan broke off negotiations and both sides prepared to renew the war. A.A. Zimin, A.L. Khoroshkevich, *Rossiia vremeni Ivana Groznogo* (Russia at the Time of Ivan the Terrible) (Moscow, 1982), pp. 110-114. Crummey, p. 165.

16. Mikhail Ivanovich Vorotynsky (1510-1573) was a brilliant military commander who took an active part in the capture of Kazan in 1552, but like many

powerful figures he too fell victim to the capricious nature of Ivan IV. Because of his association with Alexis Adashev, Vorotynsky fell into disfavor but in 1569 he emerged to become director of the frontier service in Kolomna and Serpukhov. He initiated important regulations in this aspect of national defense. In 1572 he led the forces which defeated Devlet-Girey, but in 1573 he was accused of having secret relations with the Crimean khanate and was executed. See V.I. Buganov, "Vorotynskii, Mikhail Ivanovich," MERSH, Vol. 43, pp. 70-71.

17. The solemn prayers or *moleben* is an occasional service performed at the request of the people or in accordance with circumstances. It may take place in the church building before or after the Divine Liturgy or at other times and places. The moleben can be a *Te Deum* or thanksgiving, or a solemn prayer of intercession and is comprised of a canon to Christ, the Mother of God or other saints, litanies, psalms and appropriate readings. Martine Roty, *Dictionnaire russe-français des termes en usage dans l'Église russe* (A Russian-French Dictionary of Terms Used in the Russian Church) (Paris, 1980), p. 71.

18. Elena Vasilievna Glinskaia, second wife of Vasily III Ivanovich, functioned as regent for Ivan IV after his father's death in 1533. During her regency a mint was established in Moscow and a currency reform was undertaken. The rival Belsky, Shuisky and Glinsky families barely concealed their hostility towards each other during Elena's tenure of office, and upon her death by poison in 1538 engaged in a protracted campaign of annihilation. Crummey, pp. 146-147. S.M. Kashtanov, "Glinskii Family," MERSH, Vol. 12, pp. 200-202.

19. Stefan Bathory (1533-1586) was born in Szilagysomlyo, Transylvania. In 1556 he entered the service of Prince Sigismund Zapolya of the newly independent Transylvania in the capacity of commander-in-chief of the army. Chosen prince in 1571, Bathory hoped to liberate all of Hungary from Habsburg control, but enjoyed only limited success. On May 1, 1576 Bathory was crowned king of Poland, having been elected the previous year by the Polish Diet. Though unable to speak Polish when crowned king, he quickly became an ardent and successful Polish patriot, defending the crown and Catholicism against Protestant incursions, and actively promoting the Counter-Reformation in Poland. His reign was marked by a series of conflicts with Ivan IV over the Baltic regions. Together with his commander-in-chief Jan Zamoyski he captured Polotsk in 1579 and turned over all but one of its churches to the Jesuits. In 1580 he took Velikie Luki and laid siege to Pskov in 1581. A truce with Muscovy was negotiated in 1582 by Antonio Possevino at Yam Zapolsky. The Zapolsky truce, ten years in duration, recognized Poland's annexation of Livonia and all territories taken by Moscow from Lithuania, but left Smolensk in Russian control.

20. Matvey Ivanovich Rzhevsky, with the nickname "diak" (crown secretary), was a commander of the musketeers during the conquest of Kazan in 1552. He led a successful attack against the forces of the Crimean khan Devlet-Girey in 1556, taking the stockaded town of Ochakov. In 1558 he served as governor of Chernigov. His nickname is thought to refer to his above average level of education or, as Soloviev thinks, to his service title.

21. Prince Ivan Mikhailovich Shuisky (died 1559) led a distinguished military career during the minority and early years of Ivan IV. In 1531 he bore the rank of commander of the great regiment, and served as governor in Kholmogory during Elena Glinskaia's regency. He was made a boyar in 1535 with the rank of Moscow governor and advanced to become commander-in-chief of the great regiment by 1552. Until 1547 Shuisky was almost continually involved in military campaigns. He died childless.

22. Around the year 1562 Ivan IV composed a new testament which regulated the succession to the throne and named a number of boyars to a council of regents who were obliged to protect the interests of the heir, Ivan Ivanovich. Among these boyars figured Daniel Romanovich Yuriev (died 1564), who together with P.I. Gorensky headed the sovereign's court. Daniel Romanovich Yuriev was a member of the powerful Zakharin family which rose to power in the middle of the sixteenth century. After the Kazan campaign of 1552 he was named majordomo of Kazan, but retained his Moscow title. Daniel Romanovich was considered by his contemporaries to have inspired and promoted the institution of the oprichnina. The Yuriev-Zakharins are later and better known as the Romanovs. Zimin, *Oprichnina,* pp. 86, 88.

23. Grigory A. Chodkiewicz (1505-1572) was hetman of Lithuania. In 1565 he gave refuge to the first printers of Moscow, Ivan Fedorov and Peter Mstislavets, on his estate in Zabludov.

24. Ivan Petrovich Fedorov Cheliadnin belonged to an ancient aristocratic family, but the early death of his father obliged him to fight to preserve his rank among the Muscovite aristocracy. After serving as commander of the right flank in various campaigns between 1536 and 1541, Ivan Petrovich attained the rank of boyar and master of the horse sometime before 1546; that same year, however, he fell into disgrace and was exiled to Beloozero. He regained the rank of boyar and master of the horse as a member of the Chosen Council of boyars. In the crisis of 1553, occasioned by Ivan IV's near death, Ivan Petrovich swore allegiance to Dmitry, the infant son of Ivan IV and Anastasia Zakharina (Romanova), but the uncertain loyalties of the boyar council worried the tsar so much that he suppressed the office of master of the horse and sent Ivan Petrovich into exile. For ten years was absent from the capital, but served as vicegerent and governor in numerous towns, including Pskov (1554), Sviiazhsk (1556), Smolensk (1559) and Yuriev/ Dorpat (1563). The initial stages of the oprichnina found Ivan Petrovich back in favor at the Moscow court, and he served once again as chief of the boyars in Moscow. Fortunes shifted yet again for the aging Cheliadnin; suspected by Ivan IV of desiring the throne, Ivan Petrovich found death at the hands of the enraged tsar himself in 1577. Zimin, *Oprichnina,* pp. 270-282.

25. The boyar Prince Ivan Dmitrievich Belsky (died 1571) served Ivan IV loyally as boyar and general of the great regiment. He married Marfa Vasilievna, daughter of Prince Vasily Vasilievich Shuisky, in 1554. When Ivan IV retired to Alexandrov Village in 1564, Belsky was one of the first leaders of a delegation from Moscow to petition Ivan not to renounce the throne. His loyalty was rewarded

with a high rank in the zemshchina lands (Land domains) during the period of the oprichnina. In 1571 he had to return hastily to defend Moscow against Devlet-Girey, but perished in the conflagration which engulfed the city in the course of the Tatar attack.

26. Ivan Fedorovich Mstislavsky (1530-1586) served for over twenty-five years in the military. His marriage to Irina Aleksandrovna Gorbataia-Shuiskaia produced four children, one of whom, Anastasia Ivanovna, in 1573 was chosen by Tsar Ivan IV to marry Simeon Bekbulatovich, whom Ivan IV chose as puppet ruler of Moscow in 1575. Although he had a long career, two curious incidents brought him close to disgrace. He confessed to having disobeyed the tsar's orders in 1561, which resulted in a defeat of Muscovite forces, and to having invited the Tatars to invade Muscovy in 1571. Together with D.I. Belsky, Mstislavsky led a delegation to Alexandrov Village in 1565 and controlled the Land domains with Belsky during the oprichnina. His fortune turned on him during the reign of Tsar Fedor Ivanovich (1584-1598) when he attempted to have Boris Godunov removed from the tsar's council. He was banished in 1586 to the monastery of St. Cyril in Beloozero, where he died. Emily V. Leonard, "Mstislavskii, Ivan Fedorovich," MERSH, Vol. 23, pp. 161-162.

27. Prince Vasily Mikhailovich Glinsky participated in a reception for the ambassadors from King Sigismund of Poland in 1542. Together with Peter Semenovich Serebriansky he defeated the Lithuanian hetman Radziwill near Pernau in 1560, and was named commander of the advance guard. Compelled to swear allegiance to the tsar and his heirs in 1561, he was named governor of Kazan with the rank of boyar in 1562. He died in 1564, and was interred in the Trinity-St. Sergius monastery.

28. See Note 22, above.

29. Ivan Petrovich Yakovlia Cheliadnin (died 1571) had a checkered military career marked by failure and suspicion. He participated with Prince Mstislavsky in the failed attempt in 1561 to take Reval. The years 1563-1564 were more auspicious for him, especially in his distinguished service against Detlev-Girey on the Oka river in 1564, but in 1566 he fell under suspicion and had to have his loyalty to Ivan IV guaranteed by a number of nobles. He joined with Prince Magnus of Denmark in a second unsuccessful attempt to capture Reval in 1570. The following year he was accused of plotting the death of Marfa Vasilievna Sobakina, Ivan IV's bride, and was executed along with his brother.

30. Ivan Ivanovich Pronsky (died 1569) enjoyed the trust of both Grand Prince Vasily III and his brother Yury Ivanovich of Dmitrov, and supported Yury's claim to the throne upon Vasily's death. His close ties with the Shuiskys eventually brought about his demise, and he remained cool towards Ivan IV throughout his life. In 1547 he fled to Lithuania but was apprehended before crossing the border; Ivan IV, however, forgave him and made him a boyar in 1549. When Ivan IV was preparing to die from a serious illness in 1553, Pronsky sided with Vladimir Andreevich of Staritsa against Ivan's young son Dmitry, but after Ivan's recovery

he suffered no penalties. Until 1568 Pronsky participated in many military campaigns, but was executed in 1569, apparently as a late retaliation for his earlier indiscretions.

31.   Ivan Bolshoy Vasilievich Sheremetev (died 1577) led an eventful career in most military campaigns between 1540-1570. The great wealth which he amassed at the end of his life earned Sheremetev the stern rebuke of Tsar Ivan IV after he was tonsured in the St. Cyril monastery in Beloozero in 1570. Soloviev includes portions of their dispute. See Chapter VI, below.

32.   Ivan Menshoy Vasilievich Sheremetev (died 1577) enjoyed the life-long favor of Ivan IV. He participated in the major ventures against Kazan, Livonia, Lithuania and Crimea from 1552 to 1577 and proved himself a courageous and daring soldier. Severely wounded during the attack on Reval on February 7, 1577, he was transported to Moscow and then to the St. Cyril monastery in Beloozero where he was tonsured and died. He was buried there in the stone church of the Dormition. Ivan IV had his name inscribed in the Moscow synodicon for eternal commemoration. His daughter Elena Ivanovna married Ivan IV's son Ivan Ivanovich.

33.   Prince Vasily Semenovich Serebriany-Obolensky (died 1570) rose from the status of junior boyar in 1537 to that of commander of the right flank in 1558. During the seige of Kazan in 1552, Serebriany-Obolensky directed the breaching of the city's walls near its secret water source.

34.   Nikita Romanovich Yuriev was majordomo in 1565 and served as vicegerent of Tver. During the 1572 campaign against Devlet-Girey, Nikita Romanovich served in the advance guard. In 1574 he assumed command of the steppe defenses.

35.   Ivan Mikhailovich Vorontsov was an army commander in the renewed war with Lithuania in 1562. In 1567 he participated in negotiations for an alliance between Muscovy and Sweden. He was not a member of the oprichnina.

36.   The lord-in-waiting Mikhailo Yakovlevich Morozov (died 1573) became a boyar in 1549. As vicegerent of Yuriev/Dorpat, he oversaw the exile of German citizens to Kostroma, Vladimir, Uglich and Kashin in 1565. Throughout the oprichnina Morozov remained a member of the boyar council in the Land domains. He participated in the fall-winter Livonian campaign of 1572-1573 which resulted in the capture of the Swedish-held fortress of Weissenstein.

37.   Cousin of Anastasia Zakharina, Boyar Vasily Mikhailovich Yuriev was appointed to the council of regents in 1562. He was closely involved in the creation of the oprichnina, of which he was himself a member.

38.   Ivan Yakovlevich Chobotov served as lord-in-waiting under Ivan IV and was present at the latter's marriage to Anastasia in 1547. He carried out a number of military and civil missions for Ivan IV, and escorted the tsar to Alexandrov Village in 1564, but was forced to return to Moscow in disgrace for undisclosed reasons. Like many of his day, Chobotov was illiterate.

39.   Little is known of Vasily Dmitrievich Danilov except that he perished during the oprichnina.

40. The boyar Semen Vasilievich Yakovlev served as vicegerent of Smolensk from July 1568 until March 1571. He was cudgeled to death in the reprisals of 1571 after the great Moscow fire together with his relative, the crown estates boyar Vasily Petrovich Yakovlev. Their estates in Kolomna district were confiscated by the tsar.

41. Ivan I Danilovich (died 1340), known to history as Ivan Kalita, was prince of Moscow from 1325 until 1328 and grand prince of Vladimir from 1328 until 1340. His nickname means "Moneybag" and is thought to derive from his service as tax-collector for the Tatars and his generosity towards the poor. See Emily V. Leonard, "Ivan I Danilovich," MERSH, Vol. 15, pp. 35-40.

42. The Trachaniotes family were Greek immigrants living in Muscovy. Yury Dmitrievich Maly was keeper of the seal during the reign of Ivan III and treasurer under Vasily III. His son Vasily Yurievich was already a boyar at the wedding of Anastasia and Ivan IV, and served as crown steward in Dmitrov in 1550-1551. The learned Dmitry Trachaniotes the Elder, an advisor to Archbishop Gennady of Novgorod, wrote at Gennady's request a tract entitled "Missive Concerning the Seventh Millennium" in which he tried to explain the discrepancy between Latin and Russian calendaric calculations pertaining to the expected end of the world in 1492 (the year 7000 from the creation of the world according to Russian reckoning). N.A. Kazakova, Ya.S. Lur'e, *Antifeodal'nye ereticheskie dvizheniia na Rusi XIV-nachala XVI veka.* (Antifeudal Heretical Movements in Russia from the Fourteenth to the Beginning of the Sixteenth Century) (Moscow and Leningrad, 1955), p. 135. A.M. Kleimola, "Patterns of Duma Recruitment, 1505-1550," *Essays in Honor of A.A. Zimin* (Columbus, Ohio, 1985), p. 247, Note 52.

43. Soloviev refers to Prince Dmitry Mikhailovich Pozharsky (1578-1642) who was the military commander of the second national militia formed in Nizhny Novgorod in 1611 during the Time of Troubles. He drove the Polish garrison out of Moscow in October 1612, and formed a provisional government which ruled until the election of Mikhail Romanov as tsar in 1613. See Volume 15 of this series. The principality of Starodub, situated in Northeastern Russia on the Kliazma river was originally ruled by Ivan, the younger son of Prince Vsevolod of the Big Nest. In the fourteenth century the princes entered the service of Moscow, and by the fifteenth century the principality broke apart into smaller units controlled by a number of princes including the Pozharsky, Riapolovsky, Romodanovsky, Paletsky and Kovrov families.

44. The validation charter (dokladnaia gramota) was a document used in the transfer of any type of legal action from a lower to a higher court for re-examination and final decision.

CHAPTER II

1. The Russian army of the fifteenth and sixteenth centuries was dominated by the cavalry. This massive force of several thousands of men was subdivided into five large divisions: the great regiment or main corps, the advance and rearguards,

and the left and right flanks. Additional flexibility was provided by a number of auxiliary units. Artillery played an increasingly important role in the sixteenth century, as did the creation of infantry units of musketeers and arquebusiers. Crummey, pp. 10-11, 107-110.

2. Fedor Ivanovich Troekurov after a distinguished military career was exiled to Kazan in 1565 for reasons as yet unclear.

3. The hundredman (sotskii) was the elected head of a hundred in civil administration who executed police duties. The name was adopted from the military practice of dividing the regiment of a thousand men into units of tens, fifties and hundreds. The fiftyman and tenman were subordinate to the hundredman in the civil administration and with him shared the responsibility of maintaining public order.

4. Quitrent villages (obrochnye derevni) were those which paid the quitrent instead of taxes. The quitrent (obrok) was originally a rent paid in kind by a peasant for the use of land, but from the sixteenth century it was paid in cash or through labor. In some cases, and especially for cotters and the poor, the quitrent resembled a simple tax (tiaglo). The Viatka district was divided into tax-paying and quitrent-paying regions.

5. The areal (obzha) was the area of land one man with a horse could plough in one working day.

6. In the fifteenth-century legal system, graft (posul) was a contractual payment by the litigants to the trial judge as recompense for his work. It later came to signify bribe. Pominok is a gift "in memory of the donor" but also official fees or a bribe.

7. Sigismund II Augustus (1520-1572) was the only son of King Sigismund I of Poland (1467-1548) and Queen Bona. Throughout his reign he contended with the hostile Polish nobility, although he did manage to exercise a greater measure of control over it than had his father. Sigismund Augustus reigned over a Poland which saw upheaval from below and the incursion of Protestantism destabilize an already unsteady domestic political situation. His marriage to Barbara Radziwill, daughter of the leading Lithuanian Calvinist Prince Nicholas Radziwill, seemed to augur well for the fortunes of Protestantism in Poland, but Sigismund II remained a firm Roman Catholic. After the Diet of 1564 he authorized the decrees of the Council of Trent, and banished foreign heretics from Poland. In 1565 he invited the Jesuits into Poland to restore Catholicism. Sigismund's skilled diplomacy spared his country much of the Turkish threat, while his disciplined and efficient army thwarted the advances of Muscovy. His principal achievement was the Union of Lublin in 1569, which made out of Lithuania and Poland a single body politic with one Diet, a common elected head and currency. Sigismund II was the last of the Jagiellonian dynasty, his three marriages having produced no heirs.

8. See Chapter I, Note 34.

9. Ostafy Dashkovich (Daszkiewicz, Dashkevych), the commander of the cossack company at Kanev, won renown for his success in defending Kanev against Turkish and Tatar assaults. In 1533 he was consulted by King Sigismund

I of Poland about establishment of a system of defense on the Dnieper river. Dashkovich advised the settlement of cossacks on the Dnieper islands, but the Polish nobility ultimately rejected his suggestion. For information on the cossacks and Dashkovich's involvement see Orest Subtelny, *Ukraine. A History* (Toronto, 1988), pp. 108-115.

10. Prince Dmitry Ivanovich Vishnevetsky was a former magnate in Russian Lithuania who entered service in Muscovy. In 1553-1554 he united disparate cossack groups and built a fort on the Mala Khortitsia island below the Dnieper rapids as a bulwark against Tatar raids into Ukraine. After some daring raids into the Crimea and against the Ottoman Turks, Vishnevetsky settled in Muscovy but seems to have left around 1561 to become involved in Moldavian affairs. He was betrayed to the Ottoman Turks by some Moldavians and executed in 1563. See V.A. Golobutskii, "Vishnevetskii, Dmitrii Ivanovich," MERSH, Vol. 42, p. 126.

11. A murza is a Tatar princeling.

12. Henry of Valois (Henryk Walezy) (1551-1589) was elected to the Polish throne on May 11, 1573 by the national assembly in Warsaw and through the influence of his mother, Catherine de Medici. King Henry reigned in Poland for thirteen months. Upon learning of the death of his brother Charles IX he fled Poland on June 18, 1574 and became King Henry III of France that same year. His lack of political involvement, his love of pleasure and his effeminacy aroused the disfavor of his French subjects, culminating in his assassination on August 1, 1589. A thorough study of Henry's life is given by Pierre Chevalier, *Henri III. Roi shakespearien* (Paris, 1985). For the Polish experiment, pp. 181-254 and Norman Davies, *God's Playground. A History of Poland in Two Volumes* (New York, 1982), Vol. I, pp. 413-420.

13. The word *podkova* means "horseshoe" in Russian.

14. In 1579 Stefan Bathory launched a counter-offensive against Northwestern Russia in the ongoing conflict over Livonia. He took Polotsk in August 1579, Velikie Luki in September 1580 and laid seige to Pskov in September 1581. Thanks to the carefully planned defense of Pskov by Prince Ivan Petrovich Shuisky, the town did not fall, and Bathory eventually agreed to a truce negotiated by Antonio Possevino in 1582.

CHAPTER III

1. The commercial ordinance was a document which regulated trading, the level of duties on goods, which goods were dutiable and who collected the duties. Penalties for customs infractions were included in this document. It also could be a document granting a monastery the right to establish a market and collect excise at it.

2. The judicial escort fee (khozhenoe) was the money paid to the official who brought the accused to trial.

3. The text reads "more" but, as the Soviet editor notes in parentheses, "less" makes more sense.

4.   A longboat (strug) is a wooden flat-bottomed river boat with vertical sides in use since the eleventh century. It was roughly 20-50 m long, 4.5-9 m wide, and could be propelled either by oars or a sail.

5.   The Volkhov river neatly cuts Novgorod into two sections. The left side of the river was known as St. Sophia's Side, named after the cathedral of St. Sophia (Holy Wisdom) built in 1045. With the residence of the archbishop, the Sophia Side was the political center of Novgorod. The other side of the river was known as the Merchants' or Market Side where the commercial enterprises of the city were centred. The main church in this section was the cathedral of St. Nicholas, built in 1113.

6.   The church of St. John the Baptist-in-Opoki was apparently the last princely building erected within the city limits of Novgorod. Its builder, Prince Vsevolod Mstislavich (died 1138), erected the church in 1127-1130 in a vain attempt to shift the political focus of Novgorod away from St. Sophia.

7.   A moskovka was a small silver coin minted in sixteenth-century Moscow similar to the Moscow denga and worth one half a novgorodka or copeck.

8.   An *izba*, translated here as shed, is the typical Russian peasant house or hut, constructed of interlocking logs. In a restricted sense the word also can refer to the living quarters of such a dwelling. It also can mean an office.

9.   The shop levy (polavochnoe) was collected in the sixteenth century for the use of the prince's shops and selling stalls, its value determined by the size of the business space and the type of goods being sold.

10.   The tax on trade and industry in the fifteenth and sixteenth centuries known as *pozem* or floor space tax perhaps was levied for the use of land on which a business stood.

11.   The prow tax (nosovoe) was a late fifteenth-century customs duty placed on boats and ships carrying goods. The name derives from the word for prow of a boat, nos.

12.   A morgen (morga) is the area of land which a farmer can plow in one morning, roughly 1,300 square sazhens (about 1 hectare).

13.   Soloviev explains that one stone weighs 32 *funt*, which equals roughly 29 lb. or 13 kg.

14.   The plowland (voloka) in Lithuania was a parcel of land roughly 15 desiatinas or 20 hectares in size.

CHAPTER IV

1.   The constables (nedel'shchiki) were officials in Muscovy who performed their duties on a weekly basis. Into the sixteenth century they were entrusted chiefly with organizing judicial duels. Later they subpoenaed parties and witnesses for court appearances, helped in the arrest and guarding of thieves and organized the general questioning of witnesses for both parties in a suit. They ranked equal to or slightly above the bailiff (pristav).

2. In an effort to control the supply of peasant labor a two-week period in autumn around the feast of St. George (November 26) extending from November 17 until December 3 was inaugurated during which time peasants legally were permitted to move from one landowner to another. This period coincided with the end of harvest and other agricultural labor and so allowed for a minimum of disruption in service.

3. In the thirteenth century the Novgorod lands of Torzhok and Volok were divided into halves (poloviny), one of which was run by the prince's official and the other by the vicegerent of Novgorod. The other territories belonging to Novgorod known as "fifths" (piatiny) were subdivided into districts (volosti). After the annexation of Novgorod by Moscow in the sixteenth century, the fifths also were subdivided into halves.

4. The word *otkup* means buying of freedom from service obligations. In the middle of the sixteenth century the "vicegerent's franchise" (namestnich'ii otkup) replaced the fees paid by the local population in natural products for the upkeep of the governor.

5. In the fourteenth and fifteenth centuries the court costs (prisudy) were those paid by the unsuccessful plaintiff to the judge, and were levied at a set percentage of the contested value.

6. Dmitry Fedorovich Paletsky (died 1561), also surnamed Shchereda, was a member of the Starodub princely family. He had a long and distinguished military career, serving in the campaigns against Polotsk, Vitebsk and Wilno in 1535 and played an important role with Adashev in the conquest of Kazan in 1552. He twice was named military governor of Kazan.

7. The future archbishop Gury of Kazan was born Grigory Rugotin of a poor noble family. He served Prince Ivan Penkov, but was accused falsely of having improper relations with the prince's wife and was imprisoned for two years in a dungeon. Grigory spent his confinement as a copyist, selling his products and giving his earnings to the poor. Upon his release he entered the monastery of St. Joseph of Volokolamsk where he was tonsured with the name Gury. He later served as abbot of that monastery. Ivan IV compelled him to assume the abbacy of the Selizharov monastery, a position he held for two years. In 1555 he was consecrated as the first archbishop of Kazan and enjoyed great success as a pastor and missionary bishop.

8. Bogdan-Feofan Yurievich Saburov (died 1598) occupied a number of important positions in the military and was made a boyar in 1572. His daughter Evdokia Bogdanovna married Ivan IV's son Ivan.

9. Mikhailo Bitiagovsky (died 1591) was a crown secretary and director of the fiscal administration of Uglich. He supervised the grand princely estates at Uglich and regulated the finances of Maria Nagaia, the last wife of Ivan IV. He owed his office in Uglich to Boris Godunov. The Nagoy family resented his tight control of Maria's finances and looked for an opportunity to discredit him. That moment arrived with the sudden death of Prince Dmitry Ivanovich. The Nagoy clan spread a rumor that Bitiagovsky's son Daniel and his nephew Nikita Kachalov murdered the young Dmitry. While attempting to defend his relatives against these false

accusations, Bitiagovsky was seized by the crowd and lynched. "Bitiagovskii, Mikhail," MERSH, Vol. 4, p. 190. See also Volume 13 of this series.

10. The passage deals with *mestnichestvo* or service hierarchy, which Soloviev discusses in Chapter I , above. The system of assigning ranks to boyars serving in the military, court and other administrative situations was developed during the fifteenth, sixteenth and seventeenth centuries. With it, the higher nobility sought to protect their privileges as members of a duty-bound service contingent against lower nobility and commoners. The boyars did not engage in rivalry for the best postings in the service hierarchy, but rather for the postings appropriate to their rank in comparison with other boyars. Genealogy, service rank and length of service were the criteria for determining position in the service hierarchy. Members of the grand princely family outranked Moscow boyars and lesser princes in genealogy. A boyar genealogically equal in rank with another boyar received a higher rank in the service hierarchy if his ancestors occupied a superior service rank and performed it for a lengthier period of time than the other boyar's ancestors. The system impeded the good administration of the realm; in times of war conflicts over proper service rank frequently distracted military commanders from their duties. As the text shows, in crisis situations the grand prince or tsar could suspend the service hierarchy altogether for the duration of a campaign. The servitors then were required to perform their duties as though "without rank."

11. For information on Prince Andrei Kurbsky, see Chapter VI.

12. Timofey Ivanov Teterin was a junior boyar from Mozhaisk. A commander of regiments, Teterin was tonsured forcibly in the monastery of St. Anthony on the Sii river sometime after 1558 and fled to Lithuania around the year 1563.

13. Soloviev lists the following terms for town garrison commander: *gorodnichi, gorodovy prikashchik, gorodchik.*

14. Soloviev uses the term *sosed* ("neighbor"), which signifies those who did not have their own homesteads and were not registered for taxes, but lived with tax-paying peasants as hired hands, a boarder.

15. Merchants resettled by the grand prince were known as "resettled merchants," *gosti vvedennye.* Soloviev uses *gosti vedenye* in the text.

16. The term *nizovye goroda,* downstream towns, refers to towns situated on or near the upper and middle Volga river, including Suzdal, Rostov, Vladimir, Nizhny Novgorod, Gorodets-Radilov, and Murom.

17. The *zemshchina* or non-crown Land domains was the larger part of Muscovite territory which remained after Ivan IV set up his own special state, the oprichnina or crown domains, in 1565. It was governed by boyars and officials from pre-1565 Muscovy, and had its own troops. The Land domains were continually expropriated by the crown estate troops. In 1575-1576 Ivan IV installed a puppet tsar for the Land domains, the Tatar prince Simeon Bekbulatovich. Ivan IV was absolute ruler of the crown domains from their inception in 1565 until their dissolution in 1572. His permanent residence for the duration of the crown estates was Alexandrov Village, which also housed the administration and judiciary. The crown estates were not a cohesive territory, but comprised crown lands, former free peasant lands and estates of executed or exiled boyars. Occupying roughly one

third of Muscovite territory, the crown estates lay in North and Central Russia; parts of Moscow belonged to the crown estates, as did parts of Novgorod. See Volume 10 of this series.

18. The fancy bread or kalach is a type of round festive loaf usually made of wheat flour and sweetened with honey.

19. The *gostinyi dvor*, merchant square or trading house, was usually an enclosed and covered market space housing a number of individual shops. Trade, which could be conducted legally only in this market space, was subject to various fees.

20. Beginning in the fourteenth century a woodland settlement (pochinok) was a type of habitation built during the clearing of wooded land. It retained this name for the duration of the tax exemption granted to promote agricultural use of the land. Once this expired, the *pochinok* was called *derevnia* (village or hamlet).

21. Yuriev was the Russian name for Dorpat. It was named after its founder Yaroslav the Wise, whose baptismal name was Yury. Its modern name is Tartu.

22. For both the Code of Law (sudebnik) and the statute charter (ustavnaia gramota), see Chapter VII, below.

23. In the fourteenth and fifteenth centuries the representative of an appanage prince in towns divided into three parts was known as the *tretchik* (administrator of the "third"). In Muscovy from the middle of the fifteenth century the grand prince's representative, the *bol'shoi namestnik* (great vicegerent) supervised the other two administrators.

24. Vladimir Andreevich (1533-1569), cousin of Ivan IV, was the last prince of Staritsa. His father, Andrei Ivanovich, was the fourth son of Grand Prince Ivan III Vasilievich. After his father's rising against Ivan IV in 1537 failed, Vladimir Andreevich was placed under house arrest for three years, together his mother Evfrosinia Khovanskaia, but in 1541 Vladimir received his freedom and his estates in Staritsa. Relations between the two cousins proceeded cordially for the time, Vladimir serving in the conquest of Kazan in 1552. After Ivan's serious illness in 1553 Vladimir suffered the same fate as many former allies. He had to swear oaths of loyalty in 1554 to Ivan's son Ivan Ivanovich, renounce all claims to the throne and take up residence in Moscow, where a specially assigned retinue could keep him under surveillance. Although relations improved, in 1563 Vladimir and his mother were accused of speaking against the tsar and were brought to trial before Metropolitan Makary. Found guilty, they were pardoned by Ivan, though Evfrosinia was forced to enter a convent. In 1566 Ivan seized Vladimir's estates for the oprichnina. Vladimir's name was linked with I. P. Cheliadnin-Fedorov and other prominent boyars suspected of plotting Ivan's overthrow. Cheliadnin-Fedorov and four Kolychevs were hanged in 1568. In 1569 Vladimir and his family were arrested and forced to take poison; his mother was removed from the convent and put to death. Only Vladimir's eldest son and two daughters were spared. See Graham, "Staritskii, Vladimir Andreevich," MERSH, Vol. 37, pp. 86-88.

25. When a peasant left his landlord legally he was required to pay him the departure fee (pozhiloe) in compensation for the use of the house and farm.

26. The word "recruiter" (otkazchik) designates an agent employed by wealthier landowners to lure peasants away from other landowners by offering cash payment for the peasants.

27. Soloviev digresses at this point to explain the meaning of the phrase. "This expression *raspakhivat' derevniu* (plough up the hamlet) gives us an indication of the original meaning of *derevnia* (hamlet) and its relation to *selo* (village). The word *derevnia* derives from *derevo* (wood, tree) thus signifying a place only recently claimed from the forest and cleared for ploughing. To this notion corresponds the well-known West Russian expression *syroi koren', sest' na syrom korniu* "damp root, to sit on a damp root."

28. In this case the term *doklad* means a confirmed slavery document, that is, a document attesting to the slave status of the bearer and officially recorded as such.

29. Presumably the children of monks and nuns are the offspring they had before entering monastic life. It is also possible that Soloviev refers to the spiritual children of monks and nuns, for although acting as a godparent in baptism was canonically unusual for a monk or nun, it was by no means rare. Godchildren were then treated as one's legal offspring, particularly in marriage law.

30. Anyone holding a position of trust in the government of the grand prince or in the management of princely estates was a slave. The reduction of such officials to the status of slavery was adopted by private landowners as well. In the present case, the free man becomes a slave because he "holds the key," that is, he performs the duties of a steward for the landowner in question. See Richard Hellie, *Slavery in Russia,* 1450-1725 (Chicago, 1982), p. 37.

CHAPTER V

1. The Great Court (Bolshoi Dvorets) oversaw economic affairs of the court and the people who lived on rural properties owned by the court from 1534 until 1728. It also administered the provisioning of the tsar's court with wheat, fodder and beverages.

2. The name Novaia Sol' means "New Salt" which Soloviev takes as an indication of the age of the saltworks there.

3. Soloviev uses three obscure terms for the stone, *zheleznitsy, golubitsy and krasny,* which presumably refer to their color: ferreous, bluish and red.

4. Gustav I Eriksson (1496-1560), member of the Swedish Vasa family, became king of Sweden in 1523 after the expulsion of the Danes from Sweden. In 1537 together with the Danes he freed himself and his country from dependence on the wealthy merchants of Lübeck who were influential in promoting him to the Swedish throne. He alienated his other faction of supporters, the peasantry, when he forcibly broke religious allegiance with Rome after 1527 and introduced Protestantism. Throughout his reign Gustav I fought to establish a fully independent Sweden. See Michael Roberts, *The Early Vasas. A History of Sweden,* 1523-1611 (Cambridge, 1968), Chapter 2.

238 NOTES TO CHAPTER V

5. Prince Anton Mikhailovich Romodanovsky-Riapolovksy was sent to Denmark on August 18, 1562 as part of an embassy to renegotiate a treaty pertaining to Livonia. He figured prominently at the marriage of Ivan IV and Anastasia Romanovna in 1547, being one of the principal torch bearers in the procession.

6. Sir Jerome Bowes was sent as ambassador to Moscow in June 1583 to continue the negotiations concerning a possible marriage between Ivan IV and Lady Mary Hastings. He was also to discuss Ivan IV's requests about an mutual military alliance with England and the possibility of England providing him with refuge in the event of an insurrection. Bowes was instructed to promise fulfillment of the last request only. In addition to Russian interests, Bowes was to obtain a trade monopoly for the Russia Company at the monastery of St. Nicholas of Kholmogory, but he was unsuccessful. When Ivan IV died March 18, 1584 Bowes was detained two months. He finally reached England in September 1584. T.S. Willan, *The Early History of the Russia Company*, 1553-1603 (Manchester, 1956, reprinted New York, 1968), pp. 162-166. See also Volume 10 of this series.

7. The Russia Company was a joint-stock company whose members were also shareholders. Though many of them were merchants, they were forbidden by the Company statutes from trading as individuals in Russia. Trade for the Company was conducted by its employees, known as agents or factors. The headquarters of the Russia Company was Moscow House in London. There was a London agent who supervised the shipment of goods to Russia and received the return cargoes. Originally the agents in Russia were instructed to live together in one trading center, but by 1577 they lived in Kholmogory and Moscow, and in 1589 the Company had five houses in Russia: in Vologda, Kholmogory, Yaroslavl, Moscow and St. Nicholas. The agents or factors were assisted by employees who were junior clerks and novice merchants. These could advance to the position of agent. For a detailed history of the Russia Company see Willan, cited above.

8. Christopher Hoddesdon entered the Russia Company in 1553 and went to Vologda and Yaroslavl in 1555. As Soloviev notes, he was very successful in his business ventures, returning to England in 1562. The Company convinced him to act as its agent in Narva in 1566.

9. A forecourt (podvore) of a monastery is a smaller offiliate located some distance from the monastery itself, for example, in the fields cultivated by monastery peasants, or in a town where business could be conducted.

10. One *grivenka* measures 205 grams, and the merchant bought 15 grivenkas, or 3,075 grams.

11. Devlet-Girey was khan of the Crimean Tatars from 1551 to 1577. Though a vassal to the Turkish sultan, Devlet-Girey was not keen on having the Ottoman empire established in the Crimea, and maintained satisfactory relations with Muscovy. This changed with Moscow's conquest of Kazan and Astrakhan. Raids into Muscovy increased until a state of war seemed inevitable. In 1571 the Crimean Tatars under Devlet-Girey inflicted a devastating blow to Muscovy, sacking and burning Moscow itself. Had the Tatars been interested in more than booty they could well have put an end to the nascent Russian empire; but they left Muscovy,

enabling the Russians to regroup. The following year the Tatars suffered a decisive defeat at Molodi under the armies of Ivan IV. Devlet-Girey died in 1577. Graham, "Devlet-Girei," MERSH, Vol. 9, pp. 104-106. See also Volume 10 of this series.

12. The False Dmitry is generally held to have been Yury Otrepiev (1582-1606), the son of a junior boyar from Galicia. Orphaned early in life, Yury travelled from one monastery to another, finally taking up residence in the Miracles monastery where he became a copyist. He enjoyed the favor of Patriarch Job and seems to have been introduced in the tsar's court, but an accusation of treason forced him to flee Moscow. In 1603 he appeared in Brahin in the service of Prince Adam Wisnowiecki to whom he declared himself to be none other than Dmitry Ivanovich, the deceased son of Ivan IV. He managed to convince Wisnowiecki and the Polish court that he escaped death and was now laying claim to the Moscow throne. It was at this time that he met and fell in love with Marina, daughter of the palatine of Sandomierz, Jerzy Mniszech. Taking advantage of the turmoil in Russia, and in particular of Boris Godunov's unpopularity, Otrepiev succeeded in winning over the Muscovite populace and entered Moscow on June 20, 1605 as their tsar. The boyar class hoped that Otrepiev would be an ineffectual puppet but he proved to have some ideas of his own, including a reform of the administration and laws pertaining to the peasantry. The boyars were displeased and rumors quickly spread discrediting Otrepiev. A revolt led by Vasily Shuisky brought death to Otrepiev on May 16, 1606, only nine days after his solemn marriage to Marina Mniszech. See G. Edward Orchard, "Dmitrii Ivanovich," MERSH, Vol. 4, pp. 164-169. See also Volume 14 of this series. R. G. Skrynnikov, *Boris Godunov* (Academic International Press, 1982) and *The Time of Troubles* (Academic International Press, 1988). Both the Skrynnikov volumes are translated by Hugh F. Graham.

13. Soloviev refers to the reign of terror inflicted on Novgorod in 1570 by Ivan IV and his crown estates henchmen. Aroused by suspicions that Novgorod planned secretly to switch its allegiance to Poland, Ivan IV set off with an army towards Novgorod in December 1569. On the way the army tortured and murdered selected victims in the countryside and towns, including Tver. Once in Novgorod, Ivan IV began the systematic annihilation of its leading residents, with perhaps as many as 2,200 people perishing.

14. The "fatal mark" refers to boils or buboes which were the typical physical manifestations of an infection with the plague. Contemporary literature abounds with references to these marks. For example in the *Volokolamskii Paterik* of Dosifey Toporkov we read that "in the days when there was a great plague, in 1427, people died from sores which were called buboes. On him who was to die the buboe was blue, and after three days of sickness, he would die." See T. Allan Smith, *The Volokolamskiy Paterik. A Study, Translation and Commentary* (Ph.D. diss., Toronto, 1989), p. 87. N. Langer, "Black Death in Russia," MERSH, Vol. 4, pp. 192-196, provides useful information on the plague in Russia.

15. King Sigismund I "the Old" (1467-1548) was the fifth son of Casimir IV of Poland and Elizabeth of Austria. He was elected grand prince of Lithuania in 1505 and king of Poland in 1506. His reign was marked by ongoing warfare with

Muscovy and Tatar raids, which were encouraged by the Turks and Russians. In an effort to deliver his country from the extremely debilitating Tatar raiding forays Sigismund I attempted to enlist the cossacks as a type of front line defence by having them settle on islands in the Dnieper river. He was rebuffed by the Polish nobility in this venture. Sigismund I treated his non-Catholic subjects with fairness, protecting the rights of the Orthodox Christians living in Poland and Lithuania. He was less favorably disposed towards Protestantism and democracy but undertook no measures to prevent their establishing a foothold in his realm.

16. Bona Sforza, granddaughter of the king of Aragon and related to Emperor Maximilian I, became the second wife of Sigismund I of Poland in 1518 after the death of his first wife Barbara Radziwill. Together they produced four daughters and one son, the heir Sigismund Augustus. Bringing with her a dowry of two hundred thousand ducats and considerable financial talents, she exercised no small measure of influence on the policies of her husband. In order to protect her vast holdings in Podolia and Volhynia against Tatar raids, Queen Bona converted the castles of Krzemieniec and Bar into mighty fortresses under the command of her Silesian steward Pretficz. Her success led to the settlement of the area by cossacks who acted as a front line of defence for Poland. Because of her greed and maltreatment of her children, Queen Bona did not enjoy popular support. She was suspected of having poisoned Barbara Radziwill, Sigismund Augustus's first wife, in 1550.

17. Magdeburg Law originated in the German town of Magdeburg and was adopted in a number of towns in Germany, Poland and Bohemia. The law secured administrative independence for those municipalities following it.

18. The prefect (voit) was the mayor of cities in Lithuania holding a position above that of the town manager and councillors. He presided over the council for police and economic affairs and judged criminal cases.

19. The unit of measurement used by Soloviev is the *kad*, which equals four chetverts or about 505 lbs.

20. The circuit tax (poliude) was the tax collected in the Kievan period when the prince and his retainers travelled about the principality on official visitation to collect taxes and administer justice. The practice was maintained into the sixteenth century in Lithuania.

21. *Shirokie groshei* were large silver Lithuanian coins worth twenty Moscow copecks.

22. In the Orthodox church Cheesefare week is the last week before Great Lent when dairy products may be used. It is preceded by Meatfare week, the last time meat may be eaten until Easter.

23. Grand Prince Alexander (1461-1506) was the fourth son of King Casimir IV of Poland-Lithuania. At the death of his father in 1492 he was elected by the Lithuanians as their grand prince, an act which temporarily ended the political union with Poland. When it became clear that independent Lithuania was threatened by Muscovy, the Lithuanians proposed a marriage between Alexander and Ivan III's daughter Elena. Ivan III agreed on condition that his daughter be free to practice her Orthodox faith. The peace which came with the marriage in 1495

lasted barely five years, after which Ivan III captured a third of Lithuanian territory on the pretext that Orthodox subjects were being persecuted.

CHAPTER VI

1. The bishop of Krutitsa acted as the second-ranking bishop in Moscow. His place of residence was the Krutitsky (New Savior) monastery, founded around 1272 by Prince Daniel Alexandrovich as the residence for the bishops of Saray while they were on business in Moscow. After the Golden Horde's power diminished the Krutitsky monastery became the permanent residence of the bishop of Saray in 1460. When Moscow became a patriarchate in 1589, Krutitsa was elevated to the status of a metropolitanate.

2. Hilarion was made metropolitan of Kiev and all Rus in 1051, and held that post until 1055 at the latest. He is generally considered the author of the *Sermon on Law and Grace,* at the end of which is the prayer referred to by Soloviev. For a thorough study of the entire sermon, see *Des Metropoliten Ilarion Lobrede auf Vladimir den Heiligen und Glaubensbekenntnis* (Metropolitan Hilarion's Eulogy for St. Vladimir and his Confession of Faith), edited, introduced and annotated by Ludolf Müller, (Wiesbaden, 1962). See also Volume 1 of this series.

3. For forecourt, see Chapter V, Note 9. Giving the neophytes kvas and mead was perhaps symbolic of their renunciation of Islam, which forbade consumption of alcoholic beverages.

4. Feodorit of Kola (1480-1577) had an eventful life as an anchorite and missionary in Russia's Far North. He entered the Solovetsk monastery at the age of fourteen and spent fifteen years there under the direction of a monk named Zosima. After a brief stay in the monasteries of St. Alexander Svirsky and St. Cyril of Beloozero he returned to the Solovetsk community around 1529. When his teacher Zosima died Feodorit took up the life of an anchorite, living twelve years on the Kola river with a companion named Mitrofan. In 1540 both monks presented themselves in Novgorod to Archbishop Makary, who ordained Feodorit to the priesthood and took him as his confessor. In 1542 Feodorit returned to the Kola region and founded a monastery in honor of the Holy Trinity. His familiarity with the Lapp language enabled him to preach with great success to the surrounding indigenous people. Feodorit eventually came in contact with Abbot Artemy of the Trinity-St. Sergius monastery, an association which brought him opprobrium and imprisonment in the monastery of St. Cyril of Beloozero in 1554. In 1557 he was again in favor with Tsar Ivan IV, who sent him to Constantinople to obtain ratification from the patriarch of his coronation as tsar. Feodorit ended his days in the Kola region as a missionary preacher. Igor Smolitsch, *Russisches Mönchtum. Entstehung, Entwicklung und Wesen, 988-1917* (Russian Monasticism. Origins, Development and Nature, 988-1917) (Amsterdam, 1978), pp. 292-293.

5. St. Trifon of Pechenga undertook the conversion of the Pechenga Lapps in the Kola region some time before Feodorit. He erected a church on the Pechenga

river and was tonsured a monk. Later he established a monastery near his church and obtained from the tsar charters in 1556 granting the monastery some land and fisheries. Until his death in 1583 Trifon worked among the indigenous people to establish Christianity.

6. Since the end of the fifteenth century Novgorod's rural territory was divided into fifths (piatiny), likely in imitation of the division of Novgorod town into five sectors. The five fifths were the Votskaia, Shelonskaia, Derevskaia, Obonezhskaia and Bezhetskaia. The last two named fifths were incorporated into the crown estates in 1571.

7. According to Eastern Orthodox practice and doctrine, the sacramental blessing of the bridal couple culminates in the solemn crowning of the groom and then the bride by the officiating priest. Tradition holds that the crowning symbolizes the triumph of premarital chastity over lust. Since 993 imperial Byzantine legislation held the crowning as necessary for the validity of a marriage between two free citizens.

8. Archbishop Feodosy of Novgorod (1491-1563) was tonsured in the monastery of Joseph of Volokolamsk. In 1532 he became abbot of the Khutyn monastery and then returned to his home monastery as abbot. From 1542 to 1551 he was archbishop of Novgorod and Pskov. A participant in the Hundred Chapters Council of 1551, Feodosy retired shortly afterwards to the monastery of St. Joseph of Volokolamsk because of ill health. A number of works are attributed to his pen.

9. The Solovetsk monastery was founded in the late 1420s or early 1430s by a group of monks from the St. Cyril of Beloozero monastery among whom figured Savvaty, German and Zosima. Situated on the shore of Solovetsk Island in the White Sea, the monastery rapidly evolved into the commercial and political center of the region. Under its third abbot, Jonas, the monastery obtained perpetual ownership of all the Solovetsk islands. Though first and foremost a religious community, the Solovetsk monastery played a key role in the defence of Northeastern Russia, owing to its massive fortifications. It also served as a prison for enemies of the tsar and the Orthodox church. In 1667 the monks of Solovetsk refused to accept the new liturgical books being promoted in the Russian church, joining forces with the Old Believers. After a lengthy siege the monastery was captured, some of the rebellious monks were exiled or imprisoned, and others were executed. V.I. Buganov, "Solovetskii Monastery," MERSH, Vol. 36, pp. 140-141.

10. The man who eventually became Metropolitan Philip was born Fedor Stepanovich Kolychev (1507-1569), a member of an ancient boyar family connected with the princes of Staritsa. In 1537 Fedor entered the Solovetsk monastery, where he took the name Philip. It is speculated that his decision to enter monastic life was motivated by the failed revolt against Elena Glinskaia led by Prince Andrei Ivanovich, in whose service Fedor was at that time. Philip proved to be a devoted, ascetically-minded monk and served as abbot of the monastery from 1548 to 1566. During that period he vigorously improved the financial status of the monastery, acquiring tax concessions, developing the fisheries, agriculture and saltworks. In 1566 he was consecrated metropolitan, having promised Ivan IV that he would not

criticize the crown estates or Ivan's private affairs, but he soon found himself unable to adhere to this agreement. The ever-increasing cruelty of Ivan IV finally led Philip in 1568 to rebuke the tsar during a Divine Liturgy for his lawless behavior. He was quickly removed from office and imprisoned in the Otroch monastery near Tver, where he was strangled by Ivan's loyal executor Maliuta Skuratov in December 1569. In 1652 he was canonized as a martyr. See Graham, "Filipp," MERSH, Vol. 11, pp. 131-133.

11. On December 17, 1521, Grand Prince Vasily III deposed Metropolitan Varlaam because of various conflicts, notably his refusal to grant the grand prince a divorce from Solomonia Saburova so that he could take a second wife. Varlaam was replaced by Daniel of Riazan, whom the Shuiskys deposed in 1539. His successor Joseph was removed from the metropolitan throne in 1542 and replaced by Makary, until then archbishop of Novgorod.

12. In 1529 Joseph Skripitsyn was appointed abbot of the Trinity-St. Sergius monastery. A council under the close control of the Shuisky family chose him to replace the deposed Daniel as metropolitan in 1539. In 1542 he too fell victim to the power struggle between the Shuiskys and Belskys and was imprisoned in the monastery of St. Cyril of Beloozero. He was transferred to the Trinity-St. Sergius monastery after 1547 and died there July 27, 1555.

13. The "Holy God" is the Trisagion, a Trinitarian hymn sung during the Divine Liturgy at the Little Entrance, after the Gospel Book has been carried in procession into the sanctuary and before the deacon reads the Epistle. At this point in the Liturgy ordinations and monastic professions take place. In English the hymn goes "Holy God, Holy and Mighty, Holy Immortal One, have mercy on us (repeated three times). Glory be to the Father and to the Son and to the Holy Spirit. As it was in the beginning, is now and shall be for ever and unto the ages of ages. Amen. Holy Immortal One, have mercy on us. Holy God, Holy and Mighty, Holy Immortal One, have mercy on us."

14. The sanctuary (bema or altar') is the elevated part at the east end of an Orthodox church where the altar (prestol, literally "throne") is located. The sanctuary is separated from the rest of the church by a wall or barrier with spaces for icons, known as an icon screen or iconostasis. Normally three doorways lead through the screen into the sanctuary; the middle, double-leaved door, which leads directly to the altar, is referred to as the royal doors. In Russian churches the royal doors are painted with icons of the four evangelists and a depiction of the Annunciation. A cross decorates the top. It is thought that the royal doors (tsarskie dveri) get their name from their liturgical symbolism, since through them Christ the King of Glory passes at the moment of communion. Only the priest and bishop, and on rare occasions, the deacon, may enter the sanctuary through the royal doors. The lesser clergy do so through the side doors.

15. Soloviev refers here to the Council of Florence attended by Patriarch Joseph of Constantinople, numerous Eastern bishops including Metropolitan Isidore of Kiev and all Rus and the Byzantine emperor John VIII Palaeologus. After much debate and discussion a formula of union was promulgated on July 6, 1439

formally ending the schism between Byzantine and Latin Christianity. Isidore initially was an opponent of the union but at the council became one of its most vocal proponents, for which he was rewarded with the dignity of cardinal. The union was never officially enacted in the East until December of 1452 and died with the capture of the imperial capital on May 29, 1453. Grand Prince Vasily II of Moscow was unfavorably disposed towards such a church union because it did not accord well with his own ecclesiastical politics; he hoped to create an autonomous church with its principal see in Moscow, and already tried to appoint Jonas as its metropolitan. When Isidore attempted to proclaim the decree of union in Moscow he promptly was arrested, but managed to escape shortly afterwards and fled Russia. The Council of Florence is not recognized as an ecumenical council in the Orthodox world. See Joseph Gill, *The Council of Florence* (Cambridge, 1959).

16. Daniel of Riazan (1490-1547) became metropolitan under unusual circumstances in 1522 after his predecessor Varlaam was removed forcibly from office for failing to grant a divorce to Grand Prince Vasily III Ivanovich. Daniel was trained in the monastery of Joseph of Volokolamsk and is generally, though not universally, considered a faithful disciple of the strict abbot. Although he played no significant role in the monastery, at the behest of Grand Prince Vasily III he was elected as abbot in 1515 after Joseph's death. He proved to be a servile creature of the grand prince with little tolerance for divergent theological opinions. Under his reign both Maxim the Greek and Vassian Patrikeev were convicted of heresy and sentenced to life imprisonment. Daniel was a prolific and persuasive writer, considered by the eminent church historian E.E. Golubinsky as one of the most outstanding of all Russian metropolitans. Involvement in dynastic struggles eventually toppled the ambitious prelate in 1539. The fundamental study of Daniel's life and writings remains V. Zhmakin, *Mitropolit Daniil i ego sochineniia* (Metropolitan Daniel and his Works) (Moscow, 1881).

17. The kamelaukion is the special headgear of Eastern Orthodox bishops, derived from the monastic habit. In its simplest form it is a black conical hat with a black veil.

18. The deed of enthronement (nastol'naia gramota), was given to metropolitans, bishops and abbots, containing details of their election and granted them the full authority and honor due them in their respective offices.

19. Archbishop Pimen of Novgorod was exiled in 1570 to the Venevshy monastery near Tula, where he died in confinement. Together with many others in Novgorod, he was suspected by Ivan IV of secretly plotting to hand over the city to the Poles in 1569. He was elected to the see of Novgorod in 1552 and functioned as a diligent pastor and administrator. He was for a time close to Ivan IV, urging him in a letter dated 1563 to fight against the Lithuanians and Lutherans. D.M. Bulanin, "Pimen," *Slovar' knizhnikov,* No. 2, Part 2, pp. 185-188.

20. The *prosfirnia* was a woman of proven moral and religious stature entrusted with the duty of baking the prosphora, or altar bread, for the eucharistic liturgy. In the Byzantine tradition the bread used at the eucharist resembles a small round leavened loaf. Some of the bread is consecrated during the eucharist, while

the remainder is blessed, though not consecrated, and distributed to the faithful as the antidoron at the conclusion of the service.

21. A Russian church council in 1503 decreed that widowed priests must relinquish their pastoral duties and either enter a monastery or revert to the lay state. Since Orthodox canons forbade marriage after ordination, the decision reached in 1503 was logical if somewhat harsh. The priest who chose the monastic route could function as a priest in the monastery; whoever preferred the world could serve as a cantor in his former parish and receive a small share of the new incumbent's income, provided he remain celibate. See Jack Edward Kollmann, Jr., "The *Stoglav* Council and Parish Priests," *Russian History* 7 (1980), pp. 65-91.

22. Remarriage (digamy) is the taking of a second wife after the divorce or death of one's first wife. This is what is meant here, though the Russian word *dvoezhenets* also means bigamist, that is, a man who has two wives simultaneously. The Orthodox church permits second and third marriages although the marriage rite differs considerably from the first marriage, being heavily penitential in tone. Similarly "trigamist" in this context means one who has contracted a third serially monogamous union.

23. A commendation letter (gramota otpusknaia) was issued by the bishop for clerics transferring to another diocese, commending them to the care of their new bishop.

24. The Council of 1551, known in history as the *Stoglav* or Hundred Chapters, was one of the most important ecclesiastical events in the Muscovite era. The council understood itself as a reform council with a decidedly conservative Muscovite tendency. For the next century the decisions of this council dictated church and social life in Muscovy. See Jack Kollmann, *The Moscow Stoglav ("Hundred Chapter") Council of 1551* (Ph.D. diss., Michigan, 1978) for a full treatment of this topic.

25. The typikon is a liturgical book which explains in detail how the various canonical hours and liturgies are to be celebrated, and how to coordinate movable feasts with saints' days and fixed feasts. Monastic typika include the rule of life for a given monastery.

26. The antimension is a rectangular cloth placed on the altar for the celebration of the Divine Liturgy. Though physically resembling the Latin corporale, an antimension serves the same purpose as the altar stone required in all fixed altars of the Latin rite. Originally the antimension served as a portable altar, a reminder of which is the fact that relics are sewn into it. A depiction of the burial of Christ covers most of the cloth, with the four evangelists displayed in the corners. In order for the Liturgy to be celebrated a priest must use an antimension. Thus Ivan complains that granting of this essential liturgical furnishing was losing its religious significance and becoming a profit-making venture for the bishops.

27. A charter of legal exemption (nesudimaia gramota) grants jurisdictional privilege to certain groups, in particular the church, monasteries and some secular landowners, removing them from the normal legal system and placing them directly under the jurisdiction of the ruler or his highest judge.

28. The minor clergy would include the lectors, cantors, and subdeacons.

29. In some respects the Russians followed the Jewish dietary laws, according to which animals slaughtered for food must have their throats slit and their blood drained. This law also applied to gentiles living among the Jews. See Leviticus 17:10-14.

30. Kutia is a dish of boiled wheat, rice or other grains with raisins and honey, usually eaten at funeral repasts.

31. The paskha is a very rich cheesecake in the form of a tall cylinder decorated with the initials X B for the traditional Easter greeting *"Khristos voskrese,"* "Christ is risen." As the name itself indicates, the paskha is an Easter food.

32. Karavai are round loaves.

33. A kuteinik is a side table on which the kutia and other foods were placed in a church.

34. In the sanctuary are found two sacred tables, the prothesis or credence table (predlozhenie) and the altar (prestol, trapeza). The word *zhertvennik* (from zhertva, sacrifice), which is used in the text, is occasionally a synonym for both prothesis and altar. At the prothesis the officiating priest and deacon prepare the bread and wine for use in the eucharist in a richly symbolic ritual which recapitulates the sacrificial life and death of Jesus Christ and anticipates the sacramental commemoration of His death and resurrection to be celebrated on the altar (prestol). Tsar Ivan's point is that Muscovites showed such disregard for religious propriety that they brought ordinary food into the sanctuary and set it on the prothesis.

35. The aer (air) or great veil is the third veil used to cover the liturgical vessels after they have been prepared for the Eucharist. The small veil is placed on the asterisk to cover the diskos or paten; the second or chalice veil covers the chalice and the aer covers the other two veils. The name derives from the waving of the great veil over the gifts during the recitation of the creed as a symbol of the breath of the Holy Spirit, who will descend to transform the bread and wine. The asterisk consists of two pieces of bent metal, joined in the middle, from which a small star is suspended. The asterisk prevents the small veil from touching the particles of bread on the diskos.

36. This complaint refers to shamanist belief that a child born with its shirt (v sorochkakh), that is, a caul, is destined to be a shaman.

37. A poltina equals half a ruble or 50 copecks.

38. The monk Andrei Rublev (1370-1430) has become one of the most popular figures of medieval Russia, thanks to his exquisite icon of the Holy Trinity, which he painted around 1411 for the Trinity-St. Sergius monastery. Little is known of his life. Around 1405 he assisted Theophanes the Greek and Prokhor in painting the Annunciation cathedral in Moscow. In 1408 he and Daniel Cherny painted the cathedral of the Dormition in Vladimir. He lived in both the Trinity-St. Sergius and Andronnikov monasteries. In 1988 he was canonized a saint in the Russian Orthodox church as part of the celebrations marking the millennium of the Christianization of Rus. The Soviet film director Andrei Tarkovsky (died 1986) interpreted his life and times in a film entitled *Andrei Rublev*. Despite his renown,

no major study of Rublev as yet has appeared in English. See George P. Majeska, "Rublev, Andrei," MERSH, Vol. 31, pp. 228-232; also the review of the Tarkovsky film by Joseph C. Bradley, Jr., Kritika. *A Review of Current Soviet Books on Russian History,* 10 (1974), pp. 111-120.

39. St. Piatnitsa (Friday) is the popular Russian name for the early Christian martyr, Paraskeve (Preparation Day, Friday). According to pious legend, she was born on a Friday to parents who had a special devotion to the day of Christ's passion and death. As with St. Anastasia (Resurrection, Sunday), and St. Pistis, Elpis, Agape and their mother St. Sophia (Faith, Hope, Charity, and their mother Wisdom), St. Paraskeve-Piatnitsa may be nothing but a personification of a holy day or religious virtue. Shrines containing an icon of St. Piatnitsa frequently were erected along roads and crossings. She was venerated as the patroness of commerce in Novgorod.

40. The decade priest (desiatskii sviashchennik) was subordinate to the dean of priests, and was in charge of ten churches.

41. The miracle workers Peter, Alexis and Jonas were influential metropolitans of Moscow. Peter (died 1326) was an abbot in Galicia before his nomination in 1308 to the office of metropolitan of Kiev and all Russia, against the wishes of Grand Prince Mikhail Yaroslavich of Tver. Peter eventually moved the residence of the chief hierarchs of the Russian church from Vladimir-on-the-Kliazma to Moscow in 1325 in accordance with the wishes of Ivan I Kalita, and laid the foundation for the cathedral of the Dormition there. The close political connections with the local Muscovite princes were intensified by Alexis (died 1378), who was metropolitan from 1354 to 1378. After the death of Prince Ivan II Ivanovich in 1359 Alexis acted as regent for the heir Dmitry Ivanovich, effectively ruling both church and state, and secured recognition of Dmitry as grand prince from the current khan of the Golden Horde in 1362. Metropolitan Jonas (died 1461) was chosen by a local Russian synod for the office in 1431; he was prevented, however, from taking possession of the title by domestic political strife and church events. In 1435 Constantinople had settled on Isidore as metropolitan of Moscow. After a brief appearance in Moscow Isidore hastened to attend the Council of Florence at which the union of Greek and Latin Christendom was promulgated in 1439. When Isidore finally returned to Moscow in 1441 to proclaim the union, he was arrested by Grand Prince Vasily, but just as quickly escaped custody. Jonas was installed as metropolitan unilaterally by a local Russian council in 1448. Though plans were made to seek the necessary confirmation of his election in Constantinople, its acceptance of church union with Rome and its fall to the Turks in 1453 gave Vasily and his like-minded churchmen the opportunity they were waiting for all along, in that the church in Moscow was deemed autocephalous, enjoying the right of electing its own head without outside intervention. See Joseph T. Fuhrmann, "Aleksei," MERSH, Vol. 1, pp. 112-114.

42. The work identified by the Hundred Chapters Council as *Aristotle's Gates* (Aristotelevye vrata) is thought by most scholars to be the same as the *Mystery of Mysteries* (Tainaia tainykh), the Slavonic version of the widely read *Secreta*

Secretorum. This was originally an Arabic work of the eighth or ninth century containing practical advice on topics ranging from politics to alchemy to personality which Aristotle supposedly gave to his pupil Alexander the Great. The Slavonic version closely resembles a twelfth or thirteenth century Hebrew translation of the Arabic short redaction. For bibliography in English, see D.M. Bulanin, "Tainaia Tainykh," *Slovar' knizhnikov,* No. 2, Part 2, pp. 227-230.

43. The *shestokryl* or "Six Wings" was a lunar table originally used, it seems, to calculate the date of Easter, but later figured as a tool for fortune-telling.

44. Soloviev omits the expletive.

45. The Great Canon of St. Andrew of Crete is a Lenten liturgical composition recited in its entirety at Thursday orthros of the fifth week of Great Lent, and in parts at great compline during the first four days of Lent. The name *efimon* derives from the first words of the Greek, "meth imon." Alexander's depravity is obvious.

46. The text of the letter with a modern Russian translation can be found in *Poslaniia Ivana Groznogo* (The Letters of Ivan the Terrible), ed. D.S. Likhachev and Ya. S. Lur'e (Moscow and Leningrad, 1951), pp. 162-192; commentary, pp. 632-639.

47. The reference is to the high priests Annas and his son-in-law Caiaphas mentioned in Luke 3:2, John 18:13, and Acts 4:6-22. According to these texts, they were involved in the death of Jesus and in prohibiting the Apostles from preaching.

48. Ivan Bolshoy Vasilievich Sheremetev (died 1577) participated in all major military campaigns between 1540 and 1570 in the service of Ivan IV but entered the monastery of St. Cyril of Beloozero in 1570 shortly after the murder of Metropolitan Philip. A man of immense wealth, Sheremetev made large donations to a number of important monasteries in Muscovy, including the Trinity-St. Sergius monastery, the monastery of St. Joseph of Volokolamsk and that of St. Cyril of Beloozero. Sheremetev had close connections with Ivan Viskovaty, some whose conservative religious ideas he seems to have shared. He may have considered the procession or a*krestnyi khod* an unwarranted religious innovation and hence refused to participate. Ivan Ivanovich Khabarov was a boyar and general; when he entered St. Cyril's monastery is unknown.

49. Varlaam Sobakin (died 1574), in the world Vasily Stepanovich the Lesser, belonged to the boyar family of Sobakins who served the princes of Tver before entering the service of Grand Prince Ivan III Vasilievich in 1495. On the occasion of the marriage of his cousin Marfa Vasilievna Sobakina to Ivan IV in 1571, Vasily Stepanovich was elevated to the rank of lord-in-waiting. He apparently entered monastic life voluntarily, receiving the name Varlaam, and lived for a time in the monastery of St. Cyril of Beloozero.

50. No information is available concering the *desiatyi kholop,* "tenth slave." The phrase might also be translated by "tithe slave."

51. Ivan IV names monastic figures who promoted the Russian style of cenobitic life in their monasteries, namely Sergius of Radonezh (died 1392), Cyril of Beloozero (died 1427), Varlaam Khutynsky (died 1192), Dmitry Prilutsky (died 1392) and Pafnuty Borovsky (died 1478).

52. This likely would be Vladimir Vorotynsky who died in the 1550s and in whose honor a church was erected in the monastery of St. Cyril of Beloozero. See *Poslaniia Ivana Groznogo,* p. 635, Note 7.

53. Dionisy Glushitsky (died 1437) came from the Vologda region and was tonsured in the Spaso-Kamenny monastery by Abbot Dionisy the Hagiorite. After spending ten years there he was given permission to establish his own monastic center. He first went to Sviataia Luka on Kubensk lake where he erected a church dedicated to St. Nicholas. A short distance from there he founded the Intercession monastery on the Glushitsa river. In 1420 he was granted permission by Dionisy, his former abbot who was now bishop of Rostov, to establish the St. John the Forerunner monastery in Sosnovets, five versts from the Intercession monastery. Dionisy was known for his gentleness and humility, and may have been a practitioner of hesychasm, thanks to his training under Dionisy the Hagiorite. Of special note is Dionisy's renown as an iconographer and maker of liturgical vessels. He was canonized for general veneration in 1547 by Metropolitan Makary. Smolitsch, *Russisches Mönchtum,* pp. 98, 142. In the Orthodox tradition, John the Baptist is known as John the Forerunner (Predtech), a name based on Matthew 3:2 which depicts him as one who precedes Jesus and prepares the way.

54. Alexander Svirsky (1448-1533) began his monastic life in the Valaam monastery on Lake Ladoga. After thirteen years there he withdrew to dense woods near the Svira river to live as a hermit. He eventually was discovered and a community of monks soon grew up around him. In 1508 Archbishop Serapion of Novgorod consecrated him as hieromonk and abbot of the new monastic community dedicated to the Trinity. Alexander remained true to his strict ascetical life even while abbot, sharing in the menial tasks of the common life. A life was written by his pupil Irodion in 1545 and he was canonized in 1547. Smolitsch, *Russisches Mönchtum,* p. 137.

55. Ivan Mikhailovich Viskovaty rose from humble origins to play a leading role in Muscovite foreign affairs. He was put in charge of the office of foreign affairs in 1549 and in 1561 was promoted to the dignity of keeper of the seal (pechatnik). In 1554 Viskovaty was condemned by a church council for his views on iconography. He took exception to the departure from traditional Eastern Orthodox canons of sacred art in which certain iconographers were indulging. In particular he criticized complex allegorical icons dealing with the Creed and other articles of faith, correctly pointing out that, among other things, Orthodox canons forbade the depiction of God the Father. He also protested the political use of sacred symbols. Though condemned, he retained his high political office. In 1570, he fell victim to the oprichnina terror and was hacked to death publicly in Moscow after refusing to confess to false accusations. See Graham, "Viskovatyi, Ivan Mikhailovich," MERSH, Vol. 42, pp. 129-132.

56. This is the monastery of the Nativity of the Virgin founded by Savva Storozhevsky (Sabbas the Guardian) in 1404 outside Moscow. The monastery later was co-dedicated to its founder.

57. The cell-monk was a junior monk who lived in the cell with a senior monk, sometimes as a servant, sometimes in the status of a novice, sometimes as a guardian of morality.

58. Anthony, archbishop of Polotsk, was chosen to succeed Cyril (1568-1572) as metropolitan of Moscow in May 1572. At heart a monk, Anthony was ill suited for the demanding post of chief hierarch during the last decade of Ivan IV's reign. Two councils (1573 and 1580) held during his tenure of office placed restrictions on the right of the church to acquire and own property. The retiring Anthony seems to have kept a low profile while metropolitan, but was unable to avoid entirely the tsar's cruelty, as the heads of Ivan's latest victims purportedly were tossed into the metropolitan's courtyard, no doubt to remind him of the cost of meddling in the tsar's affairs. Anthony died in office in 1581.

59. The word *nemets*, which means "German" in modern Russian, was used as a generic term for foreigners.

60. Soloviev uses the word *krestets* which can mean "crossing, crossroads, intersection." The special fee levied on visiting priests would thus take its name from the intersection in the Ilyinsk street market in Moscow where they assembled. The fee granted the priests the same privileges as a *celebret* in the Latin church. Such a document permits a visiting priest to celebrate the eucharist and perform other sacraments outside his own diocese.

61. With a memorial request (vkladnaia gramota) the donor requested that a monastery or parish church commemorate a deceased relative in return for money, property or other type of donation.

62. The bow (luk) was the basic taxation unit in Northern Russian presumably because it was the principal income-producing tool, just as the plow was the basic taxation unit in the South. Though the bow generally equalled two obzhas for taxation purposes, it was not a land unit but an assessment of the productivity of non-agricultural peasant workers such as fishermen and hunters.

63. The names "prince" and "princess" allude to the ritual crowning which occurs during an Orthodox wedding. See Note 7, above.

64. The residence tax (pokhoromnoe) was paid by a peasant when he moved from one district to another and from one lord to another.

65. The monetary unit to which a given plot of land corresponded for taxation purposes was known as *perevod*, conversion, commutation.

66. The saltpan (tsren), used in the production of salt, came to be the name for a taxation unit.

67. The Bulgarian monk Cyprian, envoy of Patriarch Philotheos to Russia, was consecrated metropolitan of Kiev, Russia and Lithuania on December 2, 1375 but a series of incredible misadventures and intrigues prevented Cyprian from assuming full jurisdiction over the metropolitanate until 1390. His consecration was a doubly unusual move on the part of Patriarch Philotheos since the title broke with the traditional formula "metropolitan of Kiev and all Rus," and the incumbent, Metropolitan Alexis, was still alive. The title reflects the disarray in which the metropolitanate found itself at the end of the fourteenth century, a situation exacerbated by the political instability in the region, and was an attempt by Constantinople

to restore unity to the Kievan metropolitanate. The political rivalry between an emerging Muscovy and expansionist Lithuania made such an undertaking extremely risky, since both powers laid claim to speak for and defend Orthodox Christians in the disputed territories of Southwestern Rus, and both hoped to bolster their claims by maintaining a metropolitan see in their respective capitals. Cyprian seems genuinely to have been committed to executing the wishes of Patriarch Philotheos, and even after the union of Krewo in 1386, which saw Lithuania turn westward and embrace Roman Catholicism, Cyprian continued to act as the ecclesiastical head of Orthodox Christians in Poland-Lithuania. Besides his ecclesiastical career, the former Athos monk promoted hesychast spirituality in the Russian church, translated a number of spiritual texts into Slavonic, and edited an all-Russian compilation of chronicles of great significance for Russian history. For a very thorough discussion of Cyprian and the ecclesiastical turmoil of his day, see John Meyendorff, *Byzantium and the Rise of Russia* (Cambridge, 1981), pp. 197-260.

68. Gennady was archbishop of Novgorod from 1484 until 1504, when he was deposed, allegedly for practising simony. Soloviev refers to a letter written by Gennady in which he complained graphically about the very low level of education among candidates for the priesthood. According to Gennady, many of his priests could not even read the liturgical books from which they were to celebrate religious services; some candidates for the priesthood committed to memory the necessary texts. The complaint may be found in *Akty istoricheskie*, Vol. I (St. Petersburg, 1841), No. 104.

69. The sixteenth century priest and monk Vasily (Varlaam), about whom little biographical information has survived, was an author active at the turn of the century. He wrote the *Life of Evfrosin* at the request of the monks of the Pskov Eleazar monastery founded by Evfrosin around 1450. Vasily drew upon information contained in a first redaction of the *Life*, which was composed between 1481 (the year of Evfrosin's death) and 1510. This first redaction is considered more properly a tale relating to the double-alleluia controversy between Evfrosin and the defrocked priest Job. Vasily's version added descriptions of miracles and other biographical details gleaned from monastic records and eyewitness accounts.

70. Theodoret of Cyr (393-466 AD) was one of the most important theologians of the Greek church in the fifth century, author of over thirty-five works on a variety of subjects ranging from biblical commentaries to treatises on the Trinity and liturgical questions. Some of his writings were condemned at the Three Chapters Council in 553 and his orthodoxy is debated.

71. See Note 16, above, for information on Metropolitan Daniel.

72. *The Book of Enoch the Righteous,* better known as *The Book of the Secrets of Enoch* (2 Enoch) is an apocalypse which describes Enoch's ascent into the seven heavens, his vision of God, and his return to earth. Its probable author was a Hellenistic Jew living in Alexandria in the first century AD, but it survives only in two Old Church Slavonic translations. The shorter of these versions likely was translated in the eleventh or twelfth century. This text was used frequently in other compilations. For the Slavonic text, see *Le livre des secrets d'Hénoch. Texte slave*

et traduction française (The Book of the Secrets of Enoch. Slavonic Text and French Translation), ed. André Vaillant (Paris, 1952). Excerpts translated into English are available in *The Other Bible,* ed. Willis Barnstone (San Francisco, 1984), pp. 4-9, 495-500.

73. The Schismatics in question are the Old Believers who proved to be the first and most long-lasting rupture in the unity of the Russian church. During the reign of Tsar Alexis Mikhailovich a sizable minority of laity and clergy rebelled against changes in ritual instituted by Patriarch Nikon after 1654. The principal leaders of the protest were Bishop Paul of Kolomna and the archpriests Ivan Neronov and Avvakum. Among the laity Boyarina Feodosia Morozova played a significant role. The Old Believers objected to the use of three instead of the traditional two fingers when making the sign of the cross, to the new manner in which the name of Jesus was spelled, and to the number of alleluias which were to be sung at certain prayers. Though the modern Westerner might find these ritual changes insignificant, to the protesters they symbolized the abandonment of sacred Russian religious tradition and were understood by some to be a warning of the imminent appearance of the Antichrist. The Old Believers suffered severe persecution at the hands of the tsarist government and church, and were one of the few Christian groups who benefited from the Bolshevik revolution of 1917. See G. Douglas Nicoll, "Old Believers," MERSH, Vol. 25, pp. 228-237.

74. The Judaizers were purportedly a strong heretical sect in the fifteenth century which rejected traditional church teachings on the Trinity, holy orders and the eucharist. Though at one time they were regarded as a homogeneous and dangerous threat to church authority, recent studies now argue that the circle was relatively small and had more political than religious aims. Scholars have attempted for a long time to unravel the true doctrine and aims of this group of free-thinkers. The name "Judaizer" has led scholars to search for Jewish elements but this has proved largely fruitless. The word itself is an ancient Christian epithet for anyone who rejected the divinity of Christ or the doctrine of the Trinity and need not say anything about the ethnic background of those espousing such beliefs. In the nineteenth century the term was applied indiscriminately to what are now recognized as two distinct groups of political and/or religious heterodox thinkers, a Novgorod and a Moscow group. Both groups suffered trial and execution. For the traditional view of the Judaizers see David M. Goldfrank, "Judaizers," MERSH, Vol. 15, pp. 143-146. A different opinion is given by J.R. Howlett, *The Heresy of the Judaizers and the Problem of the Russian Reformation* (Ph.D. diss., Oxford, 1976).

75. The fire occurred on June 21, 1547 and unleashed a wave of popular protest against the Glinsky family, ending in the lynching of Prince Yury Glinsky, Ivan's uncle.

76. A more apt epithet for Sylvester (died around 1577) would have been "elusive" because the true personality and activity of this priest and author has continued to escape scholarly definition. He has been considered an ally of the boyar class and a leader of their opponents in the mercantile sector; as a friend of the Non-Possessors and a partisan of the Possessors. Little is known with certitude

about his life. Originally from Novgorod, where he busied himself with the training of skilled iconographers, calligraphers and cantors, Sylvester appeared in Moscow sometime around 1545 and served as a priest at the Annunciation cathedral in the Kremlin. Though he long has been considered the confessor of Ivan IV, this view now has been largely abandoned. Exactly how much influence he exerted at the court of Ivan IV remains uncertain, though he does seem to have enjoyed the favor of the tsar. He retired of his own volition in 1560 to the monastery of St. Cyril of Beloozero, where he was tonsured with the name Spiridon. Kurbsky's information that Sylvester was exiled to the Solovetsk monastery after 1560 because of his association with Adashev has been called into question. It is known that both Sylvester and his son Anfim were commemorated by the St. Cyril monks, and that his famous library ended up in that monastery. Sylvester was the author of three works: a 1553 letter to Prince A.B. Gorbaty, the governor of Kazan, a life of Princess Olga, and a letter and instruction to a son, included as Chapter 64 in the *Household Manager*. Sylvester seems to have been the editor of the final redaction of that encyclopedic work. See D.M. Bulanin, V.V. Kolesov, "Sil'vestr," *Slovar' knizhnikov*, No. 2, Part 2, pp. 323-333.

77.   Canon 64 of the sixth ecumenical council in 692, also known as Quinisext or Trullan Council, states, "It does not befit a layman to dispute or teach publicly, thus claiming for himself authority to teach, but he should yield to the order appointed by the Lord...." A full English translation is available in *The Seven Ecumenical Councils. Nicene and Post-Nicene Fathers*, Second Series, Volume 14 (Grand Rapids, 1977), p. 394.

78.   Matvey Bashkin was a minor noble who numbered among the thousand noble servitors chosen by Ivan IV in 1550 to have estates near Moscow. Along with Feodosy Kosoy, a runaway slave, he was convicted of heresy in 1553. Bashkin apparently rejected a number of church doctrines including the divinity of Jesus Christ and the validity of church tradition as a norm for Christian life. Soloviev draws attention to Bashkin's social thought when he points out that he demanded that slavery be outlawed because it was contrary to Gospel values. The monk Artemy likely was tonsured by Kornily Komelsky some time before 1536. He resided for a while in the Pskov Caves monastery and was made abbot of the Trinity-St. Sergius monastery during the Stoglav council. Artemy shared the religious opinions of the Non-Possessors and likely found some support from Maxim the Greek and Joseph, both imprisoned in the Trinity-St. Sergius monastery. Soloviev reproduces the main events of the trial against Artemy in 1554; most scholars agree that Artemy was innocent of the charges against him. He was imprisoned in the Solovetsk monastery but he managed to escape and flee to Lithuania, perhaps with the assistance of Abbot Philip. There at the court of Prince Yury of Slutsk he defended Orthodoxy against Calvinist, Lutheran and anti-Trinitarian attacks. See V.I. Koretskii, "Bashkin, Matvei Semenovich," MERSH, Vol. 3, p. 144.

79.   Alexis Fedorovich Adashev (died 1561) belonged to a wealthy family of Tatar origin which owned extensive properties in Kolomna and Pereiaslavl and owed its wealth to the salt trade. His father Fedor Grigorievich, a diplomat, took

Alexis with him in 1538 on his mission to the Turkish sultan, after which Alexis entered the tsar's service. In 1547 he was appointed ceremonial chamberlain and joined forces with Sylvester in an attempt to influence the young tsar. His star continued to rise until 1555 when he was named lord-in-waiting, a position he held until his death. With Sylvester he encouraged Ivan IV to institute reforms in the provincial government and taxation, as well as certain reforms in the church. As a diplomatic adviser Adashev opposed Ivan's desire to invade Livonia, arguing that control of the Crimean Tatars would be more advantageous. Ivan did not listen to his advice, but when Adashev brokered a truce of six months in 1559 he convinced Ivan to attack the Crimea. The military fortunes of Muscovy suffered important setbacks and Adashev began to fall into disfavor. In 1560 he and Sylvester were charged with hastening the death of Ivan's wife Anastasia through sorcery. Both men were tried in absentia; Adashev was imprisoned in Dorpat where he died in 1561, perhaps from poison. Others close to Adashev perished, including his brother Daniel and son Torkh, who were executed in 1562 or 1563. See Graham, "Adashev, Aleksei Fedorovich," MERSH, Vol. 1, pp. 28-30.

80. The Epistle or Apostle is the collection of the New Testament Letters and Acts of the Apostles used in the Divine Liturgy.

81. John 15:13.

82. Galatians 5:14-15

83. Joseph of Volokolamsk (1439-1515) was a leading monastic theologian and reformer who became involved in a conservative reassessment of Russian church tradition. His monastery of the Dormition of the Virgin, later co-dedicated to him, flourished for over a century as a center of theological learning and produced many bishops during the sixteenth century. Beginning with the foundation of his monastery in 1479 Joseph found himself at odds with the grand princes Ivan III and Vasily III throughout his life. He defended the biblical legitimacy of monasticism and its independence of secular control. He is most famous as a theological and spiritual writer and left behind an impressive number of letters, a monastic rule and a large volume of Orthodox theology, *The Book Against the Novgorod Heretics,* better known as *The Enlightener* (Prosvetitel'). It is to this work that Artemy refers. The chapter in question is based on a much earlier writing of Joseph while he was still a novice in the monastery of St. Pafnuty of Borovsk, around 1470. In this letter Joseph discussed the possiblity of a pre-incarnational revelation of Jesus Christ as an angel, one of the three who appeared to Abraham at the oak of Mamre according to biblical tradition (Genesis 18:1-21). Although their followers had nothing but animosity for each other, Joseph was an admirer of Nil Sorsky, the other great monastic figure of late fifteenth century Russia. In his declining years Joseph was involved in a bitter and public dispute with Archbishop Serapion of Novgorod which caused him to lose many of his life-long friends. For a different, more traditional picture of Joseph see David M. Goldfrank, "Iosif Volotskii," MERSH, Vol. 14, pp. 229-232. The most recent examination of the Prosvetitel' is still Irene Holzwarth, Der *«Prosvetitel'» des Josif von Volokolamsk* (The Enlightener of Joseph of Volokolamsk) (Ph.D. diss., Berlin, 1944). Further detailed study comprises part of the massive work by Thomas Seebohm, Ratio und

Charisma, *Ansätze und Ausbildung eines philosophischen und wissenschaftlichen Weltverständnisses im Moskauer Russland (Reason* and *Charisma.* Approaches and Development of a Philosophical and Scholarly Comprehension of the World in Muscovite Russia) (Bonn, 1977). The text of the Prosvetitel' is available in Iosif Volotskii, *Prosvetitel'* (Kazan, 1903, reprinted London, 1972).

84. The personal confrontation (ochnaia stavka) was a juridical method for obtaining trustworthy and true testimony by bringing into face-to-face contact two contradictory witnesses.

85. Neuhausen (Novy Gorodok), attested as a Livonian village around 1200, is located south of Lake Peipus and east of Pskov. In 1342 Burchard von Dreileben, master of the Teutonic Knights, founded a bishop's fortress called Frouwenborch, later known as Novum Castrum, near the village. One of the mightiest fortresses in Livonia, Neuhausen was erected to defend the bishopric of Dorpat. See *Baltisches Historisches Ortslexikon. Teil I. Estland (einschliesslich Nordlivland)* (Historical Lexikon of Baltic Place-Names. Part I. Estonia (Including Northern Livonia), ed. Heinz von zur Mühlen (Cologne, 1985), pp. 382-383.

86. The monastery was built by Kornily Komelsky (died 1537) in the Komel forests of the Vologda district. Kornily began his career in the monastery of St. Cyril of Beloozero. After the typical course of events which saw him seek solitude in the wilderness only to be discovered by other ascetics, Kornily built a monastery and wrote a rule for the community. His rule draws on the *Spiritual Testament* of Joseph of Volokolamsk for regulations pertaining to the common life and on the *Instruction* of Nil Sorsky for the ascetical training of the individual monk. Smolitsch, *Russisches Mönchtum,* pp. 96-97.

87. The panikhida, or Office for the Dead, is a non-eucharistic commemorative service honouring the deceased, comprising a canon, litanies, invocations and troparia for the dead. The Office is chanted before burial and then on the third, ninth, twentieth and fortieth day after burial, as well as on the anniversary of death.

88. The Jesus Canon and Akathist of the Theotokos are poetic compositions of twelve kontakia (a sermon in verse explaining in poetic language the theme in question) and twelve oikoi (stanzas) celebrating Christ and his Mother respectively. The Akathist dates from the seventh century and was first sung, according to tradition, during an all-night vigil of thanksgiving to the Virgin for having lifted the Avar siege of Constantinople in 626. Its name means "not seated." E.M. Jeffreys, R.S. Kazhdan, "Akathistos Hymn," *The Oxford Dictionary of Byzantium,* ed. Alexander P. Kazhdan, Vol. 1 (New York, 1991), p. 44.

89. Ivan Volk Kuritsyn, Mitia Konoplev and Ivashko Maximov were burned to death in a cage in Moscow in 1504. Kuritsyn was active in the foreign service of Moscow during the reign of Ivan III. Nekras Vasilievich Rukavy was a service-estate holder from the Votskaia fifth; he was burned to death in Novgorod in 1504, first having his tongue cut out. Both men were ostensibly executed for their involvement in the heresy of the Judaizers, but some modern scholars share Artemy's scepticism. It is possible that their connections with the palace faction supporting Ivan III's grandson Dmitry as heir led to their downfall.

90. The prayer of Manasseh comprises the Book of Manasseh contained in the Old Testaments of the Orthodox and Roman Catholic bibles.

91. Prince Andrei Mikhailovich Kurbsky (1528-1583) was a descendant of the princely house of Smolensk-Yaroslavl. A well-educated young man, he was appointed in 1549 to the rank of table attendant (stolnik) by Ivan IV and spent the next fifteen years in distinguished military service. He won the trust of Ivan IV when he swore allegiance to Ivan's infant son and heir in 1553 during Ivan's nearly fatal illness. Having accompanied Ivan IV to the Trinity-St. Sergius monastery that same year he met Maxim the Greek who made a profound impression on him. His spiritual father was Feodorit of Kola. Kurbsky was appointed a boyar in 1556. After leading successful campaigns in Livonia he was named commander of the Russian rearguard in the 1563 offensive against Polotsk, but he suddenly lost Ivan's favor for undetermined reasons. On April 30, 1564 he fled to Poland and was welcomed into the Polish army by King Sigismund II. Although he acquired property in Lithuania and Volhynia, he died impoverished in 1583 after a number of misfortunes (See Chapter VIII, below). Kurbsky wrote a *History of the Grand Prince of Moscow,* a history of the council of Florence, and compiled the *New Pearl.* His correspondence with Ivan IV is generally accepted as authentic, though some scholars have declared it a later forgery. For bibliography see Karl W. Schweizer, "Kurbskii, Andrei Mikhailovich," MERSH, Vol. 18, pp. 171-174. Concerning his writings, see Chapter IX, below.

92. The Transvolga Elders or Non-Possessors were a group of monastics and other church figures who carried the teachings of Nil Sorsky concerning monastic and church property to their logical conclusion. They thought that the vow of poverty should be understood in a restrictive manner, meaning that monasteries should be stripped of their landholdings excepting what was necessary to provide the monks with basic sustenance. In addition they shared Nil Sorsky's contemplative style of monastic life and lived, by choice or as a result of persecution, in the wilderness or isolated centers. A church council held in 1531 censured their opinions. A.M. Sakharov, "Non-Possessors," MERSH, Vol. 25, pp. 45-46.

93. Vassian Kosoy, known in the secular state as Vasily Ivanovich Patrikeev (1470-1532), played an important role in the politics of the court of Grand Prince Ivan III. Together with Semeon Riapolovsky and Fedor Kuritsyn he negotiated the marriage of Alexander of Lithuania with Ivan III's daughter Elena in 1494, but the dynastic crisis of the 1490s brought a sudden reversal of fortune. The Patrikeevs sided with Ivan III's grandson Dmitry who was designated successor to the throne in 1498; in 1499 Ivan III changed his mind in favor of his son Vasily. Vasily Patrikeev was tonsured forcibly in the monastery of St. Cyril of Beloozero where he met Nil Sorsky. The encounter transformed Vassian into an ardent follower of Nil Sorsky and partisan of the Non-Possessor movement in the church. After 1509 he was given permission to move to St. Simon's monastery in Moscow where he began to write against Joseph of Volokolamsk. From 1509 until 1522 he enjoyed the approval of Vasily III Ivanovich, who at this period lent his support to the Non-Possessors. Around 1515 Vassian commenced work on an edition of the *Kormchaia*

kniga (The Book of the Pilot), a collection of canonical legislation, with a decidedly Non-Possessor bias. The appointment of Daniel of Riazan as metropolitan in 1522 spelled the end of the Non-Possessors' further development. In 1531 Vassian was condemned of heresy and imprisoned in the monastery of Joseph of Volokolamsk, where he died a short time later. The most thorough study of Vassian Patrikeev remains N.A. Kazakova, *Vassian Patrikeev i ego sochineniia* (Vassian Patrikeev and his Works) (Leningrad, 1960). See Faith C.M. Kitsch, "Patrikeev, Vassian," MERSH, Vol. 27, pp. 60-62.

94.   Antonio Possevino (1533-1611) was a member of the Society of Jesus, a skilled diplomat and forceful apologist for Roman Catholicism. He was sent to Sweden in 1577 and 1579 to try to restore Catholicism there, though without success. He secretly converted the heir to the throne, Sigismund Vasa. In 1582 he mediated the Truce of Yam Zapolsky. Of great importance for the study of sixteenth-century Muscovy is his report of his experiences in Muscovy known as the *Moscovia*. This book is especially valuable for its accurate observations about the latter part of Ivan IV's reign and presents a detailed and astutely commentated picture of the religious, political and economic realities of that era. See Graham, "Possevino, Antonio," MERSH, Vol. 29, pp. 109-114. Possevino's book is available in an English translation,*The Moscovia of Antonio Possevino,* tr. and ed. by Hugh F. Graham (Pittsburgh, 1977).

95.   Much of Ivan IV's correspondence remains unpublished. The *Drevniaia Rossiiskaia Vivliofika N.I. Novikova* (Ancient Russian Library of N.I. Novikov), Part 12 (Moscow, 1789), contains writings of Ivan IV to the sultans Selim, November 1569, p. 84; Selim, March 1571, pp. 28, 30; Murat, March 1577, p. 26. Selim Ii was sultan from 1566 to1574, and his son Murat III from 1574 to1595.

96.   See following note.

97.   Joseph was patriarch of Constantinople from summer 1556 until January 1565. He is not to be confused with Metropolitan Joseph who headed the church in Chalkis on the island of Euboea. The name used by Soloviev, *mitropolit evgripskii,* presumably derives from the Latin "Negripus" or "Euripus" current in the late middle ages. Westerners referred to the town as Negreponte.

98.   Soloviev relates here a legend composed in Muscovy concerning the origins of the title Monomakh for the Kievan grand prince, Vladimir II Vsevolodovich (1053-1125). Allegedly to ward off an attack on Constantinople by Vladimir, Emperor Constantine IX Monomachos (reigned 1042-1055) sent a metropolitan to Kiev bearing his crown. Vladimir was crowned with it and took the name Monomakh. In fact, the course of events was quite different. In 1043, for reasons not fully understood, Grand Prince Yaroslav of Kiev sent his son Vladimir Yaroslavich (died 1052) on an ultimately unsuccessful mission against Constantinople. Sometime before 1053 Yaroslav arranged a marriage between his son Vsevolod Yaroslavich and a daughter of Emperor Constantine IX Monomachos. It was because of this alliance that their son Vladimir could style himself Monomakh. Princess Anna was the wife of Vladimir I Sviatoslavich of Kiev (died 1015).

99. In 1303-1305 Niphon was named first metropolitan of Galicia, directly subordinate to the patriarch of Constantinople. The see became vacant in 1391, which gave the current metropolitan of Kiev and all Russia, Cyprian (1375-1406) a long-awaited opportunity to press Constantinople for the suppression of the Galician metropolitanate and its annexation to Kiev. He was not successful in this venture yet by 1414, the Galician metropolitanate no longer figures in historical records. See John Meyendorff, *Byzantium and the Rise of Russia* (Cambridge, 1981), for a full discussion of the ecclesiastical situation in Galicia, Lithuania and Russia until the early fifteenth century. Not until the reign of Metropolitan Joseph II Soltan (1507-1521) was the title "Metropolitan of Galicia" appended to the title "Metropolitan of Kiev." See Albert M. Ammann, *Abriss der ostslawischen Kirchengeschichte* (A Sketch of East Slavic Church History) (Vienna, 1950), pp. 195-215, for church-historical developments in Poland-Lithuania from 1451-1613.

100. The precentor (ustavnik or ustavshchik) functioned as a type first cantor in a choir whose duty it was to sing the verses of a given liturgical composition, which then were repeated by the choir. The office arose at a time when books were rare and most choristers unable to read. In larger churches and monasteries the choir was headed by a canonarch (kanonarkhist), assisted by a precentor and a subprecentor (golovshchik). See Vol. 17, Chapter VI, Notes 6-7.

101. Mikhail Vasilievich Ragoza was tonsured in the Ascension monastery in Minsk. In 1589 he was consecrated metropolitan of Kiev by Patriarch Jeremiah II, a position he held until 1596. Ragoza was an indecisive figure when the times demanded decisiveness. He was sympathetic towards the Roman Catholic church and convened the Council of Brest-Litovsk in 1596 at which formal union of the Orthodox church in Ruthenia with Rome was accepted. He remained as Uniate metropolitan until 1599, when he was succeeded by the much more energetic Hypatius Pociej (1600-1613).

102. Reliable biographical information about Metropolitan Onisifor Devochka is unavailable. He was named metropolitan of Kiev in 1579 while still a layman and was ordained only in 1583. During his reign Roman Catholicism, spearheaded by Jesuit missions, made serious inroads into the traditionally Orthodox population. Onisifor did little to assist his fellow Orthodox countrymen and seems to have been uncooperative with the Orthodox Brotherhood in Kiev in its work to print and disseminate Orthodox theological literature. He did in 1586 secure for the Orthodox of Poland-Lithuania the right to maintain the Julian calendar after the introduction of the Gregorian calendar there. Onisifor was twice married, a fact which made his appointment to the metropolitan's throne canonically irregular. When Patriarch Jeremiah of Constantinople made a pastoral visitation of Kiev and Russia in 1588-1589, Onisifor stepped down, and took up residence in the Trinity monastery in Wilno.

CHAPTER VII

1. Soloviev refers to the Code of Law (Sudebnik) of 1497 prepared during the reign of Ivan III. This Code of Law drew on a number of earlier legal sources for its statutes, including the *Pskov Judicial Charter,* grand princely edicts, *The Russian Justice,* and *The Metropolitan's Law Handbook.* Only one copy of the 1497 Code, discovered in 1817, survived the middle ages. The 1497 code dealt with judicial and administrative personnel and the fees owed to them for their service, court procedures, bail and pledges. A translation is available in Horace W. Dewey, *Muscovite Judicial Texts, 1488-1556* [Michigan Slavic Materials, No. 7] (Ann Arbor, Michigan, 1966), pp. 7-21. See Richard Hellie, "Sudebniki," MERSH, Vol. 38, pp. 15-21, for bibliography and further discussion.

2. The character witness (poslukh) gave a testimonial to the honesty and credibility of one of the parties and also attested to the correctness of their claims even though he had no firsthand knowledge of the case.

3. Compare the conveyance in which the heir is obligated not to redeem a sold hereditary estate, in *Sobranie gosudarstvennykh gramot i dogovorov, khraniashchikhsia v Gosudarstvennoi Kollegii Inostrannykh Del* (Collection of State Charters and Treaties Preserved in the State College of Foreign Affairs), Part 1 (Moscow, 1813), No. 173. Nevolin (see Introduction, Note 2) says in evaluating the right of redemption that "the indeterminacy in which redemption by relatives appears at the first reference can scarcely convince us of its great antiquity, but it is perhaps quite ancient...like the very situations out of which it arose." Further on he rejects the explanation that redemption is a remnant of that common ownership of land in which relatives were sometimes involved. He does not recognize the existence of common ownership by relatives among us, for if in ancient times relatives occasionally owned properties jointly this was by no means the sole form of land ownership. On the contrary, alongside this form could have existed, and in fact did exist, the other form of separate possession. The indication that in ancient times, alongside joint possession, there also existed separate possession can only prove that the first form was not exceptional, but there still arises the question as to which form was older? Nevolin suggests that in the legendary information about Kii, Shchek and Khoriv, the three brothers lived independently of each other in their own places, and with their own economies, but this suggestion does not hold since the three brothers could have occupied in each other's proximity different places for economic convenience. From this it does not at all follow that they were divided. Do we not now see that brothers live in different places, in different houses and nevertheless have undivided property? There is nothing to say about princes' allotments in parcels of land, for we know that princes looked at these parcels as a temporary possession, and forsook them for others as they strove for seniority on the family ladder, recognizing the indivisibility of family and family property, the

patrimonial nature of the whole Russian land for everyone. With the appearance of the retinue, and in keeping with its very character, separate property had to appear of necessity alongside of family property, just as the family way of doing things generally began to weaken with the appearance of princes and their retinues, though its ultimate collapse was still a long way off. It gave way only with difficulty and left behind visible traces. Nevolin further says that "given the existence of common ownership, by its very nature a participant in litigation cannot alienate his share of the property without the consent of the other participants. Alienation of property undertaken by him without their consent must have as its consequence not the right of redemption for the other co-participants but the invalidity of the alienation. If, however, consent to this alienation was given by the co-participants, then after this there exists for them no right of redemption." We already remarked that with the appearance of princes and their retinues the family way of doing things was dealt a blow, and it must have been weakened, but as usually happens in the battle of two forms if the old form is so strong that it cannot be annihilated entirely by the new a compromise is reached between them, so to speak, or mutual concessions are made. The right of redemption belongs to such an arrangement. The owner could alienate his property without the consent of relatives, but they maintained the right to redeem the alienated property. Concerning the battle between the old and new form and the arrangements between them is the extraordinarily significant resolution which we introduced in the text, that an owner could alienate only one half of the hereditary estate without the heirs, otherwise the alienation was invalid. We see the same thing in Lithuanian legislation. (Soloviev's note)

4. The pro forma testament (nariadnyi dukhovnyi) was drawn up at the instruction of a third party, and was often considered counterfeit.

5. Reinhold Heidenstein (1553-1620) was born in Königsberg. In 1583 Margrave Georg Friedrich of Ansbach appointed him as his agent at the Polish court. The year before he had been named secretary to Stefan Bathory, a post he retained under the reign of King Sigismund III owing to his close relationship with Grand Chancellor Jan Zamoyski. After Zamoyski's death in 1605 his influence at court waned, and he eventually retired to his estates in West Prussia in 1612. A diplomat and jurist, Heidenstein also gained renown as a chronicler of his age, leaving behind invaluable writings in Latin in which he glorified both Zamoyski and Bathory.

6. Great Hetman Stanislaw Zolkiewski was a distinguished Polish military commander and negotiator. During the First Swedish War (1601-1602) together with Zamoyski and Jan Karol Chodkiewicz (1560-1621), he drove the Swedes out of Livonia into Estonia. The fame to which Soloviev alludes was the result of Zolkiewski's actions during the Time of Troubles in Moscow. After numerous intrigues and shifts of fortune, Vasily Shuisky replaced the first False Dmitry on the tsar's throne in Moscow in 1606, but in 1610 a new threat appeared on the horizon in the figure of the second False Dmitry, also known as the Brigand of Tushino. The Brigand's supporters included some eighteen thousand Polish fighters hostile to King Sigismund III. When in 1609 Shuisky renounced a treaty signed

with Sigismund III in favor of an alliance with Sigismund's enemy Karl IX of Sweden, the Polish king decided to march against Muscovy. Hetman Zolkiewski advised a direct attack on Moscow, but the king chose instead to assault the fortress of Smolensk. The possible threat to Sigismund's campaign posed by the Brigand of Tushino was diffused in February 1610, when Sigismund signed an agreement with the Brigand which guaranteed freedom for the Orthodox faith in Polish-controlled territory and promised that Sigismund's son Wladyslaw would be elected tsar of Moscow. In the meantime Shuisky was apprised of the dissolution of the Brigand's forces, and led a Russian army of forty-six thousand men towards Smolensk to relieve the beleaguered town. Zolkiewski was sent to head off the Russians, and on June 23, 1610 he won a decisive victory over Shuisky at Klushino. Shuisky was deposed in July and Zolkiewski marched into Moscow. Hetman Zolkiewski met his death on October 6, 1620 in a battle against the Turks at Cecora. See *The Cambridge History of Poland to 1696*, ed. W.F. Reddaway, et al. (Cambridge, 1950), pp. 461, 463-471; Norman Davies, *God's Playground. A History of Poland in Two Volumes*, Volume I (New York, 1982), pp. 454-460, 477.

7. Reference unknown.

8. The kalghay was the heir apparent or deputy of the Crimean khan, normally his son or brother. He frequently led Tatar raids into Poland-Lithuania and Muscovy on behalf of the khan, and received one tenth of the booty taken on such expeditions. Although the kalghay tended to remain in the Crimea when the khan was leading an army, on occasion he joined the campaign, in which case he served as commander of the right wing of the army. The kalghay was permitted to send his own envoys on missions with those of the khan and could negotiate certain deals on his own. See C.M. Kortepeter, "Kalghay," *The Encyclopaedia of Islam,* New Edition, Vol. 4, pp. 499-500.

CHAPTER VIII

1. Savva Vishersky (died 1460) was a fifteenth century ascetic from the Novgorod region. He began his monastic career in the Savva hermitage in Tver, where later he became abbot. He subsequently travelled to Mount Athos before finally settling on the Vishera river around 1414. He apparently brought back a copy of *The Book of the Pilot* (Kormchaia kniga) which was used by Archbishop Vassian of Rostov. On the Vishera river Savva founded his monastery around 1418. A life was written for Savva by Abbot Gelasy of the Savva-Vishersky monastery. See V.O. Kliuchevskii, *Drevnerusskiia zhitiia sviatykh kak istoricheskii istochnik* (Old Russian Lives of Saints as a Historical Source) (Moscow, 1871; reprint London, 1969), pp. 123, 156-158.

2. The *Russian Justice* (Russkaia Pravda) is a collection of early Russian legal standards which focuses on criminal and procedural law. Punishments meted out for murder, insults and theft of property, the organization of trials, and laws of inheritance are all dealt with in considerable detail. The *Russian Justice* survives in copies dating from the thirteenth to eighteenth centuries, and was compiled in

three different redactions. The Short Version, composed sometime in the 1030s, is generally held to reflect the legal mind of Yaroslav the Wise. The Expanded Version has been dated to the early twelfth century, perhaps during the reign of Vladimir Monomakh or his son Mstislav. The Abbreviated Version has been dated as a twelfth or fifteenth-century composition. All three redactions were published in *Pravda Russkaia,* 3 vols. (Moscow-Leningrad, 1940-1963). An English translation is available in George Vernadsky, *Medieval Russian Laws* (New York, 1947), pp. 26-56.

3. See Chapter I, Note 2, for Tsarevich Ivan Ivanovich's death.

4. September 1 was dedicated to St. Simeon the Stylite, and there were special prayers said on the square in front of the church for the New Year.

5. The "fools for Christ" are a category of saint going back to the early Byzantine period in church history. Inspired by the statement in 1 Corinthians 1:25, "...for God's foolishness is wiser than human wisdom," the holy fools took it upon themselves to glorify God through acts of self-humiliation. In Russia the fools for Christ were revered by the common people and feared by the merchant and noble classes who bore the brunt of their derision. Sharing with their ancient counterparts severe asceticism and simplicity of spirit, the Russian holy fools attacked religious hypocrisy and social injustice by by acting in an outrageous fashion, including public nakedness, theft and ribald mockery of religious rites. The holy fool frequently had the gift of clairvoyance or prophecy, and used it to excoriate political and religious leaders. Even Ivan IV, who normally tolerated no criticism, allowed the stinging words and actions of a holy fool to stand. According to the legend, Nikola of Pskov (died 1576) offered Ivan IV meat upon his arrival outside Pskov in 1570. When the tsar refused to eat the food because it was Lent, Nikola denounced him as a devourer of Christian flesh. The death of a favorite horse, prophesied by Nikola, further convinced the tsar to leave Pskov relatively unharmed. Vasily the Blessed (died 1552) attained such popularity in Moscow that the cathedral of the Intercession on Red Square was renamed by the people in his honor. Ivan Big Cap (died 1589) was a northerner who worked in the salt trade before retiring to Rostov, where he practised his foolishness. He wore heavy chains and fetters on his body, donning his big cap, likely a hooded cloak, for the street. Shortly before his death he was active in Moscow. See Elisabeth Behr-Sigel, *Prière et sainteté dans l'église russe* (Prayer and Holiness in the Russian Church), 2nd edition (Abbaye de Bellefontaine, 1982), pp. 98-108.

6. Mikhalon Litvin (dates uncertain) served as a diplomat in the Crimean khanate. His *Memuary, otnosiashchiesia k istorii iuzhnoi Rusi* (Memoirs Relating to the History of Southern Rus), describing life in Lithuania, Southern Russia and the Crimea, were published in Kiev in 1890.

7. For information on Kurbsky in Poland-Lithuania, see Oswald P. Backus, "A.M. Kurbsky in the Polish-Lithuanian Commonwealth," *Acta Balto-Slavica,* 6 (1979), pp. 29-50.

8. The theological and spiritual development of the Russian church owes much to the fourth century archbishop, ascetic and theologian John Chrysostom.

A Byzantine collection of his works known as *Margaritai* (Pearls), translated perhaps in the thirteenth century into Slavonic, enjoyed immense popularity in Russia from the fifteenth to seventeenth centuries under the name *Margarit*. Although the original Greek collections vary in their structure, the Slavonic versions in use in Russia all follow the same format in the arrangement of Chrysostom's writings. Kurbsky's *New Pearl* (Novyi Margarit) departs from the traditional Russian *Pearl* both in structure and content. Many of the selections from Chrysostom compiled by Kurbsky were previously unknown in Slavonic, or as he explains, were very poorly translated. The *New Pearl* contains sixty-seven works by Chrysostom and five smaller writings including Kurbsky's preface and a short treatise on punctuation. The collection has been preserved in two copies. A.I. Gladkii and A.A. Tsekhanovich, "Kurbskii, Andrei Mikhailovich," *Slovar' knizhnikov*, No. 2, Part 2, p. 499. T.V. Chertoritskaia, "Margarit," *Slovar' khizhnikov*, Part 2 (Leningrad, 1989), pp. 100-102. See also Andrej Michajlovic Kurbskij, *Novyj Margarit*, ed. Inge Auerbach (Giessen, 1976). The latter edition is based upon the best-preserved copy of the work at the Herzog August Bibliothek, Wolfenbüttel, Germany, Codex Guelph 64.43 Extravagantes.

CHAPTER IX

1. In 1472 Sophia (Zoë) Paleologue, the niece of the last Byzantine emperor Constantine XI and daughter of Despot Thomas of Morea became the second wife of Grand Prince Ivan III, who hoped to reap political gains from such a union. The papacy, under whose guardianship Sophia lived since her flight from Constantinople, hoped that the carefully negotiated marriage would induce Ivan III to place the Russian church under papal jurisdiction, but Ivan remained a firm supporter of Orthodoxy, and no church union occurred. Vasily, the son of Sophia and Ivan III, eventually assumed the grand princely dignity, though not without difficulty. In 1490 the heir Ivan Ivanovich died. Grand Prince Ivan III hesitated in choosing between his grandson Dmitry Ivanovich and his second son Vasily as successor to the throne. In 1498 he solemnly crowned Dmitry co-regent and heir, temporarily frustrating Vasily's aspirations. It seems that Vasily and Sophia had the support of a group of lesser courtiers who wanted to put an end to the monopoly held by the Patrikeev family. In 1499 Ivan III arrested Prince I.Yu. Patrikeev, his two sons, and son-in-law Prince S.I. Riapolovsky, executing the latter and forcibly tonsuring the Patrikeevs. Dmitry was imprisoned and Vasily was named co-regent and heir in 1500. See Crummey, pp. 85, 110-111; also J.V.A. Fine, "The Muscovite Dynastic Crisis of 1497-1502," *Canadian Slavonic Papers*, 8 (1966), pp. 197-215.

2. See Chapter VI, Note 74, above.

3. For Joseph of Volokolamsk see Chapter VI, Note 83.

4. For Transvolga Elders see Chapter VI, Note 92.

5. See Chapter VI, Note 93, for information on Vassian Kosoy (Prince Vasily Patrikeev).

6. Information about Metropolitan Daniel may be found in Chapter VI, Note 16.

7. Romans 13:2.

8. Prince Fedor Rostislavich, who reigned 1260-1299 over the principality of Yaroslavl, had very close ties with the Golden Horde. He married a daughter of the khan and became his cupbearer and favorite. Like a number of princes at the end of the thirteenth century, Fedor Rostislavich accepted the overlordship of the Tatar khan, marching in his army against Russian and possibly Lithuanian towns. He was buried in the Yaroslavl monastery of the Transfiguration, to be joined later by his sons David and Konstantin. According to report, his remains and those of his sons were unearthed in 1463, after which a number of miraculous healings occurred. All three were canonized, their memorial being September 19.

9. Ivan is accusing Kurbsky of drawing the parallel between Anastasia and the Byzantine empress Eudoxia who was the bitter enemy of St. John Chrysostom.

10. John 8:39

11. Luke 3:8

12. Romans 4:16.

13. Mark 4:5-6.

14. Vasily Grigorievich Griaznoy-Ilyin was a trusted crown estates henchman who was made commander of the Donets army in 1573. He was taken prisoner by the Crimean Tatars sometime afterwards and was ransomed from captivity only in 1577. *Poslaniia Ivana Groznogo,* pp. 456-457.

15. The Muscovite frontier town Aleksin, situated roughly ninety kilometers south of Borovsk on the Oka river, was the site of a protracted seige which saw the town fall to Khan Ahmed in 1572.

16. Jan Rokyta (died 1591) was a member of the Czech Brethren. Renowned as an excellent orator and defender of the Brethren, Rokyta participated in a number of religious disputations aimed at preserving unity and a measure of theological orthodoxy within the dissident Protestant groups. In 1564 he debated anti-Trinitarian doctrine in the presence of King Sigismund I Augustus and traveled as chaplain for the Czech Brethren with the diplomatic mission sent to Moscow in 1570 by King Sigismund. On May 10, 1570 he engaged in a formal dispute with Ivan IV concerning the beliefs of the Czech Brethren. Roughly one month later, Ivan presented him a written response in which Rokyta's hopes for gaining a foothold in Muscovy were dashed. For a general discussion of Rokyta and Ivan's response see Valerie A. Tumins, *Tsar Ivan's Reply to Jan Rokyta* (The Hague, 1971).

17. Matthew 7:6.

18. Ivan makes a pun here: *Liuter* is the Russian form for Luther; the adjective *liutyi* means wild, cruel, fierce, ferocious.

19. Soloviev may be thinking of B. Vilentas (1525-1587), whose *Gospel and Epistles* became a standard Lithuanian translation of the four Gospels and excerpts from the book of Acts, used by Protestants and Catholics alike. He also translated Luther's Catechism into Lithuanian in 1575. Vilentas studied at the university in

Königsberg in 1545 and was made pastor of an Evangelical Lutheran parish in Königsberg in 1550. *Encyclopedia Lituanica*, Vol. IV, ed. S. Suziedelis, A. Vasaitis (Boston, 1978), p. 127. The Russian word *volan* means "flounce, shuttlecock."

20. Giles Fletcher (1546-1611) was the English ambassador to Muscovy in 1588-1589. He was sent on a goodwill mission to settle disputes which arose between England and Russia after the death of Ivan IV in 1584. Chief among these were the English demand that no other English traders except those belonging to the Muscovy Company be allowed to trade in Russia, and the Russian demand that the Company be held accountable for any debts incurred by English traders in Russia. The latter charge arose after a former company agent named Marsh, who traded as a private individual, failed to meet his debt obligations to a number of Russian merchants. The Russian government ordered the Muscovy Company to pay the entire amount owed. Fletcher was able to reduce the sum by half and arrange that the Company would henceforth be responsible only for the debts of its own merchants. He was unable, however, to retain the trade monopoly for the Company in Northeast Russia. Detained for two months in Vologda, Fletcher began to write down his experiences of Moscow. It was published in 1591 but quickly withdrawn because its negative portrayal of life in Muscovy might jeopardize the future of the Company. Only in 1643 could it appear in its entirety. The book, entitled *Of the Russe Commonwealth,* begins with a description of the geography of Muscovy, moving on to treat the government, judiciary, revenue, military and church institutions, the nobility and peasantry, Russia's neighbors and the manners and customs of the people. It was the first English-language book to describe Muscovy. The text is available in *Rude and Barbarous Kingdom,* ed. L.E. Berry and R.O. Crummey (Madison, 1968). See also Samuel H. Baron, "Ivan the Terrible, Giles Fletcher, and the Muscovite Merchantry. A Reconsideration," *Slavonic and East European Review,* 56 (1978), pp. 563-585.

21. Ivan may be referring to his membership in the Riurikid dynasty founded by the Varangian prince of Novgorod, Riurik, around 860. According to the saga preserved in the *Russian Primary Chronicle,* the native Slavs of Northern Russia invited three Scandinavian brothers to establish law and order in their region. Riurik took control of Ladoga, his younger brother Sineus ruled in Beloozero and the third brother Truvor held sway in Izborsk. After the death of his brothers, Riurik became sole ruler and established headquarters in Novgorod on Ilmen lake. In 879, just before his death, Riurik entrusted his domain to his relative Oleg, who expanded Varangian control over other East Slav tribes and united Novgorod and Kiev into a powerful principality. The saga maintains that Riurik's son Igor assumed control of the realm in 912/913 and reigned until 945. Igor and the Varangian princess Olga were the grandparents of Grand Prince Vladimir Sviatoslavich of Kiev (died 1015). The saga accurately retains the foreign provenance of the ruling dynasty of Rus. Ivan calls himself a German, but the word used, *nemets,* can also mean "foreigner."

22. The *Paremia* is a reading from the Old or New Testament chosen with regard to the liturgical feast being celebrated. The paremia is read at vespers after the office hymn and prokeimenon.

23. Kurbsky compares Vassian Patrikeev with the traditional founder of monasticism, St. Anthony of Egypt (251-356 AD). John the Baptist was imprisoned because he condemned Herod for marrying his brother Philip's wife Herodias, according to Mark 6:17-18. When Vasily III divorced Solomoniia Saburova in 1525 because she did not bear him any children, and married Elena Glinskaia in 1526, Vassian Patrikeev and many other church figures protested vehemently. Kurbsky would be suggesting that one of the reasons for Vassian's ultimate demise could be found in this act of protest.

24. While the phrase *filosof iskusnyi* can be translated as "an expert philosopher" it should be realized that in the Byzantine tradition, true philosophy ("love of wisdom") is the Christian life, and the true philosopher is one entirely devoted to this, namely a monk.

25. See Chapter VI, Note 78, for Artemy.

26. Prince Konstantin Ostrozhsky (1526-1608) was a very wealthy nobleman who did much to protect and promote the interests of his fellow Orthodox in Poland-Lithuania. In 1580 he founded an academy in Ostrog in which Latin, Greek and Slavonic were taught. Under his aegis the first complete version of the Bible in Church Slavonic was published in 1581 on the printing press which he had established in Ostrog. At first mildly sympathetic to plans for church union in Ukraine, he became a passionate opponent after the Union of Brest-Litovsk in 1595, and convened an Orthodox synod in Brest in 1596 which succeeded in hindering the full implementation of the union.

27. St. John of Damascus (657-749 A.D.) earned theological renown for his comprehensive presentation of Greek Christian doctrine in his work *De Fide Orthodoxa* (Concerning the Orthodox Faith) and for his strong defense of icons during the iconoclast controversy of the early eighth century. Recognized as an authority by medieval theologians, John of Damascus may have earned the scorn of radical Protestants for his forceful teaching on the Real Presence in the Eucharist, his fully developed Mariology and his defense of icons.

28. The image of the "seven-pillared dogmas" likely derives from Proverbs 9:1 which states that divine wisdom "has built her house, she has hewn her seven pillars." It could also be an allusion to the Seven Ecumenical Councils recognized by the Orthodox church as authoritative. These were Nicaea I (325), Constantinople I (381), Ephesus (431), Chalcedon (451), Constantinople II (553), Constantinople III (680-681), Nicaea II (787).

29. Kurbsky makes a pun here using the Graeco-Latin loan word *feologiia* for Latin theology and the Slavic *bogoslovie* for Orthodox theology. Thus the phrase reads, "...to newly-invented and lame Latin theology from true Orthodox theology."

30. St. Gregory Palamas (ca.1296-1359) became archbishop of Thessalonica in 1347. His *Triads in Defence of the Holy Hesychasts* is a defence of Athonite hesychasm against the overly rationalistic attacks of Barlaam the Calabrian, and became a fruiful source for Trinitarian theology in the Eastern church. St. Neilos of Thessalonica (died 1361) succeeded Palamas as archbishop but died before

assuming office. He was a resolute opponent of Latin Christianity, and penned a number of works dealing with the schism, papal primacy and the procession of the Holy Spirit.

31. Princess Czartoryska was a member of the ancient Ruthenian family of Czartoryski who intermarried with the Jagiellons. Political acumen brought the family to prominence. The family eventually joined the Roman Catholic church.

32. The Jesuit priest and polemicist Peter Skarga (1536-1612) served as the court preacher for Sigismund III and forcefully defended the claims of the king and aristocracy against democratic tendencies among members of the szlachta grouped around Chancellor Jan Zamoyski. Skarga accused the szlachta (nobility) of corrupting Polish burghers and peasants, and promoting Protestantism. He used his considerable intellectual skills to wage a relentless war against the Orthodox in Poland-Lithuania and advocated the conversion of the entire populace of Ukraine and Belorussia to Catholicism.

33. Though Soloviev adopts the term "Arian" from Kurbsky's letter, a more correct term would be "anti-Trinitarian," "Socinian" or "Unitarian." From the early Byzantine period onward, Arianism was considered the root of all heretical teaching in the church, and commonly was attributed to anyone propounding heterodox doctrine. Anti-Trinitarian thought entered Poland along with certain strands of Protestantism in the middle of the sixteenth century. George Blandrata of Piedmont headed a group of anti-Trinitarians or Unitarians within the Reformed church in Poland in 1558 until their expulsion from the church in 1565. Fausto Paolo Sozzini (1539-1604), after whom the Socinians were named, took up residence in Poland in 1579 and actively spread Unitarian thought among the upper classes.

34. Nikephoros Kallistos Xanthopoulos (1256-1335) belonged to a circle of anti-Latinizers centered around Emperor Andronikos II. Xanthopoulos's principal work, the *Church History,* narrates in eighteen books events from the birth of Christ to the death of Emperor Phocas in 610. A summary of five planned books which were to extend the history down to 912 and the death of Leo the Philosopher was added to the introduction. Since it was translated into Latin only in 1555, Kurbsky shows himself well-informed about what works would be beneficial to his cause of defending Orthodoxy. Hans-Georg Beck, *Kirche und theologische Literatur im byzantinischen Reich* (The Church and Theological Literature in the Byzantine Empire) (Munich, 1977), pp. 705-706.

35. Maxim the New Confessor is Kurbsky's title for Maxim the Greek, comparing him with St. Maximus the Confessor (died 662) who was imprisoned ostensibly for treason, but in fact for his refusal to submit to the theological opinions supported by Emperor Constans II.

36. *The Heavens* is the title of the partial translation of John Damascene's *The Source of Truth* produced by the Bulgarian John the Exarch in the tenth century.

37. Selivan (Sil'van), a monk of the Trinity monastery, was attached to Maxim to assist him in his work as a translator. Together with Maxim he was tried by Metropolitan Daniil in 1525. According to one source he was imprisoned in the

monastery of Volokolamsk with Maxim, where he was put to death; yet another source indicates that he died a natural death." Fennell, *Kurbsky's History of Ivan IV*, pp. 82-83, Note 2.

38.   Zinovy Otensky (1500-1568) was apparently a disciple of Maxim the Greek. The year after his teacher's condemnation as a heretic in 1425 Zinovy was sent to the Otnia hermitage located in a marshy area some thirty miles northeast of Novgorod. There he composed his *Istiny pokazanie* (Demonstration of the Truth), a treatise of roughly one thousand pages in which Zinovy refuted the heterodox teachings of Feodosy Kosoy. Graham, "Zinovii Otenskii," MERSH, Vol. 46, pp. 105-107.

39.   Galatians 1:8.

40.   The pun derives from Feodosy's surname Kosoy, which means crooked, askew, squint-eyed.

41.   The date refers to the year in which the book was composed. (Soloviev's note) The strange phenomenon Zinovy describes is a waterspout.

42.   See Chapter VI, Note 74, above.

43.   Zinovy is referring to the story of the prophet Daniel and his three companions Hananiah, Mishael and Azariah taken prisoner by the Babylonian king Nebuchadnezzar. The four young men, who refused to eat the fine foods and wines served at the royal table, dined on vegetables and water instead, and turned out healthier than those men who ate the royal fare. For their self-control, they were rewarded by God with the gift of knowledge and learning. See Daniel 1:1-21.

44.   Romaneia is a sweet liqueur made from Frankish wine, hence a type of brandy.

45.   The discussion centres on the meaning of the verbs *chaiat'* and *zhdat'*.

46.   The exposited Psalter, *tolkovaia psaltyr,* is an edition of the principal psalms used in the liturgies, provided with commentaries drawn from the writings of St. John Chrysostom, St. Basil the Great and other Church Fathers.

47.   The *Domostroi* or *Household Manager* originally was composed in Novgorod. Sylvester edited and revised this version to reflect Muscovite political and ecclesiastical realities. His version stressed reverence for the authority of the tsar and exudes an at times stifling religious conservativism. The text is available in A.S. Orlov, *Domostroi po konshinskomu spisku i podobnym* (The Household Manager, Following the Konshinsk and Similar Copies) (Moscow, 1909-1910, reprint The Hague, 1967). The work is divided into three sections. The first deals with the Orthodox faith and one's duties to the state; the second treats home life and the third handles practical matters. As even the excerpts cited by Soloviev demonstrate, the *Household Manager* presents the reader with very detailed regulations pertaining to all aspects of life in middle-class Moscow of the sixteenth century.

48.   A Menology is the Eastern Christian version of the *Proprium Sanctorum* (Proper of the Saints). It contains the office for all feasts having a fixed date, providing the formulary for the saint being commemorated. Hagiographical information normally is included in the canon for the saint in question. Menologies begin on September 1, the Byzantine New Year, and often appear in twelve

volumes. Some menologies, such as Makary's *Great Menology,* contain extensive hagiographical material of a variety of genres including lives, sermons, instructions, and selections from patristic writings and paterika. Makary's *Great Menology* was completed in 1552 after roughly twenty-five years of work, and comprises approximately 27,000 pages in twelve folio volumes. He employed the leading hagiographers, copyists, translators and writers of the day in the production of the *Great Menology.* In addition to supervising the copying and correcting existing lives of saints, Makary commissioned a number of new compositions, especially for those newly canonized. A scholarly edition of the Great Menology was partially completed by the Commission for the Study and Publication of Ancient Texts between 1863 and 1916. See N.F. Droblenkova, "Velikie Minei Chetii," *Slovar' knizhnikov,* No.2, Part 1, pp. 126-133; D.B. Miller, "The Velikie Minei Chetii and the Stepennaia Kniga of Metropolitan Makary," *Forschungen zur osteuropäischen Geschichte,* 26 (1979), pp. 262-382.

49. Vladimir II Vsevolodovich Monomakh (1053-1125) became prince of Kiev in 1113. An astute ruler, Vladimir Monomakh left behind a number of writings, among which figures his Instruction written shortly before his death in 1125. The *Instruction* contains the prince's advice to his children on the duties of a Christian prince, tempering secular wisdom with Christian religiosity. The work opens with quotations from the Psalter pertaining to damnation and salvation, then moves on to give political advice and concludes with an autobiography.

50. The panagia is bread blessed in honor of the Mother of God which is used in a ritual marking the end of a meal in monasteries. The name, which means "all-holy," is a typical epithet for the Mother of God in the Eastern Orthodox church.

51. The hymn honoring the Mother of God "It is meet and right" occurs in the Divine Liturgy after the consecration of the bread and wine as part of the commemoration of those individuals for whom the Eucharist is being offered. Its text reads, "It is meet and right to bless thee, Theotokos, the ever-blessed and most pure Mother of our God, more honorable than the cherubim and beyond compare more glorious than the seraphim, who without defilement didst bear God the Word, true Theotokos, we magnify thee."

52. The great book of Nikon likely refers to the *Pandektai* of Nikon of the Black Mountain (eleventh century), a compilation of excerpts from the writings of the Church Fathers, conciliar decisions and other theological compositions. The *Pandektai* is organized into sixty-three chapters and was designed to give monks access to otherwise hard to obtain theological and spiritual texts. Nikon also compiled the *Taktikon* which includes canonical, liturgical and ascetical writings linked with matters of church discipline, arranged in forty chapters. Both his works were translated into Slavonic in the thirteenth or fourteenth century. Their great popularity in medieval Russia is demonstrated by the fact that almost no collections or original writings lack excerpts from one or the other work. Nikon was born around 1025 in Constantinople and entered the monastery of the *Theotokos tou Rhoidiou* (Theotokos of the Pomegranate) on the Black Mountain in Syria. See Hans-Georg Beck, p. 600.

53. Briefly stated, a paterikon is a collection of writings describing the ascetical triumphs and failures of a group of monks. Scholars trace the origins of this literary genre to the *Apophthegmata Patrum* (Sayings of the Desert Fathers). The Russian paterika can be thought of as spiritual chronicles recording for posterity the religious history of a given monastic foundation. Like secular chronicles, the paterika can and do include a variety of literary genres such as sayings, anecdotes, tales, legends, saint's lives, letters and spiritual testaments. Makary mentions the important paterika available to him, the *Alphabetical* is an alphabetical collection of sayings; the *Jerusalem* is a collection of sayings arranged thematically; the *Egyptian* is a composite work based on the *Alphabetical* paterikon and the *Historia monachorum in Aegypto, Epistola de indicis gentibus de bragmantibus* and *Historia lausiaca* (A History of the Monks in Egypt, A Letter Concerning Brahmans, The Lausiac History); the Sinaitic is a translation of John Moschus' *Pratum spirituale* (The Spiritual Meadow); the *Sketic* paterikon is a translation of *The Book of Holy Men*. The *Kiev Caves Paterikon* originated in the monastery of the Caves in Kiev and is the work of the monks Polikarp and Simeon.

54. The *Stepennaia kniga tsarskogo rodosloviia,* usually referred to as *Stepennaia kniga* (Book of Generations), belongs to the circle of Makary. It is a sacred history of Russia traced through the ancestral line of the tsars of Moscow, beginning with Rurik and culminating seventeen generations later in Ivan IV. The text reworks information from the chronicles, and incorporates much apocryphal and folkloric material to produce what is ultimately a forgery. See Dmitrij Čiževskij, *History of Russian Literature* (The Hague, 1971), pp. 302-305.

55. Eleazar Bomelius was born in Westphalia (not in the Netherlands as Soloviev asserts), and studied medicine in England. He became a confidant of Ivan IV after being rescued from English prison by the Russian ambassador Sovin. Sir Jerome Horsey gives a gruesome description of Bomelius's end in 1579. See Sir Jerome Horsey, "Travels," in *Rude and Barbarous Kingdom,* pp. 292-293.

56. Sultan Mehmet II (1429-1481) conquered Constantinople on May 29, 1453 with an army of over one hundred thousand soldiers. Mehmet permitted his soldiers the traditional three-day looting period foreseen in Islamic legal practice for a city which resisted attack, though he put a stop to the plundering at the end of the first day. As Sultan, Mehmet II pursued a relatively liberal policy towards the conquered peoples and granted protection to numerous Christian churches and monasteries throughout the vast territories under his sway. He composed poetry in Persian and was a patron of the arts.

57. Ivan Semenovich Peresvetov was a sixteenth century publicist who emigrated from Lithuania to Muscovy in the 1530s. Earlier he served the Hungarian king Jan Zapolya and then switched allegiances to support the Habsburg Ferdinand I. In addition to the *Skazanie o Magmete saltane* (The Story about Sultan Mehmet) referred to by Soloviev, Peresvetov also wrote the following works: *Skazanie o knigakh* (The Story about Books), *Pervoe predskazanie filosofov i doktorov* (The First Prophecy of Philosophers and Doctors), *Malaia chelobitnaia* (The Small Petition), *Vtoroe predskazanie filosofov i doktorov* (The Second Prophecy of

Philosophers and Doctors) *Skazanie o tsare Konstantine* (The Story about Emperor Constantine) and *Bol'shaia chelobitnaia* (The Great Petition). Although not always presenting a consistent ideology, Peresvetov's writings generally display an anti-aristocratic bias and promote the common lot shared by all "children of Adam" as he terms the human race. He argued against indenture and slavery but promoted the idea of a strong ruler who will not shrink from using military force to achieve his goals. The highest good of any state should be justice, and Peresvetov can excuse a monarch's brutality provided that his subjects are all treated fairly. This notion is particularly evident in his narrative about Sultan Mehmet II, the conqueror of Constantinople. Peresvetov may have perished during the terror of the latter part of Ivan IV's reign. Ya.S. Lur'e, "Peresvetov, Ivan Semenovich," *Slovar' Knizhnikov*, No. 2, Part 2, pp. 178-182. The principal study of Peresvetov remains A.A. Zimin, *I.S. Peresvetov i ego sovremenniki* (Ivan Peresvetov and His Contemporaries) (Moscow, 1958).

58.   Yermak, a cossack leader who had fought against the Poles in the Livonian war, was recruited along with a force of fifteen hundred men by the Stroganov family to assist in the conquest of the Siberian Tatars whose khanate was located in the Ob river basin. In 1582 he launched a successful attack on the Tatar capital, but fell in a subsequent battle while waiting for reinforcements from Moscow. The Stroganovs were merchant adventurers who controlled the northeastern part of European Russia and made a fortune from salt and furs.

59.   The church of St. Nicholas the Miracle Worker of Gostun, located in the Kremlin in Moscow, played an important role in Muscovite religious and political society. The pastor of the church, Archpriest Amos, participated in the trial of Matvey Bashkin in 1553. The parish clergy were literate men who donated various books to monastic centers. Archpriest Michael sent a copy of the works of Dionysius the Areopagite to the Trinity-St. Sergius monastery. It has been suggested that the first printing press in Moscow was built near the church of St. Nicholas of Gostun. Information is very scarce about Ivan Fedorov before he came to St. Nicholas. Scholars surmise on the basis of his artistry that Fedorov may have worked on the production of books prior to printing the *Apostle* with his associate Peter Timofeev Mstislavets. As Soloviev points out, both men were forced to flee Moscow in 1565 after publishing the *Chasovnik* (Book of Hours), though the reasons for their departure remain unknown. One school of thought held that Fedorov and Mstistlavets were suspected of heresy, but there is little evidence to support this contention. Another school argued that as a widowed deacon Fedorov was expected to take monastic tonsure; his refusal to do so would have cast doubts on his orthodoxy. Still another group of scholars maintain that the two printers fell into disfavor because their edition of the *Chasovnik* contained textual corrections which could have been interpreted as corruptions. See A.I. Rogov, "Vozniknovenie i razvitie knigopechataniia"("The Origin and Development of Book Printing") *Ocherki russkoi kul'tury XVI veka* (Essays on Russian Culture of the Sixteenth Century), Part 2 (Moscow, 1977), pp. 270-277.

60.   The Catholic Epistles is a title used of the New Testament Letters of James, 1 and 2, Peter, 1 John and Jude, indicating that they were addressed to a general or

universal readership. This distinguishes them from the letters of St. Paul, which are addressed to individuals or specific churches. Although 2 and 3 John do have addressees, they usually are counted among the Catholic epistles. The term may have been used to describe their canonicity during the formation of the New Testament.

61. The *Chasovnik* (Book of Hours) contains texts for the celebration of the eight canonical hours into which each day is divided, beginning with vespers.

62. The Triodions are liturgical books which contain the services for the Paschal Cycle. There are two such tridions, the Lenten Triodion, which covers the period of Lent up to Holy Saturday, and the Pentecostarion, which extends from Easter to the Sunday following Pentecost. The name Triodion derives from the three odes which make up the canons sung at this time of year. The Oktoikh contains eight series of seven offices, one office for each day of the week. Each series corresponds to one of the eight liturgical tones or modes according to which hymns are sung. The series is sung for eight weeks, one tone per week, and then the cycle begins again. The text of a hymn for a given day remains the same, but its melody and the form of the chant vary according to the tone.

63. See Chapter I, Note 23, for Hetman Grigory Chodkiewicz.

Additional information on personalities and topics found in the text and notes is available in George N. Rhyne and Joseph L. Wieczynski, eds., *The Modern Encyclopedia of Russian, Soviet and Eurasian History* (MERSH) and *Supplement*; Harry B. Weber, ed., *The Modern Encyclopedia of Russian and Soviet Literatures (Including Non-Russian and Emigre Literatures)* (MERSL); Paul D. Steeves, ed., *The Modern Encyclopedia of Religions in Russia and the Soviet Union* (MERRSU); and David R. Jones, ed., *The Military Encyclopedia of Russia and Eurasia* (formerly *The Military-Naval Encyclopedia of Russia and the Soviet Union*), all published by Academic International Press.

INDEX

THE EDITOR AND TRANSLATOR

T. Allan Smith was born in Brampton, Ontario, on May 7, 1953. Upon receiving his B.A. in Russian and French in 1976 at the University of Toronto, he was accepted as a Junior Fellow in Massey College and earned his M.A. in Russian literature from the University of Toronto the following year. He taught at St. Mary's College, Sault Ste. Marie, Ontario, for one year and then entered the novitiate of the Basilian Fathers in Rochester, New York. In 1983, after successfully obtaining the M.Div. from the University of St. Michael's College, he was ordained to the priesthood and went to West Germany to pursue doctoral studies. Under the guidance of Frau Dr. Fairy von Lilienfeld, chairwoman of the Institute for Eastern Christian History and Theology at Friedrich-Alexander Universität Erlangen, he earned his D.Th. (summa cum laude) in 1988, with a thesis entitled *The Volokolamskii Paterik. A Translation, Study and Commentary.* He returned to Toronto and spent two years as a research assistant at the Pontifical Institute of Mediaeval Studies. He was a lecturer in church history at the Toronto School of Theology and taught a summer course in patristic thought at Newman Theological College in Edmonton, Alberta. In 1990-1992 he was assistant professor of Religious Studies at St. Thomas More College, University of Saskatchewan, and then moved to Montreal to conduct private research. He currently teaches church history and foundational theology at Newman Theological College in Edmonton.

FROM ACADEMIC INTERNATIONAL PRESS*